Encyclopaedia of British
Railway Companies

Encyclopaedia of British Railway Companies

Christopher Awdry

Foreword by Rev W. Awdry

PATRICK STEPHENS LIMITED

Front endpaper *The old Chester & Holyhead Railway station at Llandudno stood to the west of the present one, which replaced it in 1896. The number of staff pictured reflects the station's importance.* (Gwynedd Archives Service)

Rear endpaper *The bridge across the River Wye at Chepstow, opened by the South Wales Railway in 1851. An up train crosses during rebuilding in 1962.* (Rev W. Awdry)

First published in 1990

British Library Cataloguing in Publication Data
Awdry, Christopher
   Encyclopaedia of British railway companies.
   1. Great Britain. Railway services –
   Encyclopaedias
   I. Title
   385'.03'21

ISBN 1-85260-049-7

Patrick Stephens Limited is part of the
Thorsons Publishing Group, Wellingborough,
Northamptonshire NN8 2RQ, England.

Printed by Butler & Tanner Limited, Frome,
Somerset
10 9 8 7 6 5 4 3 2 1

Contents

For my Father, with grateful thanks for passing his love of railways into the third generation, and for his continual encouragement while this book was in preparation.

Foreword *by Rev W. Awdry*

It is not generally realised how utterly haphazard was the way in which railways in Britain developed. After the success of the Stockton & Darlington and the Liverpool & Manchester, railway schemes began to proliferate. Businessmen and others formed committees to build lines between two or more neighbouring towns in the belief that a railway would be a profitable investment. Eventually nearly a thousand of these local companies were formed. Each had its Act of Parliament, Seal of Incorporation and Board of Directors. They were mostly minor, low-mileage lines, generally under-capitalized and managed by inexperienced Directors who had great hopes of profit but little idea of how to run a railway.

The independent life of these lines was often short. Before long economic pressures forced the Directors to lease or sell their concerns to larger, more ambitious companies. These, well-engineered and managed, were backed by adequate finance, and had deliberately set out to be trunk lines — the Great Western, the Grand Junction and the Great Northern were typical. The process of absorption, thus begun, continued for nearly a century, until, by 1921, the Railway Clearing House map showed 19 main-line companies, with some 20 smaller ones. The map also, however, shows that at that date there were still about 150 separate railway concerns in Britain operating as self-contained units. Thus, besides the large railways mentioned there were some 111 others. These included lines of narrow gauge, Light Railways and Joint concerns managed by Committees drawn from two or more larger companies. Some were, of course, swallowed at the Grouping of 1923,

but many, such as the Somerset & Dorset and the Midland & Great Northern, retained their identity for some years.

In writing this book, Christopher has set out to supply a long-felt want. It throws light on an obscure part of British railway history, and is the product of some three years of careful research. Its subject is complicated: just how complex is only realised when an attempt is made to trace what may have started as a small railway through various expansions, amalgamations and changes of name, until finally it becomes part of one of the 'Big Four' in 1923. A further difficulty is that authorities do not always agree over dates. More research is then needed to determine the most reliable. Be that as it may, original sources, where available, have been consulted to ensure a reliable book of reference.

· For convenience the information is arranged in five sections covering railways in Britain as they were at the Grouping — GWR, LMS, LNER, SR, Independent and Joint — and within each section entries are arranged alphabetically. A series of 'genealogy' tables helps to show how a system grew, enhancing a fully indexed and illustrated text.

This book is an important one. We have often longed for one like it, to help in researches we have undertaken. We would not recommend it for light reading; but as a work of reference we have found it excellent and deserving of high commendation. We have every hope that it will come to be regarded as a classic.

W. Awdry
Stroud

Acknowledgements

A book like this would be impossible to compile without help from many people in many ways — to all who have given me time, information, photographs, or anything else, my very grateful thanks. Among them are: Nigel Bowman (Launceston Steam Railway), Mark and Veronica Chambers, T. J. Edgington (NRM), Andrew C. Ingram, John James, A. E. Jarvis, (Liverpool Museums), Fred Landery (Caledonian Rly Assoc), John Lewis, M. Little (Salisbury Library), Klaus Marx (Bluebell Railway), John Miller (Col Stephens Museum, Tenterden), Tim Petchey (Winchcombe Railway Museum), J. H. Price, R. D. Penhallensick (Royal Institution of Cornwall), Peter Rowe (Falkirk DC), Brian Stewart (Canterbury Museums), K. L. Taylor, J. G. Vincent (Talyllyn Railway, NGRM), Alan P. Voce (Tiverton Museum Society), Tony Warren, Prof H. P. White, Noel Williams, Rhian Williams (Meirionydd Area Library), Gareth Haulfryn Williams (Gwynedd Archives Service), Mike Wood, S. J. Woodward (Swindon Museums) and Peter van Zeller (Ravenglass & Eskdale Railway). Also the staff at Peterborough Central Library and Cambridge University Library, who made the relevant areas of their material available to me. And in the very possible event that I have failed to remember everyone, I combine apologies with thanks to any whose names I have inadvertently omitted. Photographs are individually acknowledged: those lacking such information are by the author or from his collection.

There are also three people, not so far mentioned, to whom I am particularly grateful. The first is my father, whose 'library' I have used widely: indeed, without the knowledge of its availability I doubt whether I should have taken the job on. Allan Mott has put his photographic collection at my disposal, has gone to some trouble to supplement it as asked, and has used a photo-technician's skills to make acceptable some of my own dubious offerings. Thirdly my wife Diana, who has borne patiently with jaunts to libraries and on photographic trips, has offered both encouragement and useful suggestions, and, not least, come to the rescue on occasions when word-processor problems threatened. My thanks to you all.

Introduction

It is hoped that readers will find the layout of this volume easy to follow. Railways are listed alphabetically within the Group to which they were attached in 1923; a fifth section includes independent and Joint railways, and those lines that made up the LPTB in 1933.

I have tried to keep abbreviations to a minimum, though space limits demand that some companies be treated in this way — a list of these appears below. It may be taken for granted that there is an entry for each of these in the text, and in such cases the expression 'qv' has also been dispensed with. Companies appearing more than once in the same entry are abbreviated also. Closure dates given, particularly those after 1923, should not be taken as exhaustive — I have used those readily available, but the subject is comprehensively covered elsewhere.

The Index lists, individually, all places which feature in a company name: ie the Manchester & Leeds Railway appears with the appropriate page number under both Manchester and Leeds, and it should be possible for a reader with an incomplete knowledge of the company name to find the railway he seeks with the minimum of trouble. It must also be said that no work of this kind can ever be entirely free of error, not only because of conflicting evidence arising from early railway records, but because research is making new discoveries daily. For any discrepancy herein I hold myself entirely responsible, and would ask any reader who can correct or supplement information, to write to me c/o the Publishers, including, if possible, details of the source of the new material.

Abbreviations

B&DJR	Birmingham & Derby Junction Railway
B&ER	Bristol & Exeter Railway
B&GR	Birmingham & Gloucester Railway
B&MTJR	Brecon & Merthyr Tydfil Junction Railway
BoT	Board of Trade
BR	British Rail (British Railways)
BRB	British Railways Board
Br&GR	Bristol & Gloucester Railway
CambR	Cambrian Railways
C&GWUR	Cheltenham & Great Western Union Railway
C&HR	Chester & Holyhead Railway
CLC	Cheshire Lines Committee
CR	Caledonian Railway
dmu	diesel multiple unit
DR	District Railway
EAR	East Anglian Railways
E&GR	Edinburgh & Glasgow Railway
E&MR	Eastern & Midlands Railway
ECML	East Coast Main Line
ECR	Eastern Counties Railway
ELR	East Lancashire Railway
emu	electric multiple unit
EP&DR	Edinburgh, Perth & Dundee Railway
ESR	East Suffolk Railway
EUR	Eastern Union Railway
FR	Furness Railway
G&SWR	Glasgow & South Western Railway
GCR	Great Central Railway
GER	Great Eastern Railway
GJR	Grand Junction Railway
GNR	Great Northern Railway
GNER	Great North of England Railway
GNSR	Great North of Scotland Railway
GPK&AR	Glasgow, Paisley, Kilmarnock & Ayr Railway
GVR	Gwendraeth Valleys Railway
GWR	Great Western Railway
H&BR	Hull & Barnsley Railway
HH&BR	Hereford, Hay & Brecon Railway
HR	Highland Railway
I&AJR	Inverness & Aberdeen Junction Railway

IoWCR	Isle of Wight Central Railway
L&BR	London & Birmingham Railway
L&CR	London & Croydon Railway
L&MR	Liverpool & Manchester Railway
L&NWR	London & North Western Railway
L&OR	Llynfi & Ogmore Railway
L&SWR	London & South Western Railway
L&YR	Lancashire & Yorkshire Railway
LB&SCR	London, Brighton & South Coast Railway
LC&DR	London, Chatham & Dover Railway
LD&ECR	Lancashire, Derbyshire & East Coast Railway
LMS(R)	London, Midland & Scottish Railway
LNER	London & North Eastern Railway
LPTB	London Passenger Transport Board
LR	Light Railway
LRO	Light Railway Order
LTE	London Transport Executive
M&BR	Manchester & Birmingham Railway
M&GNJR	Midland & Great Northern Joint Railway
M&LR	Manchester & Leeds Railway
M&SWJR	Midland & South Western Junction Railway
MCR	Midland Counties Railway
MDR	Metropolitan District Railway
MetR	Metropolitan Railway
MR	Midland Railway
MS&LR	Manchester, Sheffield & Lincolnshire Railway
N&DJR	Newcastle & Darlington Junction Railway
NA&HR	Newport, Abergavenny & Hereford Railway
N&BR	Neath & Brecon Railway
N&CR	Newcastle & Carlisle Railway
NCB	National Coal Board
NBR	North British Railway
NDR&DC	North Devon Railway & Dock Company
NER	North Eastern Railway
NLR	North London Railway
NMR	North Midland Railway
NR	Norfolk Railway
NSR	North Staffordshire Railway
NUR	North Union Railway
NWR	North Western Railway

ole	overhead line equipment
OR	Official Receiver
OVR	Ogmore Valley Railways
OW&WR	Oxford, Worcester & Wolverhampton Railway
P&WR	Preston & Wyre Railway
PD&SWJR	Plymouth, Devonport & South Western Junction Railway
PTR	Port Talbot Railway
RETB	Radio Electronic Tokenless Block
RP	Running Powers
RPS	Railway Preservation Society
RS	Railway Society
S&CR	Shrewsbury & Chester Railway
S&DR	Somerset & Dorset Railway
St&DR	Stockton & Darlington Railway
S&HR	Shrewsbury & Hereford Railway
S&MJR	Stratford-upon-Avon & Midland Junction Railway
SMJR	Scottish Midland Junction Railway
SD&LUR	South Durham & Lancashire Union Railway
SDR	South Devon Railway
SE&CRCJMC	South Eastern & Chatham Railway Company Joint Management Committee
SER	South Eastern Railway
SR	Southern Railway
SUR&CC	Shropshire Union Railways & Canal Company
SWR	South Wales Railway
TA	Traffic Agreement/Arrangement(s)
TVR	Taff Vale Railway
VNR	Vale of Neath Railway
WA	Working Agreement/Arrangement(s)
WCML	West Coast Main Line
wef	with effect from
WLR	West London Railway
WM&CQR	Wrexham, Mold & Connah's Quay Railway
WMR	West Midlands Railway
WS&WR	Wiltshire, Somerset & Weymouth Railway
WYR	West Yorkshire Railway
Y&NMR	York & North Midland Railway
YN&BR	York, Newcastle & Berwick Railway

PART 1

The Great Western Railway group

The crests and arms of London (left) and Bristol form the insignia of the Great Western Railway. (Allan Mott)

Overleaf *Isambard Kingdon Brunel died in 1859, but his spirit lives on. As his statue surveys the 'lawn' at Paddington, it might well claim, like Sir Christopher Wren at St Paul's Cathedral: 'If you seek a memorial, look around you'. (Allan Mott)*

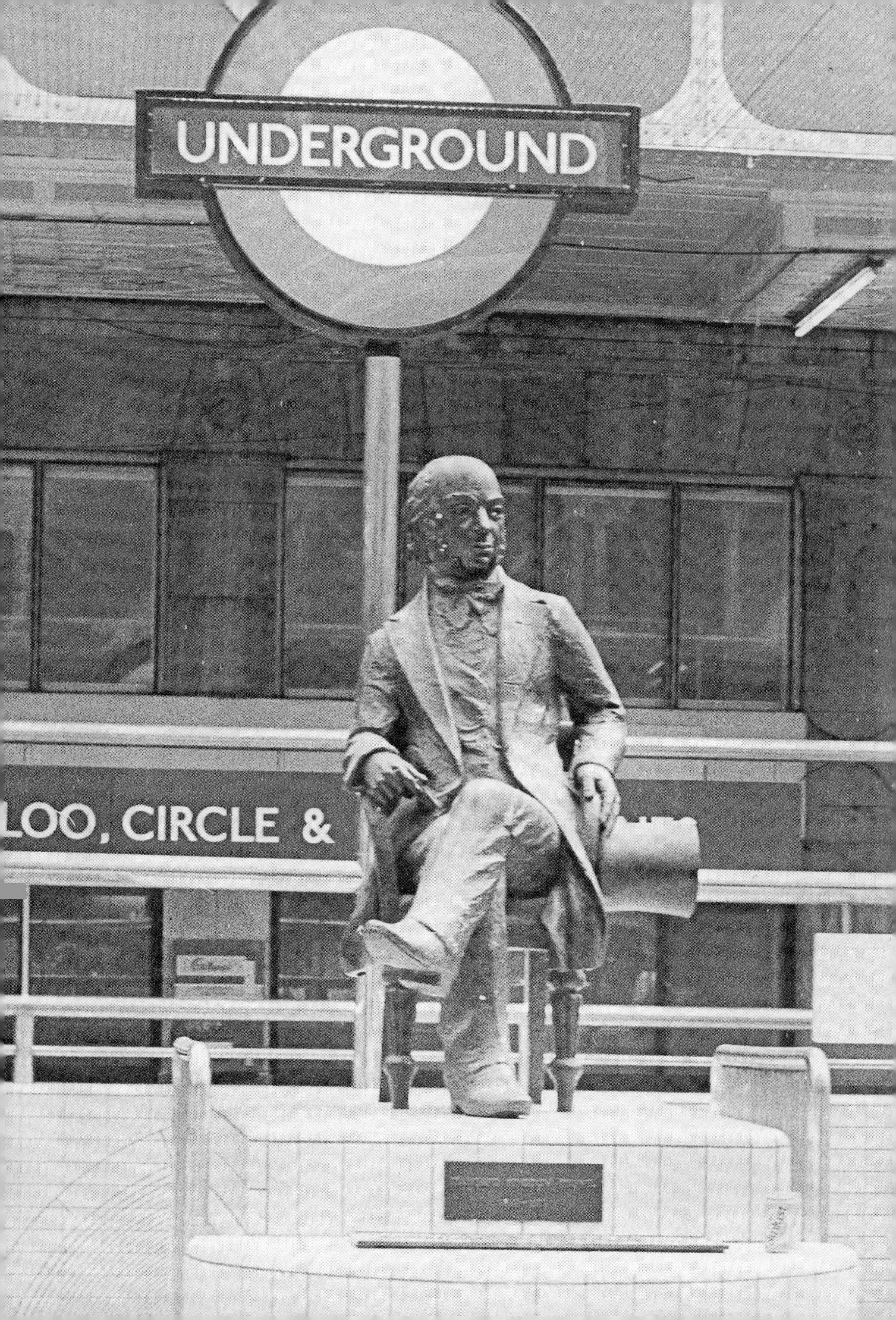
UNDERGROUND
LOO, CIRCLE &

GREAT WESTERN RAILWAY

Incorporated on 31 August 1835 to link Bristol with London, it had been planned to join the L&BR at Kensal Green and share a terminus, but the GWR opted for a separate station at Paddington, opened on 4 June 1838, on the site of the present goods station. A new station, designed by I. K. Brunel, was opened on 16 January 1854 (departure side), 29 May (arrival). The line was broad gauge, but standard gauge was also laid into Paddington. The first standard gauge train left for Birmingham via Oxford on 1 October 1851, reaching its destination only 3 minutes late amid speculation that it would not arrive at all! The last broad gauge train left Paddington on 20 May 1892, the 5.00 pm to Plymouth, hauled by 4–2–2 *Bulkeley*, which returned with the last up train early next morning. The system expanded through amalgamations and absorptions, until by 1918 the track mileage was 6,743, including sidings. Under the Railways Act of 1921, almost 50 more companies joined the 150 or so already collected. The GWR became the only member of the 'Big Four' to retain its original title.

ABBOTSBURY RAILWAY

The Company was authorised on 6 August 1877 to build a line ' . . . 6 miles 3 furlongs 6.10 chains' long from the Dorchester–Weymouth line at Upwey Junction to Abbotsbury, near the Dorset coast. It was not a profitable venture; opening on 9 November 1885, the line joined the GWR by Act of 7 August 1896. It closed to passengers on 1 December 1952.

ABERCARN RAILWAY

See Hall's Tramroad.

ABERDARE RAILWAY

Promoted by the South Wales ironmasters Crawshay Bailey and Sir John Guest, this 7.5-mile line, authorized on 31 July 1845, ran from Aberaman Ironworks to the TVR at Aberdare Junction. A half-mile branch from Cwmbach Junction also connected with several collieries. It opened on 6 August 1846 and was leased by the TVR for 999 years wef 1 January 1849. A branch to Roath, authorized on 6 August 1885, was opened on 23 April 1888. Authority to amalgamate was granted to the TVR by an Act of 26 August 1889, but actual vesting did not happen in this case until 30 June 1902, by an Act dated 31 July.

ABERDARE VALLEY RAILWAY

Incorporated on 2 July 1855, this line bridged the 1.5-mile gap between a canal basin at Hirwain and the Middle Dyffryn colliery. Authorized in broad gauge, the line was sponsored by the VNR which was empowered to work it from its opening in November 1856. Formal transfer was authorized by an Act of 21 July 1859, carried out under an Agreement dated 2 April 1864.

ABERYSTWITH (sic) & WELSH COAST RAILWAY

Incorporated on 22 July 1861 to build a line north from Aberystwyth to Pwllheli via Tywyn, Barmouth and Porthmadoc, the railway was to bridge the Dyfi estuary and connect with the Newtown & Machynlleth Railway (qv) at Machynlleth. An Act of

Barmouth bridge, as built, with a lifting span; replacement with a swinging span began in 1899. A Cambrian Railways train is crossing, consisting mostly of oil-lit four-wheelers, and signals bear the customary Cambrian disc instead of a stripe. The buildings at the bridge's end are almost unchanged today. (Gwynedd Archives Service)

27 July 1862 gave powers to build from Barmouth to Dolgellau. The Machynlleth–Aberystwyth section (21 miles) was begun first, but firm foundations for the Dyfi bridge could not be found; the crossing was abandoned and the line built along the estuary shore instead. It opened in stages (Machynlleth–Borth 1 July 1863, to Aberystywth 23 June 1864). The line north opened throughout on 10 October 1867, but before it was finished the Company had amalgamated with the CambR wef 5 August 1866 (Act of 5 July 1865). The original Pwllheli station was rebuilt nearer the town centre in 1907; though the layout has been modified under BR, the buildings (Listed) remain intact.

ABINGDON RAILWAY

A branch from the projected Oxford–Didcot line was offered to the folk of Abingdon in 1837 — they refused then, but later an independent company was formed to build a 2-mile line to Culham. Authorized on 15 June 1855 and laid to broad gauge, it was opened on 2 June 1856 and converted to standard gauge in 1872. The next year it was extended ¾ mile to the Oxford–Didcot line at Radley. It was worked from 19 April 1860 by the GWR and vested in it by an Act of 15 August 1904.

ALCESTER RAILWAY

The line was authorized on 6 August 1872 as a branch from the Stratford-upon-Avon Railway at Bearley to Alcester on the Evesham & Redditch Railway (both qv). The 6.5-mile line was greatly influenced by the GWR, which worked it from opening (4 September 1876) and took over maintenance from 4 September 1877. The Company was vested jointly in the GWR and the Stratford-upon-Avon Railway from 22 July 1878, and the GWR took over completely wef 1 July 1883. The line, single throughout, was closed as an economy in 1917, the track being lifted and sent to France. After the war, the GWR relaid it, re-opening from Bearley to Alne on 18 December 1922, to Alcester on 1 August 1923. It closed finally to passengers on 25 September 1939.

ALEXANDRA (NEWPORT & SOUTH WALES) DOCKS & RAILWAY

This was incorporated in 1865 as the Alexandra (Newport) Dock Company, opening on 13 April 1875. It launched the Pontypridd, Caerphilly & Newport Railway (qv) in 1878 and changed its title on 18 August 1882, rising above initial financial problems. Between 1884 and 1906, mineral traffic to Newport was worked by the TVR, after which the Company worked its own, using locomotives from the newly-electrified Mersey Railway. Passenger traffic began on 28 December 1887; its working was much more complex, being either by the company, the GWR or the Rhymney Railway, depending upon

The seal of the Alexandra (Newport & South Wales) Docks & Railway. (Roy Nash/Swindon Museums)

whether the traveller was using a local or through service. Working was taken over by the GWR from 1 January 1899. Services were withdrawn as an economy from 1 January 1917 but reinstated later. The Company became a GWR constituent at the Grouping. Passenger services between Pontypridd and Caerphilly were finally withdrawn on 17 September 1956.

AVON & GLOUCESTERSHIRE RAILWAY

Authorized on 19 June 1828, this 5.25-mile, 4 ft 8 in gauge tramway ran from the R Avon below Keynsham to collieries at Rodway Hill (Mangotsfield). The owner was the Kennet & Avon Canal, but the Bristol & Gloucestershire Railway (qv LMS) contributed. On 10 January 1831, 2.5 miles were usable, and connection with the Br&GR was made on 5 June. The line came to the GWR on its take-over of the Canal wef 1 July 1851 (Act of 30 June 1852). Authority to abandon the line was given on 5 July 1865, though the track remained for some years.

BALA & DOLGELLY (sic) RAILWAY

Authorized on 30 June 1862, the line linked Bala with Dolgellau, the county town of Merioneth, and on 12 July 1870 the Company was authorized to extend to Penmaenpool, where it met a branch (opened on 3 July 1865) from Barmouth at an end-on junction. The line served nowhere of importance except at either end, and the GWR, which worked it from its opening on 4 August 1868, absorbed it on 23 July 1877. The Bala Lake Railway, a narrow gauge tourist line opened throughout in 1976, uses the track-bed along the S shore of Lake Bala, and has its headquarters at Llanuwchllyn.

BALA & FESTINIOG RAILWAY

GWR-backed and incorporated on 28 July 1873, this was an attempt to reach the slate-quarries of Blaenau Ffestiniog before the L&NWR, but it was a year too late. The line opened to Llan Ffestiniog on 1 November 1882, and Blaenau on 10 September 1883, its 22 miles of single track winding through bleak country to join the Festiniog & Blaenau Railway (qv) end-on at Llan Ffestiniog. The line was leased to the GWR in 1879, which absorbed the Company under an Act of 26 July 1910, wef 1 July. Later the line served the nuclear power station at Trawsfynydd, but when, in 1961, it was to be cut above Bala by a reservoir, it was decided to close the line rather than deviate, and to serve the power station via the ex-L&NWR line (see Conway & Llanrwst Railway – LMS). The last passenger train ran on 2 January 1960, the last goods on 27 January 1961.

BANBURY & CHELTENHAM DIRECT RAILWAY

Incorporated on 21 July 1873, this was an amalgam of several schemes – the Bourton-on-the-Water and the Chipping Norton (both qv), and lines from Cheltenham to Bourton (opened on 1 June 1881) and from Chipping Norton to Kings Sutton (on the GWR's Oxford–Worcester line) opened on 6 April 1887. The line was 33 miles long, and was joined at Andoversford by the M&SWJR on its opening in 1891. It was worked by the GWR, which absorbed it wef 1 July 1897. Kings Sutton–Chipping Norton closed to passengers on 4 June 1951.

BARRY DOCK & RAILWAY

A mixed gauge line between Barry and Peterston (SWR), it was first incorporated on 5 July 1865, abandoned by BoT certificate in 1878–9 and re-incorporated on 14 August 1884. Powers were for 76 miles of railway from Barry Dock to the Rhondda Valley, with branches. One of its engineers was Henry Marc Brunel, son of Isambard. It opened from Barry to Barry Dock (passengers) on 8 February 1889, St Fagans–Cadoxton and Barry–Cogan (goods) on 13 May, with the Dock and remainder of the line to goods ceremonially opened on 18 July. On 5 August 1891 the company changed its name to the Barry Railway (qv).

BARRY RAILWAY

Incorporated on 5 August 1891 out of the Barry Dock & Railway (qv). A ¾-mile extension to Barry Island opened in July 1896, replacing an unbuilt tramway authorized in 1893 with, later, another ½-mile to Barry Pier. The company began to run steamers, but these lost money and were sold in 1909, the extension closing to passengers on 28 October 1971.

The Bala & Festiniog Railway in GWR days. In about 1920, a Dean 2-4-0T No 1491, with a mixed train of elderly stock, waits at Bala to begin its journey north. (John Roberts/Gwynedd Archives Service)

Above *The seal of the Barry Railway, its device neatly encapsulating its intentions.* (Roy Nash/Swindon Museums)

Below *The courses of canals were used in railway construction more than is usually realised—the Berks & Hants Extension Railway, for example, seen here at Crofton. Crofton lock (Kennet & Avon Canal) is on the right, just below the railway. The building on the left houses a Newcomen atmospheric pumping engine, still occasionally steamed.*

Between 1913–1920 dividends never fell below 9.5 per cent, and in 1913 Barry shipped almost one-third (11:37 million tons) of the coal exported from South Wales. Route mileage on 1 January 1922, when the Company became a GWR constituent, was 68 miles (300 track miles).

BERKSHIRE & HAMPSHIRE RAILWAY

Although nominally independent (incorporated on 30 June 1845), the company was backed by the GWR, which absorbed it by an Act of 14 May 1846. It continued the GWR's Newbury branch to Hungerford and a 13.5-mile line ran from Southcote Junction, Reading, to a separate station at Basingstoke. Opening from Reading to Hungerford was on 21 December 1847, and to Basingstoke on 1 November 1848. Broad gauge to begin with, authority to 'adapt the broad gauge' was obtained on 21 July 1873. It was extended to Devizes as the Berkshire & Hampshire Extension Railway (qv).

BERKSHIRE & HAMPSHIRE EXTENSION RAILWAY

The line was authorized on 13 August 1859 to extend the Berkshire & Hampshire Railway (qv) along the Kennet Valley for another 24.5 miles from Hungerford to Devizes. It was opened on 11 November 1862 and absorbed by the GWR on 10 August 1882, having been further extended to the

WS&WR at Westbury under Authority of 28 June 1866.

BIRMINGHAM & HENLEY-IN-ARDEN RAILWAY

A GWR-influenced company, incorporated on 7 August 1888, it took over the abandoned Henley-in-Arden & GW Junction Railway, opened it on 6 June 1894 (passengers), 2 July (goods), and worked it. It retained nominal independence until taken over by the GWR wef 1 July 1900. The line closed to passengers between Rowington Junction and Henley on 1 January 1915, and to goods on 1 January 1917, when the three miles of track went for wartime use. The line's terminus at Birmingham Moor Street was projected as a terminal for a steam link with the Standard Gauge Steam Trust's activities at Tyseley.

BIRMINGHAM, NORTH WARWICKSHIRE & STRATFORD-UPON-AVON RAILWAY

Originally part of a much larger scheme, the company finally settled for one authorized on 25 August 1894 which left the GWR S of Tyseley. When no capital was forthcoming, the GWR took over the company's powers from 30 July 1900, under an Act of 6 August. The route was revised to join the GWR's own Stratford line at Bearley N, and when it opened on 9 December 1907 (goods), 1 July 1908 (passengers), it was 18 miles long.

BIRMINGHAM & OXFORD JUNCTION RAILWAY

Incorporated on 3 August 1846, the line was to run from the Oxford & Rugby Railway (qv) at Knightcote (2 miles N of Fenny Compton) to the L&NWR at Birmingham. However, because it preferred broad gauge, the company agreed to amalgamate with the Birmingham, Wolverhampton & Dudley Railway (qv), with a lease to the GWR. Learning of this, the L&NWR used dubious tactics to effect a take-over — the resulting Parliamentary Inquiry permitted lease of both companies to the GWR. By the time the 24.75 miles from Oxford to Banbury were open (2 September 1850), the company had been absorbed by the GWR (Agreement of 12 November 1846) along with the BW&DR, on 31 August 1848. The Birmingham line opened on 1 October 1852, double track mixed gauge — broad gauge was abolished N of Oxford on 1 April 1869.

BIRMINGHAM, WOLVERHAMPTON & DUDLEY RAILWAY

Incorporated on 3 August 1846 to build a broad gauge line, the company was already leaning towards the GWR in regard to a lease. Following an Agreement of 12 November 1846, however, the company came into GWR hands by purchase and Act of Parlia-

ment of 31 August 1848. Construction began in 1851, and the line opened on 14 November 1854.

BLAENAVON TRAMROAD

First incorporated on 3 June 1792, this was a tramroad from Blaenavon Ironworks to the head of the Monmouthshire Canal at Pontnewydd. It was laid to 3 ft 4 in as an edge-railway, opening in 1795–6, and rebuilt in 1829 as a 4 ft 2 in gauge plateway, on which a 'tram' engine was used. In 1845 the company was re-incorporated as the Monmouthshire Railway & Canal Company (qv), and the line was later rebuilt as an extension of that company's Newport & Pontypool Railway (qv).

BOURTON-ON-THE-WATER RAILWAY

This line, authorized on 14 June 1860, was to run 6.5 miles from Chipping Norton Junction (Kingham, OW&WR) to Bourton. The line was worked by the GWR and the WMR (as the OW&WR had by then become) from opening, to stations only partly finished on 1 March 1862. Extension to Cheltenham, authorized on 25 July 1864 but abandoned in 1867, presaged the Cheltenham & Banbury Direct Railway (qv). The GWR absorbed the company from 1 February 1874.

BRECON & MERTHYR TYDFIL JUNCTION RAILWAY

An Act of 1 August 1859 authorized the Talybont–Brecon section only, but the rest was sanctioned on 15 May 1860 and 28 July 1862. The line opened from Brecon to Talybont on 23 April 1863, to Merthyr on 1 August 1868 and to Dowlais on 23 June 1869 — the Merthyr–Dowlais section was authorized jointly with the L&NWR. Amalgamation with the HH&BR under an Act dated 5 July 1865 was ruled illegal as improperly processed, and was never re-made. On 28 July 1863 the Company acquired the Rumney Railway (qv) in an effort to reach Newport, a link being finally made on 1 September 1868. The Company became a GWR subsidiary in 1922. Beacon, or Summit, tunnel was once the highest in the UK at 1,312 ft, with a 7-mile climb at 1 in 38 to the N portal. The line closed to passengers on 31 December 1962, and to goods on 4 May 1964, but is not dead, for the Pant–Torpantau section now carries the Brecon Mountain Railway — the Pant–Pontsticill section opened 8 June 1980.

BRIDGEND RAILWAY

This 4.5-mile line of 4 ft 7 in gauge ran between Cefn Cribbwr (W of Tondu, Dyffryn Llynfi & Porthcawl Railway, qv) and Bridgend. The line, authorized on 19 June 1828 and opened on 22 February 1830, was not a success, and after abandonment in 1854 was acquired for £3,000 by the LVR, which was authorized to use part for its Tywith branch, opened on 10 August 1861.

Talybont-on-Usk station, B&MTJR. The line this solid stone station served has gone, but the building is now a study centre. Old photographs show that the extension at the near end originally supported a water-tank.

BRIDPORT RAILWAY

Incorporated on 5 May 1855, this line ran from Maiden Newton (WS&WR) for 9.25 miles to Bridport. It opened on 12 November 1857, and was leased for 21 years from 1 July 1858 by the GWR, which obtained powers to adapt the gauge on 21 July 1873. Re-leased to the GWR from 1 July 1882, it was extended on 31 March 1884 to Bridport Harbour, renamed West Bay in the hope that tourism might result. It didn't — the GWR, which had absorbed the company by Act of 26 July 1901, withdrew the passenger service during the Great War, then permanently from 22 September 1930. The line closed completely on 5 May 1975.

BRISTOL & EXETER RAILWAY

This scheme was proposed by Exeter businessmen encouraged by the success of the GWR. Broad gauge was authorized on 19 May 1836, but the company was soon in financial trouble and unable to buy rolling-stock. Leased to the GWR, the line opened from Bristol to Bridgwater on 14 June 1841, to Taunton on 1 July 1842 and to Exeter on 1 May 1844. In 1845 the GWR offered to buy; it was turned down, and by the time the lease expired on 30 April 1849, the company had stock of its own and 85.5 miles of railway. In 1859 it began to build its own locomotives at Bristol. The Chard & Taunton (1863), Cheddar Valley &

Yatton (1865) and Exe Valley Railways (1875) — all qv — were absorbed, the Company eventually working 213.5 miles of line, of which it owned 138.5 miles. Various circumstances forced the laying of a third rail, standard gauge trains reaching Taunton on 30 May 1875, and Exeter (goods) in March 1876 (passengers in 1877). The line was re-leased to the GWR wef 1 January 1876, and amalgamated with that Company on 1 August (Act: 27 June).

The seal of the Bristol & Exeter Railway. (Roy Nash/Swindon Museums)

BRISTOL HARBOUR RAILWAY

This 1-mile line, authorized on 28 June 1866 and backed by the GWR, B&ER and Bristol City Corporation, ran from Wapping (Bristol) Wharf and the floating harbour to join the GWR main line just E of Temple Meads. Opened on 11 March 1872, it was worked by a joint committee. Its powers, vested in the GWR and B&ER on 30 June 1874, passed to the GWR when that company absorbed the B&ER. On 4 October 1906 it was extended ¾ mile to the Canons Marsh branch, opened on the same day.

BRISTOL & NORTH SOMERSET RAILWAY

Authorized on 21 July 1863, this 20-mile line ran between Radstock and Bristol. Its first sod was cut at Clutton on 7 October 1863, but the company had difficulty raising money, and the line did not open until 3 September 1873. Single track throughout, it was worked by the GWR from opening under an Agreement made in 1870, and vested in it under an Act of 7 August 1884. The GWR built the Camerton branch from Hallatrow (opened on 1 March 1882), and extended it to Limpley Stoke on 9 May 1910, using intact the Combe Hay tunnel, built in 1805 for the Somerset Coal Canal. The passenger service ceased on 22 March 1915, but was restored on 9 July 1923, after public pressure, to cease again on 21 September 1925. Camerton station was renamed 'Fal Vale' during the filming of 'The Ghost Train' in 1935. The last goods to Camerton ran on 14 February 1951, and in 1952 Monkton Combe station and village were used in the Ealing comedy feature film 'The Titfield Thunderbolt'. The branch was lifted in 1958. The 'main' line's last passenger train ran on 31 October 1959, the last goods on 11 July 1968.

BRISTOL & PORTISHEAD PIER & RAILWAY

The company was incorporated on 29 June 1863 to build a pier at Portbury and a 10-mile railway to the B&ER at Bedminster Downs. Broad gauge, it replaced an unbuilt Portbury Pier & Railway scheme of 1846, opening on 12 April 1867 (railway), 5 July 1879 (docks). After the GWR absorbed the B&ER (1876), it worked the line for 40 per cent of receipts and later bought it under an Act of 14 August 1884, wef 1 July.

BRISTOL & SOUTH WALES UNION RAILWAY

A line authorized on 27 July 1857 between Bristol and a 'steam-ferry' across the Severn estuary — broad gauge, it was opened by the GWR on 8 September 1863. Probably a detached section on the opposite bank, joining the ferry to the SWR, opened then too, though the date often quoted is 1 January 1864. The company was absorbed by the GWR from 1 August 1868 which then built the 4.628-mile Severn Tunnel

The Bristol & South Wales Union Railway plaque at Bristol, Temple Meads, is a caption in itself. (Allan Mott)

to supersede the ferry. This, authorized on 27 June 1872, is the longest 'surface railway' tunnel in the UK and was, for some time after opening, the longest underwater tunnel in the world. It saw its first train on 9 January 1886, and opened to regular goods traffic on 1 September, to passenger trains on 1 December.

BRITON FERRY FLOATING DOCK & RAILWAY

Incorporated on 3 July 1851 this short, ½-mile line linked the SWR with a wharf on the R Neath at Briton Ferry. It was leased to the VNR from opening in about 1852, and was absorbed by the GWR under an Act dated 28 July 1873.

BUCKFASTLEIGH, TOTNES & SOUTH DEVON RAILWAY

Incorporated on 25 June 1864 to build a broad gauge branch from Totnes to Buckfastleigh, powers were obtained the following year for an extension to Ashburton. Its 9 miles 20 chains included branches to quays at Totnes, the line being worked by the SDR from opening (1 May 1872) as part of its own system. It was bought for £22,450 by the GWR on 1 July 1897 having been converted to standard gauge in May 1892. Though closed by BR from 3 November 1958 (passengers), 10 September 1962 (goods), it survives between Totnes and Buckfastleigh as the Dart Valley Railway, opened on 21 May 1969.

BULLO PILL TRAMWAY

Incorporated on 10 June 1809, this tramway in the Forest of Dean was of uncertain gauge — authorities vary between 3 ft 6 in and 4 ft. It linked mines in the Forest with a quay on the Severn at Bullo Pill. The company was re-incorporated in 1826 as the Forest of Dean Railway (qv).

BURRY PORT & GWENDREATH (sic) VALLEY RAILWAY

Incorporated on 5 July 1865, by 1866 it had amalgamated with the Kidwelly & Burry Port Railway (qv) and had absorbed the Burry Port Harbour Company, giving it 21 miles of single track — 13 miles were 'main' line, the rest branches. Always short of money, the Company charged for baggage, since it could not legally charge fares. Though in Receivership twice, matters improved at the turn of the century, and the GWR took over a comparatively prosperous company wef 1 July 1922. The line was notable for its restricted loading gauge.

BUTE DOCKS COMPANY

A local concern at first, it was incorporated on 25 June 1886 and included railways in and around the Bute Docks at Cardiff. The TVR tried to take over the Company in 1888 but were turned down. In 1896 the Glamorganshire and the Aberdare Canals were acquired, but an amalgamation with the Rhymney Railway failed. By an Act of 6 August 1897 it changed its name to the Cardiff Railway (qv).

CALNE RAILWAY

Authorized on 15 May 1860, this broad gauge single line ran for 5.25 miles from the GWR at Chippenham. It opened on 3 November 1863 — the GWR gained powers for conversion to standard gauge on 21 July 1873, but did not take over until 1 July 1892. Passenger trains were used for sausage traffic from Calne, and the line retained this service (until 20 September 1965) longer than its goods trains, which ceased in November 1964.

CAMBRIAN RAILWAYS

Note the plural title — the Company was formed on

The Cambrian Railways were among the first to run buses from stations to villages not on the railway. From 1906 two Orions linked Edern and Nefyn with Pwllheli, a service used by both residents and visitors. (Gwynedd Archives Service)

25 July 1864 from the Oswestry, Ellesmere & Welshpool, the Oswestry & Newtown, the Llanidloes & Newtown and the Newtown & Machynlleth Railways; on 5 July 1865 the Aberystwyth & Welsh Coast Railway was also absorbed (all qv). By 1870 the company's financial affairs were in chaos, but had recovered by 1880. Tourist traffic grew during the next decade, improvements were made and Barmouth Bridge was rebuilt. The Mid-Wales Railway was absorbed in 1904, the Vale of Rheidol Railway in 1913, and the Tanat Valley LR (all qv) in 1921, just before the company itself became part of the GWR. Though threatened with closure, the Machynlleth–Pwllheli section saw steam specials in 1987, following renewal of Barmouth Bridge, and RETB was introduced from October 1988.

CARDIFF RAILWAY

Originally incorporated as the Bute Docks Company (qv), this was the sixth and last railway into the city of its title. Authorized on 6 August 1897 to build lines to the docks, it actually built only one, remaining a 6.5-mile local branch, because its main competitor, the TVR, managed to stifle its traffic potential. It opened for goods on 15 May 1909 and for passengers on 1 March 1911, retaining independence until it became a constituent of the GWR from 1 January 1922. The Coryton–Rhydfelin section closed to passengers on 20 July 1931, and about two-thirds of the Company's route is now beneath the A470 Cardiff–Merthyr road.

The seal of the Cardiff Railway—the Welsh motto means 'From Water and Fire'. (Roy Nash/Swindon Museums)

CARDIFF & OGMORE RAILWAY

The company was authorized on 21 July 1873 to build a line of 8 miles 1 furlong 5 chains from a junction in the parish of Llangeinor (Glamorgan, OVR) to Llanharan (GWR). A mineral-only line, opened on 2 October 1876, it had but a brief existence before amalgamating with the L&OR on 1 July 1876. The line closed on 28 July 1938.

CARMARTHEN & CARDIGAN RAILWAY

Incorporated on 7 August 1854 to build a line between the two towns, Cardigan was never reached, and it was left to the GWR to attain Newcastle Emlyn. The Carmarthen–Conwil section opened on 3 September 1860, worked by the SWR with GWR engines, but the company could not meet line charges, and closed the railway on 31 December. It re-opened on 12 August 1861, with extensions to Pencader on 28 March 1864, and Llandyssul on 3 June, but an OR was appointed in November 1864 and though the directors regained control in 1867 (using hired GWR locos), the Receiver was not discharged until 1878. The company was wound up and sold by Act of 22 August 1881 to the GWR, which opened a line to Newcastle Emlyn on 1 July 1895. This line closed to passengers on 15 September 1952, Pencader–Carmarthen on 22 February 1965 and to goods throughout on 28 September 1973. Two sections still have steam trains, however — the Abergwili & Llanpumpsaint LRO of 24 October 1977 authorized 8 miles of track between those places. The line was opened to the site of a workmen's platform at Llwyfan Cerrig in 1987, and an extension is planned. Nine miles of the Newcastle Emlyn branch have been bought by the Teifi Valley Railway, presently operating from Henllan.

CARMARTHENSHIRE RAILWAY

Incorporated on 3 June 1802, and opened between 1804 and 1806, this horse-worked tramway between Llanelli and Gorslas was laid with flange-rails on stone blocks. Less than a mile of the projected 16 was built, and the line was not a success, going into voluntary liquidation in 1844, after which it was dismantled. In 1875 the works were bought by the Llanelly & Mynydd Mawr Railway (qv) for £1,400.

CEFN & PYLE RAILWAY

This private line opened in 1798 to link local collieries with Waterhall Junction (PTR). It was acquired by the PTR for use as a branch under Acts of 27 July and 7 August 1896.

CHARD & TAUNTON RAILWAY

Incorporated on 6 August 1861, this line was built by the B&ER, (powers transferred on 8 June 1863), and laid beside a canal cut in 1842. It opened as a broad gauge line on 11 September 1866, serving Ilminster

The elegance and symmetry of the B&ER signal boxes is demonstrated by this one at Yatton West (Somerset), one of the large type. (Robert Humm)

as well as the named places. The GWR converted it to standard gauge on 19 July 1891.

CHEDDAR VALLEY & YATTON RAILWAY

The Act, dated 14 July 1864, for this line was obtained by the S&DR, but an Act of 19 June 1865 transferred powers to the B&ER. Broad gauge, the line opened to Cheddar on 3 August 1869, and to Wells on 5 April 1870, and was converted to standard gauge by the GWR in 1875. The GWR absorbed the company, with the B&ER, on 1 August 1876.

CHELTENHAM & GREAT WESTERN UNION RAILWAY

Incorporated on 21 June 1836, the first section to Kemble and Cirencester was opened on 31 May 1841. The Gloucester extension from Kemble met the Br&GR at Standish (opened 12 May 1845), 42 miles from Swindon. The line was leased to the GWR for seven years from the date of opening under an Agreement of April 1840, but was absorbed from 10 May 1844, making it, with the Oxford Railway (qv), absorbed on the same day, the first of many amalgamations by that company.

CHIPPING NORTON RAILWAY

Authorized on 31 July 1854, powers for this 4.5-mile branch from Chipping Norton Junction (renamed Kingham in 1909) were obtained by the OW&WR. The line was standard gauge and single; space was allowed for doubling but remained unused. Opening day (passengers) was 10 August 1855 — it had opened for goods on 1 June — and was a public holiday in Chipping Norton. In 1859 the OW&WR made an Agreement to pay a 4 per cent dividend to owners of

branch line shares, and the company amalgamated with the GWR in 1863 in company with the WMR as the OW&WR's successor. The line closed to passengers on 3 December 1862 (see also Banbury & Cheltenham District Railway).

CLEOBURY MORTIMER & DITTON PRIORS LIGHT RAILWAY

This 12-mile line lying E of Ludlow, authorized by LRO on 23 March 1901, took seven years to build, opening for goods on 19 July 1908, and passengers on 20 November. The company retained independence until absorption by the GWR on 1 January 1922; the line eventually had four owners, passing from BR to the Admiralty wef 1 May 1957. Though it lost its passenger service on 26 September 1938, the armaments depot it ultimately served prevented complete closure until 16 April 1965.

COLEFORD RAILWAY

With powers granted on 18 July 1872 to refurbish an old tramway from Coleford to the E bank of the R Wye near Monmouth, the company found that the Severn & Wye Railway's completion of its Lydbrook Junction line, plus a general depression, gave little incentive to build. On 30 June 1874 the GWR obtained permission to subscribe, but it was 1 September 1883 before the line's 5.25 miles opened for passengers. The company was absorbed by the GWR on 7 August 1884. Services ceased on 1 January 1917 (passengers), and 11 August 1967 (goods).

COLEFORD, MONMOUTH, USK & PONTYPOOL RAILWAY

Promoters of this link between the Forest of Dean and the S Wales coalfield were headed by Crawshaw Bailey MP, and the company was authorized on 20 August 1853 to build its line and to take over the Monmouth Railway (qv). The line opened from

Pontypool to Usk on 2 June 1856, and the remaining 17.5 miles to Monmouth (Troy) on 12 October 1857, worked from the start by the NA&HR. A viaduct was built across the Wye and opened on 1 July 1861, the day on which the line was leased to the WMR for 1,000 years (by an Agreement dated 31 January 1861, Act of 22 July). By then, however, the WMR had other things to think about, and it went no further towards Coleford. The company was transferred to the GWR by an Act of 22 August 1881. The line closed to passengers on 13 June 1955 (also for goods between Usk and Monmouth), the remainder closing on 13 September 1965.

CORNWALL RAILWAY

This railway W from Plymouth was authorized on 3 August 1846 and backed by the GWR, B&ER and SDR, who contributed £337,000 between them. The company was empowered to buy the Bodmin & Wadebridge Railway (qv – Southern Railway) but was beaten to it. Work began slowly, but the line opened from Plymouth to Truro on 2 May 1859 (officially) and 4 May (to the public), with the Falmouth branch opening for passengers on 24 August 1863 (goods 5 October). The backers leased the line until the B&ER and SDR were absorbed by the GWR; the GWR worked it from 1 January 1877. Despite efforts by the GWR to buy the company, it remained independent until dissolved by an Act of 24 June 1889.

CORNWALL MINERALS RAILWAY

This line was authorized on 21 July 1873 to take over or build several goods lines: the Newquay & Cornwall Junction Railway (qv), Fowey–Newquay, Bugle–Carbus, Treloggan Junction–E Wheal Rose. They were open by 1 June 1874 and a passenger service was begun on the Newquay–Fowey section on 20 June 1876. The line was leased to the GWR wef 1 July 1877 (Act of 10 August), and the company was absorbed by an Act of 7 August 1896. Part of the Treloggan–E Wheal Rose section was included in the Perranporth–Newquay passenger line, but the rest was closed in 1917. Re-opened in 1926, it quickly became disused again; the passenger service was cut back to St Blazey on 8 July 1929, and though never officially closed, the rest was dismantled after the Second World War. Under a 1987 plan, Newquay passenger traffic may be re-routed from the main line at Burngullow, W of St Austell, via St Dennis Junction.

CORRIS RAILWAY

Originally incorporated as the Corris, Machynlleth and River Dovey Tramroad (qv), the company changed names on 25 July 1864 under an Act which also permitted use of steam engines. The Imperial Tramways Company of Bristol acquired the line in 1878, relaid it and supplied locomotives — passenger working was authorized from 9 July 1880, and by

The Corris Railway's locomotive shed at Maespoeth Junction features in a preservation scheme. The track runs through the gate on the right towards Lower Corris, ¾ mile up the valley.

steam from 18 June 1883. A service opened on 4 July. The line was bought by the GWR in 1930, which promptly closed the passenger service wef 1 January 1931. Flooding caused final closure on 20 August 1948; two locomotives, some rail, goods rolling-stock and, later, a carriage went to the nearby Talyllyn Railway (qv – Jt/Ind) where locos and stock are still in service. A small museum has been opened in the station at Corris, and there are plans to re-open a stretch of line.

CORRIS, MACHYNLLETH & RIVER DOVEY TRAMROAD

Incorporated on 12 July 1858, the line linked slate quarries at Aberllefenni with a quay on the R Dyfi at Derwenlas, 2 miles downstream of Machynlleth. Built to a gauge of 2 ft 3 in, the line was gravity and horse-worked. An Act of 25 July 1864 authorized a change of name to the simpler Corris Railway (qv).

CORWEN & BALA RAILWAY

This line, incorporated on 30 June 1862, continued the Llangollen & Corwen Railway (qv) along the Dee valley. The 4.75-mile section to Llandrillo opened on 16 July 1866, and the line reached Bala on 1 April 1868. It was backed by the GWR, which worked it from the outset and absorbed it by an Act of 7 August 1896.

COWBRIDGE RAILWAY

This single-track branch, authorized on 29 July 1862, ran between Cowbridge and the SWR at Llantrisant. The line opened for goods in February 1865 and to passengers on 18 September, the company running its own services, using hired engines, though WA

Left *This embankment and bridge of the Cowbridge & Aberthaw Railway's formation are now completely dwarfed by the gigantic cement plant at Aberthaw.*

Below *The seal of the SDR, which wasted no time in taking over the Dartmouth & Torbay. Exeter (right) is linked with Plymouth, with Devon in attendance, all depending on the railway.* (Roy Nash/Swindon Museums)

with the GWR had been authorized on 21 July 1873. In 1876 the TVR leased it, though they could reach it only via GWR rails and reversal at Llantrisant, and it came officially into TVR hands by an Act of 26 August 1889. The line closed to passengers on 26 November 1951, and to goods on 1 November 1965, though the Llantrisant–Llanharry section remained open for ore trains until 1975.

COWBRIDGE & ABERTHAW RAILWAY
Authorized on 12 August 1889, this was an extension S of the Cowbridge Railway (qv), built to counter a threat from the Barry Railway (qv) which never materialized. It was opened on 1 October 1892 and absorbed by the TVR on 17 August 1894. The 6.5-mile line closed to passengers on 4 May 1926, but re-opened on 11 July 1927, closing finally on 5 May 1930. Goods traffic ceased on 1 November 1932, though the track remained until 1947.

CULM VALLEY LIGHT RAILWAY
The company was granted a Light Railway Act on 15 May 1873 by a rarely-used provision in the Regulation of Railways Act of 1868. Though well-supported locally, the line cost twice as much to build as forecast and opened two years later than promised, on 29 May 1876. Traffic was disappointing too, and disillusioned shareholders, authorized on 19 July 1875 to sell the concern to the B&ER, sold it to the GWR in April 1880 for £33,000.

DARE VALLEY RAILWAY
Promoted by the TVR and authorized on 21 July 1863, this line ran for 3.5 miles from the TVR's line at Dare Valley Junction to collieries in the upper Dare valley. The line was worked by the TVR, leased

wef 1 January 1871 and absorbed by Act of 26 August 1889. Motor trains were introduced in 1906, lasting until September 1924. The upper end has been landscaped to form part of the Dare Valley Country Park.

DARTMOUTH & TORBAY RAILWAY
This line was sanctioned on 27 July 1857, an extension of the SDR branch to Torre. It opened to Paignton on 2 August 1859, Brixham Road on 14 March 1861 for passengers (1 April for goods) and Kingswear on 16 August 1864. The line was worked by the SDR from the start, which leased it wef 1 January 1866 and

absorbed it shortly after. The line between Paignton and Dartmouth re-opened as a preserved line in the autumn of 1972, run by the Paignton & Dartmouth Steam Railway.

DEVON & SOMERSET RAILWAY

This 42.25-mile line ran from Norton Fitzwarren (near Taunton) to Barnstaple, and was authorized on 29 July 1864. Built cheaply (and slowly) to the broad gauge, it opened to Wiveliscombe on 8 June 1871, and to Barnstaple on 1 November 1873, worked by the B&ER. The line gained an appalling reputation, but after conversion to standard gauge in 1881 things improved. A spur to the L&SWR from Barnstaple Junction, authorized on 31 August 1885, opened on 1 June 1887 and through running over the Barnstaple & Ilfracombe Railway (qv – Southern Railway) became possible. The Company passed to the GWR by an Act of 26 July 1901.

DIDCOT, NEWBURY & SOUTHAMPTON RAILWAY

Authorized on 5 August 1873 to link the GWR at Didcot with the L&SWR near Micheldever, the two big companies wasted so much time arguing about connections that the company obtained powers for its own route into Southampton on 10 August 1882. Money was a problem, but while the GWR and L&SWR bickered the company pushed on to Winchester (opened on 1 May 1885), adding 27.5 miles to the 17.5 opened between Didcot and Newbury on 13 April 1882. At last the L&SWR agreed to a connection at Winchester, worked by itself, the GWR working the rest: it opened on 1 October 1891. The company remained independent until Grouping, when it went to the GWR.

DUDLEY & OLDBURY JUNCTION RAILWAY

This was the original title of a company incorporated on 21 July 1873 to build 1.5 miles of railway from Langley Green, Dudley, to Halesowen, with two branches. WA with the GWR were made in 1876, and, before opening, an Act of 11 August 1881 authorized a change of name to the Oldbury Railway (qv).

DULAS VALLEY MINERAL RAILWAY

This was the incorporative name (20 July 1862) of what became the Neath & Brecon Railway (qv), though the first plan was simply to open up the area between Neath and Onllwyn, 10 miles to the NW. However, before this initial line was opened, on 2 October 1864, the company changed its name to suit an ambition to become a through route between Swansea and the Midlands.

DYFFRYN LLYNFI & PORTHCAWL RAILWAY

This 4 ft 7 in gauge tramway, almost 17 miles long,

There are no railways at Porthcawl now, but this short length of one of the earliest lines in Wales, the Dyffryn Llynfi & Porthcawl Railway, last used in its original form in 1847, has been preserved in situ *on the quay.*

was authorized on 10 June 1825, engineered by John Hodgkinson using edge-rail. It opened in 1828 or 1829, linking Dyffryn Colliery with a harbour at Porthcawl, one of the earliest instances of a railway company opening its own harbour. Though the company chose an unfortunate site for its harbour, the Llynfi Valley Railway (qv) was not deterred from taking over the tramway on 22 July 1847: no doubt the anticipated traffic in coal, iron, limestone and general goods outweighed the disadvantages.

EAST GLOUCESTERSHIRE RAILWAY

Incorporated on 7 July 1862, this was a 50-mile, GWR-backed plan to link Witney with Cheltenham. The GWR backed out, and the company decided to go it alone, but only 14 miles between Witney and Fairford were ever opened, on 15 January 1873. It was worked (for 50 per cent of receipts) by the GWR as an extension of the Witney Railway (qv), the Banbury & Cheltenham Direct Railway (qv) later using abandoned earthworks at the Cheltenham end. The company was transferred to the GWR wef 1 September 1890 (Act of 4 August), which used the line, with the WR, as a guinea-pig for ATC experiments in 1906.

EAST SOMERSET RAILWAY

The company was authorized on 5 June 1856 to build a broad gauge line from Witham Junction to Wells. It opened to Shepton Mallet on 9 November 1858 and to Wells on 1 March 1862. The GWR obtained authority to convert the gauge on 21 July 1873, taking over the line the next year under an Act dated 30 June 1874. Passenger traffic ceased between Witham and Yatton on 9 September 1963, but the Witham end remains open for stone traffic from Merehead, and Cranmore is a steam preservation scheme centre under the company's old name, its stock including locomotives owned by the painter David Shepherd.

EAST USK RAILWAY

This was a revival, authorized on 6 August 1885, of an unsuccessful E Usk Railway & Docks scheme of 20 years before, to make a 4 miles 50 chains feeder to the GWR. The powers were transferred to the GWR on 28 June 1892, and the line was opened on 4 April 1898, with an extension to Uskmouth in August 1901. The line was doubled in the 1970s in order to serve Uskmouth Power Station.

ELY & CLYDACH VALLEYS RAILWAY

Sanctioned on 5 August 1873, this short extension of the Ely Valley Railway (qv) ran from Penygraig to Blaenclydach. The line opened on 10 August 1878 — the GWR was authorized on 13 July 1876 to subscribe, and, on 6 August 1880, to absorb the company.

ELY VALLEY RAILWAY

An Act of 13 July 1857 authorized a broad gauge line from Llantrisant (SWR) to Penrhiwfer, with branches — one went to 'Mynydd Gellyrhaidd' (sic), whence sprung the Ely Valley Extension Railway, another going to Glanmychydd (Penygraig), where it spawned the Ely & Clydach Valleys Railway (both qv). The line was opened to Tonyrefail on 2 August 1860 and Penygraig on 10 August 1878 (goods) and 1 May 1901 (passengers). It was leased to the GWR (which had worked it from the start) for 999 years wef 1 January 1861, and absorbed by an Act of 11 August 1903. The line closed to passengers on 9 June 1958, and to goods on 12 October 1964.

ELY VALLEY EXTENSION RAILWAY

Incorporated on 28 July 1863, this broad gauge line was worked by the GWR and ran from Gelli'r hiadd to Gilfach Goch. It opened for goods on 8 January 1862 and for passengers on 16 October 1865, and the company amalgamated (Act of 5 July 1865) with the OVR. The line closed to passengers on 22 September 1930, and to goods on 5 June 1961.

EXETER RAILWAY

This was the name taken by the Exeter, Teign Valley & Chagford Railway (qv) when its branch to Chagford was abandoned on 12 August 1898. Opening on 1 July 1903, the line linked Exeter with the Teign Valley Railway (qv) at Christow; it became known as the Teign Valley line, proving a useful diversionary route when the coast line via Dawlish was blocked, and for goods during the wars. Always leased/worked by the GWR (which absorbed it at Grouping), it closed to passengers on 9 June 1958, and to goods exactly ten years later.

EXETER, TEIGN VALLEY & CHAGFORD RAILWAY

Incorporated on 20 August 1883, the line was to run 8.75 miles from Exeter St Thomas via Doddiscombesleigh to Christow, where it would make an end-on junction with the Teign Valley Railway, and a 10-mile branch to Chagford was also authorized. The first sod was cut on 7 November 1894 — money problems caused the eleven-year delay — by Lady Northcote, wife of the MP for Exeter. More financial trouble caused abandonment of the Chagford branch, and in 1898 the company renamed itself the Exeter Railway (qv).

EXE VALLEY RAILWAY

The original authority for a line along the Exe valley had lapsed, but a company was incorporated on 30 June 1874 to build 7 miles 3 furlongs 1 chain 37 links between Tiverton and Thorverton, with a branch to Stoke Canon (B&ER). The powers passed to the B&ER by an Act of 19 July 1875, but that company was taken over by the GWR in 1876, and it was the GWR which actually built the line. It opened, standard gauge, on 1 May 1885, and closed to passengers on 7 October 1963.

FARINGDON RAILWAY

Authorized on 13 August 1860 in broad gauge, single track, it was the last purely broad gauge line E of Bristol. Opening between Faringdon and Uffington Road (GWR) on 1 June 1864 and worked by the GWR from the outset, it was converted to standard gauge on 10 August 1878. The company remained nominally independent until absorbed by the GWR under an Act of 25 June 1886. The line closed from 31 December 1951.

FESTINIOG & BLAENAU RAILWAY

A 3.5-mile line built without statutory powers (though the company was registered under the Limited Liability Act, 7 August 1862) to a gauge of 1 ft 11.75 in, it ran S to Llan Ffestiniog, from an end-on junction with the Festiniog Railway at Blaenau Ffestiniog, opening on 29 May 1868. Though worked at first by the FR, the Company was vested in the Bala & Festiniog Railway (qv) wef 13 April 1883 under a GWR Act of 6 August 1880. The B&FR converted the track to standard gauge (re-opened on 10 September 1883), the GWR using it as a link with Blaenau — see Bala & Festiniog Railway.

FOREST of DEAN RAILWAY

The company was formed on 5 May 1826 when the

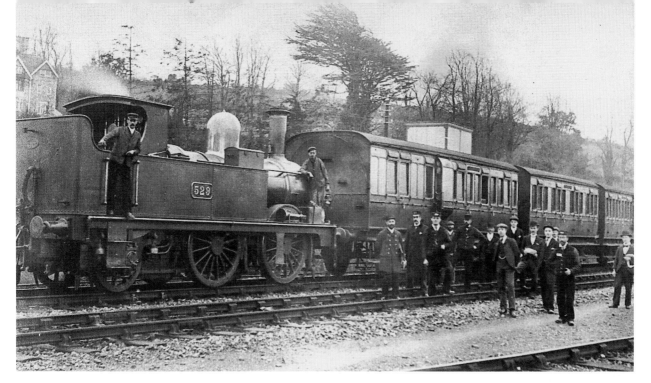

The Exe Valley Railway lost its independence long before it opened—this is believed to be the first train into Tiverton, GWR worked, on 1 May 1885. (Tiverton Museum Society)

Bullo Pill Tramway (qv) was re-incorporated. An Act of 2 July 1847 authorized the SWR to lease or buy the company, so that it could rebuild; the line re-opened on 24 July 1854 as 7.25 miles of broad gauge tramway serving a small harbour at Bullo Pill.

FOREST of DEAN CENTRAL RAILWAY

The company's aim was to link collieries with a dock planned at Brimspill on the R Severn — this was never built, and the Company had money problems immediately after incorporation (11 July 1856) because several shareholders omitted to pay up. When work began, the company was virtually in the hands of the GWR — the 4.75 miles were among the last in the country to be built to the broad gauge. On opening, 25 May 1868, the line joined the GWR at Awre; the gauge was converted in 1872. The company retained nominal independence, however, not falling officially to the GWR until 1923.

GLOUCESTER & DEAN FOREST RAILWAY

GWR-supported, the company was authorized on 27 July 1846 to build about 8 miles of railway from Gloucester to Grange Court Junction, with a 7.5-mile extension to Awre (SWR). The Gloucester–

Oakle Street, on the one-time Gloucester & Dean Forest Railway, was 5 miles from Gloucester, and though now closed, clearly had a respectable milk traffic in 1933. Note the 'stepped' platform ramp, no doubt to aid horses like that on the up platform. (Rev W. Awdry)

Grange Court section was opened on 19 September 1851 and leased in perpetuity to the GWR from the opening day. When money ran out, the SWR built the Awre extension, and the GWR a branch to Llanthony, Gloucester, opened on 20 March 1854. The line remained broad gauge until 1869, and the company was absorbed by the GWR under an Act of 30 June 1874.

GOLDEN VALLEY RAILWAY

This 18.75-mile line, authorized on 13 July 1876, ran along Herefordshire's Golden Valley from Pontrilas to Hay-on-Wye. Because of financial problems, the service between Pontrilas and Dorstone lasted only from 1 September 1881 to early July 1885 — it re-opened on 3 August 1885, but re-closed on 20 April 1898. The Dorstone–Hay section (authorized on 7 August 1884) opened on 27 May 1889 and closed on 23 August 1897. Under an Act dated 1 August 1899, the company was acquired by the GWR, and the line re-opened throughout on 1 May 1901. It closed finally on 15 December 1941.

GREAT MARLOW RAILWAY

Owned by local businessmen and authorized on 13 July 1868, this line of 2 miles 6 furlongs 5 chains 23 links had the support of the GWR and that company's assistance at the opening, on 28 June 1873: WA were authorized by Act of 21 July 1873. An extension to Henley was proposed, but dropped in the face of local opposition, and the company was absorbed by the GWR under an Act of 6 August 1897.

GREAT WESTERN & BRENTFORD RAILWAY

Incorporated on 14 August 1855, this 4-mile broad gauge branch from Southall to Brentford Dock, opened for goods on 15 July 1859, and was leased to the GWR that year — passenger opening was on 1 May 1860, and in 1861 a standard gauge track was laid beside the broad one, which was converted in 1876. It was an important goods route, but passenger traffic was light and the service was withdrawn on 4 May 1942. The company was vested in the GWR wef 1 January 1872.

GREAT WESTERN & UXBRIDGE RAILWAY

This line between W Drayton and Uxbridge, authorized on 16 July 1846, was laid to the broad gauge and single. It opened on 8 September 1856, was converted to standard gauge in 1871, and was doubled in 1880 by the GWR, which had acquired the company by an Act of 22 July 1847. Re-singled on 18 October 1962, the line closed to passengers on 10 September, and to goods on 13 July 1964.

GROSMONT RAILWAY

Incorporated on 12 May 1812, this 7-mile plateway was engineered by John Hodgkinson to a gauge of 3 ft 6 in. It opened in 1818–19, extending the Llanvihangel Railway from Llanvihangel to Monmouth Cap, where, in 1829, the Hereford Railway (both qv) joined it, making a continuous line between Abergavenny and Hereford. It was bought by the NA&HR in 1846, which used the track-bed for a line between Hereford and S Wales.

GWENDRAETH VALLEYS RAILWAY

Promoted as a goods line by the Carmarthen & Cardigan Railway (qv), and authorized on 30 July 1866 to serve lime-kilns, silica and tinplate works, it opened in 1871, but an OR was appointed 1892–1903; during this time the Burry Port & Gwendreath Valley Railway (qv) worked the line by Agreement. In 1904 the line was sold to the Kidwelly Tinplate Works — this company supplied two locomotives, and when the line became the smallest subsidiary of the GWR at Grouping it owned 3 miles of track and two engines. Official closure was on 28 August 1960, though the last train ran in February 1959.

HALL'S TRAMROAD (later known as ABERCARN RAILWAY)

This plateway was built privately and opened about 1811 by Benjamin Hall, son-in-law of Cyfarthfa ironmaster Richard Crawshaw. Thought to have been approximately 3 ft gauge originally, an affidavit of 1879 states that about 1828 '. . . a wider gauge was substituted'. This was 4 ft 2 in, the same as the Monmouthshire Railway & Canal (qv). The line was an outlet for Manmoel Colliery, above Argoed in the upper Sirhowy valley, running downstream and E into Ebbw Vale near Newbridge, before joining the MR&C a little N of Risca. An Act of 13 July 1876 authorized the GWR to lease or buy the line; it opted for a 1,000-year lease at the end of 1877, and, after conversion to a standard gauge railway, re-opened it from Manmoel to Penar Junction in March 1886, throughout in September 1912. A passenger service at the lower end began on 14 March 1927, and the line survived until 31 December 1979, becoming one of the oldest lines to remain in use: it had still not been dismantled in 1986. Hall's son, Benjamin, was responsible, as Chief Commissioner of Works, for the clock tower at the Houses of Parliament, and gave his name to the bell, 'Big Ben'.

HAYLE RAILWAY

Slightly unusual in that the line was authorized (27 June 1834), and the company named afterwards, this was a standard gauge line between Hayle and Tresaveen (Gwennap) — 12 miles, with 5 miles of branches. The Portreath branch opened first, for goods on 23 December 1837 (passengers in 1841), with Carn Brea Mines–Redruth (goods) on 11 June 1838, Redruth–Hayle (passenger) 23 May 1843. The Portreath arm did such business with ore and coal

that it needed enlarging in 1846. The passenger service on the main line was operated by William Crotch, but he soon passed the responsibility to the Railway. Part of the main line became incorporated into the Paddington–Penzance line, via the W Cornwall Railway (qv), which absorbed the company on 3 December 1846. Regular traffic to Portreath ceased about 1930, and the line closed officially from 1 April 1938.

HELSTON RAILWAY

Locally promoted, and sanctioned on 9 July 1880, this 8 miles 67 chains line between Gwinnear Road and Helston required extension of time and extra capital (31 July 1885) before completion. It was opened on 9 May 1887, and is notable mainly for the fact that the first GWR buses ran in connection with it. An LRO for extension to the Lizard was obtained, but buses saved the £85,000 expense of building it; they began running on 17 August 1903, the company having been absorbed by the GWR five years earlier, under an Act of 2 August 1898.

Left *The incline at Portreath, photographed in 1934, and in good condition considering that regular traffic had ceased four years before. Note the wagon turntable in the foreground, and the rollers (to prevent the cable snagging) still in place on the incline. (Royal Institution of Cornwall)*

Below *A posed photograph of train crew and station staff of Gwinnear Road, believed to have been taken on the day the Helston Railway opened, 9 May 1887. (Royal Institution of Cornwall)*

HENLEY-in-ARDEN & GREAT WESTERN JUNCTION RAILWAY

Powers under the original Act of 5 August 1873 were revived on 23 June 1884 for a 3-mile line between Rowington Junction and Henley. The Company became the Birmingham & Henley-in-Arden Railway (qv) on 7 August 1888.

HEREFORD RAILWAY

This line from Monmouth Cap to Hereford, authorized on 26 May 1826, opened on 2 September 1829; by continuing the Grosmont Railway (qv) it linked the Abergavenny & Brecknock Canal with Hereford. The company was bought by the NA&HR in 1846, the track-bed being used as part of its route.

HEREFORD, ROSS & GLOUCESTER RAILWAY

The company was incorporated on 5 June 1851 to build 22.5 miles from Grange Court (W of Gloucester) to Hereford via Ross-on-Wye. The Grange Court–Hopesbrook (near Longhope) section was opened on 11 July 1853, but it was 2 June 1855 before the rest was ready. Financial support came from the GWR via the Gloucester & Forest of Dean Railway (qv), which had acquired the authorising Act, and the line was built broad gauge. An Act of 29 July 1862 transferred the Company to the GWR, which mixed the gauge and doubled the track in 1866. Three years later the line was used as the guinea-pig for the GWR's gauge conversion programme.

KIDWELLY & BURRY PORT RAILWAY

The Company was incorporated on 5 July 1865 to take over the track-bed of the Kidwelly & Llanelly Tramroad, and convert it to a railway. It amalgamated with the Burry Port & Gwendreath Valley Railway (qv) on 30 April 1866.

KINGSBRIDGE & SALCOMBE RAILWAY

Incorporated on 24 July 1882, this GWR-backed company took over powers granted to the Kingsbridge Railway on 29 May 1864 to build from Brent (SDR) to the places named. Alas, it never saw its railway opened independently, being dissolved and absorbed by the GWR on 13 August 1888. The line opened — to Kingsbridge only — on 19 December 1893 and closed to passengers on 16 September 1963.

KINGTON TRAMWAY

An early (23 May 1818) horse-drawn tramway 14 miles long from limestone quarries at Burlinjob, 3 miles from Radnor, to join the Hay Railway (qv – LMS) end-on at Eardisley. It opened on 1 May 1820 between Eardisley and Kington, and throughout on 7 August. In 1862 the route was acquired by the Kington & Eardisley Railway (qv) for use as part of its own line.

KINGTON & EARDISLEY RAILWAY

Part-adapted from the Kington Tramway (qv), acquired at incorporation (30 June 1862), the 7-mile line did not open until 3 August 1874; the proprietors' plan was to link with the HH&BR at Eardisley, about 10 miles NE of Hay. A 6.5-mile extension to New Radnor opened on 26 September 1875, the company passing to the GWR from 1 July 1897.

LAMBOURN VALLEY LIGHT RAILWAY

This short, privately-promoted line had a long gestation — work was not begun on its 12 miles until five years after authorization (2 August 1883), and another ten passed before opening, on 2 April 1898. All rolling-stock was withdrawn in 1904, after which passenger traffic was carried in motor railcars lent by the GWR. That company took over by Act of 4 August 1905, and in the 1930s tested, very successfully, a diesel railcar on the line; built specifically, it was equipped to haul a wagon or horsebox. The line closed to passengers on 4 January 1960.

LAMPETER, ABERAYRON & NEW QUAY LIGHT RAILWAY

Authorized by LRO on 9 October 1906, the first sod of this line was cut on 20 October 1908, but only 12 miles were built, from Lampeter to Aberayron. It was opened on 10 April 1911 (goods), 12 May (passengers), by the GWR, under WA made in February 1909. The company did, however, retain independence until 1923. The line closed to passenger traffic temporarily from 12 February 1951, and permanently from 7 May, and to goods between Aberayron and Felin Fach from 5 April 1965 and completely on 1 October 1973.

LAUNCESTON & SOUTH DEVON RAILWAY

The Act (30 June 1862) authorized a 19-mile line from Tavistock to Launceston, extending the S Devon & Tavistock Railway (qv). It opened (officially) on 1 June 1865, and to the public a month later, passing to the SDR by an Act of 24 June 1869.

LEOMINSTER & BROMYARD RAILWAY

Incorporated on 30 July 1874 as a substitute for the abandoned section of the Worcester, Bromyard & Leominster Railway (qv), it was to join it from the S&HR at Leominster. Powers for extension into Leominster and Bromyard were obtained on 8 August 1878 and 7 August 1884 respectively, and the 12-mile line, opened on 1 March 1884 and worked from the outset by the GWR, was vested in it wef 1 July 1888.

LEOMINISTER & KINGTON RAILWAY

This 13.25-mile line was incorporated on 10 July

'There was once a road through the woods . . .' Nature had taken over the trackbed at Titley Junction (Leominster & Kington Railway) in May 1988, though the platform (right) is in fair shape, and the station house is lived in.

1854 to link the towns; it opened throughout on 2 August 1857, worked by Thomas Brassey, its contractor. From 1 July 1862, the WMR and GWR took over joint working. A branch from Titley to Presteign was authorized on 31 July 1871, opening on 10 September 1875. TA with the GWR were sanctioned on 23 July 1877, and absorption followed under an Act dated 2 August 1898.

LISKEARD & CARADON RAILWAY

Incorporated on 27 June 1843 as a standard gauge, gravity-worked feeder for the Liskard & Looe Canal, horses were used for the uphill runs. It opened from Moorswater to S Caradon on 28 November 1844, and to Cheesewring in March 1846. The company worked the Liskeard & Looe Railway (qv) from 1862, leasing it in 1901; passengers travelled free in mineral wagons, provided they bought a ticket for their umbrella, parcels, hat, etc, a system not abandoned until 31 December 1916. From 1909, the line was worked by the GWR, which absorbed the company under an Act of 25 May that year.

LISKEARD & LOOE RAILWAY

Originally incorporated on 22 June 1825 by the Liskeard & Looe Canal Company, this 7-mile line joined the two towns, opening about 1828. The Company was reconstituted to build a link with the Liskeard & Caradon Railway (qv) from Moorswater to Looe Bridge on 11 May 1858; this was worked by the L&CR from 1862. A passenger service began in 1879, and a lease was made from 1901. A line, still used, was built between Coombe and Liskeard (GWR) in 1901, and WA were made with the GWR by an Act of 25 May 1909. The company was independent until Grouping.

LLANELLY (sic) RAILWAY & DOCK

Often known as the Llanelly Railway, this undertaking was authorized in two sections — docks (19 June 1828) and railway (21 August 1835). The Docks–Dafen section opened in 1833, and the railway to Pontardulais on 1 June 1839. The company expanded over the years, stretching tentacles to Llandilo (24 January 1857), Carmarthen (1 June 1865), and to Swansea from Pontardulais on 14 December 1867. After authority was given on 26 June 1868 to lease the Vale of Towy Railway (qv) jointly with the L&NWR's Central Wales companies, the L&NWR pressed for a new company to take over the Llandilo–Abergwili and Pontardulais–Swansea lines, with the Penclawydd branch; these were reincorporated as the Swansea & Carmarthen Railway (qv). The Penclawydd branch became known as the 'Cockle' line for obvious reasons, though it had been built to serve collieries. The L&NWR persuaded the company to grant it RP over all lines, which the company later regretted. The GWR took over working from 1 January 1873 under Agreement, absorbing the Company by an Act of 24 June 1889. The Dafen branch closed on 4 March 1963.

LLANELLY & MYNYDD MAWR RAILWAY

Incorporated on 19 July 1875, it was the successor to the Carmarthenshire Railway (qv), having bought that concern's works for £1,400. Its final length was a little over 12 severely-graded miles, 7 miles of it at 1 in 40 — it was not unusual to see three locomotives on a train. The line opened on 1 January 1883, the company passing to the GWR at Grouping; coal traffic still flows from Cynheidre.

LLANGOLLEN & CORWEN RAILWAY

Incorporated on 6 August 1860 to continue the Vale of Llangollen Railway (qv) along the Dee Valley, like the earlier line this 9 miles 50 chains section was backed and worked from opening (1 May 1865) by the GWR, being formally absorbed by that company under an Act of 7 August 1896. All services ceased between Llangollen and Bala on 13 December 1964,

a month earlier than the official closure date because of a bridge wash-out at Llandderfyl, near Bala. The Llangollen Railway Society has a steam centre at Llangollen — the line has reopened to Berwyn, and the Society, like the GWR in 1860, has its sights on Corwen.

LLANIDLOES & NEWTOWN RAILWAY

This 14-mile line, authorized on 4 August 1853 and isolated until the coming of the Oswestry & Newtown Railway, opened for goods on 30 April 1859, and to passengers on 2 September. In 1864 the company joined the O&NR, the Newtown & Machynlleth and the Oswestry, Ellesmere & Welshpool Railways (all qv) to form the Cambrian Railways. Substantial coal traffic to Scapa Flow used the line during the Great War; it closed to passengers on 31 December 1962, and to goods on 2 October 1967.

LLANTRISANT & TAFF VALE JUNCTION RAILWAY

Though nominally independent, this company, incorporated on 7 June 1861, was promoted by the TVR to run between Pontypridd and Llantrisant, tapping the area W of its own line and keeping its rivals in their place. It opened for goods in December 1863, and for passengers in 1865, and was worked by the TVR, which leased it (for 999 years from date of opening, though this was not ratified until 20 June 1870), and absorbed it on 26 August 1889. Passenger services ceased on 31 March 1952.

LLANVIHANGEL RAILWAY

Incorporated on 25 May 1811 and opened in 1814, this was a 3 ft 6 in gauge line running from a wharf on the Brecknock & Abergavenny Canal at Govilon to Llan Crucorney (6.25 miles), and an end-on junction with the Grosmont Railway (qv). The company was bought by the NA&HR on 3 August 1846, but part reverted to the Merthyr, Tredegar & Abergavenny Railway after 1859.

LLYNFI & OGMORE RAILWAY

Formed on 28 June 1866 by amalgamation of the Llynfi Valley Railway (qv) and the OVR, agreement was made with the GWR to work and manage the line wef 1 July 1876. Also from that date the Cardiff & Ogmore Railway (qv) joined the group. Despite its disadvantages, the harbour at Porthcawl prospered until the PTR and the Barry Railway tapped its business. The GWR, which had formally absorbed the Company wef 1 July 1883, closed the harbour in 1898, but not the railway — yet. The harbour was turned into an esplanade, and Porthcawl began to develop as a resort, the GWR opening a new station on the dock site in 1916. Closure of the railway came on 9 September 1963 (passengers) and 1 February 1965 (goods) — nothing can now be seen of the line there.

LLYNFI VALLEY RAILWAY

Incorporated on 7 August 1846, the company bought two connecting tramroads, the Dyffryn Llynfi & Porthcawl Railway (22 July 1847), and the Bridgend Railway (both qv) for £3,000 in 1855, with powers to use the BR track-bed for a new line. In 1861 the company began to convert its acquisitions into railways suitable for passenger traffic, the line opening for goods on 1 August 1861 and for passengers exactly four years later. Amalgamation with the OVR by an Act of 28 June 1866 formed the L&OR. Closure to passengers was on 9 September 1963.

LOSTWITHIEL & FOWEY RAILWAY

Incorporated on 30 June 1862, this was a broad

Left *Berwyn was the Llangollen & Corwen Railway's first station to the west. It is seen here on 3 October 1987, as a Llangollen Railway Society train draws into the platform.* (Diana Awdry)

Right *The GWR extended the Llynfi & Ogmore Railway across the Afan valley by a lattice girder bridge. N of the bridge it joined the S Wales Mineral Railway, whose trackbed is on the right of the valley. On this side were the Swansea & Rhondda Bay Railway and a GWR branch to Cymmer.*

gauge line from Lostwithiel to Carne Point, a mile upsteam from Fowey. It opened on 1 June 1869, with china clay as the main traffic, but the company ran out of funds (it had been undercutting the rates of the rival Cornwall Minerals Railway — qv) and it had to close on 1 January 1880.*

MALMESBURY RAILWAY

This 6.5-mile line from Dauntsey to Malmesbury, authorized on 25 July 1872, was promoted by an independent company, though the GWR subscribed half the capital. The line opened on 17 December 1877, the company being absorbed by the GWR under an Act of 6 August 1880.

MANCHESTER & MILFORD RAILWAY

Incorporated on 23 July 1860, this was a grandiose scheme to link Manchester with Milford Haven, its independent line running from Llanidloes to Pencader while the remainder would have required RP. It never linked the places, though a line from Pencader was opened to Lampeter 1 January 1866, to Strata Florida on 1 September, and to Aberystwyth on 12 August 1867. Neither was it viable financially; an OR was appointed in 1880, and the line was leased to the GWR wef 1 July 1906, before absorption under an Act of 2 June 1911. It closed to passengers on 22 February 1965, and to goods on 30 September 1973: its bay platform at Aberystwyth is now used by the Vale of Rheidol LR (qv).

* The Company was transferred to the CMR by an Act of 27 June 1892, and when the line re-opened on 16 September 1895, it was a standard gauge branch of the GWR, which had absorbed the CMR in the meantime.

MARLBOROUGH RAILWAY

Sanctioned on 22 July 1861, this was a heavily-graded line from Savernake to Marlborough, more than one-fifth of its 5.5 miles being at 1 in 58. Broad gauge, it was opened on 14 April 1864 and converted in 1874; the GWR absorbed the company by an Act of 7 August 1896. Duplication with the M&SWJR ended when the GWR closed Marlborough station to passengers wef 6 March 1933, and incorporated part of the route into the M&SWJR.

A line that never was—the Manchester & Milford built S from Llanidloes to Llangurig, but never connected with the arm coming N from Pencader. The remains of a shallow cutting are seen from the site of what might, in time, have been Llangurig station.

MARLBOROUGH & GRAFTON RAILWAY

This 6.75-mile line was authorized to the M&SWJR on 7 August 1896, as a link between the Swindon, Marlborough & Andover and the Swindon & Cheltenham Extension Railways (both qv), to bypass the GWR whose lines were causing a bottleneck at Marlborough. Incorporated as a subsidiary, since the parent company was bankrupt, it was absorbed by an Act of 1 August 1899, after the line had opened on 26 June 1898. A curve to join the Berkshire & Hampshire Railway (qv) was opened on 6 September 1905.

MAWDDWY RAILWAY

The Act (5 July 1865) spelt the name 'Mowddwy', favouring the phonetic rather than the accurate. The line's 6.75 miles began at Dinas Mawddwy and ran down the Dyfi Valley to the CambR at Cemmaes Road, serving the Hendre Ddu Tramway (qv — Jt/Ind) *en route*. It was worked by the contractor on opening (1 October 1867), but traffic was disappointing, and the line closed to passengers on 17 April 1901, and to goods on 8 April 1908. Lt-Col David Davies bought out the company, promoted an LRO (confirmed on 2 March 1910), and the line re-opened to the public on 31 July 1911, worked by the CambR. The line passed to the GWR at Grouping, and the passenger service ceased wef 1 January 1931 (goods from 1 July 1951). A woollen-mill and cafe now occupy the station site at Dinas Mawddwy.

Rails still enter the locomotive shed at Dinas Mawddwy, terminus of the Mawddwy Railway, but it is many years since an engine watered at the column. An attempt to establish a narrow gauge tourist venture on the site in 1975 failed for financial reasons.

MIDLAND & SOUTH WESTERN JUNCTION RAILWAY

This was formed on 23 June 1884 by the fusion of the Swindon, Marlborough & Andover and the Swindon & Cheltenham Extension Railways (both qv). The line served a sparsely populated area, but military camps gave good business, particularly during the Second World War. RP into Southampton had been authorized, but were not used until 1 November 1892 (goods) and 1 June 1894 (passengers). The company became bankrupt, but recovered thanks to Sam Fay, later Sir, who came from the L&SWR and went on to the GCR. He promoted the Marlborough & Grafton Railway (qv), and established a locomotive, carriage and wagon works at Cirencester. The S section, between Eling and Fawley, was taken over by the S Hampshire Railway & Pier (qv), and the whole by the GWR in 1923, which thus gained the entry to Southampton it had wanted for so long. The passenger service to Southampton ceased on 11 September 1961. Blunsdon station was re-opened on 29 August 1982 by the Swindon & Cricklade RS, which plans to restore part of the line.

MID-WALES RAILWAY

The line was authorized in two sections — the N end, Llanidloes–Llandovery, on 1 August 1859, the S length (Newbridge-on-Wye to Three Cocks) on 3 July 1860. The company also gained control of the Three Cocks–Talyllyn section, hitherto owned by the HH&BR. The first sod was cut in a downpour on 2 September 1859, but further work on the 46.75 miles was delayed until 1862. Formal opening took place on 23 August 1864, and the line opened to goods on 1 September. The company worked the HH&BR while that company was sorting out its 'illegal' amalgamation with the B&MTJR, but then had money trouble. Locomotives and rolling-stock were sold, WA with the CambR were signed, wef 2 April 1888, and vesting followed from 24 June 1904. The line was used intensively by coal traffic going N to Scapa Flow during the Great War.

MILFORD RAILWAY

Incorporated on 5 June 1856 to build a 4-mile broad gauge line from docks at Milford Haven to an SWR branch at Johnston, it opened on 7 September 1863. It was worked under Agreement to Rent by the GWR, which was lessee of the SWR, and was absorbed by the GWR under an Act of 7 August 1896.

MINEHEAD RAILWAY

Originally incorporated on 5 July 1865 as an independent extension of the W Somerset Railway (qv) from Watchet, the company was dissolved in 1870. The scheme was revived by the WSR on 29 June 1871, after which work began and the line was finally

opened on 16 July 1874. It was managed, maintained and worked by the B&ER from opening, and was converted to standard gauge in October 1882. The company was absorbed by the GWR under an Act dated 6 August 1897.

MITCHELDEAN ROAD & FOREST of DEAN JUNCTION RAILWAY

This was incorporated on 13 July 1871 to extend the Bullo Pill Railway to the Hereford, Ross & Gloucester Railway (both qv) at Mitcheldean Road, 4.75 miles away. Heavy engineering was involved and the line was never finished, despite the company's absorption by the GWR under an Act dated 6 August 1880. The first 1.75 miles to Speedwell opened in July 1885, and to Drybrook on 4 November 1907, but the rest, though built and maintained, was not. Unused track went for scrap in 1917.

Above Rhayader (Mid-Wales Railway) lost its train service (officially) on 31 December 1962, an event perhaps foreshadowed by the right-hand poster on the end wall, headed 'TRANSPORT ACT', which was possibly giving notice of closure. Prospects for the station seemed as dismal as the weather.

Right A substantial stone overbridge near Drybrook (Mitcheldean Road & Forest of Dean Junction Railway). This section opened on 4 November 1907, but closed on 7 July 1930. Note the bridge-rail fencing, still extant in August 1988.

MONMOUTH RAILWAY

Though authorized on 24 May 1810 and opened on 17 August 1812, the line was probably not completed until early 1817. It was a 3 ft 6 in horse-drawn plateway, linking Howler's Slade in the Forest of Dean with Coleford and Monmouth. Little used after 1850, the Monmouth–Coleford section was bought by the Coleford, Monmouth, Usk & Pontypool Railway (qv) in 1853.

MONMOUTHSHIRE RAILWAY & CANAL

Incorporated on 31 July 1845, this line had its beginnings in the Blaenavon Tramroad (qv) re-incorporated and re-titled. The company's Pontypool to Newport line extended the original one S, opening on 1 July 1852; it re-opened from Pontypool to Blaenavon (North) on 2 October 1854. In 1860 the WMR tried to lease it but was refused — it got RP, however, in 1862. From 1 August 1875, the GWR was granted a 99-year lease and use of all fixed assets — formal amalgamation came wef 1 August 1880. Two short, steep branches fed the line, to Cwmfrwdoer (1 in 22) and Cwmnantddu (1 in 19), both opened in 1870. A third, opened on 18 September 1879, climbed on a tight semicircle to cross them, heading N to Abersychan and Talywain. Amongst S Wales companies, the MR&C has the distinction shared only with the TVR in S Wales, of building its own engines. Pontypool–Blaenavon closed to passengers on 30 April 1962, the mineral branches on 7 April 1969 and the Talywain branch on 3 May 1980.

MORETONHAMPSTEAD & SOUTH DEVON RAILWAY

This broad gauge branch, authorized on 7 July 1862, ran N from Newton Abbot and was worked from opening (4 July 1866) by the SDR, which absorbed it by an Act dated 18 July 1872. From Heathfield (see also Teign Valley Railway) it followed the Bovey valley, ending its 12-mile journey at Moretonhampstead, 550 ft higher than it began. The line closed to passengers on 2 March 1959, but the Newton Abbot–Heathfield stretch still has occasional use.

MUCH WENLOCK & SEVERN JUNCTION RAILWAY

Incorporated on 21 July 1859 to build a 3.25-mile line from a branch of the Severn Valley Railway (qv) at Buildwas to Much Wenlock, it opened on 1 February 1862. It was worked by the WMR, which passed it to the GWR by an Act of 7 August 1896.

NANTWICH & MARKET DRAYTON RAILWAY

Incorporated on 7 June 1861, it was a 10.75-mile line between the towns. It opened on 20 October 1863, and on 21 July 1873 the GWR was authorized to

'. . . make financial arrangements', absorbing the Company wef 1 July 1897 by an Act of 6 August.

NARBERTH ROAD & MAENCLOCHOG RAILWAY

Built under a BoT certificate dated 24 June 1872, this line served slate quarries at Rosebush, in the Preseli Hills. It was opened on 19 September 1876, and in 1881 a scheme to extend the line to Fishguard led to an arrangement with the Rosebush & Fishguard Railway (qv); this, however, came to nothing until revived as the N Pembroke & Fishguard Railway (qv).

NEATH & BRECON RAILWAY

Formed on 13 July 1863 when the Dulas Valley Mineral Railway (qv) changed its name, the line, from Onllwyn to Brecon (authorized on 29 July 1864) opened on 3 June 1867 across 23 miles of bare land. Because the BoT forbade passenger traffic across a bridge at Brecon, the company emptied trains short of it, and transferred travellers to the engine, which then crossed, light, to a point nearer the B&MTJR station. When the MR leased the HH&BR in 1874, it used Swansea Vale Railway RP, bought at the same time, to reach Swansea. The service was worked by the MR and continued by the LMS despite the fact that the company had actually passed to the GWR wef 1 January 1922. The line closed to passengers on 15 October 1962, and to goods N of Craig-y-Nos. The section to Colbren Junction closed to goods on 7 October 1963, but re-opened on 1 July 1964 to serve a quarry. The quarry company has restored the waiting room at Craig-y-Nos station, used by Dame Adeline Patti, the opera singer. The line near Craig-y-Nos was used in 1971 during the making of the feature film 'Young Winston', together with the Great Western Society's 0–4–2T No 1466, heavily disguised.

NEWENT RAILWAY

Incorporated on 5 August 1873, a few days after the Ross & Ledbury Railway (qv), it joined the latter in building a line from Over Junction (Gloucester) to Dymoke (12.75 miles). In 1874 and 1885 the GWR was authorized to subscribe, the line opening on 27 July 1885, and passing to it on 1 July 1892, again in company with the R&LR. Part of the line's course near Newent had been a canal, and, now a bypass, is marked with a plaque noting the continuity of the route.

NEWPORT, ABERGAVENNY & HEREFORD RAILWAY

This line grew out of a grandiose scheme for a Welsh Midland Railway running from Worcester to Merthyr Tydfil. Incorporated on 3 August 1846, the company bought the Hereford, the Llanvihangel and

The Neath & Brecon Railway signal box, now minus its GWR nameboard, at Onllwyn. Note the decorated bargeboards, and the fact that the near finial appears to have lost its tip, perhaps when the timber extension was built. (Robert Humm)

the Grosmont Railways (all qv) for the sake of their track-beds, but construction was suspended during the money crisis of 1847–51, and the L&NWR tried to buy the company. Parliament prevented this, but when the line opened (Abergavenny–Pontypool on 2 January 1854, Hereford–Barton on 16 January) it was the L&NWR which worked it. A TVR extension to Quakers Yard was authorized on 9 July 1847 and opened on 11 January 1858, a notable feature being Crumlin Viaduct, 1,658 ft long, 208 ft high and designed by the company's Engineer Charles Liddell. Costing £28,000, it was opened on 1 June 1857. Redecked by the GWR in 1928, the last train crossed it on 13 June 1964, and it was demolished the following year. The company became a constituent of the WMR in 1860.

NEWQUAY & CORNWALL JUNCTION RAILWAY

Technically this line was built to mixed gauge, since that was what the Act of 14 July 1864 stipulated, but

broad gauge rails were not laid in a usable fashion, and until 1892 there was a break of gauge at Drinnick Mill. The railway branched from the Cornwall Railway at Burngullow (W of St Austell), running N to Drinnick Mill and St Dennis Junction. Three miles opened for mineral traffic on 1 July 1869, and a new line from Newquay to Fowey opened on 1 June 1874. The company was vested in the Cornwall Minerals Railway (qv) by an Act of 21 July 1873. Between 1909 and 1922 the track was removed while china clay was extracted from beneath it, following a House of Lords ruling in a test case. A plan to use this route for Newquay passenger trains instead of the present line via Bugle has been suggested, but not confirmed at the time of writing.

NEWTOWN & MACHYNLLETH RAILWAY

The company's Act of Incorporation, 27 July 1857, sanctioned TA with the GWR, the L&NWR, the Llanidloes & Newtown, the Oswestry & Newtown, and the Shrewsbury & Welshpool Railways; another

Machynlleth station still sports much that is original on 28 May 1988, though as this picture was taken came news that it was for sale. The train shown had arrived late after a breakdown, and, having terminated, was about to return to Euston. (Allan Mott)

of 3 July 1860 narrowed the choice to the O&NR. The 22.75-mile line climbed through Talerddig (the cutting there, at 120 ft, was for some years the deepest in the world) to drop down to the Dyfi estuary and Machynlleth. The line opened on 3 January 1863, the company joining the O&NR, L&NR, and Oswestry, Ellesmere & Whitchurch Railway (qv) to form the CambR on 25 July 1864.

NORTH PEMBROKE & FISHGUARD RAILWAY

Authorized on 7 August 1884, this line left the GWR W of Clynderwen and wound towards its destination via Maenclochog and Letterston. It was begun under powers granted to the Rosebush & Fishguard Railway (qv), though work did not resume until 1893. The line opened to Letterston for goods on 14 March 1895, and to passengers on 11 April, but cash problems before completion prompted an approach to the L&NWR. A worried GWR stepped in, bought the company on 12 February 1898 and completed the line, opening it throughout 11 days later. Closed on 8 January 1917, it re-opened in stages, throughout by 9 July 1923, only to re-close on 25 October 1937. The RAF and USAF used it for wartime target practice, and Maenclochog tunnel was used for training with the Barnes Wallis 'bouncing bombs'. Despite this it re-opened (after repairs!) later in the war, between Puncheston and Clynderwen, to close finally on 16 May 1949. The Letterston–Letterston Junction section survived until 1 March 1965.

NORTH WALES MINERAL RAILWAY

The line was authorized on 6 August 1844 to run N from Wrexham to Rossett, thence to a quay on the R Dee near Saltney, with a curve to the C&HR. Powers were obtained on 21 July 1845 for a S extension to Ruabon, but by the time the 14.75-mile Ruabon–Saltney section had opened on 4 November 1846 the company had amalgamated with the Shrewsbury, Oswestry & Chester Junction Railway (qv) on 27 July 1846 to form the S&CR. This Act also authorized a branch to Minera, which opened the following July.

OGMORE VALLEY RAILWAYS

Promoted by a Tondu ironmaster determined not to be dependent upon the TVR for his trade outlet, the line, authorized on 13 July 1863, ran from Nantymoel to Tondu and Porthcawl, with powers to lay a third rail over the Llynfi Valley Railway's broad gauge line between Tondu and Porthcawl. The line opened in 1865, and in that year powers were obtained to acquire the Ely Valley Extension Railway (qv); amalgamation with the LVR on 28 June 1866 formed the L&OR.

OLDBURY RAILWAY

The company, originally the Dudley & Oldbury Junction Railway (qv), was renamed on 11 August 1881. It opened in 1884 for goods, and on 1 May 1885 for passengers, and was worked by the GWR which had agreed to this in 1876. Amalgamation came under an Act of 31 July 1894, and passenger traffic ceased on 3 March 1915.

OSWESTRY, ELLESMERE & WHITCHURCH RAILWAY

Incorporated on 1 August 1861, the railway opened from Whitchurch to Ellesmere for goods on 20 April 1863, to passengers on 4 May, and throughout on 27 July 1864. On 25 July, however, the company had amalgamated with the Oswestry & Newtown, the Llanidloes & Newtown and the Newtown & Machynlleth Railways (all qv) to form the CambR. Oswestry became the CambR headquarters, and is now the home of the Cambrian RS which holds steam days in the station yard.

OSWESTRY & NEWTOWN RAILWAY

This line, authorized on 26 June 1855, became the link between the world and the isolated Llanidloes & Newtown Railway (qv). Lady Williams-Wynn cut the first sod at Welshpool on 4 August 1857, and the line was built single on a double formation; it opened from Oswestry to Pool Quay (Welshpool) on 1 May 1860, into Welshpool on 14 August, and to Newtown on 10 June 1861. After various ideas for amalgamation, the company joined the L&NR, the Oswestry, Ellesmere & Whitchurch, and the Newtown & Machynlleth Railways (all qv) to form the CambR on 25 July 1864. An Act of 17 May 1861 authorized the company to build the Kerry and

Headquarters of the Oswestry & Newtown at one time was Welshpool. As is apparent from the attendant vans, the station building, though externally unchanged, is no longer used by BR.

Llanfyllin branches — the latter opened on 10 April 1863, following the R Can for 8.75 miles to Llanfyllin. The Kerry branch, 3.75 miles long, opened to passengers on 2 March 1863, and to goods on 1 July. They closed on 18 January 1965 and 1 May 1956 respectively.

OXFORD RAILWAY

There was a branch to Oxford in the GWR's 1833 prospectus, but the University would have none of it. It took a nominally independent company, incorporated on 11 April 1843 and supported by the GWR, to crack the façade. This company was absorbed by the GWR on 10 May 1844, just before the line opened on 12 June as a 9.75-mile branch from Didcot Junction to a timber terminus remote from the city centre. A bigger station was built in 1852, and lasted until the early 1970s.

OXFORD & RUGBY RAILWAY

Although authorized on 4 August 1845 to build a 24.75-mile line between the towns, before the first section, from Oxford to Banbury, had opened (2 September 1850), the company had become part of the Birmingham & Oxford Junction Railway (qv), itself absorbed by the GWR under an Act of 14 May 1846.

OXFORD, WORCESTER & WOLVERHAMPTON RAILWAY

Incorporated on 4 August 1845 for 89 miles of broad gauge railway connecting the places named, there were also branches to Tipton and Kingswinford. The GWR subscribed, no doubt hoping to boost its influence in the Midlands, but the cost of the line was underestimated, and the company was always to be short of funds. During building there was trouble when a sacked (but unpaid) contractor refused to leave a site at Mickleton. Brunel massed 2,000 navvies, and troops were called from Coventry, but the contractor backed off after a minor skirmish. Help from the L&NWR and MR finished the line, and an Agreement dated 21 February 1851 gave them joint powers to work it, but the GWR had this declared void in Chancery, and offered the company another on similar terms. The first section was opened on 5 October 1850 (Worcester–Abbots Wood), extended to Stoke Works on 18 February 1852. Droitwich–Stourbridge was opened on 1 May 1852, Stourbridge–Dudley on 16 November (goods), 20 December (passengers), and throughout on 1 July 1854. The company amalgamated with the Worcester & Hereford Railway (qv) and the NA&HR from 1 January 1860, to form the WMR.

PEMBROKE & TENBY RAILWAY

The line was authorized on 21 July 1859 to link the named towns. Powers were obtained to extend to

The seal of the Oxford, Worcester & Wolverhampton Railway, bearing the arms of the three centres, Oxford top left and Worcester top right. Could the ingenious motto—loosely translated as 'Persevere through difficulties to true things'—have been devised by an Oxford don? (Roy Nash/Swindon Museums)

Whitland also, and this line opened on 4 September 1866. The main line had opened on 30 July 1863, with an extension to Pembroke Dock on 8 August 1864. On 6 August 1866 a line to Carmarthen and Milford Haven was sanctioned, with authority to lease the Llanelly Railway & Dock (qv). The GWR opposed this; terms were agreed, the Carmarthen branch abandoned, and the GWR worked the line after gauge conversion in 1872, though the company remained independent until the GWR took over by an Act of 6 August 1897. The line survives as BR's Pembroke Dock branch, though Pembroke Dock station closed to coal traffic on 31 December 1978.

PENARTH EXTENSION RAILWAY

Authorized on 11 August 1876, this was, as implied, an extension of the Penarth Railway into Penarth. It opened on 20 February 1878; its 1 mile 10 chains was leased to the TVR wef 1 January 1878, but the company retained independence until Grouping.

PENARTH HARBOUR DOCK & RAILWAY

Incorporated as the Ely Tidal Harbour & Railway (21 July 1856), a fresh Act of 27 July 1857 re-incorporated the company under a new name. It was to link the TVR at Radyr (5.25 miles N of Cardiff) with the Ely Tidal Basin. The line opened in July 1859, and the TVR agreed to work its 11 miles for a guaranteed 5.25 per cent; a lease in perpetuity was granted, wef 1 January 1864. The Bute Trustees, owners of the

Harbour, took the company to the House of Lords over the matter, but lost their case. It became a GWR subsidiary at Grouping.

PONTCYSYLLTE TRAMWAY

This feeder tramway, part of the SUR&CC system, became, after the lease of that company to the L&NWR (Act of 2 July 1847), an isolated section of its line. The L&NWR converted it to a locomotive railway in 1863, adding several branches and re-opening it (goods only) in January 1867. The Pontcysyllte section was bought for £51,000 by the GWR, wef 1 February 1896 (Act of 20 July 1896), and joined to its system via the Ponciau branch at Legacy. A passenger service with railmotors began on 5 June 1905, and closed on 22 March 1915. The Pontcysyllte–Pant section closed completely in 1953, the Pant–Rhos line on 14 October 1963.

PONTYPOOL, CAERLEON & NEWPORT RAILWAY

Conceived to duplicate the Monmouthshire Railway & Canal Company's line (qv), which was becoming congested, it was authorized on 5 July 1865, opening for goods on 17 September 1874, and for passengers between Pontypool and Maindee on 21 December. The GWR was authorized to subscribe by Acts of 21 July 1873 and 15 July 1876; absorption powers had been granted two days before.

PONTYPRIDD, CAERPHILLY & NEWPORT RAILWAY

A nominally independent company, incorporated on 8 August 1878, it was backed by the Alexandra Dock Company of Newport as a way of expanding its business. By RP interspersed with lengths of its own track, the company eventually reached Pontypridd, but never owned locomotives, stock or stations. It was absorbed by its parent company, by then the Alexandra (Newport & S Wales) Dock & Railway (qv) under an Act of 6 August 1897. An attempt to open the line on 7 July 1884 was blocked for 18 days by the GWR, but it opened for goods on 25 July 1884 and for passengers on 28 December 1887. It closed on 17 September 1956 (passengers) and 31 July 1967 (goods).

PORT TALBOT RAILWAY & DOCKS

Incorporated on 31 July 1894, and usually known as the Port Talbot Railway, it was born out of the slow progress of a Vale of Gwendraeth scheme and was promoted by the mine owners. The company enlarged the dock at Port Talbot and reached the Garw valley via the Vale of Dyffryn. An Ogmore valley extension, authorized in 1896, required take-over of two tramways, the Cefn & Pyle (qv) and the Morfa. On completion, the line served more than 50 collieries, and connected with the S Wales Mineral Railway (qv) at Tonmawr. It opened from Port Talbot to Lletty Brongu on 31 August 1897, to Pontrhyll on 17 January 1898, and for passengers on 14 February. TA wef 1 January 1908 involved the

The Port Talbot Railway swung across the Afan valley at Pontrhydyfen on an impressive red-brick viaduct to reach Tonmawr and its link with the S Wales Mineral Railway.

GWR in working both the company's line and the SWMR for 67.5 per cent of gross receipts. Associations with the GWR became closer, though the company retained independence until 1923. The line closed from Maesteg to Pontrhyll on 12 September 1932, Port Talbot–Maesteg on 11 September 1933 (both to passengers), though goods services lasted until 31 August 1964 on the Dyffryn Junction–Cwmdu section. The Cwmdu–Maesteg stretch was transferred to the NCB.

PRINCETOWN RAILWAY

Part of the track-bed of the defunct Plymouth & Dartmoor Railway (qv — Southern Railway) was bought by the GWR for £22,000 and used for this 10.5-mile line from Yelverton into the heart of Dartmoor. Authorized on 13 August 1878, and opened on 11 August 1883, the GWR worked the line, the company passing into its hands in 1922.

RHONDDA & SWANSEA BAY RAILWAY

Like the S Wales Mineral Railway (qv), this line, sanctioned on 10 August 1882, used the Afan valley via a tunnel from the Rhondda, the longest wholly in Wales. It also ignored Port Talbot, turning instead towards Swansea, though it did not reach a Swansea terminus for some years. The line opened to Pontrhydyfen on 26 February 1885, from Aberafan to Cymmer on 2 November, and throughout on 14 March 1895. Building costs were high, but rewards eventually enabled profitable terms to be made with the GWR when that company took over working and management by Agreement, wef 1 July 1906. The company passed to the GWR as a subsidiary in 1922. Passenger traffic ceased on the closure of Rhondda tunnel on 26 February 1968, buses taking over until the official closing date (14 December 1970).

RHONDDA VALLEY & HIRWAIN JUNCTION RAILWAY

Authorized on 12 August 1867 to link Hirwain (spelt Hirwaun from 1926) with Blaenrhondda, only the upper section, from colliery to branch junction, was completed. It opened in 1878, authority to abandon the rest being granted on 17 June 1878. The line was leased from opening by the TVR, and vested in it from 26 August 1889.

RHYMNEY RAILWAY

The company was incorporated on 24 July 1854 to build a 9.5-mile line from Rhymney Ironworks to a junction with the NA&HR at Hengoed. Powers to extend to the TVR at Taff's Well were obtained in 1855, and a line from Crockherbstown to Bute E Dock. Lack of capital and escalating costs made early years difficult — the Dock line opened in September 1857, but was not linked with the main line, which

The seal of the Rhymney Railway. The maritime motif indicates the intent to aim for Bute Docks from the start. The bee-skep device is perhaps intended to represent a blast-furnace. (Roy Nash/Swindon Museums)

opened on 25 February 1858 (goods), 31 March (passengers). Trouble flared with the TVR over the shared Crockherbstown line, and on 25 July 1864 the company obtained powers for a direct Cardiff–Caerphilly route and granted RP to the L&NWR — it opened officially on 5 September 1871, and to the public on 2 October. The 9-mile Taff–Bargoed line, built jointly with the GWR, opened for goods on 20 December 1875, and to passengers on 2 February 1876. The company went to the GWR as a constituent in 1922, and the former loco works at Caerphilly is now the home of the Caerphilly RS.

ROSEBUSH & FISHGUARD RAILWAY

Incorporated on 8 August 1878 to build a 13 miles 70 chains line from Rosebush to Goodwick, near Fishguard, the company made an arrangement with the Narberth & Maenclochog Railway (qv) in 1881, but the scheme lapsed. Powers were revived on 7 August 1884 by the N Pembroke & Fishguard Railway (qv).

ROSS & LEDBURY RAILWAY

Incorporated on 28 July 1873, the company built only 4.75 miles of its projected line, and joined the Newent Railway (qv) to continue to Gloucester. The GWR was authorized to subscribe on 30 June 1874, the line opening on 27 July 1885. The company, with its ally, passed to the GWR on 1 July 1892.

ROSS & MONMOUTH RAILWAY

This line along the Wye valley, authorized on 5 July 1865, was opened on 4 August 1873 and operated by the GWR from the start. The GWR extended it to Monmouth (Troy), though the company retained nominal independence until passing to the GWR in 1922. The line closed to passengers on 5 January 1959, and parts of the track-bed now form the Wye Valley walk.

RUMNEY TRAMROAD

Incorporated on 20 May 1825, this 21.75-mile plateway built by George Overton to a gauge of 4 ft 2 in ran from the Rhymney Ironworks to the Monmouthshire Railway (qv) at what later became Bassaleg Junction. Like the Sirhowy and the Monmouthshire Railways (both qv) it delayed the change to proper railwayhood too long; re-incorporated on 1 August 1861, with WA with the WMR, it began conversion in 1863. It was, however, too great a task for the company's finances, and it sold out on 28 July 1863 to the B&MTJR, which used it to continue its own drive towards Newport. This section was taken over by the GWR wef 1 July 1922 and closed to passengers on 31 December 1962.

SEVERN VALLEY RAILWAY

Incorporated on 20 August 1853, this 39.5-mile line between Shrewsbury and Hartlebury (OW&WR) ran along the Severn Valley. It was leased from opening on 1 February 1862 by the WMR (under an Act of 14 June 1860), passing into GWR hands by an Act of 18 July 1872. The GWR added a 3-mile link from Bewdley to Kidderminster, which opened on 1 June 1878. The 16 miles from Bridgnorth to Kidderminster is now one of the country's best-known preserved lines.

SHREWSBURY & BIRMINGHAM RAILWAY

Authorized on 3 August 1846 after much haggling, this was a truncated line between Shrewsbury and Wolverhampton, with a branch to Coalbrookdale. The 10 miles between Wellington and Shrewsbury were to be shared with the SUR&CC and the company was given a quarter share in the Birmingham, Wolverhampton and Stour Valley Railway (qv), with RP. The line opened from Shrewsbury to Oakengates on 1 June 1849 and throughout on 12 November. The company established a Works at Stafford Road, Wolverhampton, about 1849, the forerunner of the GWR Works there; its first locomotive, designed by Joseph Armstrong, was built in 1859. The company was absorbed by the GWR wef 1 September 1854, as authorized by an Act of 7 August. Part of this line became the first ex-GWR line to go 'under the wires' when the spur from Wolverhampton High Level to the carriage sidings at Oxley was electrified.

SHREWSBURY & CHESTER RAILWAY

This company was formed on 27 July 1846 when the Shrewsbury, Oswestry & Chester Junction Railway united with its promoter, the N Wales Mineral Railway (both qv). When the first section opened (Saltney–Ruabon, 4 November 1846) the company had temporary possession, by Agreement, of a short length of the C&HR into Chester. Works were heavy S of Ruabon, including viaducts at Cefn and Chirk, 148 ft and 106 ft high respectively – the line was designed by Francis Thompson and built by Thomas Brassey. It opened throughout on 16 October 1848. A station at Chester was managed jointly by the L&NWR, the C&HR and the Birkenhead, Lancashire & Cheshire Junction Railway (qv – Jt/Ind), but trouble broke out between the L&NWR and GWR over traffic via

Left *The parapet of this bridge at Bedwas has been renovated, but a girder bears the inscription EAGLE FOUNDRY CARDIFF (left) and RUMNEY RAILWAY 1863 (centre).*

Right *The Shrewsbury & Chester Railway's magnificent viaduct at Cefnmawr strides 148 ft above the R Dee, S of Ruabon.*

Shrewsbury, and there were appalling scenes at Chester. At length the company, with the Shrewsbury & Birmingham Railway (qv), made TA with the GWR in January 1851. An Amalgamation Bill with the GWR was rejected in 1852, but passed wef 1 September 1854. Shrewsbury station opened formally on 12 October 1858, and to the public two days later.

SHREWSBURY, OSWESTRY & CHESTER JUNCTION RAILWAY

Incorporated on 30 June 1845, this was a N Wales Mineral Railway (qv) promotion against possible L&NWR opposition via a cut-off line linking Ruabon with Chester. Extensions were authorized (27 July 1846) from Leaton to Wem and from Gobowen to Crickheath, but only the Oswestry–Gobowen section was built — it opened on 23 December 1848. By an Act of 27 July 1846, the company amalgamated with the NWMR to form the S&CR '. . . from and immediately after the day on which the present Session of Parliament shall end'. The Liverpool & Bury Railway's (qv — LMS) Act carried similar conditions; the relevant date has been quoted as 1 October 1846.

SOUTH DEVON RAILWAY

Originally called the Plymouth, Devonport and Exeter Railway, but authorized as above on 4 July 1844, it was backed by the B&ER, GWR and the Br&GR for almost half of its capital. The line was engineered by Brunel and built for atmospheric traction — one of IKB's few failures. Exeter to Teignmouth opened on

One of the last remaining relics of Brunel's atmospheric experiment on the SDR, where the Italianate pumping house at Starcross is now a Museum. (Allan Mott)

30 May 1846, to Newton Abbot on 30 December and to Totnes on 20 July 1847. Locomotive working began between Exeter and Teignmouth on 13 September 1847, to Newton Abbot on 10 January 1848 and between Newton and Laira (Plymouth) on 5 May, the day that section opened. A 5-mile branch to Torre was opened on 18 December 1848. As soon as the GWR had control of the B&ER, the company approached it and the line became GWR-worked under a 999-year Agreement wef 1 January 1876. The company was dissolved and absorbed by the GWR from 1 August 1878 — it had itself absorbed the Dartmouth & Torbay (1862), the S Devon & Tavistock (1865), the Launceston and S Devon (1869) and the Moretonhampstead & S Devon railways (1872) (all qv). The line is noted for the sea-wall route between Starcross and Teignmouth, and for the heavy banks between Newton Abbot and Plymouth.

SOUTH DEVON & TAVISTOCK RAILWAY

A 13-mile line along the Plym valley, linking Plymouth with Tavistock, and incorporated on 24 July 1854, it had six viaducts, three tunnels and was laid to the broad gauge. It was opened on 22 June 1859, worked from the start by the SDR, and amalgamated with it from 1 July 1865 (Act of 5 July). In 1866, powers were granted to lay a standard gauge rail when required by the Devon & Cornwall Railway (qv) — the first L&SWR train to reach Plymouth ran on 17 May 1876. That company used the route until its own (PD&SWJR — qv Southern Railway) via Bere Alston opened. The line was converted to standard gauge with the rest of the GWR in 1892. Because closure night, 29 December 1962, coincided with the worst blizzard of the century in W Devon, the 'final' train did not run, and two earlier trains were abandoned in mid-line. Part of the route N from Marsh Mills forms the Plym Valley Railway, a preservation project.

SOUTH HAMPSHIRE RAILWAY & PIER

This was incorporated on 25 June 1886 to take over the S section of the Swindon, Marlborough & Andover Railway (qv), since 1884 part of the M&SWJR. It was authorized to complete the section by an Act dated 21 July 1891 — a line from Eling (on the L&SWR's Southampton–Dorchester branch) to Stone Point, Fawley, a branch to join the Southampton line, and a pier and jetty at Stone Point. Not completed as planned, the link with Fawley was built by the Totton, Hythe & Fawley LR (qv — Southern Railway).

SOUTH WALES RAILWAY

Incorporated on 4 August 1845, this was supported by the GWR, which was aiming at Ireland. Its first section (Swansea–Chepstow, 75 miles) opened on 18 June 1850. The building of Brunel's bridge across the Wye delayed opening E to Gloucester until 19 September 1851 (the company was authorized in 1847 to lease or buy the Forest of Dean Railway, (qv), and W extensions opened to Carmarthen on 11 October 1852, to Haverfordwest on 2 January 1854, and to Neyland on 15 April 1856. The line was leased to the GWR in 1846 at a guaranteed 5 per

Another Brunel relic, this time the bridge across the R Wye at Chepstow, opened by the SWR in 1851. An up train crosses during rebuilding in 1962. (Rev W. Awdry)

cent, and amalgamated with it wef 1 August 1863. Broad gauge, however, did not suit the valley lines, for which sharp curves were often necessary, and by 1866 freighters were petitioning for conversion; this had reached Cardiff by 1872.

SOUTH WALES MINERAL RAILWAY

A broad gauge line authorized on 15 August 1853 and engineered by Brunel, it included a rope-worked incline, a 1,109-yd tunnel at Gyfylchi, and gradients of 1 in 22. It ran from Glyncorrwg down the Afan valley to Briton Ferry, and was costly to build. Completion was delayed until 10 March 1863 by the tunnel, but it opened to that point on 1 September 1861. From 25 May 1855 it had been leased to the Glyncorrwg Coal Company for 30 years, but when that failed the railway did too – T. J. Woods, the OR, kept the line going from 1878–1880, and it remained in his hands for 29 years. By Agreement the PTR worked and managed it from 1 January 1908 until Grouping. A passenger service was introduced on 28 March 1918, and though this ceased on 22 September 1930, mineral traffic continued until 1970 on the Abercreggan Sidings–Cymmer Junction section. The tunnel closed on 13 July 1947 following a landslip.

STOURBRIDGE RAILWAY

This was incorporated on 14 June 1860, and before building began, a 5-mile extension to join the Birmingham, Wolverhampton & Stour Valley Railway (qv) at Smethwick had been authorized on 6 August 1861. The line was then extended further to the GWR at Handsworth, giving a direct link with both New Street and Snow Hill stations. The company was closely related with the OW&WR and was worked by it (or more precisely by the WMR) from opening, to Cradley Heath on 1 April 1863, Old Hill on 1 January 1866 and Smethwick on 1 April 1867. An Act of 16 July 1866 (29/30 Victoria c221) authorized amalgamation with the GWR five years after completion, but this was amended by 32/33 Victoria c109 (12 July 1869) which implied that union could take place earlier, without specifying when. Some authorities take this to be 1870, but WA were made on 31 July 1871, unnecessary if amalgamation had already happened. Perhaps 1872, as intended by the original Act, is the answer.

STRATFORD & MORETON RAILWAY

This horse-drawn tramway (16 miles), authorized on 28 May 1821, linked Moreton-in-Marsh with the Stratford Canal and was laid to what appears to be one of the earliest uses of 'standard' gauge. It opened on 5 September 1826, and a branch to Shipston-on-Stour was authorized on 10 June 1833, opening on 11 February 1836. The Act incorporating the OW&WR included a clause for permanent lease at £2,537.10s pa, and it took possession on 1 May 1847, from 1 January 1852 assuming entire management. It upgraded the line, re-opening it on 1 August 1853, but the N end became redundant when the OW&WR's Stratford–Honeybourne line opened on 12 July 1859, and was probably little used after the

A wagon of the Stratford & Moreton Railway, preserved at Stratford-upon-Avon. The inscription on the wheel-hub reads 'Smith & Willey, Windsor Foundry, Liverpool'. (Rev W. Awdry)

turn of the century. Lifted during the Great War, it was officially abandoned in 1928. The Shipston section, thanks to public opposition to the WMR which wanted to close it, was retained, horse-drawn until 1882. The GWR obtained powers to upgrade it and use steam on 7 August 1884 — the original Act forbade this. Re-opened on 1 July 1889, passenger traffic was withdrawn on 8 July 1929, though a goods service lasted until 3 May 1960. The line was lifted in July of the following year.

STRATFORD-UPON-AVON RAILWAY

Incorporated on 10 August 1857, this mixed gauge line, 9 miles long, ran from Hatton (GWR) to Stratford. Built by the GWR, it opened on 10 October 1860. The Alcester Railway (qv) was vested in it, jointly with the GWR, on 22 July 1878, and the company was itself absorbed by the major one from 1 July 1883 (Act of 29 August).

SWANSEA & NEATH RAILWAY

Authorized on 6 August 1861, this was a standard gauge line from an end-on junction with the VNR, NW of Neath, to the N Dock at Swansea, via the Crumlin Burrows. It opened on 15 July 1863, the VNR working it from the start and acquiring it by an Act of 13 July 1863 wef the fourth Wednesday after the date of the Act — 5 August.

SWANSEA VALE & NEATH & BRECON JUNCTION RAILWAY

The company was incorporated on 29 July 1864 to build a 7.5-mile link between Ynysgeinon Junction (SVR) and Colbren Junction (N&BR). It was steep (1 in 48/55) and expensive. On the opening day, 26 July 1869, the N&BR obtained powers to take over, but by then the SVR had already obtained RP over the entire N&BR system, perhaps its intention in the first place. . . !

SWINDON & CHELTENHAM EXTENSION RAILWAY

A line authorized 18 July 1881 and linking Swindon with Cheltenham via Andoversford, it opened from Rushey Platt to Cirencester on 18 December 1883, and to Andoversford on 1 August 1891. On 23 June 1884 the company merged with the Swindon, Marlborough & Andover Railway (qv) to form the M&SWJR.

SWINDON & HIGHWORTH RAILWAY

The original scheme for a LR between Swindon and Lechlade was dropped in favour of a shorter line, authorized on 29 June 1875. Maybe this was lucky, since the company had financial troubles before it reached Highworth, and went no further anyway. Despite misgivings, the GWR bought the company

on 10 August 1882, opening the line on 9 May of the following year.

SWINDON, MARLBOROUGH & ANDOVER RAILWAY

This line, its Act gained on 21 July 1873 by the GWR, opened from opposite ends — Red Post Junction–Grafton on 1 May 1882, and Swindon–Marlborough on 5 February 1884. A link was provided by the Grafton & Marlborough Railway (qv). On 23 June 1884 the company amalgamated with the Swindon & Cheltenham Extension Railway (qv) to form the M&SWJR.

TAFF VALE RAILWAY

Authority for a line from Cardiff Docks to Merthyr Tydfil was given on 21 June 1836, the original being laid out by Brunel to standard gauge because broad gauge would not suit the terrain. Opening to Abercynon on 9 October 1840 and to Merthyr on 12 April 1841, it became one of the most prosperous railways in S Wales, at one time declaring a dividend of 17.5 per cent. Its 24.5 miles were doubled from 1845, completion to Merthyr being by 1861. The Penarth Harbour Dock & Railway was leased wef 1 January 1864, the Penarth Extension Railway from 1878, and eight other Companies were acquired: the Llantrisant & Taff Vale Junction, the Cowbridge, the Dare Valley, the Rhondda Valley & Hirwain, the Treferig Valley, the Cardiff, Penarth & Barry Junction Railways (all 1889), the Cowbridge & Aberthaw Railway (1894) and the Aberdare Railway (1902) — all qv. These gave a route mileage of 124.5 at its maximum (411.5 single track miles, including sidings). The company became a constituent of the GWR at Grouping, and closure of other lines has made it the last survivor, albeit singled, of the six to Merthyr.

TANAT VALLEY LIGHT RAILWAY

A LRO was confirmed on 4 January 1899, and sods were cut on 12 September 1899 to describe 'TVLR' in the turf, the first of them by Lady Powis. The line opened on 5 January 1904, ceremonially, and to the public the next day, worked by the CambR. Mineral traffic was good, but the company remained in debt until it passed into CambR hands wef 12 March 1921, by the Tanat Valley LR (Transfer) Order. Passenger services ceased from 15 January 1951, goods W of Llanrhaiadr from 1 July 1952, and the line closed completely from Blodwell Junction to Llanrhaiadr on 5 December 1960 after heavy flooding damaged the Tanat Bridge.

TEIGN VALLEY RAILWAY

This line, authorized on 13 July 1863 in broad gauge between Bovey Tracey and Doddiscombesleigh, needed nine Acts before it finally opened on 9 October 1882, standard gauge between Heathfield (S Devon

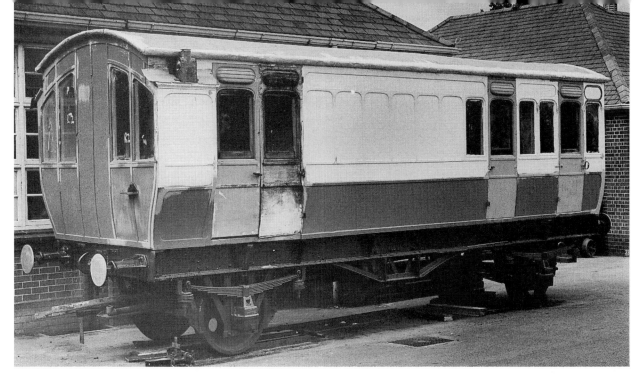

Above *Taff Vale Railway coach No 220, built in 1891 and rescued by the Gwili Railway from a Herefordshire field after 50 years, seen on 15 July 1988 at Brynteg Comprehensive School, Bridgend. It is being restored by the School's Preservation Group, and pupils taking Certificate of Education courses.* (Deryck Lewis)

Right *Christow, on the Teign Valley Railway, looking S in 1986. The building, platform and lamp-post on the right are original: on the down side the station building has been extended towards the camera to create a desirable residence.* (Mark Chambers)

& Moretonhampstead Railway, qv) and Ashton. An extension to Teign House, Christow, was opened later. The line was built under GWR protection (the L&SWR had expressed interest), and the GWR worked it, despite its isolation, until the conversion of the SD&MR to standard gauge (23 May 1892). Ashton station had a timber platform and a raised causeway for access when the Teign flooded, and the site of Chudleigh station is now beneath the A38 trunk road. The Exeter Railway (qv) gave the line a link with Exeter in 1903. The last passenger train ran on 7 August 1958, the last goods to Christow on 1 May 1961, the line closing completely on 4 December 1967.

TENBURY & BEWDLEY RAILWAY

This 14-mile branch W from the Severn Valley Railway (qv) at Bewdley was authorized on 30 July 1860, and ran through the Wyre Forest to Tenbury. It opened officially on 13 August 1864, and to the public the next day, worked by the WMR; the company amalgamated with the GWR by an Act of 12 July 1869.

TIVERTON & NORTH DEVON RAILWAY

This was re-incorporation (19 July 1875) of a scheme authorized ten years earlier and abandoned in 1868. The company's powers went only from Bolham, N of Tiverton, to Morebath (Devon & Somerset Railway, qv) though in practice its trains ran to Dulverton. The line was built to standard gauge, opening on 1 August 1884; the company had WA with the B&ER and TA with the GWR, authorized on 23 July 1877, to raise further funds. It amalgamated with the latter from 1 July 1894 (Act of 31 July).

TORBAY & BRIXHAM RAILWAY

The company was incorporated on 25 July 1864, and a Brixham man, R. W. Wolston, took 1,770 of the

1,800 shares when the Contractor defaulted. The broad gauge line was 2 miles long, was let to the SDR and from its opening in 1868 continually made a loss. Legal measures resulted in an award of £2,000, the company working it thereafter until sale to the GWR for £12,000 (Agreement of 19 May 1882) was ratified by Parliament on 24 July.

TREFERIG VALLEY RAILWAY

A 2 miles 56 chains goods-only line authorized on 21 July 1879, it served Glyn Colliery. This branch off a branch of the Ely Valley Railway (qv) opened in April 1883; leased to the TVR by an Act of 14 July 1884, it was absorbed by that company under a General Powers Act dated 26 August 1889. It closed about 1924 and was lifted some ten years later.

TREFFRY ESTATES TRAMWAY

John Thomas Treffry built a canal from Par harbour to St Blazey, and a horse-tramway along the Luxulyan valley to china clay workings. The line was opened in 1842, and in 1844 an Act authorized extension to Newquay, reached in 1849: inclines there were rope-worked. In 1857 the Trustee of the Treffry Estate was authorized to work the line, and in 1872 W. R. Roebuck leased both the company and the Newquay & Cornwall Junction Railway, resulting in the formation of the Cornwall Minerals Railway (both qv).

VALE OF GLAMORGAN RAILWAY

Though nominally independent, the Barry Railway, thinly disguised, was responsible for this line, authorized on 26 August 1889, from Coity Lower (L&OR) to Barry, 21 miles including branches. WA with 'the Barry' gave that company 60 per cent of gross receipts and a guaranteed dividend of 4 per cent. Despite its sponsor, the company retained independence to become a GWR subsidiary at Grouping. Cowbridge Road–Coity Junction closed on 15 June 1964, except for ½ mile serving Bridgend and Coity Goods until 28 November 1977. The Barry–Bridgend passenger service ceased on 15 June 1964, but the line remains open for goods, notably coal for Aberthaw CEGB, and as a diversionary route.

VALE OF LLANGOLLEN RAILWAY

The first sod was cut on 1 September 1859, exactly a month after incorporation, and the line was open for goods on 1 December 1861, and passengers on 2 June 1862, running from Ruabon (S&CR) to Llangollen. The GWR worked it from the start, seeing it as a route to the W coast; plans for extension towards Corwen were being made in 1861 (see Llangollen & Corwen Railway). The company was absorbed by the GWR under an Act of 7 August 1896, and the line closed to passengers on 18 January 1965, and to goods on 1 April 1968.

The basic material of the Vale of Glamorgan Railway's bridges was the local limestone, and they were built to last. This solid specimen near St Athan serves merely as an occupation crossing.

VALE OF NEATH RAILWAY

Authorized on 3 August 1846, it was a 16.25-mile railway along Glyn Neath to Gelli Tarw, with branches to Aberdare and Merthyr Tydfil. Laid to broad gauge, it joined the B&MTJR at Rhydycar Junction, opening to Quakers Yard, Merthyr, on 24 September 1851, and its own extension to Mardy Junction gave entry to Merthyr High Street via RP on 2 November 1853. The NA&HR proposed a standard gauge link as part of a third-rail scheme over the Company's system, but by the time this was completed the WMR was already part of the GWR. The company absorbed the Swansea & Neath (1863) and the Aberdare Valley Railways (1864) (both qv) and that year the track became mixed gauge. The company then followed the WMR into the GWR net, first making WA from 1 February 1865, and then amalgamating by an Act of 10 August 1866. The through line via Pontypool was to become a vital goods route, particularly during the Great War when coal was moving N to Scapa Flow. It closed to passengers on 13 June 1964.

VALE OF RHEIDOL LIGHT RAILWAY

This 1 ft 11.5 in line takes roughly the route authorized on 11 July 1861 to the Manchester & Milford

Vale of Rheidol locomotives share Aberystwyth station in 1959. No 7 Owain Glyndwr *has a Machynlleth shedplate (89C) on its smokebox door, but No 9* Prince of Wales *is without.*

Railway (qv), from Aberystwyth up the Rheidol valley to Devils Bridge. The Company got its own authorization on 6 August 1897, and opened on 22 December 1902. On 1 July 1913 it amalgamated with the CambR (Act of 4 July); the GWR acquired it in 1922, with the harbour at Aberystwyth in 1924. Mines in the valley had closed after the First World War, but tourist traffic increased and in 1938 the carriage stock was renewed. The line closed from 31 August 1939 to 23 July 1945, and was realigned at Aberystwyth in 1968 to use the abandoned Manchester & Milford bay. For some years it remained the only steam part of BR's operation, but in 1988 was bought by the Brecon Mountain Railway.

VAN RAILWAY

Built under a BoT Certificate of 3 June 1870, this 6.5-mile line linked lead mines with the main CambR line at Caersws, opening for goods on 14 August 1871, and to passengers on 1 December 1873. The mines closed in the early 1890s, and the railway also, in 1893, but the CambR undertook to work it, for the use of the weed-free stone spoil, crushed as ballast. It re-opened 1 August 1896, along with mines, which remained in business until 1920, the line retaining independence until Grouping. Final closure came on 2 November 1940 — a short-lived passenger service had expired in July 1879.

WALLINGFORD & WATLINGTON RAILWAY

Incorporated on 25 July 1864, this was the first

standard gauge branch off the GWR. It failed to reach the length authorized (9 miles), stopping short at Wallingford and abandoning the river crossing. Opening on 2 July 1866, the line was worked by the GWR, which bought the company for £16,750 under an Act of 25 July 1872. The line was closed on 1 June 1981, and is the site of a preservation scheme, the Cholsey & Wallingford Railway, now authorized to run into Cholsey station.

WATLINGTON & PRINCES RISBOROUGH RAILWAY

This 8.75-mile line, authorized on 26 July 1869, was opened on 15 August 1872. When it became clear that the Wallingford & Watlington Railway (qv) was not going to cross the Thames, the GWR, which rarely missed such a chance, stepped in — the company was dissolved and vested wef 1 July 1883 (Act of 20 August).

WELLINGTON & DRAYTON RAILWAY

Incorporated on 7 August 1862, this line linked the GWR at Wellington with the Nantwich & Market Drayton Railway (qv — LMS). It opened on 16 October 1867, and though an Act of 14 July 1864 had authorized transfer of the company to the GWR on completion, full amalgamation was not ratified until an Act of 12 July 1869, after an Agreement dated 16 December 1868. Traffic was never heavy along the line's 16.25 miles, its passenger service ceasing on 9 September 1963, but it became a diversionary route during the WCML electrification. It closed completely on 8 May 1967.

WELLINGTON & SEVERN JUNCTION RAILWAY

Incorporated on 20 August 1853, this line ran from Wellington to Ketley and Coalbrookdale via Madeley, with an extension to Lightmoor authorized the following year. It opened on 1 May 1857, worked for the first four years by the Coalbrookdale Iron Company; negotiations led to its lease by the GWR and WMR jointly for 999 years wef 1 July 1861 (Act of 1 August). Amalgamation with the GWR was from 1 July 1892 by an Act of 28 June; the line closed to passengers in 1962.

WELSHPOOL & LLANFAIR LIGHT RAILWAY

A scheme authorized on 23 August 1887 for a LR from Welshpool to Llanfair Caereinion collapsed, but a LRO of 8 September 1899 had more success. The CambR agreed to build, work and maintain the line, and the first sod was cut by Viscount Clive on 30 May 1901, using an engraved spade now in the Powysland Museum, Welshpool. The railway, 9 miles 10 chains long, opened to goods on 9 March 1903, officially on 4 April and for passengers two days later, and though worked by the CambR, the company remained independent until taken over by the GWR

Llanfair Caereinion on 3 August 1964, with both the line's original locomotives—No 1 The Earl in front of No 2 The Countess.

at Grouping. The passenger service ceased on 9 February 1931, and goods on 3 November 1956. On 6 April 1963, a Preservation Society re-opened the line from Llanfair to Castle Caereinion. It re-entered Welshpool on 16 May 1982, when the Earl of Powis planted a tree at the new Raven Square terminus, using the 'first sod' spade.

WENLOCK RAILWAY

Projected as the Much Wenlock, Craven Arms & Coalbrookdale Railway, but incorporated on 22 July 1861 with an easier title, it was 14 miles long, with a branch from Buildwas to Coalbrookdale Ironworks. Opened from Coalbrookdale to Presthorpe on 1 November 1864, and to Craven Arms on 16 December 1867, the line was worked from the start by the GWR, which absorbed the company under Act of 7 August 1896.

WEST CORNWALL RAILWAY

Authority was given on 3 August 1846 to rebuild the Hayle Railway (qv), extending it either way, to Truro and Penzance. Opening from Redruth to Penzance on 11 March 1852, and to Truro on 16 April 1855, this formed the earliest part, in Cornwall, of what became the Paddington–Penzance main line. The

The first broad gauge train into Redruth (West Cornwall Railway) from the west on 1 March 1866. The locomotive, Lance, was delivered to the company in October 1851 and withdrawn in December 1873. (Royal Institution of Cornwall)

line was stipulated as broad gauge, but when the company made no progress it requested leave to use standard gauge in order to utilize track already there. This was allowed, provided it be altered should the Cornwall Railway (qv) so request. When it did so in 1864, the company could not afford the work, and the broad gauge companies (GWR, B&ER and SDR) took over wef 1 January 1866, under an Act of 5 July 1865. The line was then worked by them until the GWR swallowed the two lesser companies. The WCR remained in being, however, until dissolved at Nationalization.

WEST MIDLAND RAILWAY

This company was formed on 14 June 1860 by the union of the OW&WR, NA&HR and the Worcester & Hereford Railway (qv). During a short independent life, the company worked or leased the Witney, the Bourton-on-the-Water, the Severn Valley, the Stourbridge, the Tenbury & Bewdley, and the Much Wenlock & Severn Junction Railways. It also took over working of the Leominster & Kington and the Coleford, Monmouth, Usk & Pontypool Railways (all qv), so that when it was itself absorbed by the GWR, from 1 August 1863 (Act of 13 July), it owned 200 miles of line and controlled more. It had, itself, been under a 999-year lease to the GWR since 30 May 1861.

WEST SOMERSET RAILWAY

Though authorized on 14 August 1857, construction of this broad gauge line did not begin until 1859, and

because of money problems it was another three years before the line opened to Norton Fitzwarren from Watchet on 31 March 1862. Worked by the B&ER, it was converted to standard gauge in 1882 and retained independence until 1922, when the GWR took it on. With the erstwhile Minehead Railway (qv) this line is now a preserved railway under its original title, at the time of writing being the longest such scheme in the country.

WHITLAND & CARDIGAN RAILWAY

Originally incorporated as the Whitland & Taf Vale Railway (qv), this proved to be Cardigan's only rail link with the outside world. Its Act (2 August 1877) authorized extension to Cardigan, and the GWR was responsible both for the opening, on 1 September 1886, and working. It was also given leave to subscribe on 13 August 1888, absorbing the company under an Act dated 4 August 1890. The line closed to passengers on 10 September 1962, and to goods on 27 May 1963.

WHITLAND & TAF VALE RAILWAY

This 14-mile line, authorized on 12 July 1869, followed the Taf valley to a terminus at Crymmych Arms, a small market town at its head. It opened for goods to Llanfarnach on 24 March 1873 and to Crymmych Arms in October 1874, but because the BoT Inspector failed to do his duty within the prescribed time, the passenger service opening on 12 July 1875 was without official sanction. In 1877, when powers were obtained to extend 11 miles to Cardigan, the company changed its name to the Whitland & Cardigan Railway (qv).

WILTSHIRE, SOMERSET & WEYMOUTH RAILWAY

Though nominally an independent company, incorporated on 30 June 1845, this broad gauge project was actually backed by the GWR. Originally proposed as a line from Bath to Weymouth, financial problems and indifference delayed and changed plans, but the first section opened was between Thingley Junction and Westbury on 5 September 1848. The company was dissolved and vested in the GWR on 3 July 1851, which opened 19.5 miles of single track from Warminster to Salisbury on 30 June 1856, the Frome–Yeovil section opening on 1 September. Broad gauge trains began to run between Yeovil and Weymouth on 20 January 1857, the same day as standard gauge ones reached Weymouth from Dorchester. Earthworks were built for doubling, which was done in 1885 — conversion to standard gauge had been made in 1874. In 1876 the GWR began running its own boats into Weymouth, at first in partnership with a French company, but, from August 1889, on its own.

WITNEY RAILWAY

The OW&WR was authorized to build an 8-mile branch from Yarnton to Witney in 1846, but it came to nothing; an independent company was incorporated on 1 August 1859, opening a line on 14 November 1861. There were demands for extension, but the resultant project was over-ambitious (see E Gloucestershire Railway) and only reached Fairford. The Company was absorbed by the GWR under an Act of 4 August 1890.

WOODSTOCK RAILWAY

Authority was given on 25 September 1886 for a 2 miles 4 furlongs 7 chains railway to Woodstock from a junction 1 mile N of Kidlington. It was financed by the Duke of Marlborough, whose seat is at Blenheim Palace, Woodstock. It opened on 19 May 1890, and on 4 August 1890 the GWR obtained powers to extend the branch, parallel to its own line, from the junction to Kidlington (Woodstock Road) station, the same Act authorizing it to work the line. Official absorption of the company came by an Act of 6 August 1897.

WORCESTER, BROMYARD & LEOMINSTER RAILWAY

A railway between these towns was authorized on 1 August 1861, but in 1869 the Bromyard–Leominster section was abandoned. The GWR agreed to work the rest — it opened from Worcester to Yearsett on 2 May 1874 and to Bromyard on 22 October 1877, and the company was duly absorbed wef 1 July 1888. The abandoned section was re-incorporated as the Leominster & Bromyard Railway (qv).

WORCESTER & HEREFORD RAILWAY

This was one of several schemes which aimed to link the Midlands with S Wales. The 29.75-mile line was authorized on 15 August 1853 to connect Worcester with the NA&HR, but heavy engineering problems (there were to be two long tunnels) were beyond the company's finances. In 1858 Parliament gave subscription powers to the OW&WR, NA&HR and MR, and on 1 January 1860 the company became a constituent of the WMR. The line, which had opened in stages, was open throughout on 25 July 1860.

WREXHAM & ELLESMERE RAILWAY

Incorporated on 31 July 1885, this 12.75-mile line between the two towns shared a station with the WM&CQR at Wrexham. It was seven years, however, before the first sod was turned (11 July 1892) and when the line eventually opened on 2 November 1895 the CambR worked it. The company remained independent until going to the GWR at Grouping. Between 10 June 1940 and 6 May 1946 the passenger service was suspended because of munitions traffic from a Royal Ordnance factory at Marchwich.

WREXHAM & MINERA RAILWAY

This company was incorporated on 17 May 1861 to build 3.25 miles of line from Croes Newydd (S&CR) to the Minera branch at Brymbo. The line opened for minerals on 22 May 1866, and on 11 June amalgamated jointly with the GWR and L&NWR, to create the Wrexham & Minera Joint Railway (qv – Jt/Ind). An attempt to open for passengers in July 1866 failed because of weak bridges and faulty works. The part of the undertaking not already jointly owned was vested solely in the GWR in 1871, and it was that company which began a passenger service from 24 May 1882. That between Wrexham and Brymbo ceased on 1 January 1931.

WYCOMBE RAILWAY

This was a system built up from various branches radiating from High Wycombe. The oldest line, author-

Left *The timber station and its overall roof survive at Frome (WS&WR). Opened in 1856, it was still busy in June 1988.*

Right *Colwall station, on the Worcester & Hereford Railway, is a shadow of its former self, though a footbridge to the disused second platform still honours a right of way.*

ized on 27 July 1846, ran W to Bourne End and thence to Maidenhead — it was single, broad gauge and engineered by Brunel. The system was worked by the GWR from the start; it was opened to Maidenhead on 1 August 1854, Thame on 1 August 1862, between Princes Risborough and Aylesbury on 1 October 1863, and to Oxford on 24 October 1864. The GWR absorbed the company by an Act of 23 July 1866, wef 31 January 1867, and the Princes Risborough–Aylesbury branch gained the distinction of being one of the shortest-lived of all broad gauge lines. It was converted to standard gauge a mere five years after opening. The goods service between High Wycombe and Maidenhead was withdrawn on 11 September 1967, the passenger service lasting until 4 May 1970.

The track-bed has been filled in and turfed over, but the station building and signal cabin (behind the camera) at Tintern, ex-Wye Valley Railway, have been beautifully restored to house a small museum of the line.

WYE VALLEY RAILWAY

Incorporated on 10 August 1866, this 15.5-mile line ran N to Monmouth along the Wye valley from a junction with the SWR near Chepstow. It opened on 1 November 1876, and was vested in the GWR under an Act of 4 August 1905. It closed to passengers on 5 January 1959, and to goods in January 1964. Tintern station and signal box have been restored as a picnic site, and house a small museum of the line, while other parts of the route have become the Wye Valley Walk.

PART 2

The London, Midland & Scottish Railway group

The insignia of the LMS, combining the English rose, the Scottish thistle and the crest of the City of London. (Allan Mott)

Overleaf *Ironwork at Llandudno Junction; by echoing the style of its constituents, the LMS tried to re-create an age that was fast disappearing.* (Allan Mott)

LONDON, MIDLAND & SCOTTISH RAILWAY

Formed by the amalgamation, wef 1 January 1923, of the FR, G&SWR, HR, L&NWR, MR and NLR. Many smaller companies were absorbed at the same time including several in Ireland, previously owned by the MR. The CR and NSR, because of certain legal requirements not completed by the due date, entered the fold from 1 July 1923. This gave the LMS lines stretching from Thurso to Bournemouth (via the S&DR) and from Holyhead to Lowestoft (via the M&GNR), and access to Southend (LT&SR) and South Wales (via the ex-N&BR).

ABERDEEN RAILWAY

Incorporated on 31 July 1845 for a line from Guthrie (Arbroath & Forfar Railway, qv) to Aberdeen, with branches to Brechin and Montrose, it was promoted by GNSR supporters, who arranged for amalgamation should it be thought appropriate. However, by the time half the capital was paid up and spent, the companies had drawn apart. The line opened from Guthrie to Dubton Junction and Montrose, and from Bridge of Duns to Brechin on 1 February 1848, from Dubton Junction to Portlethen on 1 November 1849, to Aberdeen (Ferryhill) on 1 April 1850 and to Aberdeen (Guild Street) on 2 August 1853. It was worked by the SCR between 12 May 1851 and 31 July 1854, and the company amalgamated with the SMJR on 29 July 1856 to form the SNER.

ALLOA RAILWAY

Authorized on 11 August 1879, this 3-mile branch ran from the CR's S Alloa branch, across the R Forth to Alloa. The CR paid for the line, absorbing the Company wef 1 September 1884, the Act (14 July) also authorizing extension. The line opened on 1 October 1885 — the NBR had RP.

ALYTH RAILWAY

This line, sanctioned on 14 June 1858, ran 5.25 miles from Meigle (SNER, between Coupar Angus and Forfar) to Alyth. It was worked by the SNER from opening (12 August 1861), and the company was vested in it wef 1 February 1863, by an Act of 23 June 1864. The company was re-vested, this time in the CR, by an Act of 19 July 1875. Passenger traffic ceased 2 July 1951.

ANGLESEY CENTRAL RAILWAY

Incorporated on 13 July 1863 to build a railway between Gaerwen and Amlwch, the first 4.5 miles

A glassy River Forth and a line of bridge stanchions, reflecting, perhaps, on times past. They once carried the Alloa Railway to the industrial town on the north bank.

(Gaerwen–Llangefni) opened on 16 December 1864, though not to the public; that was on 12 March 1865, and on 3 June 1867 throughout. The company tried to persuade the L&NWR to buy or lease the line; it decided to buy, for £80,000 wef 1 July 1876 (Act of 24 July). The line closed to goods on 1 December 1964 and to passengers on 7 December, but is still open for chemical traffic from Amlwch.

ARBROATH & FORFAR RAILWAY

Incorporated on 19 May 1836 to link the two towns, there was also a branch to Almericloss (Dundee & Arbroath Railway, qv – Jt/Ind), making 15.25 miles in all. The 5 ft 6 in gauge line, single with passing places, was engineered by Grainger and Miller; it opened from Arbroath to Leysmill on 24 November 1838, and throughout on 3 January 1839. Locomotives came from the Dundee Foundry Company, owned by James Stirling, uncle of the Patrick who became well-known later. The line was leased in perpetuity to the Aberdeen Railway from 1848, but the company was absorbed by neither that concern nor its successor the CR, surviving independently until Grouping.

ARDROSSAN RAILWAY

This was formed on 23 July 1840 by an Act which divorced the Ardrossan & Johnstone Railway (qv) from its canal company, and authorized conversion of the line to standard gauge, doubling and upgrading for steam haulage. Its first locomotive, *Firefly*, built by Barr & McNab of Paisley, was delivered on 27 July

1840, and conversion was achieved in less than a week. On 20 August, a steamer service to Liverpool began, connecting with Glasgow trains. Though not successful at first, and subsequently abandoned, it was renewed with better results after the completion of Fleetwood harbour. The company, with branches, was vested in the G&SWR from 24 July 1854.

ARDROSSAN & JOHNSTONE RAILWAY

A 4 ft 6 in gauge line which grew from the Glasgow, Paisley & Ardrossan Canal, it was authorized on 20 June 1806 and opened from Glasgow to Johnstone on 6 November 1810. It was decided to build a railway to Ardrossan, so a company was incorporated 14 June 1827. Finance was difficult, however, and the line ran out of steam, as it were, at Kilwinning, opening in 1831. Its 5.5 miles of main line, with four branches, made a total length of 22.5 miles. In 1840 the company shook off its canal interests, changing its name to the Ardrossan Railway (qv).

ASHBY & NUNEATON JOINT RAILWAY

The L&NWR proposed a line from Ashby to Nuneaton via Market Bosworth in conjunction with the Nuneaton–Wigston line (see S Leicestershire

The Ashby & Nuneaton Joint Railway was the only joint MR/L&NWR project. Market Bosworth station, now used as a garage, is also the S limit of the Battlefield Line, which aims to extend along the track-bed beyond the station towards Shenton and Bosworth battlefield.

Railway) opened in 1864, but the MR had already obtained powers for an identical line in 1846, which had lapsed at the time of the purchase of the Leicester & Swannington Railway (qv). Now, however, it revived the plans, the result being a joint project, authorized on 17 June 1867. The line, opened on 1 September 1873, was worked by both partners, becoming part of the LMS in 1923. Three miles of track-bed between Shackerstone and Market Bosworth are now the preserved 'Battlefield Line'.

ASHTON, STALYBRIDGE & LIVERPOOL JUNCTION RAILWAY

This line, authorized on 19 July 1844, was connected with the L&MR from the start via M&LR rails. It opened from Miles Platting to Ashton on 13 April 1846, and to Stalybridge on 5 October, to be vested formally in the M&LR on 9 July 1847.

AYLESBURY RAILWAY

An Act was obtained on 19 May 1836 with the help of Sir Harry Verney, a local landowner, for a 7-mile, single line branch from Cheddington (L&BR). A rival scheme delayed building, but it resumed in May 1838 under Robert Stephenson — opening day, 10 June 1839, was a public holiday in Aylesbury. The line was worked by the L&BR, which absorbed the company on the day the L&NWR was formed.

AYR & DALMELLINGTON RAILWAY

An authority of 4 August 1853 extended lines already built along the Doon valley by the Ayrshire & Galloway (Smithstown & Dalmellington) Railway (qv) from Waterside to Falkland Junction (G&SWR) and from Sillyhole to Dalmellington. They opened for goods on 15 May 1856 and to passengers on 7 August, and the company was vested in the G&SWR under an Act of 28 June 1858, wef 1 August. Closure to passengers came on 6 April 1964.

AYR & MAYBOLE JUNCTION RAILWAY

Incorporated on 10 July 1854 to build a 5.25-mile line between the two towns, it opened on 15 September 1856 (goods) and 13 October (passengers). It was worked by the G&SWR, which received further RP and authority to work and maintain the line wef 1 August 1863 (Act of 13 July). It absorbed the company wef 1 February 1871 (Act of 29 June).

AYRSHIRE & GALLOWAY (SMITHSTOWN & DALMELLINGTON) RAILWAY

This was authorized on 8 June 1847 to build lines to Sillyhole and Waterside, SE of Ayr. By the time they opened, on 18 March 1854, the company had changed its title to the Ayr & Dalmellington Railway (qv) by an Act of 4 August 1853.

AYRSHIRE & WIGTOWNSHIRE RAILWAY

Formed on 23 May 1887 to take over and work the

Girvan & Portpatrick Railway (qv), the company was vested in the G&SWR wef 1 August 1892 (Act of 20 June). That company had actually taken over working and management on 1 February.

BAILEY'S TRAMROAD

A 5.5-mile plateway linking Nantyglo Ironworks with the canal at Govilon, it was laid to a gauge of 4 ft 4 in and opened in 1822. Its owner, Crawshay Bailey, sold it to the Merthyr, Tredegar & Abergavenny Railway (qv) under an Agreement of 1 February 1859, hoping no doubt that the larger company (of which he was a director) would turn it into an even more effective outlet via the Brecknock & Abergavenny Canal.

BANGOR & CARNARVON (sic) RAILWAY

Incorporated on 20 May 1851 to build between the two towns, the junction with the C&HR, which was authorized to work the line, was actually at Menai Bridge. It was an 8.5-mile single line, with a 1-mile branch to Port Dinorwic (Y Felinheli), which opened on 1 March 1852 for goods. The line opened throughout for passengers on 1 July, and for goods on 10 August. Agreement to lease the line to the C&HR for 999 years was made wef 1 July 1852, but the company was instead transferred by an Act on 10 July 1854; dissolution was delayed until 15 July

The North Wales Chronicle of 25 June 1852 carried notice of the opening of the Bangor and Carnarvon Railway, issued, of course, from the offices of the already-controlling C&HR in Chester. (Gwynedd Archives Service)

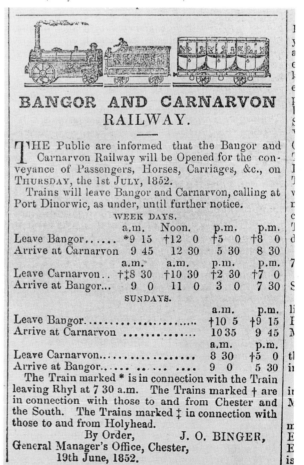

1867. The line was doubled in 1872, re-singled in 1966, and closed to goods on 4 August 1969, and to passengers on 5 January 1970, though there was a respite when Caernarfon became a temporary freight terminal during the rebuilding of the Britannia Bridge in 1970–72.

BANKFOOT LIGHT RAILWAY
Built under LROs granted in 1898 and 1903, this 3-mile line ran from Strathord Junction (CR, N of Perth) to Bankfoot. It opened for goods on 5 March 1906, and to passengers on 15 May, the company being vested in the CR wef 1 August 1909 by an Act of 16 August. Passenger closure came on 13 April 1931, and services ceased completely on 7 September 1964.

BARNOLDSWICK RAILWAY
This was a branch to Barnoldswick from Earby, on the Skipton–Colne line; the proprietors were authorized on 12 August 1867 to build a railway of ' . . . 2 miles or thereabouts'. This opened on 8 February 1871 and was worked by the MR, which absorbed the company under an Act of 13 July 1899. Closure to passengers came on 27 September 1965.

BARRMILL & KILWINNING RAILWAY
This was a 6.5-mile line promoted by the CR and authorized on 20 August 1883 to link the jointly-owned Glasgow, Barrhead & Kilmarnock line and the G&SWR at Kilwinning, the idea being to reduce CR dependence on the G&SWR. Lord Eglinton became interested, and, with his Lordship as Chairman, the company was reconstituted as the Lanarkshire &

Ayrshire Railway (qv).

BEDFORD RAILWAY
An 1836 plan for a line between Cambridge and the L&BR via Bedford was dropped, but in 1844 George Stephenson visited Bedford to discuss a branch, which, when authorized on 30 June 1845 and opened on 17 November 1846 was a line from Bletchley to Bedford. It was built by the L&BR, and absorbed by the L&NWR on completion as provided for in the authorizing Act, though the company was not dissolved until 21 July 1879. It became the basis for the Bedford & Cambridge Railway (qv).

BEDFORD & CAMBRIDGE RAILWAY
Incorporated on 6 August 1860 as a 29.5-mile line between the two towns, the route used the track-bed of the Sandy & Potton Railway (qv, and see also Bedford Railway) which the company bought out. Opinions differ on the date of opening, some citing 1 August 1862, others October of that year. The company had close ties with the L&NWR, with which WA were made under an Act of 23 June 1864, and which absorbed it on 5 July 1865. The line closed to passengers on 1 January 1968.

BEDFORD & NORTHAMPTON RAILWAY
Authorized on 5 July 1865 to link the towns via Olney, it ran from Oakley Junction to, at first, a temporary station in Northampton, replaced when the line opened throughout on 10 June 1872. The company amalgamated with the MR by an Act of 16 July 1885, and the line closed to passengers on 3 July 1939.

The fine Midland-type canopy of the Bedford & Cambridge Railway at Potton, Beds. When this picture was taken, in July 1987, restoration was in hand with a view to use as a museum.

Brighton Road station, Birmingham, was opened on 1 November 1875, and was just under 3 miles from the Birmingham & Gloucester Railway's junction with the L&BR. An MR train hauled by a Johnson 0-6-0 No 3694 passes the timber platform during the second decade of this century.

BIRMINGHAM & DERBY JUNCTION RAILWAY

This 48.5-mile line, authorized on 19 May 1836 to link the L&BR at Hampton-in-Arden (see also Stonebridge Railway) with Derby, opened formally on 5 August 1839, and to the public on 12 August. The L&BR took the company's trains on to Birmingham until the direct line from Whitacre to Lawley Street opened to the public on 10 February 1842. A junction with the NMR at Derby was authorized, and a spur from Lawley Street to the GJR was opened on 11 April 1842. The direct line to Lawley Street was not a success, though it has since become an important goods depot. The company became a constituent of the MR at its formation on 10 May 1844, with the NMR and MCR. Two company men made names for themselves under the MR: Matthew Kirtley was once engine foreman at Hampton, while James Allport began his career as a company clerk.

BIRMINGHAM & GLOUCESTER RAILWAY

Originally conceived to link Birmingham with docks at Gloucester, a lengthy debate on the route resulted in a line (authorized on 22 April 1836) which avoided Tewkesbury and Worcester, though public pressure forced a diversion to Cheltenham. Its main bugbear was the Lickey incline, 2.5 miles at 1 in 37.5 – built as an economy, it kept the company in debt for all of its independent life. The line opened from Cheltenham to Bromsgrove on 24 June 1840, Bromsgrove–Cofton on 17 September, Cheltenham–Gloucester on 4 November, Cofton–Camp Hill on 17 December, and to Curzon St, Birmingham, on 16 August 1841. It was leased by the MR wef 1 July 1845, which absorbed the company on 3 August 1846.

BIRMINGHAM WEST SUBURBAN RAILWAY

Incorporated on 31 July 1871 to build S from Albion Wharf to King's Norton, with a junction with the ex-B&GR line, the 6.75-mile single track was vested in the MR from 1 July 1875. It was opened on 3 April 1876, and widened and extended following authority of 18 July 1881; MR expresses were diverted along it from 1 October 1885. In 1892 a triangular junction was built at Lifford (authorized on 24 July 1888), to make a circular suburban service possible.

BIRMINGHAM, WOLVERHAMPTON & STOUR VALLEY RAILWAY

Incorporated on 3 August 1846, the 'Stour Valley' got into the title because of a plan, never authorized, to reach Stourport from Smethwick. The Shrewsbury & Birmingham Railway (qv) held 25 per cent of the shares, and in 1846 the L&NWR agreed to a perpetual lease. Because it duplicated its own route, Euston made no hurry to complete it: Chancery said it must, but the L&NWR postponed the opening, claiming that the line was unsafe. Finally the S&BR met the L&NWR buffer to buffer outside New Street. Again the companies went to Chancery, after which the L&NWR opened the line (February 1852 to goods, 1 July to passengers). It absorbed the company on 15 July 1867.

BLACKBURN RAILWAY

This was the title taken by the Bolton, Blackburn, Clitheroe & W Yorkshire Railway (qv) from 24 July 1851, ratifying one used locally for some time. In 1856 the company alarmed the L&YR and ELR by proposing an extension to Long Preston; those companies hurried to take over, jointly, from 31 December 1857 (Act of 12 July 1858). It then became sole L&YR property when that company absorbed the ELR, and the extension opened from

Chatburn to Gisburn on 2 June 1879, and to Hellifield on 1 June 1880.

BLACKBURN & PRESTON RAILWAY

This line was authorized on 6 June 1844 to build from Blackburn to Farington Junction, S of Preston, there to join the NUR. The line included a notable viaduct across Hoghton Bottom, R Darwen, 108 ft high, on three 65 ft spans. Two months after opening (3 August 1846) the company was absorbed by the ELR.

BLACKBURN, BURNLEY, ACCRINGTON & COLNE EXTENSION RAILWAY

Incorporated on 30 June 1845, the company was absorbed by the ELR three weeks later, wef 21 July. The line's first section, opened between Blackburn and Accrington on 19 June 1848, included Aspen Viaduct, a timber trestle which has since been buried by tipping, an embankment now standing where the viaduct did. Later openings were to Burnley (18 September 1848) and Colne (1 February 1849).

BLACKBURN, CLITHEROE & NORTH WESTERN JUNCTION RAILWAY

The company was authorized on 27 July 1846 to build along the Ribble valley to join the proposed NWR at Long Preston. The line was built by the L&YR, the first sod having been cut by Lord Ribblesdale at Clitheroe on 30 December 1846, and opened on 22 June 1850. The company had previously amalgamated with the Blackburn, Darwen & Bolton Railway on 9 July 1847 to form the Bolton, Blackburn, Clitheroe and W Yorkshire Railway (both qv).

BLACKBURN, DARWEN & BOLTON RAILWAY

Authorized on 30 June 1845, the line was to form a more direct outlet N from Blackburn and Manchester via the Blackburn, Clitheroe & NW Junction Railway (qv). The 5-mile Blackburn–Sough (Darwen) section included a 2,015 yd tunnel, and Tonge viaduct, which collapsed. Before the line opened (Blackburn–Sough 3 August 1847, throughout 12 June 1848), the company amalgamated with the BC&NWJR to form the Bolton, Blackburn, Clitheroe & W Yorkshire Railway (qv).

BLACKPOOL & LYTHAM RAILWAY

An isolated section of railway between the two towns, it was authorized on 17 May 1861 and opened on 6 April 1863. A link with the P&WR was made on 1 July 1874, and the company's station at Blackpool became Blackpool Central in 1878. The company was absorbed jointly by the L&YR and L&NWR as the property of the P&WR by an Act of 29 June 1871, wef 1 July.

BLACKWELL RAILWAY

This colliery line on the Derbyshire/Nottinghamshire border, privately built and opened in 1871, was bought by the MR under an Act of 28 June 1877. It was extended to Huthwaite, and a passenger station opened there on 17 October 1881, with a locomotive depot at Westhouses soon afterwards, but plans for extension to Sutton-in-Ashfield came to nothing.

BOLTON & LEIGH RAILWAY

Authorized on 31 March 1825, opened for goods on 1 August 1828 and to passengers on 11 June 1831, this was, technically, the first public railway to run in Lancashire. Just under 8 miles long, and engineered by George Stephenson, it was worked partly by steam (by one of his locomotives, *Lancashire Witch*) and partly by stationary engine. Hackworth's *Sans Pareil* came to the line after Rainhill. Its business was mainly mineral and agricultural, between a terminus at Bolton (Great Moor Street) and a connection with the L&MR via the Kenyon & Leigh Railway (qv) — the company was consolidated with both these and the GJR on 8 August 1845. Though closed to passengers on 29 March 1954, the line re-opened in five successive years to cope with Bolton Wakes Week traffic.

BOLTON & PRESTON RAILWAY

Authorized on 15 June 1837, the line opened from Bolton to Rawlinson Bridge on 4 February 1841, to Chorley on 22 December and to Euxton Junction on 22 June 1843. Worked by the Manchester, Bolton & Bury Railway (qv), it was quickly bought by the NUR on 10 May 1844. The L&YR opened a branch from Horwich Road on 15 July 1868 (goods), 14 February 1870 (passengers), and in 1886 established a locomotive works. From 1887, locomotives were built there well into the nationalization era — repair work continued until May 1964, and the passenger service along the branch was withdrawn on 27 September 1965.

BOLTON, BLACKBURN, CLITHEROE & WEST YORKSHIRE RAILWAY

Formed on 9 July 1847 by the amalgamation of the Blackburn, Clitheroe & NW Junction Railway and the Blackburn, Darwen and Bolton Railway (both qv), lines were opened from Sough (Darwen) to Bolton on 12 June 1848, and Blackburn to Chatburn formally on 20 June 1850, and 22 June to the public. The company changed its name to the Blackburn Railway (qv) on 24 July 1851.

BRECHIN & EDZELL DISTRICT RAILWAY

Incorporated on 25 July 1890, this 5-mile line from the Brechin branch of the CR was worked by that company from opening, on 8 June 1896. The company remained independent until 1923, and the line

Stonehouse, for Stroud and the Nailsworth branch. MR influence is apparent in this 1905 picture, but the chimneys of the original Bristol & Gloucester Railway station can be seen beyond the canopy. (Stroud Museum Association)

closed to passengers on 27 April 1931, re-opening briefly between 4 July and 26 September 1938.

BRIDGE of WEIR RAILWAY

An Act of 7 July 1862 authorized 3.5 miles of line between Johnstone and Bridge of Weir. It opened for goods on 21 April 1864, and to passengers on 20 June, but on 1 August 1865 the company was vested in the G&SWR, which closed the line on 18 May 1868. It re-opened all but the Cart Junction–Johnstone section (½ mile) on 23 December 1869 as part of the G&SWR's Elderslie–Greenock line.

BRISTOL & GLOUCESTER RAILWAY

The Incorporation Act (1 July 1839) authorized the conversion of the Bristol & Gloucestershire Railway (qv) to a main line, and the building of 22.5 miles to Standish, S of Gloucester, where it would join the C&GWUR from Swindon, and use its line to Gloucester. Built to standard gauge at first, a change to broad gauge was made in 1842; the link from Kemble was not opened until a year after the company had reached Gloucester! Formal opening was on 6 July 1844 — passenger traffic began on 8 July and goods on 2 September. However, at Gloucester break of gauge problems forced the company to unite in a Joint Board with the B&GR, and to negotiate with the GWR or another possible buyer. The MR took over working wef 7 May 1845; it absorbed the company in 1846, and converted the line to standard gauge, re-opening on 29 May 1854.

BRISTOL & GLOUCESTERSHIRE RAILWAY

Incorporated on 19 June 1828, this was a 10-mile tramway from Bristol (Cuckold's Pill), serving collieries at Shortwood, Parkfield and Coalpit Heath, in competition with the Avon & Gloucestershire Railway (qv — GWR). It opened on 6 August 1835, and merged with the Br&GR on that company's

opening, 6 July 1844 (Act of 1 July 1839).

BUCKINGHAMSHIRE RAILWAY

This was formed on 22 July 1847 by the amalgamation of two schemes, the Buckingham & Brackley Junction Railway (Claydon–Brackley), and the Oxford & Bletchley Junction Railway, both authorized in 1846; powers were granted to extend from Brackley to Banbury. The line opened from Bletchley to Banbury on 30 March 1850, and from Verney Junction to Oxford on 20 May 1851, worked by the L&NWR from the start, anxious to scotch possible incursions on Birmingham. That company leased it for 999 years from 1 July 1851 and absorbed it on 21 July 1879.

BURTON & ASHBY LIGHT RAILWAY

Authorized on 5 November 1902, this 11.5-mile electric tramway was built by the MR to a gauge of 3 ft 6 in, beginning in 1905. It opened from Burton to Swadlincote on 13 June 1906, and to Ashby on 2 July, and was worked throughout its life by the MR or its successors. That life ended, strangled by road competition, on 19 February 1927.

BURY & TOTTINGTON DISTRICT RAILWAY

Incorporated on 2 August 1877, this line opened on 6 November 1882, worked by the L&YR from the outset, and absorbed by that company under an Act of 24 July 1888, wef 1 March 1889. Mostly single track, it branched at Tottington Junction and ran for 4 steep miles to Holcombe Brook, at the N end of the town. More of a tramway than a railway, one of the first L&YR railmotors worked it from 1905, fitted with retractable steps to compensate for the lack of station platforms. The line was given ole 29 July 1913, converted to third-rail on 29 March 1918, and closed to passengers in May 1952.

The small stone building at Hairmyres (Busby Railway) has been superseded by 'bus-shelters', but at least the line is still open, thanks to local people who fought to keep it when BR threatened closure.

BUSBY RAILWAY

This was locally promoted to exploit local industries, and was authorized on 11 May 1863 to run 3 miles 43 chains from Busby Junction on the Neilston line, S of Glasgow. Extension to E Kilbride was decided upon before the first section was open (1 January 1866), the extension opening on 1 September 1868. The CR was authorized to work the line in perpetuity by an Act of 16 July 1874, and absorbed the company wef 2 February 1882 (Act of 18 July 1881). Further extension, to the Hamilton–Strathaven line near High Blantyre, was not successful — it opened on 2 July 1888, but closed on 1 October 1914. The rest remains open at the time of writing.

CAIRN VALLEY LIGHT RAILWAY

This was the outcome of several abortive schemes to build along the Cairn valley from a junction 1.25 miles NW of Dumfries to Moniave. Its LRO was confirmed on 29 December 1899, and though nominally independent, the G&SWR controlled the company. The line opened on 1 March 1905, an interesting aspect of its working being a lock and block system, using treadles in the single line worked by the trains to interact with the block instruments. The line closed to passengers on 3 May 1943 and to all traffic on 4 August 1947.

CALDON LOW TRAMWAY

Incorporated on 13 May 1776, this was the second line in the country to have an Act. It opened in 1777, a wooden wagonway running 3.5 miles from lime-stone quarries at Caldon Low to the Trent & Mersey Canal at Froghall Wharf. The line was reconditioned, with iron bars spiked to wooden sleepers, in 1780, and, after an Act of 15 April 1802, was relaid as a plateway engineered by John Rennie. In 1847 it was acquired by the NSR, which relaid it as a locomotive-worked line to a gauge of 3 ft 6 in, re-opening it in 1849.

CALEDONIAN RAILWAY

Incorporated on 31 July 1845, the Caledonian linked Carlisle and Glasgow via Annandale, Beattock and the Clyde valley. A junction at Carstairs fed a branch to Edinburgh, and the line opened from Carlisle to Beattock ceremonially on 9 September 1847 (to the public the next day), to Edinburgh on 15 February 1848, and to Buchanan Street, Glasgow, on 1 November 1849 (passengers), 1 January 1850 (goods). It was the first line to provide a journey between London and Scotland ' . . . without a change of carriage', the expresses taking 12.5 hours. An extension to Castlecary, where the line joined the SCR, was opened on 7 August 1848. By 1918, absorptions had swollen the CR system to a total track mileage, including sidings, of 2,827.75 miles, from Carlisle to Aberdeen and, via the Callander & Oban Railway (qv), to the W coast of Scotland. The company became an LMS constituent in 1923, but did not join until 1 July, after certain legal matters had been settled.

CALLANDER & OBAN RAILWAY

Though nominally independent, this company, incorporated on 5 July 1865, was supported by the CR, which agreed to work the line provided it was over 20 miles long. When funds ran out at Killin,

The seal of the Caledonian Railway quarters the arms of Scotland and England. (NRM)

only 17 had been built! However, the CR agreed to work it, reserving the right to stop at any time. Yet another injection of CR funds was required before the line could be opened on 1 July 1880. An extension from Connel Ferry to Ballachulish was authorized on 7 August 1896 and opened on 24 August 1903, with new works in Argyll authorized on 6 August 1897. The line remained independent until absorbed into the LMS at Grouping. It closed to goods on 14 June 1965, and to passengers on 26 March 1966 — dismantling began 2 days later.

CANNOCK CHASE RAILWAY
Privately built by the Marquis of Anglesey, this was a 1.25-mile line from the Cannock Mineral Railway (qv) to Cannock Chase. A company was incorporated on 15 May 1860, its Act authorizing the L&NWR to make WA with his Lordship; further arrangements (Act of 28 July 1863) gave powers to the L&NWR to absorb the company. It is probable that the line had opened that year.

CANNOCK MINERAL RAILWAY
This was the title taken by the Derbyshire, Staffordshire & Worcestershire Junction Railway on 14 August 1855, perhaps to the relief of all. Although the Act included powers to lease the line to the L&NWR, negotiations began with the NSR — they had reached an advanced stage when the NSR found that the L&NWR had pipped it by bidding slightly higher! The L&NWR took control from the date of opening, in November 1859, the line being vested by an Act dated 12 July 1869.

CARMYLLIE RAILWAY
Privately built by Lord Dalhousie, this 4.5-mile line took stone from quarries at Carmyllie to the Dundee & Arbroath Railway (qv) at Elliot Junction, near Geordiesburn. Its opening date is uncertain, but is thought to have been May 1854. The line was vested in the SNER on 19 June 1865, passing in due course to the CR, which was authorized to work it as a LR by an Order of 6 August 1898. A passenger service opened on 1 February 1900, closing on 2 December 1929.

Cannock Chase Colliery Co 0-6-0ST No 6 (Sharp Stewart 2643/1876) near Chasetown, with a home-made tender built on a brake-van frame. (Transport Nostalgia Picture Library)

CARNARVON (sic) & LLANBERIS RAILWAY

Incorporated on 14 July 1864, the first sod of a line to go 9 miles from the coast to villages at the foot of Snowdon was cut on 15 September. Building was suspended during the 1866 financial crisis, and the L&NWR offered to buy and complete the line, adding a 'persuader' by threatening an alternative Bill! The company did not succumb completely — the L&NWR got 4.5 miles at the Llanberis end, with RP over the rest, in return for allowing the company to use the L&NWR station at Caernarfon. On 13 December 1866, Agreement was reached for joint ownership of the whole line, the L&NWR working it. Opening on 1 July 1869, it was vested wholly in the L&NWR by an Act of 4 July 1870, to take place within 12 months of the Act. Though closed to passengers on 22 September 1930, the line re-opened from 18 July 1932 until 12 September; the only passenger traffic thereafter was summer excursions between 1933 and 1939, and from 1946 until 7 September 1962. The final goods train ran on 3 September 1964. The station at Llanberis has been converted into shops and a cafe, and parts of the track-bed have been used for road improvements.

CARNARVONSHIRE (sic) RAILWAY

Authorized on 29 July 1862, the line continued the Bangor & Carnarvon Railway from Caernarfon, using the Nantlle Railway (both qv) track-bed to Penygroes, and reaching Portmadoc via Afon Wen, 27 miles 50 chains. The Aberystwyth & Welsh Coast Railway (qv — GWR) agreed to build the coast section, and by 1866 the Nantlle had been converted to Penygroes. Then money problems forced the company to seek amalgamation with either the Nantlle or

CambR, which had meantime absorbed the A&WCR. The NR had no money either and the CambR was in chaos! So the NR was vested in the company on 25 July 1867, the CambR was given RP to Caernarfon, and the line was opened on 9 September. An Act of 4 July 1870 gave the L&NWR authority to make WA or to absorb the company; it chose the latter. The line closed for passengers on 7 December 1964.

CASTLE DOUGLAS & DUMFRIES RAILWAY

This nominally independent company was incorporated on 21 July 1856; the Act was obtained by the G&SWR, and authorized a line between the two towns via Dalbeattie. The line opened on 7 November 1859, worked by the G&SWR from the outset, the company being absorbed by its patron wef 1 August 1865 by an Act dated 5 July. The line closed to passengers on 14 June 1965.

CATHCART DISTRICT RAILWAY

This nominally independent company, backed by the CR, was authorized on 7 September 1880 to build a 2.5-mile line from Pollakshields E to Cathcart. It opened from Pollakshields E to Mount Florida on 1 March 1886, and to Cathcart on 25 May. The line was run by the CR as a branch from Glasgow Central — passenger traffic increased quickly and a 3-mile extension to Muirhouses Junction was authorized on 19 July 1887, opening on 2 April 1894. The CR was authorized to subscribe by Acts of 31 May 1889 and 22 May 1890, but despite this the Company retained independence to join the LMS at Grouping.

CENTRAL WALES RAILWAY

Sanctioned on 13 August 1859, this 19.75-mile line climbs from the Teme valley at Knucklas to a summit

The Castle Douglas & Dumfries Railway was influenced by the G&SWR from the start, and signal-boxes such as this (actually at Girvan) would have been typical.

(980 ft) at Llywncoch tunnel. The descent to Llangunllo is followed by another climb to the watershed above the Aran valley, the line then following the Ithon to Llandrindod Wells. It opened formally on 10 October 1865, and to the public on 17 October; the company was absorbed by the L&NWR on 25 June 1868, with the Central Wales Extension Railway (qv). The route survives, and new investment is encouraging, but it is a 'social service' line whose future cannot be taken for granted.

CENTRAL WALES & CARMARTHEN JUNCTION RAILWAY

This is what the Swansea & Carmarthen Railway (qv) became after an Act of 21 July 1873 transferred it to L&NWR control, though leaving it a nominally independent concern. The transfer took legal effect from the date of payment of £310,000, stipulated to be made by 15 September 1873. The company was completely absorbed under an Act of 21 July 1891.

CENTRAL WALES EXTENSION RAILWAY

Incorporated on 3 July 1860, this line was to extend the Central Wales Railway (qv) from Llandrindod Wells for 27.25 miles to Llandovery. The Llandrindod–Builth Wells section opened as a single line on 1 November 1866, but the length to Garth was delayed until 11 March 1867; Llanwrtyd Wells came on line on 6 May. The final run up to Sugar Loaf tunnel was 3 miles at 1 in 60/70, but once through the 1,000 yd curved bore, the line ran down to its destination, reached on 8 October 1868. The company was absorbed by the L&NWR, with the CWR, by an Act of 25 June 1868.

CHARNWOOD FOREST RAILWAY

This originated from Leicestershire's first line, a canal tramway opened in 1794, engineered by William Jessop, using smooth rails and flanged wheels. A burst reservoir caused the closure of both tramway and canal in 1799. In 1834 a railway was proposed over the route, but nothing happened until an L&NWR-backed branch to Loughborough was authorized to use part of the canal course, connections being planned with the MR at Coalville and Loughborough. Final plans changed slightly, but a 10.75-mile line was authorized between Coalville and Loughborough on 16 July 1874, which, after opening on 16 April 1883, was worked by the L&NWR for half the receipts. It was not a lucrative line, and an OR was appointed in 1885. In 1906 the L&NWR wished to connect with the GCR at Loughborough, but the company would not pay (perhaps it could not) for the flying junctions demanded. By 1909, however, it was solvent, remaining independent until absorbed by the LMS wef 1 July 1923, under an Amalgamation Order dated 14 July.

CHEADLE RAILWAY

First incorporated on 22 July 1878, and abandoned on 12 July 1882, it was re-incorporated on 7 August 1888 as the Cheadle Railway Mineral & Land Company, which built the line with financial support from the NSR. It opened to Totmanslow on 7 November 1892, and the Company was renamed the Cheadle Railway by an Act dated 7 August 1896, which also authorized the NSR to subscribe and work the line. Opening to Cheadle was on 1 January 1901, from which day the NSR leased the line until it absorbed the company wef 1 January 1908, by an Act of 21 August 1907.

CHESTER & CREWE RAILWAY

Authorized on 30 June 1837, rather more than half this line's 20.5 miles was built by Thomas Brassey, on a course which followed the Shropshire Union Canal and included the Weaver viaduct. The opening was on 1 October 1840, but it was not an independent one since the company had been absorbed by the GJR on 1 July 1840 (Act of 19 May).

CHESTER & HOLYHEAD RAILWAY

Incorporated on 4 July 1844, powers for crossing the Menai were postponed to save time, work beginning on 1 March 1845. The first section was opened jointly with the S&CR, 2 miles between Chester and Saltney Junction, on 4 November 1846. Robert Stephenson's standing as an engineer suffered when his bridge across the Dee estuary collapsed under an S&CR train on 24 May 1847, but the line was opened to Bangor on 1 May 1848, and from Llanfair PG to Holyhead on 1 August. The company ran a coach link between Bangor and Llanfair PG, using the road bridge, while the Britannia bridge was building — Conwy had been used as a practice run for the new bridge, and the first train across was driven by Stephenson on 5 March 1850, the whole line opening to the public on 18 March. The Mold Railway (qv) was absorbed in 1849, but then came financial trouble; after seeking help from the L&NWR (which had worked the line from the start), the company approached the GWR. Horrified, the L&NWR at once made an offer, accepted wef 1 January 1859. The company was not dissolved, however, until 21 July 1879.

CHESTER & WOLVERHAMPTON RAILWAY

This 45-mile project from Calveley, on the Chester–Crewe line, to Wolverhampton followed the course of the Shropshire Union Canal. Though not built, its powers (granted 3 August 1846) were transferred to the SUR&CC on formation.

CHURNET VALLEY RAILWAY

Though independent in that it had its own directors, its Act of 26 June 1846 incorporated the NSR (Churnet Valley Line), and it was regarded from the

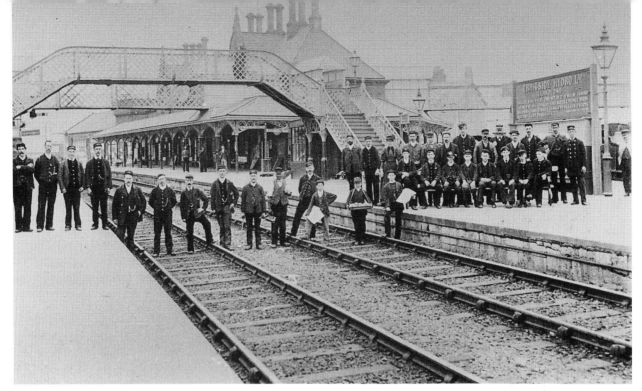

The old Chester & Holyhead Railway station at Llandudno stood to the west of the present one, which replaced it in 1896. The number of staff pictured reflects the station's importance. (Gwynedd Archives Service)

start as a constituent of the NSR. Its authorization was for a 27.5-mile line from Macclesfield to Uttoxeter, part of which was to be laid along the defunct Uttoxeter Canal. It opened on 13 June 1849, followed on 11 September by a 13-mile extension to Burton.

CITY of GLASGOW UNION RAILWAY

Eleven years from authorization (29 July 1864) to completion is a long time to build 6.25 miles of railway. However, it included St Enoch station, which, reached via the first railway bridge across the Clyde, was splendid and opened ceremonially on 17 May 1876 by the Prince and Princess of Wales. It was also the first public building in Scotland to be lit by electricity — four arc-lamps were erected in 1879, working from dynamos driven by a steam engine. The first section of line, between Pollok Junction and Dunlop Street, opened on 12 December 1870, followed by gradual extension as building progressed. St Enoch was vested in the G&SWR on 29 June 1883, and on 7 August 1896 the company was dissolved and the line partitioned between the NBR, which took the section N and W of College W Junction, and the G&SWR, which had the rest. Each retained RP over the other's portion. St Enoch station closed on 27 June 1966 and has been demolished.

CLEATOR & WORKINGTON JUNCTION RAILWAY

Authorised on 27 June 1876, this comprised 15.25 miles of line, including branches, from ironfields to Workington, promoted in an effort to bypass charges by the other companies which the ironmasters considered exorbitant. By an Act of 1877, the FR was authorized to work the line — it opened for goods on 4 August 1879, and to passengers on 1 October — and to buy shares to a maximum of £25,000. A steep, twisting branch from Distington joined the Rowrah & Kelton Fell (Mineral) Railway (qv), worked by the company. The passenger service between Moor Row and Siddick closed on 13 April 1931, the company having become a subsidiary of the LMS in 1923.

CLYDESDALE JUNCTION RAILWAY

This line, authorized on 31 July 1845, linked the Polloc & Govan and Wishaw & Coltness Railways (both qv) at Motherwell. The CR used it to reach Glasgow, having taken it over before opening, by an Act of 18 August 1846. The line was eventually opened on 1 June 1849 from Rutherglen to Motherwell, and between Newton and Hamilton on 5 September.

COCKERMOUTH & WORKINGTON RAILWAY

This 8.75-mile line, authorized on 21 July 1845, used the Derwent valley to reach the coast at Workington, the company being, incidentally, obliged to build a new vicarage at Brigham for John Wordsworth, son of the poet, through whose grounds the line cut. Early mismanagement caused problems, but after opening on 28 April 1847, much coal was carried, and a new dock at Workington was authorized in 1861, a branch to it being sanctioned on 8 June 1863. This opened in September 1864, and the company was absorbed by the L&NWR on 16 July 1866.

Though always worked by others, the Cockermouth, Keswick & Penrith Railway remained independent until 1923. Bridgeplate 13 is not, unfortunately, still in situ, but can be seen at the Winchcombe Railway Museum.

COCKERMOUTH, KESWICK & PENRITH RAILWAY

Conceived as an extension of the SD&LUR (qv — LNER) and authorized on 1 August 1861, it was a splendidly scenic line of 31.25 miles, and the only one to cross the Lake District, running from Penrith via Troutbeck, the Greta Gorge, Keswick and Bassenthwaite. It was opened on 26 October 1864 (goods), 2 January 1865 (passengers), and was worked by the L&NWR under an Act of 29 June 1863, except for mineral traffic which was worked by the St&DR as owners of the SD&LUR. Tourist traffic increased so much that the line was doubled in 1900. Diesels took over on 3 January 1955, but through goods services were withdrawn on 1 June 1964 and the line closed W of Keswick on 18 April 1966. The rest closed to passengers on 6 March 1972, and to goods on 19 June.

CONISTON RAILWAY

Though nominally independent, this company, incorporated on 10 August 1857, was a close ally of the FR, sharing the same company secretary. The 9.5-mile single line ran from Foxfield Junction, near Broughton, to Coniston, via Torver; it opened for passengers on 18 June 1859, and for goods when an extension to Copper Mines Wharf opened in 1860. The FR worked the line from opening, absorbing the company on 7 July 1862. The line was not well placed for tourists, however, and when the mines ceased work it was the first Lake District line to close, to passengers on 6 October 1958, and to goods on 30 April 1962.

CONWAY & LLANRWST RAILWAY

Incorporated on 23 July 1860 to build along the Conwy valley to Betws-y-Coed, the line's first sod was cut near Llanrwst on 25 August 1860. It opened to Llanrwst on 17 June 1863, and to Betws-y-Coed on 6 April 1868, and was L&NWR-worked; that company determined to take over, and infiltrated the Board until the company was virtually an L&NWR satellite.

The Conway & Llanrwst Railway was always prominent as a tourist line, and the L&NWR built observation cars to cater for this. No 1503, beautifully restored, is shown here before re-entering service on the Bluebell Railway. (P. Zabek)

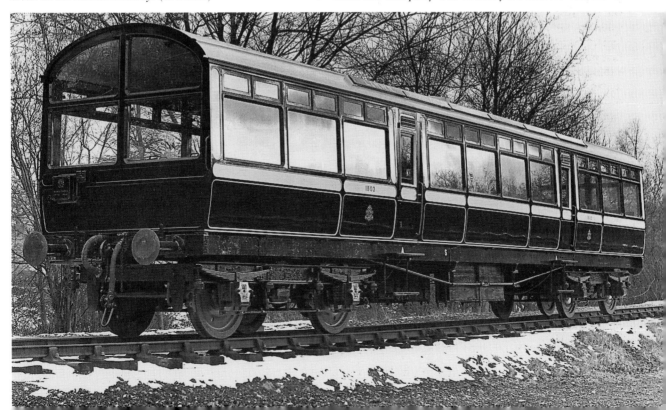

WA were authorized by an Act of 28 July 1863, and the company was finally dissolved and vested on 15 July 1867. The L&NWR planned a narrow gauge link with Blaenau Ffestiniog, but built standard gauge under powers granted on 18 July 1872: the tunnel caused problems, but the line opened on 22 July 1879. A link via the ex-Festiniog & Blaenau Railway (qv – GWR) now gives BR access to the power station at Trawsfynydd.

CRIEFF & COMRIE RAILWAY
Incorporated on 25 July 1890, this 6-mile line from Crieff Junction (CR) to Comrie took the place of an abandoned 1865 scheme. The line opened on 1 July 1893, and was worked under Agreement by the CR, which bought the company by an Act dated 2 August 1898; this stipulated that the sale, for £45,000, must take place before 1 August . . .

CRIEFF & METHVEN JUNCTION RAILWAY
Authorized on 14 July 1864, this ran from the Crieff Junction Railway (qv) outside Crieff, along the valley of Pow Burn, to join the Perth, Almond Valley & Methven Railway (qv) S of Methven. The company amalgamated with the CR on 26 July 1869, and the line closed to passengers on 1 October 1951.

CRIEFF JUNCTION RAILWAY
Powers for this 9-mile line were acquired by the SCR on 15 August 1853, to run from its own line near Loaninghead to Crieff. The line opened on 16 March 1856, and the company was absorbed by the SCR on 29 June 1865. The passenger service ceased on 6 July 1964.

CROMFORD & HIGH PEAK RAILWAY
This line of 33 miles, authorized 2 May 1825, was the result of a scheme to link the Peak Forest and Cromford Canals. The line opened from Cromford to Hurdlow on 29 May 1830, and to Whaley Bridge on 6 July 1831. Until a junction was put in at Cromford (1853) the line was isolated, and another junction, with the Stockport, Disley & Whaley Bridge Railway (qv), was made in 1857. The company was re-incorporated on 26 June 1855, and the line leased under an Act of 30 June 1862 by the L&NWR, hoping for a new route to London. In fact, the only passenger service, using a carriage attached to goods trains, ceased at the end of April 1876. Hopton incline was, at 1 in 14, the steepest solely adhesion-worked line in the UK. Absorption into the L&NWR came by an Act of 19 July 1887. The Parsley Hay–Middleton Top section closed on 1 April 1967, the rest from 11 September. A stretch of track-bed now forms part of the Tissington Trail.

DEARNE VALLEY RAILWAY
Promoted by coal-owners at Hickleton Main, Houghton Main and Carlton Main (Cudworth) collieries, this line, authorized on 6 August 1897, ran from the H&BR near Hemsworth to the GN/GE Joint line at Black Carr, Doncaster. To work their line the owners chose the H&BR, signing a 5-year Agreement. They then changed their minds and approached the L&YR, which, with reluctance, agreed to work the line and build an extension link to the Wakefield–Goole line at Crofton. Opened in stages, but throughout on 17 May 1909 (goods) and 3 June 1912 (passengers), the line was single, though increasing traffic made doubling necessary. Conisborough viaduct was a notable feature of the line.

DENBIGH, RUTHIN & CORWEN RAILWAY
The first sod of this line, authorized on 23 July 1860, was turned on 4 September. It opened from Denbigh to Ruthin on 1 March 1862, to a temporary station at Corwen on 6 October 1864, and throughout on 1 September 1865. The GWR, aiming at Rhyl, offered to lease this line and the Vale of Clwyd Railway (qv), but considered the guarantees asked by the latter too great. The L&NWR obtained WA by an Act of 28 July 1863, but repudiated them after a dispute with the contractor, who worked the line until he became bankrupt. The company bought a locomotive and tried to run things itself, but an OR was appointed in April 1866 and WA were again made with the L&NWR. The company was vested in the L&NWR by an Act of 3 July 1879, wef 1 July. The line closed to passengers from 2 February 1953, though it was used by Land Cruise trains on a circular Rhyl–Corwen–Barmouth–Caernarvon–Rhyl route during the 1950s. Goods traffic ceased on 30 April 1962.

DERBYSHIRE, STAFFORDSHIRE & WORCESTERSHIRE JUNCTION RAILWAY
Incorporated on 2 July 1847, this was to be a line of 18.25 miles between collieries in the Cannock area and Uttoxeter, but it only reached Rugeley on the Trent Valley line. Building began on 14 August 1855, when the company changed its name to the handier Cannock Mineral Railway (qv).

DINGWALL & SKYE RAILWAY
Though authorized on 5 July 1865, local objections slowed things and another Act was required on 29 May 1868 before work could begin, but the line opened to Strome Ferry on 5 August 1870 (goods), 19 August (passenger). On 2 August 1880, the company amalgamated with the HR which had worked it since opening. The HR obtained re-authorization of the Kyle section (29 June 1893), opening it on 2 November 1897. The line opened up access to the Isles, and is now a popular scenic route, carrying 5,193 passengers in its observation car during 1987, and increasing its revenue by 25 per cent that year.

Chinley station (Dore & Chinley Railway) is a shadow of former times, but something at least of the stone-built station building still survived on 30 July 1988.

DORE & CHINLEY RAILWAY

The MR liked the idea of another route across the Pennines, particularly since this one joined the MR at each end. So when engineering problems proved too much for the Dore & Chinley company, incorporated on 28 July 1884, the MR happily subscribed (up to £100,000 was authorized by an Act of 25 June 1885) and then took over, vesting the company on 24 July 1888. The line, opened on 6 November 1893 (goods), 1 June 1894 (passengers), was easily graded, but the result was two long tunnels — Totley (3 m 950 yd), at the Sheffield end, was the longest on the MR, and second only to the Severn Tunnel in Great Britain. Cowburn, at the Chinley end, is 2 m 182 yd long, and 25 per cent of line is therefore in tunnel.

DORNOCH LIGHT RAILWAY

Built under a LRO confirmed on 13 August 1898, this 7.75-mile line ran from The Mound to Dornoch. The HR worked it from opening (2 June 1902), but

the company retained independence until passing to the LMS at Grouping. It closed to passengers on 13 June 1960.

DRUMPELLER RAILWAY

Though almost 2 miles of this 4 ft 6 in gauge coal railway linking collieries with the Monkland Canal were authorized on 4 July 1843, rather less than a mile was actually built. Opened on 3 April 1847, it was little more than a wagonway, but was bought by the Forth & Clyde Navigation Company (qv) in 1846, with the Monkland Canal, under an Act of 3 July.

DUKE OF SUTHERLAND'S RAILWAY

When the Sutherland Railway (qv), planned to reach Brora, stopped at Golspie, powers for the last 6 miles were transferred to the Duke of Sutherland on 20 June 1870. The Duke built not only this section, but also acquired powers for an extra 11 miles N to Helmsdale; it opened to W Helmsdale (Gartymore)

Brora station was originally built by the Duke of Sutherland. The HR absorbed the line in 1884, rebuilding the station in 1895—when this picture was taken (22 May 1988) it was nearing its centenary. (Allan Mott)

from Dunrobin on 1 November 1870. The Duke ran the line until it was open throughout (19 June 1871), when the HR took over, absorbing the company into its own system by an Act of 28 July 1884.

DUMFRIES, LOCHMABEN & LOCKERBY (sic) RAILWAY

A CR-backed venture authorized on 14 June 1860, the line ran to a bay platform in Dumfries station, and was the springboard whence the CR reached the Portpatrick & Wigtownshire Joint Railway (qv) via RP across G&SWR territory. The line opened on 1 September 1863; the Incorporation Act allowed joint WA, but the company became CR property by an Act of 5 July 1865, wef 31 July.

DUNBLANE, DOUNE & CALLANDER RAILWAY

Originally incorporated on 16 July 1846, the company's drive languished, but after re-incorporation (21 July 1856), its line opened between Dunblane (SCR) and Callander via Doune (10.5 miles) on 1 July 1858. Powers to lease it were granted to the SCR; it took these up, and the line passed into the control of the CR when the SCR was absorbed on 29 June 1865.

DUNDEE & NEWTYLE RAILWAY

A line of almost 11 miles, authorized on 26 May 1826, it was horse-worked, though steam was introduced on the level sections in 1833. Its engineer was Charles Landale, who had converted the Elgin Wagonway into the Dunfermline & Charlestown Railway (qv – LNER). The line opened partially on 16 December 1831, and throughout on 3 April 1832; scant trade was to be had, save that of Dundee Harbour, so it did little for its shareholders, but it benefited the community greatly. Despite money problems, local people kept it open until a lease could be negotiated with the Dundee & Perth Railway (qv), dated 14 October 1846 for 999 years. The company was vested in the SCR on 28 July 1863, but maintained a separate identity until Grouping.

DUNDEE & PERTH RAILWAY

Incorporated on 31 July 1845, the company's line ran from Dundee to Perth, via Invergowrie, opening ceremonially on 22 May 1847, and to the public two days later. The company leased the Dundee & Newtyle Railway (qv) from 14 October 1846, and, with a lease of the Dundee & Arbroath Railway (qv – Jt/Ind) authorized by Parliament (31 August 1848), was empowered to change its name to the Dundee & Perth & Aberdeen Railway Junction Company (qv) wef the end of the Parliamentary Session.

DUNDEE & PERTH & ABERDEEN RAILWAY JUNCTION

The title assumed by the Dundee & Perth Railway

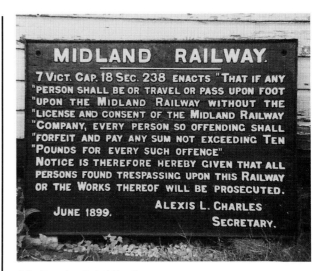

The Dursley & Midland Junction Railway was MR-influenced from the start, and warning notices of this kind would have been no uncommon sight.

(qv) from the end of the 1848 Parliamentary Session. Vested in the SCR wef 31 July 1863 (Act of 28 July), the company was dissolved and transferred to the CR by an Act dated 8 April 1881.

DURSLEY & MIDLAND JUNCTION RAILWAY

This 2.5-mile line, which obtained its Act on 25 May 1855, ran from the MR at Coaley on its Bristol–Gloucester line. Built within a year — it opened for goods on 25 August 1856, and to passengers on 17 September — it was worked initially by the MR, until a contractor took over in September 1857. The company then bought a locomotive and worked the line itself, from April 1858. The MR resumed working in 1861, absorbing the company under Parliamentary sanction of 28 June.

EAST & WEST INDIA DOCKS & BIRMINGHAM JUNCTION RAILWAY

Born from a desire of the L&BR to reach the lower Thames, the company was incorporated on 26 August 1846 and, though nominally independent, it was heavily backed by the L&NWR, which supplied 67 per cent of the capital and gave its Company Secretary an office at Euston. Construction was slow — the line opened from Bow Junction to Islington on 26 September 1850, on to Camden Town on 7 December, for coal on 20 October 1851, and for through goods on 1 January 1852. The company's Act authorized a junction with the GNR at Maiden Lane, but when it declined to make this, was taken to Chancery and compelled to do so. Before it opened, the company had changed its title to the less cumbersome North London Railway (qv).

EAST & WEST JUNCTION RAILWAY

Authorized on 23 June 1864 to build to Stratford-upon-Avon from Greens Norton (Towcester), Lady Palmerston cut the first sod of this line at Towcester on 3 August 1864. However, lack of money stopped work within two years; extensions of time and credit allowed eventual opening throughout on 1 July 1873. Income was minimal — one day the Sheriff's men arrived with a writ for £250, and, receiving no satisfaction, padlocked the locomotive to the rails. However, since the engine was the company's only source of revenue, it no doubt felt justified in breaking the padlock! An OR was appointed on 29 January 1875, and the passenger service was suspended for eight years from 31 July 1877, other services from 22 March 1885. In 1879, the company floated the Easton Neston Mineral & Towcester, Roade & Olney Junction Railway (qv), and an extension W to Broom. The company was offered for sale, but legal snags resulted in a merger with the Stratford-upon-Avon, Towcester & Midland Junction and the Evesham, Redditch & Stratford-upon-Avon Railways (both qv) to form the S&MJR (Act of 1 August 1908).

EAST LANCASHIRE RAILWAY

This was formed by the name-change of the Manchester, Bury & Rossendale Railway on 21 July 1845. On 3 August 1846 the company absorbed the Blackburn & Preston, the Blackburn, Burnley, Accrington & Colne Extension, and the Liverpool, Ormskirk & Preston Railway (all qv). An extension to

The station at Stoke Bruern (Easton Neston Mineral & Towcester, Roade & Olney Junction Railway) enjoyed a passenger service for almost less time than it takes to say the name, but its line became a valuable goods link across the Midlands.

Bacup, the summit of the system, opened to passengers on 1 October 1852, and the company was itself absorbed by the L&YR on 13 May 1859.

EASTON NESTON MINERAL & TOWCESTER, ROADE & OLNEY JUNCTION RAILWAY

This was a scheme floated on 15 August 1879 by the impecunious East & West Junction Railway to link Olney (Bedford & Northampton Railway) with the Northampton & Banbury Junction Railway at Towcester (all qv). The MR had RP for goods, but by the time 10.5 miles of line were open, the company had changed its name to the Stratford-upon-Avon, Towcester & Midland Junction Railway (qv) on 10 August 1882.

EVESHAM & REDDITCH RAILWAY

Authorized on 13 July 1863 to link Evesham (GWR) with Redditch (MR), heavy earthworks on the Alcester–Redditch section delayed things, but the line opened between Evesham and Alcester on 16 June 1866 (goods), 17 September (passengers), and to Redditch on 4 May 1868. TA with the GWR were authorized on 30 June 1874, but the line was worked from opening by the MR, which absorbed the company from 1 July 1882 (Act of 12 July). The line was used to avoid the Lickey incline (B&GR), and by much goods traffic off the S&MJR during the Second World War.

EVESHAM, REDDITCH & STRATFORD-UPON-AVON JUNCTION RAILWAY

This 7.75-mile line was authorized on 5 August 1873 to run from Broom (Evesham & Redditch Railway, qv) to Stratford-upon-Avon. It opened on 2 June 1879, worked from the outset by the East & West

Junction Railway (qv), but was soon in financial trouble, an OR being appointed on 2 January 1886. The company became a constituent of the S&MJR by an Act of 1 August 1908.

FINDHORN RAILWAY

Incorporated on 19 April 1859, this was a 3-mile line between the village and the Inverness & Aberdeen Junction Railway (qv) at Kinloss. It opened on 18 April 1860 and was run independently for two years, but the company then found itself with money problems, and working was taken over by the I&AJR from 1 April 1862. The service was withdrawn by the HR (as I&AJR successors) on 31 January 1869, the rails being lifted early in 1873.

FLEETWOOD, PRESTON & WEST RIDING JUNCTION RAILWAY

Incorporated on 27 July 1846 to link the P&WR at Maudland with the Preston & Longridge Railway, it continued from there to the Leeds & Bradford Railway (both qv) at Elslack. The company eventually agreed to go only as far as Clitheroe, but got just 1 mile, to Deepdale (P&LR), on 14 January 1850. The company absorbed the P&LR by an Act of 23 June 1856 and, at re-incorporation, opened an extension to Maudland Bridge on 1 November. It was itself absorbed by the L&NWR and L&YR jointly wef 1 July 1866, under an Act of 17 June.

FORFAR & BRECHIN RAILWAY

The company was incorporated on 4 August 1890 to build a main line of 13 m 70 yd from Forfar to Brechin (CR), another at Forfar, and a branch in Forfar. Agreement was made with the CR to work the line in perpetuity from opening, and the CR bought the concern for £168,400 under an Act of 31 July 1894. The line closed to passengers on 4 August 1952.

FORTH & CLYDE NAVIGATION COMPANY

This waterway, opened 1790–1800, linked the Scottish rivers of its title by a substantial improvement on any Scottish river navigation of the time. It carried little coal, but by an Act of 3 July 1846 bought the Monkland Canal which did, along with the Drumpeller Railway (qv). The company built the Grangemouth Railway (qv), opened in 1860, and, by an Act of 20 June 1867, was bought, railways and all, by the CR.

FURNESS RAILWAY

Seen as a link between Barrow and mines at Lindal, the company was incorporated on 23 May 1844. There was also a 3 ft 2.25 in gauge line to a slate quarry at Kirkby. Despite poetic fury from Wordsworth, the line progressed well, to be in use by 3 June 1846 and officially opened on 12 August. An extension from Kirkby to Broughton was opened in late February

The Furness Railway had a more attractive furniture motif than many lines. Its squirrel lives on in this seat from Millom, now at the Ravenglass terminus of the Ravenglass & Eskdale Railway. (P. van Zeller)

1848. The discovery of enormous deposits of haematite at Park, N of Barrow, in 1850 made the company one of the most prosperous of its time. A national slump after 1870 prompted thoughts of sale to the MR in 1875, but a change of emphasis from goods to tourists kept the company successful until the outbreak of the First World War. Absorption of smaller companies extended its system, until by 1918 it owned 428.75 track miles, including sidings. The company remained independent until the Grouping.

FURNESS & MIDLAND JOINT RAILWAY

A link between Wennington (MR) and Carnforth (FR), it was suggested by the MR which wanted a share in the rich iron ore traffic from Furness, and offered boat-train traffic to Barrow in exchange. The L&NWR, which had hitherto controlled the FR at both ends, opposed, but a company was incorporated on 22 June 1863, RP over the FR ameliorating the L&NWR. The 9.75-mile line, financed jointly by the two companies and managed by a Joint Committee, opened for goods on 10 April 1867, and to passengers on 6 June. It crossed the L&NWR N of Carnforth to a station on the W, a curve leading into the N side of the L&NWR station. The company remained independent until Grouping.

GARNKIRK & GLASGOW RAILWAY

Incorporated on 26 May 1826, the company built a line to a gauge of 4 ft 6 in from a junction with the

Borwick, on the Furness & Midland Joint Railway. The station (right distance) was built before the railway: when the line arrived, it passed 50 yd to the SE, and a second station (foreground) had to be built. (Andrew C. Ingram)

Monkland & Kirkintilloch Railway (qv – LNER) near Gartsherrie to carry coal to Glasgow. The first Scottish railway to open independent of a waterway, it gave regular goods and passenger services, both steam and horse-drawn. For the ceremonial opening on 27 September 1831 (the line had been in use since May for goods, from 1 June for passengers) two locomotives, *George Stephenson* and *St Rollox* had been supplied by Stephenson & Company, and were driven by the line's engineers, Grainger and Miller. A branch to Coatbridge opened in 1843, and by an Act of 19 July 1844 the company became the Glasgow, Garnkirk & Coatbridge Railway (qv). For ten years the company's Glasgow station was the only one serving the city.

GARSTANG & KNOT (sic) END RAILWAY

Incorporated on 30 June 1864 to build 7 miles of line from Garstang & Catterall (Lancaster & Preston Junction Railway, qv) to Pilling, the line opened on 5 December 1870. However, the passenger service lasted only until 11 March 1872; at the end of the month the line fell into disuse. An OR was appointed, and goods traffic resumed on 23 February 1875, and passenger traffic on 17 May. The line was bought wef 1 July 1908 by the Knott End Railway (qv).

GENERAL TERMINUS & GLASGOW HARBOUR RAILWAY

Authorized on 3 July 1846, the line linked the Polloc & Govan Railway with the Glasgow & Paisley Joint line, the Glasgow, Paisley, Kilmarnock & Ayr, the Glasgow, Barrhead & Neilston, and the Clydesdale Junction Railways (all qv). Though parts were open in December 1848, full opening was delayed because the main feeder, the CJR, did not open until 1 June 1849, but a grand demonstration on 16 February 1849 proved that the company's coal-handling equipment was the best in Scotland. Independence was short, and powers to vest parts of the line in the CR were granted on 24 July 1854, though final amalgamation was not until 29 June 1865.

GIRVAN & PORTPATRICK JUNCTION RAILWAY

This 32-mile link between Girvan and the Portpatrick Railway (qv) at Challoch Junction was authorized on 5 July 1865, the company planning to use RP from Challoch to Portpatrick Harbour. The line opened on 5 October 1877, but, disaster-prone (a major viaduct at Stinchar collapsed) and badly managed, it proved a liability; because tolls were unpaid, the PR barred entry on 7 February 1882, a through service not resuming until 3 August 1884. On 28 February 1886 the G&SWR ceased working the line. The company ran traffic using stock hired from the G&SWR, but closed the line from 12 March to 14 June 1886, resuming with its own stock. It was reconstituted as the Ayrshire & Wigtownshire Railway (qv) on 23 May 1887.

The Girvan & Portpatrick was a hilly road—Pinmore viaduct stands just S of the first summit, the line falling to Pinwherry before climbing across the bleak watershed by Chirmorie.

GLASGOW & RENFREW DISTRICT RAILWAY

The nominal owner of this concern, incorporated on 6 August 1897, was the Glasgow & Paisley Joint Railway, but the CR and G&SWR both had fingers in the pie, and the company was vested jointly in them by an Act of 2 July 1901. The line ran from Cardonald to Renfrew S, and opened on 1 June 1903, but never competed very successfully with the rival trams. The passenger service was withdrawn on 19 July 1926, though the line was retained for goods traffic.

GLASGOW & SOUTH WESTERN RAILWAY

Formed on 28 October 1850, an Act of 9 July 1847 stipulated that the GPK&AR and the Glasgow, Dumfries & Carlisle Railway (both qv) should, on the opening of the latter, combine as the G&SWR. The company grew to monopolize train services in Galloway, though its deadly rival, the CR, managed various incursions. The company ran a successful fleet of steamers from several piers and harbours along the coast. Track mileage in 1918, including sidings, was 1,128.5, the company becoming a constituent of the LMS in 1923.

GLASGOW, BARRHEAD & KILMARNOCK JOINT RAILWAY

This was a joint concern created on 12 July 1869 to settle differences arising from rival CR and G&SWR routes to Kilmarnock after the CR had had its own scheme authorized on 5 December 1865. The line opened on 26 June 1873, with a branch to Beith, the company's responsibility being the Glasgow,

Barrhead & Neilston Direct Railway (qv), with the Kilmarnock extension. It was absorbed jointly by the companies on 2 August 1880, the line closing to passengers between Barrhead and Neilston on 7 November 1966.

GLASGOW, BARRHEAD & NEILSTON DIRECT RAILWAY

Incorporated on 4 August 1845, the line ran from Glasgow to Crofthead (Neilston), 9 miles, with branches to Thornliebank and Househills. Opening between Glasgow, Barrhead and Spiersbridge on

The seal of the Glasgow & South Western Railway. (NRM)

27 September 1848, and to Crofthead on 5 October 1855, the line was leased to the CR by an Act of 1 August 1849; in 1865 the CR obtained powers to extend to Kilmarnock, much to G&SWR rage. It began a parallel line, but sense prevailed, and one joint line was built (see Glasgow, Barrhead & Kilmarnock Joint Railway).

GLASGOW CENTRAL RAILWAY

The CR had a large stake in this scheme, conceived as an overhead line but revised to go underground after public opposition. The 7 miles authorized on 10 August 1888 were to link Strathclyde Junction (CR) in the E with the projected Lanarkshire & Dumbartonshire Railway (qv) in the W, with a branch to Stobcross. An Act of 31 May 1889 dissolved the company and passed its assets to the CR, and in July 1891 an extension was authorized from Bridgeton Cross to Newton on the CR line to the S. Building difficulties were great, but the line, opened on 10 August 1896, gave the CR an enormous interest in Glasgow suburban traffic. Then came the trams, the 'caurs', which effectively killed it — the last steam train ran on 5 October 1964, and the system was abandoned.

GLASGOW, DUMFRIES & CARLISLE RAILWAY

This railway was authorized on 13 August 1846 to Gretna Junction (CR) from an end-on junction with

Dumfries station became part of the G&SWR as soon as it opened, but was not built by it. On 21 April 1988 it seemed to have a less austere air, though this may, in part, be due to excellent restoration undertaken by BR.

the GPK&AR's New Cumnock extension. It opened from Dumfries to Gretna on 23 August 1848, to Closeburn on 15 October 1849, and throughout on 28 October 1850, on which date it amalgamated with the GPK&AR to form the G&SWR.

GLASGOW, GARNKIRK & COATBRIDGE RAILWAY

Formed 19 July 1844 when the Garnkirk & Glasgow Railway (qv) changed its name and obtained Parliamentary sanction for an extension to Coatbridge which had already been built! The company had brief independence before sale to the CR was authorized by an Act of 3 August 1846. It was not, however, dissolved until 2 August 1880.

GLASGOW, PAISLEY & GREENOCK RAILWAY

Incorporated on 15 July 1837, the railway was straight and level from Paisley to Bishopton, where engineering problems in two tunnels delayed opening throughout until 29 March 1841 (part had been open since 15 July 1840), seven months after the GPK&AR. It reached Greenock along the riverbank, and did good business by fare-cutting, but did itself and its shareholders little good by cutting profits proportionately. Amalgamation with the CR was sanctioned on 9 July 1847.

GLASGOW, PAISLEY, KILMARNOCK & AYR RAILWAY

Authorized on 15 July 1837 to build from Ayr to Glasgow, the line also had branches to Dalry and Kilwinning (Ardrossan Railway, qv). The line opened from Ayr to Irvine on 5 August 1839, to

Kilwinning on 23 March 1840, to Beith on 21 July and Glasgow on 12 August. The Kilmarnock & Troon Railway (qv) was leased for 999 years wef 16 July 1846, with powers to improve it for steam traction. On the opening of the Glasgow, Dumfries & Carlisle Railway (qv) on 28 October 1850, the company became the G&SWR.

GLASGOW SOUTHERN TERMINAL RAILWAY
Powers were granted on 16 July 1846 to the Glasgow, Barrhead & Neilston Direct Railway (qv) for a short line from Titwood to Gushet (CR). The company was acquired before opening by its sponsor, which was authorized to buy it under an Act of 2 July 1847. It was opened on 26 September 1848.

GLOUCESTER & CHELTENHAM TRAMROAD
Though described as the Gloucester & Cheltenham Railway in the Act of 28 April 1809, it was more usually known as the above. It was promoted by Cheltenham landowners, and, 9 miles long, linked Gloucester Docks and Cheltenham, with a branch to Leckhampton quarries beyond, where there were two rope-worked inclines. It was opened in the quarries by April 1810, and reached the docks within 12 months, a 3 ft 6 in gauge, horse-worked tramway — a steam locomotive tried in 1831 was too heavy for it. The company was bought jointly by the B&GR and the C&GWUR in1837, but the B&GR bought out the other's moiety under a penal clause in the Act of

The seal of the Grand Junction Railway, using Britannia, a strange-looking engine and the Liver bird, among other things. (Allan Mott)

11 June 1838, when the C&GWUR failed to build its line to Gloucester by the stipulated date. The tramway was abandoned and the company dissolved by an Act of 1 August 1859, though parts of the line survived in Leckhampton quarries until 1924.

GRAND JUNCTION RAILWAY
Authorized on 6 May 1833, 82.5 miles long, the line ran from Curzon Street, Birmingham, via Wolverhampton, Stafford and Warrington, to join the L&MR via the Warrington & Newton Railway (qv), which it absorbed in 1834. The line opened on 4 July 1837, skirting the village of Monks Coppenhall, where a station was built taking its name from nearby Crewe Hall. Amalgamation discussions with the NUR in 1844 failed when the NUR pulled out. The company consolidated with the Bolton & Leigh, the Kenyon & Leigh, and the Liverpool & Manchester Railways (all qv) on 8 August 1845, and 11 months later with the M&BR and L&BR to form the L&NWR (16 July 1846).

GRANGEMOUTH RAILWAY
This was built by the Forth & Clyde Navigation Company under the Drumpeller Railway Amendment Act of 22 July 1848 to link the Stirlingshire Midland Junction Railway (all qv) at Grahamstown with docks at Grangemouth. Single track, it opened for goods in 1860, and for passengers in 1861, worked first by the E&GR and then the NBR. To the NBR's dismay, however, the Forth & Clyde Navigation Act of 20 June 1867 authorized the CR to buy the Canal and auxiliaries — including railways. The NBR acquired RP to Grangemouth and access to the entire canal network. The line did not come under state control until 1948.

GREENOCK & AYRSHIRE RAILWAY
Authorized on 5 July 1865 against bitter opposition from the CR, the opening of this line (minerals 1 September 1869, goods 1 October, passengers 23 December) from Greenock to Bridge of Weir (G&SWR) began a price-cutting war between the companies. When it became clear that the G&SWR had won — it was authorized to subscribe and make WA — the CR tried to improve services on its Greenock & Wemyss Bay Railway (qv). Goods traffic disappointed, and, like the Glasgow, Paisley & Greenock Railway (qv), the G&SWR found that fare-cutting did not pay dividends. A fare Agreement was reached with the CR, and, wef from 1 August 1872 (Act of 18 July), the company amalgamated with the G&SWR.

GREENOCK & WEMYSS BAY RAILWAY
Authorized on 17 July 1862 and opened on 13 May 1865, this promising scheme turned sour. Instead of continuing their journey from Greenock and catching

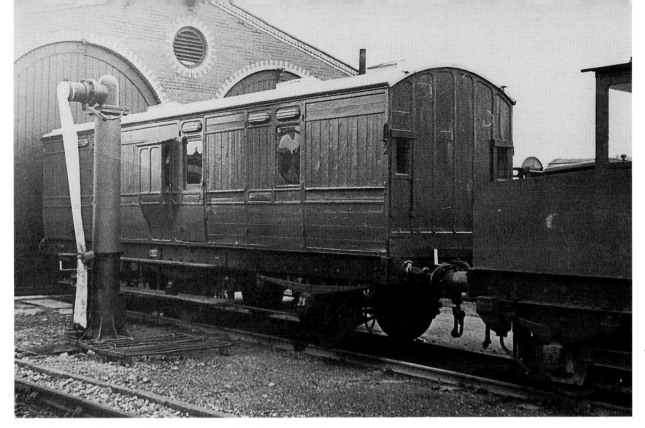

G&SWR stock, such as this nineteenth-century six-wheeled van, restored at Bo'ness, would have been in everyday use on the Greenock and Ayrshire Railway. The water-column comes from Grangemouth Docks.

boats at Wemyss Bay, as had been hoped, passengers still preferred to catch them at Greenock because of the company's unreliable timekeeping. Although no dividend was paid for 13 years after opening, the company remained independent until amalgamated with the CR, which had always worked it, by an Act of 27 July 1893, wef 1 August.

GUISELEY, YEADON & RAWDON RAILWAY

This small but ambitious company had ambitions that were ahead of its funding; its Act (16 July 1885) authorized only 1.25 miles of line between Guiseley and Yeadon, granting RP to the MR. An Act of 5 August 1891 sanctioned a name-change to the Guiseley, Yeadon & Headingley Railway, with an extension to that place, but this was abandoned in 1893. The MR agreed to buy the line and open it on 1 June 1893, but it was 26 February 1894 before the first train ran. The line closed temporarily during the Second World War, and permanently on 10 August 1964.

HAMILTON & STRATHAVEN RAILWAY

This line, authorized on 10 August 1857, ran from the CR at Clydesdale Junction (Hamilton) 10.25 miles SW to Strathaven. The CR worked it from opening, on 6 August 1860, and its absorption of the company was ratified on 25 July 1864.

HAMPSTEAD JUNCTION RAILWAY

Promoted by the L&NWR to ease congestion on the NLR, the line, authorized on 20 August 1853, was 6 miles long and included a .75-mile tunnel. It ran from Camden Town to Old Oak Junction, Willesden, and was worked by the NLR from its opening on 2 January 1860 (passengers), 1 March 1863 (goods), although WA were authorized with the L&NWR, which absorbed the company on 15 July 1867. The line closed to goods traffic on 30 September 1972.

HARBORNE RAILWAY

The 2 miles 7 furlongs 4 chains between Harborne and the L&NWR at Monument Lane, Birmingham, sanctioned on 28 June 1866, were all that was left of a much larger scheme. A three-year extension of time kept the project alive, and when the line opened on 10 August 1874 it was worked by the L&NWR. That company made three offers to buy, in vain, and the company retained its identity until becoming an LMS subsidiary in 1923. The line closed to passengers on 12 November 1934.

HARECASTLE & SANDBACH RAILWAY

These 8 miles of railway were authorized on 26 June 1846 as part of the embryo NSR, running from Harecastle to a junction with the M&BR, shortly to become part of the L&NWR. It was opened on 21 January 1852.

HARROW & STANMORE RAILWAY

This single-track branch of 2 miles 50 chains between the towns was authorized on 25 June 1886. It resulted in considerable urban growth in the area it served, and was worked from opening (18 December 1890) by the L&NWR under an Agreement dated

Left *Bridge No 60A, Hay Railway. It spans the Dulas Brook, at this point the border between England and Wales, and is seen here from the Welsh side.*

Right *The seal of the Highland Railway.* (NRM)

29 January 1891, ratified 21 July. Eight years later, wef 1 July 1899, the L&NWR bought the company for £34,000 by an Act of 9 August 1899. The line closed to passengers on 15 September 1952, and to goods on 6 July 1964.

HAY RAILWAY

A 3 ft 6 in gauge tramway, authorized on 25 May 1811, the line used a 24-mile roundabout route between Eardisley (10 miles NE of Hay-on-Wye) and Watton Wharf on the Brecknock & Abergavenny Canal. It opened on 7 May 1816, making an end-on connection with the Kington Railway (qv – GWR) at Eardisley, and giving access to limestone quarries. Bought by the HH&BR on 6 August 1860, the Three Cocks–Talyllyn Junction section was re-allocated to the Mid-Wales Railway (qv), and the Talyllyn Junction–Brecon length to the B&MTJR.

HEMEL HEMPSTEAD RAILWAY

Incorporated on 13 July 1863, the company built from Harpenden Junction (Luton) to Hemel Hempstead via Redbourn, but poor relations with the L&NWR prevented a connection at Hemel. A revision of plans (authorized on 16 July 1866) fitted in with an MR project to extend from Heath Park; though the line was not completed until 16 July 1877, the MR agreed to work it (1 December 1876), formally absorbing the company on 25 June 1886. In 1931 the line was chosen for a road/rail experiment involving a vehicle with raisable wheels which could travel on either road or rail – the creation of the LPTB in 1933 stifled the idea as it was proving itself. The line closed to passengers on 16 June 1947, and to goods in sections between August 1959 and October 1964.

HEREFORD, HAY & BRECON RAILWAY

Incorporated on 8 August 1859, the company planned to link with the S&HR, but the line actually joined the NA&HR at Barton (Hereford). Having bought the Hay Railway, the line was at once truncated when it was divided between the Mid-Wales Railway (both qv) and the B&MTJR. Hereford to Moorhampton opened for goods on 24 October 1862, on to Eardisley on 30 June 1863, to Hay on 11 July 1864 and Three Cocks on 1 September. Hereford–Eardisley opened for passengers on 30 June 1863, passenger traffic beginning to Hay on 11 July 1864. The railway opened to Brecon for goods on 1 September 1864, and to passengers on 21 September. Amalgamation with the B&MTJR (Act of 5 July 1865) was ruled improperly processed and therefore illegal, and while the legal tangle was being solved the MWR worked the line wef 1 October 1868. The MR took over from 1 October 1869, leasing the line by an Act of 30 July 1874 and absorbing the company in 1876. A short section survives at the Bulmers Railway Centre, Hereford.

HIGHLAND RAILWAY

On 1 February 1865, the I&AJR and the Inverness & Perth Junction Railway (qv) merged; on 29 June the combination was authorized as the HR. The company controlled 242 miles of railway, and subsequent amalgamations of lines N of Inverness increased this by 164.5 miles. It promoted its own direct line to Aviemore from Inverness across the Monadhliadh mountains (authorized on 28 July 1884), and opened throughout on 1 November 1898, including Slochd Mhuic summit at 1,315 ft *en route*, but saving 25.75 miles of the previous 60.25 miles between

Aviemore and Inverness. The company also worked the Dornoch and the Wick & Lybster LRs (both qv), and became an LMS constituent in 1923.

HOLYWELL RAILWAY

Sanctioned on 29 July 1864, this was a 2-mile line along the course of an old tramway to a new pier on the Dee estuary. It was completed by 1867, but after use into the 1870s lay derelict until the L&NWR bought it in late 1911/early 1912. More indecision followed, until the L&NWR was authorized to rebuild it on 7 August 1912 — it was re-opened for both passengers and goods on 1 July 1913. Steep (1 in 27) and single-track, it closed on 6 September 1954, except to textile mills, a service which survived until 11 August 1957.

HOYLAKE RAILWAY

This company was incorporated on 28 July 1863 to build a line from Poulton-cum-Seacombe to Hoylake, and from Birkenhead docks. Extensions to New Brighton (5 July 1865) and Parkgate (16 July 1866) were authorized, but only the 5.25-mile Hoylake–Birkenhead docks section was opened, on 2 July 1866. Traffic was sparse, bailiffs seized the line on 8 July 1870, and its sale was sanctioned 10 days later. The Hoylake–Leasowe Crossing section remained in use as part of the Hoylake & Birkenhead Rail & Tramway (qv).

HOYLAKE & BIRKENHEAD RAIL & TRAMWAY

Incorporated on 18 July 1872 to re-open the Hoylake Railway (qv), this was achieved on 1 August. A new dockside station opened on 1 April 1878, and an extension to Hoylake from W Kirby on the same day. From Birkenhead docks, the company owned a street tramway running to Woodside Ferry — this was sold to Birkenhead Tramways in October 1879, the company changing its name to the Seacombe, Hoylake & Deeside Railway (qv) on 18 July 1881.

HUDDERSFIELD & MANCHESTER RAILWAY & CANAL

Incorporated solely as a Canal Company in 1794, it opened its waterway through the Standedge tunnel in 1811. The company was re-incorporated on 21 July 1845 to link Cooper Bridge (M&LR) with

Huddersfield's superb station was built in 1847 for the Huddersfield & Manchester Railway & Canal Company, whose arms it carries above the left-hand pavilion. It was designed by J.P. Pritchett, architect to Earl Fitzwilliam of Wentworth Woodhouse. (Allan Mott)

Stalybridge (Sheffield, Ashton-under-Lyne & Manchester Railway, qv — LNER) via another long tunnel close to the first. The L&NWR, alarmed, acquired the company on 9 July 1847, and opened the line from Huddersfield to Stalybridge on 1 August 1849; Huddersfield–Heaton Lodge Junction had opened to passengers on 3 August 1847, and to goods on 16 November. The first train staffs were used in Standedge tunnel, introduced by the Superintendent, Henry Woodhouse, to ensure that no driver entered the tunnel without authority.

HUDDERSFIELD & SHEFFIELD JUNCTION RAILWAY

This line was authorized on 30 June 1845 to shorten the rail distance between the towns by linking Huddersfield with the MS&LR near Penistone. Its 13 miles included some heavy works, with four major viaducts and 2.25 miles of the line in tunnel. In one of these, Thurstonland (1,631 yd), the inaugural train stalled on 1 July 1850 and had to be divided. At first the MS&LR worked the line, but in 1870 the L&YR began running Sheffield–Huddersfield trains from Penistone — the company had been absorbed by the L&YR's predecessor, the M&LR, on 27 July 1846.

INVERNESS & ABERDEEN JUNCTION RAILWAY

Authorized on 21 July 1856, this line was an E extension of the Inverness & Nairn Railway (qv), planned to await the GNSR at Elgin. It opened from Nairn to Dalvey (Forres) on 22 December 1857, and to Elgin on 25 March 1858, and the GNSR offered the company £40,000 to complete the line — it opened to Keith on 18 August. At first the BoT would not pass the Spey Bridge at Orton for passenger traffic, so travellers detrained on one side and walked across the

nearby road bridge. Meanwhile the carriages were roped across the railway bridge, for reboarding by those continuing their journey. The company took over working of the Inverness & Nairn Railway in 1857, absorbing it on 17 May 1861. It absorbed the Findhorn Railway and worked it from 1 April 1862, and merged with the Inverness & Perth Junction Railway (all qv) on 1 February 1865 to form what became the HR.

INVERNESS & NAIRN RAILWAY

Incorporated on 24 July 1854, 15 miles of line were built between the towns, with a ½-mile branch to Inverness Harbour. The first sod was cut by the Countess of Seafield at Inverness on 21 September 1854, a day declared a holiday in the town. It had been hoped to open on 1 August 1855, but the contractor's plant was seaborne, and subject to the whims of the weather. Actual opening was on 5 November, and working was taken over under a ten-year Agreement from 31 December 1857 by the I&AJR, which absorbed the company on 17 May 1861. The line became the oldest section of the HR.

INVERNESS & PERTH JUNCTION RAILWAY

The first sod of this ambitious line, authorized on 22 July 1861, was cut on 17 October 1861 by Lady Seafield near Forres, and, considering the engineering difficulties, was built remarkably quickly. It opened from Dunkeld to Pitlochry on 1 June 1863, from Forres to Aviemore on 3 August, and between Pitlochry and Aviemore on 9 September. The line had two major viaducts, two tunnels (plus one built by the Perth & Dunkeld Railway, qv) and numerous bridges. Until the Leadhills & Wanlockhead LR (qv) opened, Druimuachdar was the highest summit on a UK standard gauge railway, at 1,484 ft. Wanlockhead topped it by 14 ft. The P&DR was absorbed wef

28 February 1864, under an Act of 8 June 1863, to give continuous rails from Inverness to Perth, and combination with the I&AJR on 1 February 1865 formed what became the HR. A branch to Aberfeldy, authorized in the original Act, was opened on 3 July 1865, and closed on 3 May 1965.

INVERNESS & ROSS-SHIRE RAILWAY

Incorporated on 3 July 1860 to build 31 miles of line between Inverness and Invergordon, the first sod was cut by Lady Matheson, wife of the Chairman, at Inverness on 19 September 1860. The line opened to Dingwall on 11 June 1862 and to Invergordon on 23 March 1863; on 30 June 1862, the company had consolidated with the I&AJR. The Ross-shire Extension Act (11 May 1863) authorized a line to Bonar Bridge, 26.5 miles — it opened to Meikle Ferry on 1 June 1864 and to Bonar Bridge on 1 October.

KEIGHLEY & WORTH VALLEY RAILWAY

This 4.75-mile branch line, financed locally, was sanctioned on 30 June 1862 with MR blessing. The Brontë village of Haworth gave good tourist business, the line continuing to Oxenhope. It opened for passengers on 15 April 1867, and to goods on 1 July; the MR leased it (authority of 11 August 1876), absorbing the company wef 1 July 1881, under an Act dated 18 July. On 1 January 1962 the line closed to passengers (goods 18 June), but was taken over by the Keighley & Worth Valley RPS and re-opened on 29 June 1968. Damems, its platform one carriage long, was reputedly the smallest station on the MR.

KENDAL & WINDERMERE RAILWAY

Kendal people, disappointed that the L&CR came no closer than Oxenholme, promoted a railway authorized on 30 June 1845. The line opened from Oxenholme to Kendal on 22 September 1846 (passengers),

4 January 1847 (goods), reaching Windermere on 21 April. At first the L&NWR supplied stock and engines via the L&CR, but from summer 1850 the 10.25-mile line was worked under private contract. The company assumed control in November 1851 but made such a poor showing that the L&CR lost patience and ceased to wait for late connections. This and other things caused much friction, only cured when the company agreed to be leased in perpetuity to the L&CR, wef 1 May 1858, a dealing ratified by an Act of 13 August. By then the L&CR was itself leased to the L&NWR: both companies retained their identities until dissolution and vesting on 21 July 1879.

KENYON & LEIGH JUNCTION RAILWAY

This 2.5-mile branch, authorized on 14 May 1829, ran N from the L&MR to the Bolton & Leigh Railway (qv). It opened for goods on 3 January 1831, and to the public on 13 June, private owners being permitted to work their own vehicles along it for a toll. The company was consolidated with the B&LR, the L&MR and the GJR on 8 August 1845.

KETTERING & THRAPSTONE (sic) RAILWAY

This 7.5-mile line was authorized on 29 July 1862 to link the towns. It was backed by the MR, which then floated an extension to Huntingdon and St Ives, a further 18.25 miles, sanctioned on 28 July 1863. At this point the name of the company was changed to the Kettering, Thrapstone & Huntingdon Railway (qv).

KETTERING, THRAPSTONE (sic) & HUNTINGDON RAILWAY

An 1846 scheme from the ECR at St Ives had failed, but was revived by the MR from the Thrapston end to exploit ironstone workings in Northamptonshire.

Left *Pitlochry station on the Inverness & Perth Junction Railway. The station building, pictured on 13 May 1987, has an unusual and attractive design.* (Allan Mott)

Right *The Kendal & Windermere Railway's station at Windermere is now a supermarket, but the original cast-iron* porte-cochère *has been well-integrated into the conversion.*

Quite a deal of patching up had been done to the brickwork of Kimbolton station (Kettering, Thrapstone & Huntingdon Railway) by 30 April 1988. It is now a private residence. (Allan Mott)

Sanctioned on 28 July 1863, it became an extension of the Kettering & Thrapstone Railway (qv). Opening on 21 February 1866 (goods), 1 March (passengers), the line was worked by the MR under a Perpetual Agreement — that company also had RP over the ECR between St Ives and Cambridge. The company was vested in the MR on 6 August 1897, the line closing to passengers on 15 June 1959.

KILLIN RAILWAY
Incorporated by a BoT Certificate of 1883, this line ran for 5 miles 1 chain from Killin Junction (CR) to Killin and Loch Tay, and opened in March 1886, worked by the CR. After passing to the LMS, the Killin–Loch Tay section closed to passengers on 9 September 1939, and to goods on 2 November 1964. Closure throughout came on 28 September 1965.

KILMARNOCK & TROON RAILWAY
This was the first Scottish line authorized by Act (27 May 1808). In 1807, the Duke of Portland commissioned William Jessop to survey a 10-mile route from pits at Kilmarnock to the harbour at Troon. The line, double throughout, was gauged at 4 ft, using cast-iron plates with the flange at the inner edge, taking an easy course down Irvine Water; it opened on 6 July 1812. About 1817, the Duke commissioned a steam locomotive from George Stephenson — the second Killingworth engine came to Troon, but broke the railplates. Even so, this first steam locomotive in Scotland (for 14 years the only one) remained in use until 1848. Though its Act did not authorize it, the line was also the first in Scotland to carry passengers.

It was leased by the GPK&AR on 16 July 1846, and closed four days later for relaying with edge-rail, re-opening on 1 March 1847. The company was bought by the G&SWR on 16 July 1899.

KIRKCUDBRIGHT RAILWAY
Authorized on 1 August 1861 for 10.25 miles of railway between Castle Douglas and Kirkcudbright, the line opened for goods on 17 February 1864, but the Inspecting Officer refused to pass the Portpatrick Junction for passengers. The opening was delayed until 15 August, when re-arrangement of signals and a speed restriction had been made. The company was absorbed by the G&SWR wef 1 August 1865, by an Act dated 5 July. Passenger traffic ceased on 3 June 1965.

KNIGHTON RAILWAY
This line, joining Craven Arms to Knighton, was authorized on 21 May 1858 to the S&HR with authority to make a 10-year WA. The 12.25-mile line was leased by the contractor from opening, on 1 October 1860 (Craven Arms–Bucknell) for minerals, and on 6 March 1861 for all traffic throughout. By an Act of 22 June 1863, the company merged with the Central Wales Railway (qv).

KNOTT END RAILWAY
Incorporated on 12 August 1898, this line completed the Garstang & Knot End Railway (qv) by building 4.5 miles from Pilling to Knott End. The company had bought the G&KER on 1 July 1908, and re-opened the line on 30 July, but quickly found itself in financial trouble, saved only by the opening of salt-mines at Preesall. It passed to the LMS in 1923, and ex-L&NWR railmotors ran the passenger service until withdrawal from 31 March 1930. The Knott End–Pilling section was completely closed from

A datestone in the far gable proclaims that Bucknell station (Knighton Railway) was built in 1860; it has remained virtually unchanged since. When this picture was taken (7 May 1988) the near platform was out of use, but had been planted with flowers, making an attractive display.

13 November 1950, the rest remaining open for goods between Pilling and Garstang until August 1965.

LANARK RAILWAY

This single-track branch ran from the CR main line at Cleghorn, N of Carstairs, to Lanark. It was opened on 5 January 1855, and on 23 July 1860 the CR was authorized to acquire the company. It doubled the line and extended to Douglas on 1 April 1864, and to Muirkirk for goods on 1 January 1873 (passengers, 1 June 1874). In 1923, a trade dispute in Muirkirk began a decline, and the lines did not long survive the Second World War. The system was linked to the Lesmahagow Railway by the Muirkirk and Lesmahagow Junction Railway (both qv).

LANARKSHIRE & AYRSHIRE RAILWAY

This was formed on 28 July 1884 when the Barrmill & Kilwinning Railway (qv) changed its name. Several projects were authorized by the same Act, notably branches to Ardrossan Harbour and to the G&SWR in Ardrossan, a 4 miles 10 chains line from Beith to Bervie and a 2 miles 70 chains line to Irvine from Kilwinning. The Act also authorized WA with the CR, which later subscribed, but the company retained its identity until Grouping.

LANARKSHIRE & DUMBARTONSHIRE RAILWAY

This line, authorized on 5 August 1891, became intertwined with railways already along the N bank of the Clyde. It opened from Stobcross to Clydebank on 1 May 1896, to Dumbarton E on 1 October, and became a lucrative line for goods, commuters and, in the summer, trippers to Loch Lomond. The company was vested in the CR from 1 August 1909, by an Act dated 16 August.

LANCASHIRE & YORKSHIRE RAILWAY

This company was formed when the M&LR amalgamated with the Manchester, Bolton & Bury Canal Navigation & Railway, the Huddersfield & Sheffield Junction, the Liverpool & Bury, the Ashton,

The seal of the Lancashire & Yorkshire Railway. (NRM)

Stalybridge & Liverpool Junction, and the Wakefield, Pontefract & Goole & W Riding Railways (all qv) under an Act dated 9 July 1847. Further amalgamations expanded the company's influence in the counties for which it was named, until its own merger with the L&NWR before Grouping, under Statutory Rules and Orders No 2078 of 1921, wef 1 January 1922.

LANCASHIRE UNION RAILWAY

This line was authorized on 25 July 1864 to run from the Blackbrook branch of the St Helens Railway (qv) to Adlington. By going on from Chorley (L&YR) it would reach Blackburn via Cherry Tree. The Boars Head–Blackburn section was vested jointly with the company and the L&YR on 13 July 1868, and opened for goods on 1 November 1869 (passengers, 1 December). The company was vested in the L&NWR on 16 July 1883, and became L&NWR/ L&YR joint until the Grouping, when it passed to the LMS.

LANCASTER & CARLISLE RAILWAY

Promoted with powerful support from the GJR and L&BR to build between the cities via Kendal, it was authorized on 6 June 1844. It was, at the time, the largest single contract (69 miles) ever placed, and that it opened later than the contractor had promised was due more to bad weather, land and labour problems than anything else. Opening from Lancaster to Oxenholme was on 22 September 1846, and the line was in Carlisle on 17 December, but by then the company had already passed responsibility for working the line to the GJR — and before it opened, the GJR was itself part of the L&NWR. The company was soon negotiating to take over the Lancaster & Preston Junction Railway (qv), believing that company's lease to the Lancaster Canal Company to be invalid, and began running between Lancaster and Preston on 22 September 1846. In 1856 the L&NWR terminated WA, and the company arranged to work its line wef 1 August 1857. On 10 September 1859 it absorbed the L&PJR, which it had leased from 1 August 1849, and agreed that it should itself be leased to the L&NWR. Independence lasted until formal dissolution and absorption by the L&NWR on 21 July 1879.

LANCASTER & PRESTON JUNCTION RAILWAY

This line, promoted from the Lancaster end in an attempt to increase trade from the S, was authorized on 5 May 1837. It opened ceremonially on 25 June 1840, and to the public the following day, and was run from the first by the NUR. When the NUR terminated the Agreement in 1842, the company turned to the Bolton & Preston Railway (qv) — this precipitated such repercussions with the NUR that

the company leased itself to the Lancaster Canal Company from 1 September 1842, at £13,300 pa. It then fell into such an appalling state that the Inspecting Officer instructed it to 'put its house in order' — the L&CR was running the line at the time. The company regained possession, and re-leased itself to the L&CR wef 1 August 1849, after much wheeling and dealing in which the ELR became involved. At last an Agreement was reached, the L&CR taking over from 10 September 1859.

LEADHILLS & WANLOCKHEAD LIGHT RAILWAY

Promoted by the CR under the Light Railways Act of 1898, an Order was confirmed on 5 August 1898 for a 7.75-mile line from the CR main line S of Elvanfoot to the named villages. The line was opened to Leadhills on 1 October 1901, and Wanlockhead a year later, worked by the CR; it was notable for having the highest summit (1,498 ft) on a standard gauge line in Great Britain. It closed to passengers on 31 December 1938, but a LR scheme on part of the trackbed has recently been projected.

LEEDS & BRADFORD RAILWAY

Incorporated on 4 July 1844 to build 13.5 miles of railway, the company's station at Leeds (Wellington) straddled the R Aire and was the first in the centre of the city. The line opened on 1 July 1846 (passengers) and 7 September (goods); in addition, a line was open through to Shipley by September 1846, and an extension to Colne had already been authorized (Leeds & Bradford Extension Railway, qv). In July 1846, the company withdrew abruptly from an Agreement with the M&LR and W Riding Union

The Leeds & Bradford Railway, together with its Extension, became MR property in 1851, and boundary markers such as this would have been a familiar sight in Wharfedale and Craven.

Desford, on the section of the Leicester & Swannington Railway diverted to avoid inclines at Bagworth, opened on 27 March 1848. Seen here about 1930, a Class '2P' 4-4-0 No 485 draws in with a train from Leicester. (Douglas Thompson)

Railway (qv), leasing itself to the MR from 26 August; little enough perhaps, but it left Bradford with two termini 300 yd apart instead of one through station. On 24 July 1851 the MR was authorized to buy the company for £1,800,000.

LEEDS & BRADFORD EXTENSION RAILWAY

Authorized on 30 June 1845, this line linked the L&BR at Leeds with the ELR at Colne Junction. It was leased to the MR from July 1846, opening to Keighley on 16 March 1847, Skipton on 8 September, Colne on 2 October 1848, and Colne Junction on 1 February 1849. The company was absorbed by the MR on 24 July 1851 — the line became the springboard for its route to Carlisle via Settle and Appleby opened on 1 May 1876.

LEEDS, DEWSBURY & MANCHESTER RAILWAY

This scheme to make a line between Leeds and Manchester via Huddersfield and Dewsbury was promoted in conjunction with the Huddersfield & Manchester Railway & Canal Company (qv), the first stage, to Dewsbury, being 10.5 miles long. It was authorized on 30 June 1845; the L&NWR saw it as a route to the W Riding and swiftly absorbed it, on 9 July 1847. Perhaps such summary action rankled, for the company staged its own opening ceremony on 31 July 1848. The L&NWR, unperturbed, held its 'official' opening on 18 September.

LEEK & MANIFOLD VALLEY LIGHT RAILWAY

This line (2 ft 6 in gauge) was built under an LRO confirmed on 6 March 1899, running for 9 miles from Waterhouses in E Staffordshire, N along the Manifold valley to Hulme End. It opened for passengers on 27 June 1904, and to goods in November;

the NSR worked and maintained the line from the start, for 55 per cent of the receipts under a 99-year Agreement, but was half-hearted about the scheme, perhaps because two feeder lines were required, both of which it had to build! The line passed to the LMS in 1923, and the last train ran on 10 March 1934. On Friday 23 July 1937, the company's Deed was formally handed by Sir Josiah Stamp, Chairman of the LMS, to the Chairman of Staffordshire County Council on completion of the conversion of the track-bed to a footpath. The Redhurst–Butterton section is now a road.

LEICESTER & SWANNINGTON RAILWAY

Coal owners and local traders, including William Stenson of Whitwell, met at the Bell Inn, Humberstone Gate, Leicester (now demolished), and agreed to promote a railway to carry coal between Leicester and Swannington, about 10 miles to the NW. Backed by John Ellis, a friend of George Stephenson and, later, Chairman of the MR, a company was incorporated on 29 May 1830. Robert Stephenson was appointed engineer, and after a ceremonial opening between Leicester and Bagworth on 17 July 1832 (to the public the following day), the line was extended to Ashby Road on 1 February 1833, Coalville on 22 April (coal), 27 April (passengers), and throughout (mineral) on 25 November. At the opening, the funnel of *Comet* hit the roof of the 1,796 yd Glenfield tunnel. The line was bought on 27 July 1846 by the MR, which ran it wef 1 January 1847 as part of a through route between Burton and Leicester — deviations were built to avoid inclines, though Swannington incline remained in use until 14 November 1947.

LESMAHAGOW RAILWAY

Promoted jointly by an independent company and the CR, and incorporated on 8 June 1847, the line ran from Motherwell to Coalburn, a source of the cannel coal much sought after by gasworks. It opened to Lesmahagow for goods 1 December 1856, and to passengers on 1 January 1858. A link with the Lanark Railway and the Muirkirk & Lesmahagow Junction Railway (both qv) opened in 1884. The company was absorbed by the CR under an Act dated 8 April 1881, though as early as 14 June 1860 an Act had been passed authorizing '. . . a more complete merging' with the CR, wef 31 July 1859. Amalgamation actually took place wef 11 December 1881.

LIVERPOOL & BURY RAILWAY

This line, authorized on 31 July 1845, gave alternative routes from Liverpool to Yorkshire and Manchester via Bolton. Before its 28.25 miles could be opened (20 November 1848), not only had the Company been absorbed by the M&LR under an Act of 27 July 1846 (wef 1 October) but the M&LR had become the L&YR. The line between Bolton and Bury closed in 1970.

LIVERPOOL & MANCHESTER RAILWAY

This famous railway was proposed by William James and Joseph Sanders (a partner in a local firm of corn merchants) in 1821. George Stephenson was appointed principal engineer on 3 July 1826 (the line having been authorized on 5 May), and his original plan was to use fixed engines. However, a prize was offered for the most efficient locomotive engine, so a competition was arranged at Rainhill, beginning on 6 October 1829; as a result, the winner, *Rocket*, became perhaps the best-known locomotive in railway history. The company opened its line ceremonially on 15 September 1830, for passengers two days later and for goods on 1 December, and was absorbed by the GJR on 8 August 1845. *Rocket* and *Lion* — built for the line in 1838 — survive as part of the National Collection.

LIVERPOOL, CROSBY & SOUTHPORT RAILWAY

Authorized on 2 July 1847, this line ran from Southport to Liverpool (Waterloo), opening on 24 July 1848, and extending first from Waterloo to Sandhills on 1 October 1850, then to Southport (Chapel Street) in August 1851. Financial problems delayed a planned link-up with the L&YR — it had been authorized to lease, sell or transfer by Act of 14 August 1850 — but that company took over wef 14 June 1855.

LIVERPOOL, ORMSKIRK & PRESTON RAILWAY

This scheme for a line between Walton Junction (Liverpool) and Lostock Hall (Preston) was backed by the ELR but failed in Parliament in 1845. When it was passed on 18 August 1846, the Act included powers to lease, transfer or sell to the ELR — they were put into effect that October, and the ELR opened the line on 2 April 1849.

LIVERPOOL, SOUTHPORT & PRESTON JUNCTION RAILWAY

This scheme, backed by the WLR and authorized on 7 August 1884, was for 7.5 miles of line from Meols Cop (WLR) to Hillhouse Junction. It opened to Barton for goods on 1 September 1887, to Altcar (goods) on 1 October, and for passengers throughout on 1 November, worked by the WLR. When the L&YR took over the WLR, on 15 July 1897, it absorbed the company as well.

LOCHEARNHEAD, ST FILLANS & COMRIE RAILWAY

This line was authorized on 6 August 1897 to join Lochearnhead (Callander & Oban Railway, qv) with Comrie (Creiff & Comrie Railway, qv). The line opened from Comrie to St Fillans on 1 October 1901, to Lochearnhead on 1 July 1904 and to Balquhidder on 1 July 1905 (15 miles 1 furlong 2 chains in all), and the CR was authorized to work the line in perpetuity. Dissolution and vesting in the CR followed, by an Act of 31 July 1902, wef 1 August. Passenger traffic ceased on 1 October 1951.

LONDON & BIRMINGHAM RAILWAY

The company was incorporated on 6 May 1833; the original plan was to build a terminus at Camden, but an extension to Euston was authorized on 3 July 1835, and its building behind a Doric Arch began in 1836. The station (cable haulage was used on the 1 in 77 incline up from it until 1844) and the line to Boxmoor opened on 20 July 1837, services to Tring beginning on 16 October. Tring–Denbigh Hall (Bletchley) and Birmingham (Curzon Street)–Rugby opened on 9 April 1838. A limited service was being run throughout from 24 June, a few days after the final brick was laid in Kilsby tunnel, though the line did not open officially until 17 September. On 16 July 1846 the company amalgamated with the GJR and M&BR to form the L&NWR. New Street station opened on 1 June 1854, and a month later Curzon Street closed to regular passengers, though it was still used for Sutton Coldfield excursions.

LONDON & NORTH WESTERN RAILWAY

This company was formed on 16 July 1846 by the amalgamation of the L&BR, the GJR and the M&BR. An L&BR station at New Street, Birmingham, authorized on 3 August 1846, was opened on 1 June 1854 — the MR had access, and it became a joint station on 1 April 1897. Many amalgamations stretched the company over a wide area, and it became one of the most influential of the pre-Grouping

lines. The L&YR was absorbed from 1 January 1922, and the company became a constituent of the LMS in 1923.

LONDON, TILBURY & SOUTHEND RAILWAY

This line was promoted by the London & Blackwall Railway (qv) as an extension of its line from Forest Gate via Tilbury Fort to Southend, a distance of 36 miles. Owners of shares managed to get themselves incorporated on 17 June 1852, and their line from Forest Gate to Tilbury was opened on 13 April 1854, to Leigh on 1 July 1855 and Southend on 1 March 1856. It was built in conjunction with the ECR, and leased in 1854 to the contractor, Peto, Brassey and Petts, for 21 years. When the lease expired (1875), the GER (as successor to the ECR) was no longer interested, so the company decided to fend for itself. The NLR received RP from 18 May 1869 and a line from Romford to Upminster was authorized in 1883

Above *London & Birmingham Railway works were built to last, and the bridge across the A43 at Blisworth now carries a far heavier traffic than can have been conceived at the opening in 1838.*

Above right *The L&NWR seal continues the 'Britannia' theme of the GJR, but has dispensed with everything else. (NRM)*

Right *One of Whitelegg's tank engines, built for the LT&SR service between 1923–30. No 41975 is seen here some way from Tilbury, at Peterborough in 1958, with a Class 'B17' 'Footballer', No 61654 Sunderland, in the background. (A.V. Fincham/Andrew C. Ingram)*

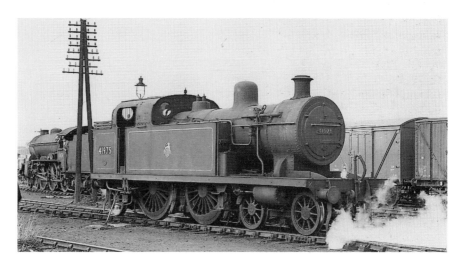

The Maidens & Dunure Light Railway used island platforms— this one, at Dunure, was barely visible in April 1988 as sur- rounding vegetation reclaimed it.

and opened on 7 June 1893, mainly to bar the GER from Southend. The company was vested in the MR wef 1 January 1912, by an Act of 7 August, but not fully merged with that company until 1 October 1920.

LONGTON, ADDERLEY GREEN & BUCKNALL RAILWAY

Built to serve coalpits in the Biddulph valley of Staffordshire, this 4.5-mile line ran from Biddulph Lane to Longton — it was later extended to Park Hall. The Incorporation Act (16 July 1866) authorized the NSR to work and maintain the line, which was opened in September 1875. In 1895 the NSR paid £22,500 for it, but disliked its circular route, and cut it in two — the S section closed in 1963, the N on 6 July 1964, and part of this length is now included in a park.

MAIDENS & DUNURE LIGHT RAILWAY

Built under a LRO dated 30 September 1899, this LR, nominally independent but actually G&SWR-controlled, was run in connection with the golf course and its hotel at Turnberry. It opened on 17 May 1906, from a junction at Alloway (S of Ayr) along a highly scenic coastal route to Girvan via Maidens, a distance of 20 miles. The 15 miles between Alloway Junction and Turnberry closed to passengers on 1 December 1930, but re-opened to a holiday camp at New Heads of Ayr on 4 July 1932.

This section closed again on 31 May 1933, re-opening in the summer of 1948. Final closure came on 14 September 1968. The remaining 5 miles had already closed on 2 March 1942.

MANCHESTER & BIRMINGHAM RAILWAY

Authorized on 30 June 1837 to link the cities, it reached only Crewe, opening from Travis Street, Manchester, to Stockport on 4 June 1840, into London Road, Manchester, on 8 May 1842 and to Crewe on 10 August. The company was a constituent of the L&NWR on 16 July 1846, the others being the GJR and the L&BR.

MANCHESTER & LEEDS RAILWAY

Incorporated on 4 July 1836, it became one of the more important of the early companies — George Stephenson was its engineer and Thomas Gooch (elder brother of Daniel) his assistant. The first section opened was Manchester-Littleborough on 4 July 1839, with Hebden Bridge–Goose Hill Junction (Normanton) on 5 October 1840, and on to Summit tunnel on 31 December. The line opened throughout on 1 March 1841. Branches to Heywood and Oldham opened on 15 April 1841 and 31 March 1842 respectively, and the line was extended to Manchester (Victoria) on 1 January 1844. Miles Platting-Ashton opened on 13 April 1846 and an extension to Stalybridge on 5 October. The company absorbed the Huddersfield & Sheffield Junction and the Liverpool & Bury Railways on 27 July 1846, and the Ashton, Stalybridge & Liverpool Junction, the Wakefield, Pontefract & Goole, and the W Riding Union

Railways, with the Manchester, Bolton & Bury Canal Navigation & Railway (all qv) on 9 July 1847, when it became the L&YR.

MANCHESTER & SOUTHPORT RAILWAY

Incorporated on 22 July 1847, a line opened between Wigan and Southport on 1 May 1855 using stations already built by the Liverpool, Crosby & Southport Railway (qv). Parts of the line were jointly vested in the ELR and L&YR by an Act of 3 July 1854. It was joined at Southport by the ELR in 1860; since that company had been absorbed by the L&YR in the previous year, the M&SR became solely owned by the L&YR.

MANCHESTER, BOLTON & BURY CANAL NAVIGATION & RAILWAY

Authorized on 23 August 1831, and though no doubt re-named (the company had been incorporated in 1791 as a Canal) with high hopes, the line never reached Manchester, at least along its own metals, though a line from Salford to Bolton was opened on 29 May 1838. Trains at first kept to the right. The company worked the Lancaster & Preston Junction Railway (qv) from 1 January 1842, and, trying to justify its title, proposed an extension to Blackfriars Bridge, Manchester, but was absorbed by the M&LR by an Act of 18 July 1846 before anything could come of it.

MANCHESTER, BURY & ROSSENDALE RAILWAY

Authorized on 4 July 1844 to build from Clifton Junction, on the Manchester–Bolton line of the

Burscough Bridge station was built by the Liverpool, Crosby & Southport Railway, but was taken over by the Manchester & Southport before opening in 1851. Apart from station 'furniture', the only change since then appears to be the chimney additions. (Robert Humm)

M&LR, to Rawtenstall via Bury, by the time it opened (28 September 1846) the company had become the ELR, wef 21 July 1845. At the time of opening the line was double to Stubbins and single for its final mile to Rawtenstall. BR closed the line in 1972, but it re-opened on 25 July 1987 as a steam railway from Bury (Bolton Street) to Ramsbottom, continuing to Rawtenstall in 1988.

MANCHESTER, BUXTON, MATLOCK & MIDLAND JUNCTION RAILWAY

This line ran through the Peak District to join Ambergate to the Nottingham, Erewash Valley & Ambergate Railway (qv – LNER). George Stephenson surveyed this ambitious project, involving heavy works and a 2.25-mile tunnel. Authorized on 16 July 1846, money problems arose from the start, and despite deviations to avoid the tunnel, the only section built was the 11.5 miles between Rowsley and Ambergate, opened to passengers on 4 June 1849, to coal on 20 August and to goods in December. The line had powerful supporters in the Duke of Devonshire and Sir Joseph Paxton, but Ruskin condemned the railway's '. . . close-clinging damnation'. Monsal Dale viaduct, 72 ft high, has been declared of historic and architectural interest. The L&NWR and MR took a joint lease from 1 July 1852 (Act of 17 June), but the MR was authorized in 1860 to build the

*A length of original Mansfield &
Pinxton fish-bellied rail. Note the
tongue and groove at the left-hand
near end, into which the adjoining
rail would slot.*

Rowsley–Buxton section (opened on 30 May 1863),
and when the joint lease expired in 1871 the MR
threatened to use its branch to Wirksworth to reach
Manchester. This would have left the L&NWR with
a useless branch, so it let the MR buy the company
alone. It was finally absorbed wef 1 July 1871 under
an Act of 20 June 1870. The Matlock–Rowsley section
closed on 1 April 1968, but part of the track-bed is
being restored by Peak Rail.

MANSFIELD & PINXTON RAILWAY

A double-track colliery line, authorized on 16 June
1817 and 8.25 miles long, it was engineered by
Outram as a feeder for the Pinxton arm of the
Cromford Canal. On the opening day, 13 April
1819, declared a public holiday, the first load of coal

was ceremonially burned in Mansfield. The line
opened for passengers in 1832 without, one hopes,
the same applying. The line, laid with edge-rails cast
at Butterley, was powered by bullocks, and the year
after passenger working began a dividend of 9 per
cent was paid. The Houses of Parliament were rebuilt
using Mansfield stone carried over the line. The MR
was authorized to buy the company on 9 July 1847,
but two London-based companies actually did so.
They readily resold (at a healthy profit, no doubt),
and the MR relaid the line for steam haulage, re-
opening it on 6 November 1851, the first locomotive
having reached Mansfield on 24 August 1849.

MARYPORT & CARLISLE RAILWAY

Humphrey Senhouse, after whose wife Maryport is

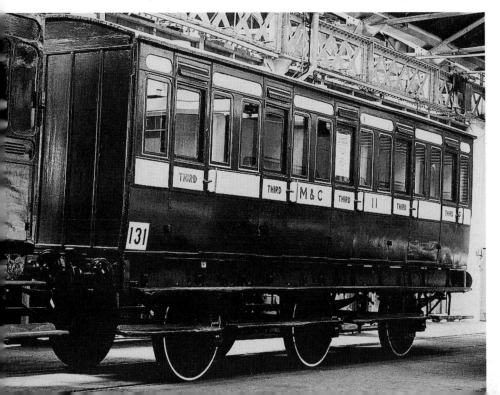

*The only surviving vehicle of the
Maryport & Carlisle Railway, a
six-wheeled third class coach of
1879. Restored on the Chasewater
LR, it is seen here at the St&DR
150 exhibition at Shildon Wagon
Works, 25 August 1975. (Transport Nostalgia Picture Library)*

named, first mooted a 28-mile link between the centres; George Stephenson was appointed engineer, and the company was incorporated on 12 July 1837. Money came in, but progress was slow — the line opened from Maryport S Quay to Arkelby on 15 July 1840, to Aspatria on 12 April 1841 and between Bogfield (Carlisle) and Wigton on 10 May 1843. Wigton–Aspatria was opened on 2 December 1844, the central link was made on 10 February 1845, and a new station opened at Maryport on 4 June 1860. The line was leased to George Hudson on behalf of the YN&BR, but the lease was never ratified and the company resumed independence from 1 January 1850, though its affairs were in confusion. It used a temporary station at Crown Street, Carlisle, a site wanted by both the L&CR and the CR for expansion. A sum of £7,005 was about to be agreed when Hudson, as 'lessee' of the M&CR, demanded £100,000. A jury valued the site at £7,171; this was paid but the company refused to go. On 17 March 1849 the Undersherriff gave possession to the L&CR and the station was demolished. From a temporary terminus at London Road, the company eventually became a permanent tenant of Carlisle (Citadel), surviving to join the LMS wef 1 January 1923.

MAYBOLE & GIRVAN RAILWAY

This line was authorised on 14 July 1856 as a continuation S of the Ayr & Maybole Railway (qv). There was talk of developing Girvan as a packet port, but Portpatrick remained the ultimate goal despite many

John Jenkins, husband of the Crossing Keeper, Mrs Emma Jenkins (seated, rear), stands beside the original apparatus at Llanelly Hill, ex-Merthyr, Tredegar & Abergavenny Railway, in 1919. Evelyn (standing, left rear) took over from her mother in 1933, and kept the crossing until 1958, when the last train, an SLS Special, ran on 5 September. (Mrs E. Francis)

barren miles which lay ahead. Like the A&MR, the line was worked from opening (24 May 1860) by the G&SWR, in which it was vested wef 1 August 1865 under an Act dated the previous 5 July.

MERTHYR, TREDEGAR & ABERGAVENNY RAILWAY

Using Bailey's Tramroad (qv) and part of the Llanvihangel Railway (qv — GWR), previously bought by the NA&HR and now reverted to a new company, incorporated on 1 August 1859, this line became known as the 'Heads of the Valleys' line. After a steep climb from Abergavenny to Tredegar, 7 miles at 1 in 34, 1 in 37 and 1 in 38 led to Dowlais, beyond which the line fell for 6.5 miles at 1 in 40 and 1 in 50. It opened from Abergavenny to Brynmawr on 29 September 1862, but it was 1 January 1873 before complete opening; the WMR applied for a lease, but it was granted to the L&NWR under an Agreement of 8 November 1861, for 1,000 years from the date of opening of any part of the line. That company, which had assisted in the building, formally absorbed the other on 30 June 1866, by an Act of 30 July. The line was doubled in 1877 and closed to through passengers in January 1958.

MIDLAND RAILWAY

The company was formed on 10 May 1844 by the amalgamation of the MCR, the NMR and the B&DJR. After 1852, John Ellis, the Chairman, began a policy of gradual expansion. A London extension was authorized on 22 June 1863; when this opened, on 9 September 1867 (goods), 13 July 1868 (passengers), Leicester became an important Midlands junction. St Pancras station, authorized on 25 May 1860, opened on 1 October 1868. Absorptions from 1844 gave the company track mileage, including sidings (but not Irish and joint lines), of 5,062.75 by 1918.

Midland Railway signal boxes were distinctive—this one, of the smaller type, survives at Manton Junction, where the goods line to Corby diverges from the Syston-Peterborough line. (Allan Mott)

MIDLAND & SOUTH WESTERN JUNCTION RAILWAY

Authorized on 14 July 1864 for a 3.75-mile link between the N end of the North & South Western Junction Railway (qv) at Acton and the MR at Cricklewood, the line opened on 1 October 1868 (goods), 3 August 1875 (passengers). It was sometimes referred to as the 'old' M&SWJR to distinguish it from the later one (qv – GWR). It was absorbed by the MR under an Act dated 30 July 1874, and proved an invaluable link in subsequent years.

MIDLAND COUNTIES RAILWAY

This line grew from a scheme for a railway between Pinxton and Leicester, an extension of the Pinxton Tramway, and it was realised that a Derby-Rugby line via Leicester, with branches to Nottingham and Pinxton would work. A prospectus was raised in 1833, but it was three years before an Act was granted on 21 June 1836. The line opened between Derby and Nottingham on 4 June 1839, from Trent to Leicester on 5 May 1840 and on to Rugby on 30 June; Thomas Cook used it on 5 July 1841 for his first excursion, a party from Leicester to a Temperance Conference at Loughborough. On 10 May 1844 the company amalgamated with the MCR and B&DJR to form the MR.

MOFFAT RAILWAY

A short line (1 mile 5 furlongs 3 chains were authorized on 27 June 1881), it was locally promoted to link Moffat and Beattock (CR). An extension into Beattock station was authorized on 19 June 1882. The line was opened on 2 April 1883, leased to the CR by an Act of 14 July 1884, and was formally vested in it by an Act of 31 May 1889 wef 11 November.

MOLD RAILWAY

Incorporated on 9 July 1847 to build from the C&HR at Pentre to Mold, with a branch to limeworks at Ffrith, shortage of funds put the scheme in jeopardy. However, the C&HR agreed to buy the line on completion, and, worked by the L&NWR, it was opened on 14 August 1849 (per Company Minutes — another official source has 14 September). The first 7.25 miles were double, but the remaining 2.75 were single. The Ffrith branch opened in November 1849, worked by the quarry owner until the C&HR and the L&NWR took over in 1852. Doubling was completed to Mold, probably by July 1870 after the opening of the Mold & Denbigh Junction Railway (qv). The line closed to passengers on 30 April 1862, and to goods from Mold Junction to Penyffordd on 1 March 1865.

MOLD & DENBIGH JUNCTION RAILWAY

Incorporated on 6 August 1861 to build a 15.75-mile link-line between Mold and the Vale of Clwyd Railway (qv) at Denbigh, it opened on 12 September 1869. Though worked by the L&NWR, the company remained independent until absorbed by the LMS at Grouping. The line closed on 30 April 1962 but was re-opened for goods between Mold and Rhydymwyn on 13 July 1974.

MORECAMBE HARBOUR & RAILWAY

Incorporated on 16 July 1846 to link Morecambe and Lancaster, the line was soon amalgamated with the NWR, one of the directors, a Mr Sharpe, becoming Secretary of the NWR and working the line, opened on 12 June 1848, under contract until 1 June 1852. Then the MR took over, leasing the line from 1 January 1859, and buying it on 1 June 1871. Electric services began on 1 July 1908 (extended to Lancaster on 14 September), and the trains supplied then lasted until steam temporarily replaced them on 17 August 1953 during renewals to the ole.

MUIRKIRK & LESMAHAGOW JUNCTION RAILWAY

Incorporated in 1881, the line was opened for goods on 2 April 1883 and to passengers in 1894, a link between Alton Heights (Lesmahagow Railway) and Poniel (Lanark Railway, both qv). The company was absorbed by the CR, and the line's 2.25 miles closed to passengers on 11 September 1939.

NANTLLE RAILWAY

The Incorporation Act of 20 May 1825 authorized a tramway from slate and copper mines along the Nantlle valley to Penygroes, then turning N to quays at Caernarfon. Its 9 miles, engineered by the Stephensons, and laid to a gauge of 3 ft 6 in, opened about 1828. On 25 July 1867, the company was vested in the Carnarvonshire Railway (qv) — during 1870 the Penygroes–Nantlle section was converted

An iron slate-wagon from the Nantlle Railway. Note the double-flanged wheels, which ran free on a fixed axle. The plate on the wagon-side shows its place of manufacture as the Glaslyn Foundry, Portmadoc.

to standard gauge, re-opening for mineral traffic on 1 August 1872, and to passengers on 1 October. The quarry line was still both horse-worked and at the original gauge when it passed to BR. The Penygroes–Nantlle section closed to passengers on 8 August 1932, and to goods on 1 December 1963, though the quarry line survived longer.

NERQUIS RAILWAY

This short private railway in Flintshire (now Clywd) served a colliery near Mold. It was bought by the L&NWR (authority of 23 July 1866, transfer 1868), which used part of it when building the Mold–Trydden branch, authorized on 16 July 1866.

NEWTOWN & CREWE RAILWAY

This scheme, authorized on 3 August 1846, for a 60-mile line from Newtown, Montgomeryshire, to Crewe, became part of the SUR&CC. It was not built, but much of its intended route was used by the Oswestry & Newtown Railway (qv — GWR).

NEWTYLE & COUPAR ANGUS RAILWAY

This company was formed under the influence of the Dundee & Newtyle Railway (qv), which wanted to extend but could not afford to; its line, almost 5 miles long, was authorized on 21 July 1835 and opened in February 1837. It was a horse-drawn concept, though experiments with wind-powered trains were made. The company's independent life was short, swallowed by the SMJR, whose Incorporation Act gave powers to buy it; the transaction was ratified by an Act of 31 July 1845, wef date of payment. The line was closed in November 1847, but re-opened from Nethermill Junction to Newtyle and from Ardler Junction to Coupar Angus on 2 August 1848, the rest on 1 August 1861.

NEWTYLE & GLAMMIS (sic) RAILWAY

This line was authorized on 30 July 1835, under the auspices of the Dundee & Newtyle Railway (qv), which wished to extend but could not afford it. The line ran for 6 miles 48 chains at a gauge of 4 ft 6.5 in, and was engineered by W. Blackadder and intended for horse-traction, though steam was tried. It opened on 4 June 1838 and was bought by the SMJR, as authorized in that company's Incorporation Act, under a ratifying Act dated 31 July 1845, wef date of payment.

NORTHAMPTON & BANBURY JUNCTION RAILWAY

Incorporated as the Northampton & Banbury Railway on 9 July 1847, powers lapsed until they were re-granted on 28 July 1863, but the company reached neither Northampton nor Banbury by its own efforts. It had a station beside the L&NWR at Blisworth, and ran W to Cockley Brake, whence it used RP to Banbury over the L&NWR metals of the Buckingham-

shire Railway (qv) — opening from Blisworth to Towcester was on 1 May 1866, and to Cockley Brake on 1 June 1872. Sanction for extensions to Blockley (Glos) in 1865 and Ross-on-Wye (1866) empowered the company to change its name to the Midland Counties & S Wales Railway, but it was soon obvious that this 96.5-mile idea was pie in the sky, and in 1870 the company reverted to its former name. Later the line was run with L&NWR engines on hire; it was bought by the S&MJR wef 1 July 1910 under an Act of 29 April.

NORTH & SOUTH WESTERN JUNCTION RAILWAY

Authorized on 24 July 1851 to link the L&NWR with the L&SWR via 3.75 miles of double track between Willesden and Old Kew Junction, the line opened on 15 February 1853 for goods, 1 August for passengers. The NLR worked the passenger service at first, though several companies operated with varying degrees of success. The line was leased to the L&NWR and L&SWR jointly until 1871, when the partners became the L&NWR, the NLR and the MR, who took a perpetual lease under an Act of 14 August 1871. The company remained officially independent until vested in the LMS.

NORTH LONDON RAILWAY

Incorporated as the E & W India Docks & Birmingham Junction Railway (qv), the company took a less cumbersome title on 1 January 1853. On 11 July 1861, it was authorized to extend to Broad Street, the L&NWR contributing substantially to an expensive project. It did well at first, but tram competition cut into traffic — common management with the L&NWR was introduced in February 1909, and the LMS took over in 1923.

NORTH MIDLAND RAILWAY

Authorized on 4 July 1836, the line was laid out by George Stephenson, who chose the Rother and Amber valleys for his route N from Derby, since he mistrusted the land between Sheffield and Chester-

field — with reason, as the MR later found to its cost. Derby–Masborough was opened on 11 May 1840, and the line reached Leeds on 1 July. Amalgamation with the MCR and B&DJR on 10 May 1844 created the MR, the company's locomotive shed at Derby becoming the nucleus for Derby Works.

NORTH STAFFORDSHIRE RAILWAY

Authorized in three Acts of 26 June 1846, for the Churnet Valley, the Potteries, and the Harecastle & Sandbach Railways (all qv), the NSR was described as a 'small octopus'. Its arms had many opening dates — between Stoke and Crewe on 9 October 1848, Stoke–Uttoxeter on 7 August, and from Colwich to Stoke in May 1849. The main line from Macclesfield to Burton was open throughout from 13 June 1849, Macclesfield–Uttoxeter opened in July 1849, and a line from Ashbourne to Rocester on 31 May 1852. The L&NWR tried to absorb the company several times, but was defeated by firm independence. Finally an Agreement was reached which gave extensive RP

over each others' systems. A branch to Market Drayton was opened 1870, and though the company was reluctant to build the Potteries loop, it proved an instant success when opened on 15 November 1875. The company became an LMS constituent, though legal matters delayed actual absorption until 1 July 1923.

NORTH UNION RAILWAY

Formed on 22 May 1834 by the amalgamation of the Preston & Wigan and Wigan Branch Railways (both qv), it produced a line of 15.5 miles. It opened to Preston on 31 October 1838, and by an Act of 10 May 1844 the company bought the Bolton & Preston Railway (qv), and a little later it was discussing terms with the GJR. An Amalgamation Bill had reached its second reading when the GJR backed out. The company was leased jointly by the GJR and M&LR, but before this was ratified (27 July 1846) the GJR became part of the L&NWR. The company was jointly absorbed by the L&NWR and L&YR by an Act dated 26 July 1889.

NORTH WESTERN RAILWAY

Incorporated on 26 June 1846, this became known as the 'little' North Western, though the title was never official. It was authorized to build from Skipton to Low Gill (L&CR) with a branch to Lancaster from Clapham — the latter became the main line, a result, perhaps, of the absorption of the Morecambe Harbour & Railway (qv) in 1846. Skipton to Ingleton (25 miles) was opened formally on 31 July 1849, and doubled within three years to Clapham. Lancaster–Wennington opened on 17 November 1849, the line was extended to Lancaster (Castle) on 19 December, and the Wennington–Bentham section opened on 2 May 1850. When the Lancaster line was complete, Ingleton was closed — the GNR showed interest, whereupon the MR agreed to work the line from 1 June 1852, an Act of 10 August 1857 authorizing lease or sale to MR or L&CR. The L&NWR took over the works beyond Ingleton; the Clapham line re-opened on 1 October 1861, and the company was leased by the MR from 1 January 1859 for 21 years.

Paisley & Barrhead District Railway services were run from the start by the CR. The electrification flash indicates a latterday picture, but the carriage is not so different, perhaps, from that used by P&BR customers.

An Act of 30 July 1874 authorized the company to be '. . . in perpetuity vested in, leased or worked by the Midland Railway'. The Ingleton–Clapham line was used as a Settle & Carlisle diversion as early as 1881, but the passenger service was withdrawn on 1 February 1954. It continued in use for goods until 1964.

NUNEATON & HINCKLEY RAILWAY
Incorporated on 13 August 1859, this 4.5-mile line revived powers granted on 27 July 1846 to the Coventry, Nuneaton, Birmingham & Leicester Railway. Powers to make WA with the L&NWR were also given. The company renamed itself the S Leicestershire Railway (qv) on 14 June 1860.

PAISLEY & BARRHEAD DISTRICT RAILWAY
This company was incorporated on 6 August 1897 to build 12.5 miles of line in Renfrewshire, primarily to link the Greenock line of the CR with the Glasgow & Paisley Joint Railway (qv) at Neilston and the G&SWR's Potterhill branch. It was vested in the CR under an Act of 31 July 1902, wef 1 August.

PAISLEY & RENFREW RAILWAY
Authorized on 21 July 1835, the railway ran from Paisley to Renfrew and the wharf there. Gauged at 4 ft 6 in, and loco-worked from the opening on 3 April 1837, it changed to horse-haulage from 7 March

1842 as an economy. On 1 July working was let to a tenant, who, finding the rent of £1,001 pa too high, had it reduced to £801. The company tried to sell itself, first to a company which had failed to build its own line! It was finally bought by the G&SWR, which completed the sale on 31 July 1852 (£34,683) but, because the line was detached from its own system and differently gauged into the bargain, it was let privately. On 23 January 1866 the passenger service was suspended to allow conversion and doubling, and a connection was made from the Glasgow & Paisley Joint Railway (qv). Steam traction was re-introduced at re-opening on 1 May 1866.

PALLEG TRAMROAD
This 1.5-mile tramway, built privately to carry coal from Palleg colliery along the N side of the Afon Twrch to Ynysgedwyn, SW of Brynamman, opened in 1807. The line was acquired by the Swansea Vale Railway (qv) under an Agreement with Lord Tredegar dated 7 June 1861, and ratified by Parliament on 22 July.

PENLLWYN TRAMROAD
Completed, after much legal argument, along the Sirhowy valley, which already contained Hall's Tramroad (qv – GWR) and the Sirhowy Tramroad (qv), it opened about mid-1824, from collieries at Rock and Penmain, near the river, to a junction with the Monmouthshire Railways (qv – GWR) near that of the Sirhowy. Traffic was drawn from Hall's Tramroad, and in September 1852 the Monmouthshire Railway & Canal made enquiries concerning a possible take-over of the Penllwyn and/or Hall's.

Penllwyn was in better condition, but by 1863 only the lower section appears to have been in use. The L&NWR converted the Ynysddu–Nine Mile Point section, acquired with the Sirhowy in 1876, using them in conjunction until 1937.

PERTH, ALMOND VALLEY & METHVEN RAILWAY

This 6-mile line, authorized on 29 July 1856 to the SMJR, ran between Dunkeld Bridge and Methven. The line opened on 1 January 1858, and the company passed to the SNER wef 1 January 1864, though it was not authorized to sell itself until the next 23 June. The 1.25 miles from Methven Junction to Methven closed to passengers on 27 September 1937, but the remainder survived as part of the line to Crieff until 1 October 1951.

PERTH & DUNKELD RAILWAY

This 8.5-mile line from Stanley Junction (SMJR) to Birnam, on the opposite bank of the R. Tay from Dunkeld, was authorised on 10 July 1854. The line was opened on 7 April 1856, worked by the SMJR and then by the SNER, but the company did not follow it into the CR. Instead it was absorbed by the Inverness & Perth Junction Railway (qv) wef 28 February 1864 (Act of 8 June 1863), becoming part of the HR system in due course.

POLLOC & GOVAN RAILWAY

Promoted privately as a partial re-alignment of his own Govan Tramway, the line was built in 1811 by William Dixon on land bought from the Corporation of Glasgow. A coalmaster, Dixon required an outlet, and this line, authorized on 29 May 1830, linked Govan with the Glasgow, Paisley and Johnstone Canal, iron deposits and the Broomielaw. It ran from Windmillcroft on the S bank of the Clyde to Rutherglen, but was slow a-building; a plan to link with the Wishaw & Coltness Railway (qv) in 1831 was rejected, as was an extension to Wellshot, near Cambusland, After opening on 22 August 1840, the systems were linked by the Clydesdale Junction Railway (qv), which bought the company on 18 August 1846. An Act of 14 March 1867 authorized the lifting of part of it.

PORTPATRICK RAILWAY

Authorized on 10 August 1857 to build from Castle Douglas to Portpatrick, the line reached its destination too late to benefit from the short crossing to Ireland – the mails were already going via Holyhead. The line opened to Stranraer on 12 March 1861 and to Portpatrick on 28 August 1862, with a harbour branch on 1 October; work continued until 1865, but a more sheltered harbour had been developed at Stranraer. It was expected that the G&SWR would work the whole S coast route but the CR offered the Board a better deal and so gained control. By 1885

the company was on the brink of collapse, only saved by amalgamation with the Wigtownshire Railway to form the Portpatrick & Wigtownshire Joint Railway (both qv) wef 1 August 1885 (Act dated 6 August).

PORTPATRICK & WIGTOWNSHIRE JOINT RAILWAY

Formed by an Act of 6 August 1885, wef 1 August 1885, this was a union of the ailing Portpatrick and Wigtownshire Railways. Though the new company came under the joint auspices of the L&NWR, MR, CR and G&SWR, the line was actually run by the two Scottish concerns. Passenger traffic ceased on 14 June 1965.

POTTERIES RAILWAY

This line was incorporated on 26 June 1846, as the third section of the trio (the others were the Churnet Valley and the Harecastle & Sandbach Railways, both qv) forming the NSR. This part was the line from Macclesfield to Colwich via Stoke, with branches to Norton Bridge, Newcastle, Silverdale and Crewe. The Stoke–Norton Bridge branch opened first, on 17 April 1848, the Stoke–Crewe and Harecastle–Congleton lines on 9 October. The S arm from Stone to Colwich opened on 1 May 1849, the line being completed to Macclesfield by 18 June.

POTTERIES, BIDDULPH & CONGLETON RAILWAY

Authorized on 24 July 1854 to the NSR, the scheme was a reply to coal owners in the Biddulph valley who proposed to build a railway themselves if the company did not. The line served collieries and ironworks E of Stoke and opened for goods on 3 August 1859, to minerals on 29 August 1860, and throughout on 1 September 1863. It was 1 June 1864, however, before the Inspector would allow a passenger service to begin.

PRESTON & LONGRIDGE RAILWAY

Incorporated on 14 July 1836, this horse-drawn tramway 6.75 miles long included a ¾-mile incline, and ran from Preston to Longridge via Grimsargh. It opened for goods on 1 May 1840 and to passengers on 2 May, and was re-opened after conversion for steam traction on 12 June 1848. The company was bought by the Fleetwood, Preston & W Riding Junction Railway (qv) for £48,000 on 31 August 1856 (authorized on 23 June). The line closed to passengers on 2 June 1930.

PRESTON & WIGAN RAILWAY

This was incorporated on 22 April 1831, but before building had begun the company amalgamated with the Wigan Branch Railway (qv) on 22 May 1834 to form the NUR. The line opened formally on 21 October 1838, and to the public ten days later.

PRESTON & WYRE RAILWAY & HARBOUR

Authorized on 3 July 1835 to develop farmland around Preston, a line was opened from Leighton Street, near Preston's canal basin, to Fleetwood, but not before the company had united with the Preston & Wyre Dock Company on 1 July 1839 to form the Preston & Wyre Railway, Harbour & Dock (qv).

PRESTON & WYRE RAILWAY, HARBOUR & DOCK

This company was formed when the Preston & Wyre Railway & Harbour amalgamated on 1 July 1839 with the Preston & Wyre Dock Company. The line to Fleetwood was opened ceremonially on 15 July 1840, and to the public the next day, with lines to Lytham and Blackpool on 16 February 1846 and 29 April respectively, worked by NUR rolling-stock and locomotives. Financial problems did not prevent the line's being doubled to Burnham Naze in 1846-7. The company had amalgamated with the M&LR from 3 August 1846, but was not actually dissolved until 1 July 1888, under an Act dated 7 August. Before opening, a steamer had been bought for sailings to Ulverston, the Isle of Man and Ireland, and in 1870 an L&NWR/L&YR joint committee was formed to run these services; those to Man and Ireland lasted until 1961.

REDDITCH RAILWAY

Authorized on 23 July 1858 to build a single-track line from Barnt Green (MR) to Redditch, it was opened for passengers on 19 September 1859 and to goods on 1 October. It was worked by the MR and absorbed under an Act dated 30 July 1874.

RUGBY & LEAMINGTON RAILWAY

The company was incorporated on 13 August 1846 to build between the two towns. Independence was short, however, for the L&NWR bought the company

three months after incorporation (17 November 1846), building the line itself. It opened on 1 March 1851, and closed for passengers on 15 June 1959.

ST HELENS & RUNCORN GAP RAILWAY

Incorporated on 29 May 1830, this 8-mile line running S across the L&MR was conceived mainly as a goods line, and became one of the busiest colliery lines in Lancashire. Opened (officially) on 21 February 1833, spurs linked it with the L&MR. The company merged with the Sankey Brook Navigation on 21 July 1845, becoming the St Helens Canal & Railway (qv).

ST HELENS CANAL & RAILWAY

This was formed on 21 July 1845 by the amalgamation of the Sankey Brook Navigation and the St Helens & Runcorn Gap Railway (qv). A 7.5-mile line was authorized on 16 July 1846 between Runcorn Gap (Eccleston) and Garston, opening on 1 July 1852. Extension to Warrington (sanctioned on 22 July 1847) was opened on 1 February 1853, and to Warrington (Arpley) on 1 May 1854. Another line, from Rainford to St Helens, authorized on 4 August 1853, opened on 1 February 1858. The Warrington–Garston line was leased to the L&NWR wef 1 July 1860, and that company absorbed the whole on 29 July 1864.

SANDY & POTTON RAILWAY

This line needed no Act since it was built on private land. It was the brainchild of Capt Sir William Peel, 3rd son of Sir Robert, and ran from the GNR at Sandy to Potton, a village 3.5 miles E. A ceremonial opening was held in June 1857, and the line opened for goods traffic on 23 June and to passengers on 9 November 1857. During its short independent life, motive power and rolling-stock were hired now and then from the GNR. The company was bought on 7 July 1862 by the L&NWR-backed Bedford & Cam-

Left *The Preston & Wyre Railway soon came under L&YR control— this example of a large L&YR signal box at Blackpool North was photographed on 8 September 1987.* (Allan Mott)

Right Shannon, *built for the opening of the Sandy & Potton Railway in 1858, served later on the Wantage Tramway and is now preserved by the Great Western Society at Didcot.*

Below *The station at Perth was designed by Sir Francis Tite and built in 1847 for the Scottish Central Railway. The practice of displaying shrubs and hanging baskets is one handed down by the CR.* (Allan Mott)

bridge Railway (qv), under powers in its Incorporation Act.

SCOTTISH CENTRAL RAILWAY
Incorporated on 31 July 1845, and running between Perth and Castlecary (45.5 miles), the line opened on 22 May 1848. Since it lay in a key position, both the CR and the E&GR were keen to control it, but amalgamation plans were dismissed three times by Parliament. In the end, the NBR got the E&GR and a ready-made route to Glasgow, while the CR got the SCR (under an Act of 5 July 1865), and a way to the N — not only that, but because the company had RP into Edinburgh from Larbert, the CR benefited there too.

SCOTTISH MIDLAND JUNCTION RAILWAY
The line was authorised on 31 July 1845 to link the SCR at Perth and the Aberdeen Railway (qv) at Forfar, 32.5 miles NE. There was also to be a branch connecting with the Dundee & Newtyle Railway (qv). The main line opened to passengers on 4

August 1848, and to goods on 11 September; branches from Coupar Angus to Blairgowrie and Kirriemuir, authorized on 8 July 1853, were opened in August and November 1855 respectively. The company merged with the AR on 29 July 1856 to form the SNER (qv).

SCOTTISH NORTH EASTERN RAILWAY

This was formed when the Aberdeen Railway (qv) amalgamated with the SMJR on 29 July 1856, giving a continuous line from Perth to Aberdeen. It was itself absorbed by the CR under an Act dated 10 August 1866.

SEACOMBE, HOYLAKE & DEESIDE RAILWAY

This was the new title taken by the Hoylake & Birkenhead Tramway (qv) on 18 July 1881, the company increasing its inheritance by opening a branch to Wallasey on 2 January 1888 and an extension to New Brighton on 30 March. A joint GWR/L&NWR committee failed to take over in 1889, but on 11 June 1891 the company was incorporated into a new Wirral Railway (qv).

SHEFFIELD & ROTHERHAM RAILWAY

Authorized on 4 July 1836 to be built from Wicker (Sheffield) to Westgate (Rotherham), it opened to the public on 1 November 1838. It was at first an isolated line until the NMR line from Derby to Masborough was opened in May 1840. Steel-making expanded, and the railway too, so that the newly-formed MR was happy to work it from 10 October 1844 and to absorb its 5.25 miles by an Act of 21 July 1845. There was also a 2-mile link between Holmes and the Greasborough Canal, opened for goods on 10 August 1839 and to passengers on 11 May 1840. The line closed between Wicker and Grimesthorpe Junction for passengers on 1 February 1870, and for

goods on 12 July 1965, and the Holmes-Westgate section closed on 6 October 1952.

SHEFFIELD, ROTHERHAM, BARNSLEY, WAKEFIELD, HUDDERSFIELD & GOOLE RAILWAY

This railway, with the longest title but by no means the longest line, was authorised on 7 August 1846 to build from the Sheffield & Rotherham Railway (qv) at Wincobank (Sheffield) to Horbury (M&LR). An Agreement of 1846 stipulated that the M&LR should have access to Goole, and that the N section was to be leased to it. This was done on 11 May 1847, the line opening for passengers on 1 January 1850 and to goods on 15 January, including a branch to Silkstone Siding. Singled during the post-Mania recession, traffic increased so much that a re-doubled track was opened on 21 April 1855. The company was sold to the L&YR by an Act of 2 August 1858, and the S section was absorbed by the S Yorkshire, Doncaster and Goole Railway (qv — LNER) on 22 July 1847.

SHREWSBURY & STAFFORD RAILWAY

This was a scheme which, when merged with the Newtown & Crewe and the Chester & Wolverhampton Railways (both qv), as authorized on 3 August 1846, formed the SUR&CC. It was the only part of the project completed as planned, opening on 1 June 1849.

SHROPSHIRE UNION RAILWAYS & CANAL COMPANY

The company was formed on 3 August 1846 by the

An SUR&CC notice on display at the Winchcombe Railway Museum. Note the omission, perhaps through lack of space, of the 'S' from 'RAILWAY'.

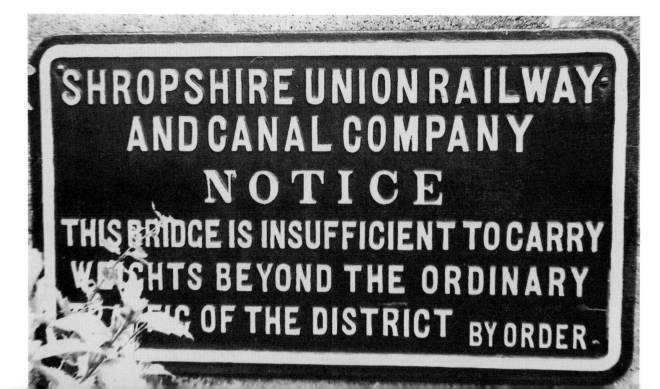

amalgamation of three canals, one of which, the Ellesmere & Chester, changed its name to the above. The company was made a partner in the Shrewsbury–Wellington section of the Shrewsbury & Birmingham Railway, and the other schemes involved were the Newtown & Crewe, the Chester & Wolverhampton and the Shrewsbury & Stafford Railways (all qv). The company was leased to the L&NWR in perpetuity from completion, by an Act of 2 July 1847, and passed to the LMS at Grouping.

SILVERDALE & NEWCASTLE RAILWAY
Built privately by Ralph Sneyd (see also Sneyd's Railway) to link his Granville Ironworks at Shelton with Etruria (Stoke-on-Trent), it opened about 1850, but did not become a public company until 13 August 1859. It was then leased to the NSR by an Act of 15 May 1860 (wef 31 August) for 999 years at £1,250 pa for the railway, £600 pa for the canal. The line's fate seems unclear — evidence of 1909 indicates that it was still under lease at that date, but it is not among the concerns listed as being absorbed by the LMS in 1923.

SIRHOWY TRAMROAD
Incorporated on 26 June 1802, this was only the third public railway to be sanctioned by Act; it ran from ironworks at Tredegar and Sirhowy to the Monmouthshire Canal, where it joined the Monmouthshire Railway (qv). The 4 ft 2 in plateway opened in 1805, and was so successful that it delayed conversion to a proper railway until 1860. When it re-opened on 19 June 1865 it was too late; others had the pickings, and the company's prosperous years were over. The L&NWR began working the line in July 1875, leasing it wef 21 August. Vesting was ratified by an Act of 13 July 1876.

SNEYD'S RAILWAY
Privately built by Ralph Sneyd, but incorporated on 28 June 1861, it had opened in January that year to give access to collieries around Talke o' the Hill, near Stoke-on-Trent. The NSR was authorized to lease it by an Act of 29 July 1864.

SOLWAY JUNCTION RAILWAY
Incorporated on 30 June 1864 to build a 20.5-mile line linking Brayton (Maryport & Carlisle Railway, qv) with Kirtlebridge (CR), the line included a 1,940 yd viaduct, then the longest in the world, across the Solway estuary. The line opened for goods on 13 September 1869, between Kirtlebridge and Bowness on 8 March 1870 and throughout on 8 August, though the first passenger train across the viaduct, an excursion, had actually run from Aspatria to Dumfries on 28 July. The CR, which had backed the line, worked it from the start, and bought the Scottish length outright (Act of 5 August 1873). The whole concern passed to the CR on 6 July 1895. The viaduct was soon troubled by ice; expensive repairs

could be done while the line was earning, but there came a time when it wasn't. Temporarily closed between 1 January 1917 and 1 February 1919, the service ceased completely from 1 September 1921. The system S of Annan had closed on 20 May, and the viaduct was demolished in 1933.

SOUTH LEICESTERSHIRE RAILWAY
The Nuneaton & Hinckley Railway (qv) changed its name on 14 June 1860, and at the same time was empowered to extend to Wigston, given RP over the MR to Leicester and authorized to build to Coventry, with a branch to Whitacre from Nuneaton. As a result, the L&NWR got access to Leicester, while the MR acquired another route to Birmingham. Nuneaton–Hinckley was opened on 1 January 1862, the line to Wigston on 1 January 1864, and to Whitacre on 1 November. The S curve at Wigston, for through running to London, was authorized in 1869 and opened in 1872. The company was dissolved and vested in the L&NWR on 15 July 1867.

SOUTH STAFFORDSHIRE RAILWAY
This was formed on 6 October 1846 when the S Staffordshire Junction Railway and the Trent Valley, Midlands & Grand Junction Railway (both qv) combined. The first 1.5 miles (Bescot–Walsall) opened on 1 November 1847, and when the other 17.5 miles to Wichnor Junction was completed on 9 April 1849 the company had access to Burton via RP. After divisions among the directors, the line was leased by an Act of 15 July 1850 to an individual (the first such authorized by Parliament), John Robinson McClean, for 21 years. He instigated entry into the Cannock coalfield, but terminated the lease after 11 years, leaving the L&NWR and MR to fight over ownership. The L&NWR won — the line was leased to it from February 1861, and the company dissolved and absorbed on 15 June 1867. The line has lost its passenger service but is still a busy goods route.

SOUTH STAFFORDSHIRE JUNCTION RAILWAY
Incorporated on 3 August 1846, this was an 8.5-mile proposal from Dudley (OW&WR) to a junction with the Trent Valley, Midlands & Grand Junction Railway (qv). Two months after incorporation, as authorized in its Act, it amalgamated with that company to form the S Staffordshire Railway (qv).

STOCKPORT, DISLEY & WHALEY BRIDGE RAILWAY
Authorized on 31 July 1854 and backed by the L&NWR, its aim was to block MR access to Manchester. The Duke of Devonshire and Sir Joseph Paxton (of Crystal Palace fame) also supported the line, but building was beset with problems, many being laid at 'Dickie's' door. A man had once been

A Beyer-Peacock 0-4-2ST (204/ 1861) shunting at Norton. The engine is named for the Paget family, Marquises of Anglesey and owners of Cannock Colliery, who were instrumental in bringing McClean's South Staffordshire Railway to the pits. (Transport Nostalgia Picture Library)

murdered at a farm through which the line passed; his skull was found and christened 'Dickie'. Tradition holds that trouble ended only after the line's engineer, Joseph Locke, had interviewed 'Dickie', promising him a free pass over the line for ever! The 10-mile railway was opened on 9 June 1857 by the L&NWR, which absorbed the company by an Act of 23 July 1866.

STONEBRIDGE RAILWAY

This was authorized on 19 May 1836 as a promotion of the B&DJR under persuasion from the MCR, which wanted a through route to Birmingham — a 6.5-mile line from Whitacre to Hampton-in-Arden would give them one via the L&BR. It opened on 12 August 1839, but heavy L&BR tolls soon forced the B&DJR to make its own route. The line closed to passengers 1 January 1917 as a wartime economy, regular goods services ceasing in 1930. The southerly 2 miles were re-opened during the Second World War to handle sand, but were finally lifted in the autumn of 1952.

STONEHOUSE & NAILSWORTH RAILWAY

Authorized on 13 July 1863, the first sod of this 5 miles 58.5 chains line was cut at Egypt Mill, Nailsworth, by the Rt Hon Edward Horsman, MP for Stroud, on 22 February 1864. It opened for goods on 1 February 1867, and to passengers three days later, but finances were soon in a poor state and an OR was appointed on 21 December. Negotiations

Left *Dudbridge Junction on the Stonehouse & Nailsworth Railway. Beyond the bridge is the MR branch to Stroud, opened on 16 November 1885 (goods), 1 July 1886 (passengers). The latter service was suspended on 14 July 1947 and ceased on 8 June 1949, and the line closed completely on 1 June 1966.*

Right *Georgemas Junction, the most northerly junction in the UK. The 12.02 ex-Wick, hauled by a Class '37' locomotive, approaches the abandoned signal box in May 1987, heading south. (Allan Mott)*

for a take-over by the MR were begun in 1872 but not finalized until an Act of 1 July 1878 ratified powers of 1874.

STRATFORD-UPON-AVON & MIDLAND JUNCTION RAILWAY

This was formed on 1 January 1909 (Act of 1 August 1908) by the fusion of the East & West Junction, the Stratford-upon-Avon, Towcester & Midland Junction, and the Evesham, Redditch & Stratford-upon-Avon Ralways (all qv) as a result of legal tangles, solvable only by an Act authorizing the sale of each concern to either the GWR, L&NWR, MR or GCR. None was interested, and the S&MJR was the result. The Northampton & Banbury Junction Railway (qv) was absorbed wef 1 July 1910 (Act of 29 April), and the company remained independent until Grouping.

STRATFORD-UPON-AVON, TOWCESTER & MIDLAND JUNCTION RAILWAY

Incorporated on 10 August 1882, this was the new name of the Easton Neston Mineral & Towcester, Roade & Olney Junction Railway. In 1883 a Joint Committee was formed with the East & West Junction Railway (qv) to run it, and the line opened for goods 13 April 1891, passengers 1 December 1892 — the passenger service died from 30 March 1893. An OR was appointed 27 May 1898, but attempts to sell the company failed and it finally amalgamated with others to form the S&MJR wef 1 January 1909 (Act: 1 August 1908).

SUTHERLAND RAILWAY

Though authorized on 29 June 1865 to run 32.75 miles from Bonar Bridge to Brora, money ran out long before completion (despite a £15,000 contribution by the HR), coming to a halt at Golspie, which was opened on 13 April 1868. Only the good

offices of the Duke of Sutherland, whose seat, Dunrobin, is 2 miles N of Golspie, allowed completion of the project — see Duke of Sutherland's Railway.

SUTHERLAND & CAITHNESS RAILWAY

This company was formed on 13 July 1871 to take over a Caithness Railway scheme authorized on 30 July 1866 for a line between Thurso and Wick, and to extend from the Duke of Sutherland's Railway (qv) at Helmsdale to Georgemas Junction. The Duke subscribed £60,000 and the HR £50,000, the latter working the line from opening on 28 July 1874. The HR also absorbed the company, exactly ten years after opening.

SWANSEA & CARMARTHEN RAILWAY

The company was formed on 16 June 1871 after an ownership battle in the House of Lords between the Llanelly Railway and Dock (qv) and the L&NWR, out of the former's Pontardulais-Swansea and Llandilo-Carmarthen branches. It was worked from the outset by the L&NWR, which bought it by an Act of 21 July 1873 for £310,000, under a stipulation that the purchase should be completed on or before 13 September 1873. The same Act changed the company title to the Central Wales & Carmarthen Junction Railway (qv).

SWANSEA VALE RAILWAY

Built as the Swansea Valley Railway (qv), it was taken over by a private company, then re-incorporated on 15 June 1855, the Act also authorizing a passenger service. It ran from Swansea to Brynamman, where it joined the Llanelly Railway & Dock (qv) line from Pantyfynnon, and opened to Pontardawe on 21 February 1860, and throughout to passengers on 18 June 1868. The Palleg Tramroad (qv) had been absorbed in 1861, and the line was leased wef 1 July 1874 (Act

SWANSEA VALLEY RAILWAY

Authorized on 2 July 1847, the line ran along the Swansea valley for 8 miles from Swansea to Abercrave Farm, Glais. In 1850 a non-statutory company was formed to take it over, opening the line (goods only) in December 1852. On 15 June 1855 this was re-incorporated as the Swansea Vale Railway (qv).

SYMINGTON, BIGGAR & BROUGHTON RAILWAY

This CR-sponsored branch E from Symington, Lanarkshire, into Tweed-dale, authorized on 21 May 1858, was opened on 5 November 1860. Extension to Peebles was authorized on 3 July 1860, opening on 1 February 1864, but by then the company had ended its brief (and nominal) independence by amalgamation with the CR under an Act of 1 August 1861. The line closed on 5 June 1950.

SYSTON & PETERBOROUGH RAILWAY

Authorized on 30 June 1845, this line from a junction N of Leicester was an attempt by George Hudson to secure Peterborough and the Fens for the MR, via the ECR. There were running battles at Stapleford Park, between Melton Mowbray and Oakham, as Lord Harborough's retainers impeded the surveyors. When a tunnel under his Lordship's Cuckoo Plantation

Though the Syston & Peterborough Railway was sponsored by the MR, it did have some autonomy, as witnessed by the SPR motif fretted in the weather-vane above Stamford station. (Allan Mott)

fell in, destroying 60 trees, Lord Harborough brought an action against the MR, sponsors of the line. A deviation (authorized on 22 July 1847) was delayed when Lord Harborough's men prevented the digging of a cutting and again obstructed surveying; the MR unsuccessfully sued 100 of his men for assault. The deviation was later eased by an agreement with Lord Harborough's successor — the earthworks may still be seen. The line opened from Syston to Melton on 1 September 1846, and from Stamford to Peterborough on 2 October, and the Melton–Stamford link on 20 March 1848 (goods), 1 May (passengers). It was part of the MR system from the first.

TEWKESBURY & MALVERN RAILWAY

The company, incorporated on 25 May 1860, was soon in financial trouble and by 1862 had had to raise more capital — the MR became shareholders, working the line from its opening on 1 July 1862 between Great Malvern and Malvern Wells, and 16 May 1864 throughout. An OR was appointed in 1866, and the next year the MR tried to lease the company but failed. In 1876, however, it acquired a vesting of assets, wef 1 January 1877 (Act of 11 August 1876). The line, single on opening, was doubled later. It was partly re-singled in 1913, and closed between Upton and Malvern in 1952. Upton–Tewkesbury closed to passengers on 14 August 1961, and to goods on 1 July 1963.

THAMES HAVEN DOCK & RAILWAY

Incorporated on 4 July 1836, the Thames Haven Railway was to build a line from Romford to Shell Haven. This scheme was dropped and the company's name was changed on 31 August 1853; the plan now was to make a line to Thames Haven and transfer it to the LT&SR for £48,000. Four miles were built from the Tilbury–Pitsea line S of Stanford-le-Hope to the river, and opened 7 June 1855 by the LT&SR, which took over on completion. Thames Haven dealt with about one-third of all cattle imports between 1850–76, when Parliament prohibited the import of live cattle, after which other industry developed.

TICKNALL TRAMWAY

Incorporated in May 1794, this 4 ft 2 in gauge plateway, laid on stone blocks and engineered by Outram, ran for about 18 miles in all. It opened between July and October 1802, serving collieries and limestone quarries on the Derbyshire/Leicestershire border. The Cloud Hill branch was rebuilt to join the Coleorton Railway (qv — Jt/Ind) at Worthington in 1839. In 1846 the MR became the owners — the line S of Ashby closed in 1850, but the Ashby–Worthington section, rebuilt to standard gauge, was re-opened on 1 January 1874 as part of the Ashby–Breedon line. The Cloud Hill branch was

The owners of Ripple station (Tewkesbury & Malvern Railway) have made a superb job of its restoration. The flamboyant bargeboards give an authentic MR flavour, though one feels, perhaps, that the hipped end to the near gable is not original.

lifted in 1891, but the Ticknall line survived until 1913.

TOTTENHAM & FOREST GATE JUNCTION RAILWAY

Promoted by the MR and LT&SR as the final link between their lines, and authorized on 4 August 1890, it ran from S Tottenham (Tottenham & Hampstead Junction Railway, qv — Jt/Ind) to Woodgrange Park (LT&SR), only 6 miles, but costly ones. The line was opened for passengers on 9 July 1894, and to goods on 1 September. The company was absorbed by the MR wef 1 January 1914 (Act of 17 August) and all goods facilities had been withdrawn by 6 May 1968.

TRENT VALLEY RAILWAY

Incorporated on 21 July 1845 to build a line along the Trent valley between Rugby and Stafford, this was a scheme to which the GJR, L&BR and M&BR were all permitted to subscribe. Before the first sod was cut by Sir Robert Peel on 13 November 1845, Agreement had been reached that the GJR, L&BR and M&BR would work the line jointly; it opened on 15 September 1847. The company had a very brief life, but it was significant because the line would clearly filter Manchester–Rugby traffic from the GJR, and it was in the GJR interest not to be in competition with it. Thus it may be said to have caused the formation of the L&NWR.

TRENT VALLEY, MIDLANDS & GRAND JUNCTION RAILWAY

This company, incorporated on 3 August 1846, built a 16.5-mile line from Walsall to Wichnor Junction (MR, near Lichfield). It merged (provided for in its Act) with the S Staffordshire Junction Railway to form the S Staffordshire Railway (both qv) on 6 October 1846.

ULVERSTONE (sic) & LANCASTER RAILWAY

This project was authorized on 24 July 1851, and cannily, perhaps, the FR let an independent company have the expense of building the link with the L&CR at Carnforth — the companies, incidentally, shared a Secretary. A notable first in engineering history was made when the engineer, James Brunlees, searching for bedrock foundations for the Kent and Leven viaducts, cleared intervening sand by using high-pressure water-jets to force it upwards. The 19.5-mile single line opened for goods on 10 August 1857, officially on 26 August, and for passengers on 1 September. The company was authorized for purchase by the FR under an Act dated 12 July 1858, but this was not effected until 21 January 1862.

VALE OF CLWYD RAILWAY

Incorporated on 23 June 1856 to build S from Foryd, on the C&HR, 10 miles to Denbigh, the first sod was cut in heavy rain on 7 August 1856. The line opened to a temporary station on 5 October 1858, and the permanent station was ready in December 1860. Working/management of the line by the L&NWR was made statutory by an Act of 25 July 1864, with full vesting and dissolution on 15 July 1867. The line closed to passengers on 19 September 1955, and to goods on 1 March 1965.

WAKEFIELD, PONTEFRACT & GOOLE RAILWAY

Incorporated on 31 July 1845, the M&LR obtained the Act, and the company had but a brief independent life. The line opened on 1 April 1848, and a branch from Pontefract to Methley was built for

Opened in 1848, Wakefield Kirkgate, which in name belonged to the Wakefield, Pontefract & Goole Railway, had, since 9 July 1847, been vested in the L&YR system. The building was largely unchanged when photographed on 23 December 1987. (Allan Mott)

access to Leeds via the MR, its first passenger traffic being Doncaster race specials on 12 September 1849. By then, however, the company had become a constituent of the L&YR.

WARRINGTON & ALTRINCHAM JUNCTION RAILWAY

Authorized on 3 July 1851 to build from the St Helens Railway (qv) at Arpley to Timperley, it reached only Altrincham, opening on 1 November 1853. Authority was obtained on 4 August 1953 for extension to Stockport, the same Act sanctioning a change of name to the Warrington & Stockport Railway (qv).

WARRINGTON & STOCKPORT RAILWAY

This was the name taken on 4 August 1853 by the Warrington & Altrincham Junction Railway (qv), on gaining powers to extend to Stockport. However, it never got there. It opened to Timperley on 1 May 1854, but then financial problems connected with the Crimean War dampened its ardour. On 1 October 1856, the Manchester S Junction & Altrincham Railway (qv) agreed to work the line for 50 per cent of revenue, meaning, in effect, that it was worked by MS&LR locomotives. Legal wrangles followed, but at length the L&NWR agreed to lease the line jointly with the St Helens Canal & Railway (qv) for 999 years from 13 August 1859. The company was vested in the L&NWR on 15 July 1867.

WARRINGTON & NEWTON RAILWAY

This 4.25-mile branch from the L&MR, running S from Newton (later Earlestown) to Warrington, authorized on 14 May 1829, was opened on 25 July 1831, the L&MR supplying locomotives and wagons. Several extensions were mooted but not built. The GJR bought the company wef 31 December 1834, but could not work the line since it was not connected, and the L&MR refused to do so. It was let privately to a Mr George Stubs until the GJR could put in its junction.

WARWICK & LEAMINGTON UNION RAILWAY

This was incorporated on 18 June 1842 to link the two towns, but on 1 July the L&BR agreed to buy the company, a step ratified by an Act of 3 April 1843. The line was opened on 9 December 1844, and on 27 July 1846 powers were granted to the L&BR to extend into Leamington. The line was built by the L&NWR, which, on 1 March 1851, also opened a branch from Leamington to Rugby made under powers granted to the Rugby & Leamington Railway (qv). Rugby–Leamington closed to passengers on 15 June 1959, Leamington–Coventry on 18 January 1965, although through trains still use the latter route.

WATFORD & RICKMANSWORTH RAILWAY

Powers were granted to Lord Ebury on 3 July 1860 for a line from Watford (L&NWR) to Rickmansworth. He also obtained powers the next year for an extension to Uxbridge, to link with a GWR branch opened in 1856. Construction began on 22 November 1860, and the line opened on 1 October 1862, but financial problems intervened and an OR was appointed on 23 February 1866. The company was bought for £65,000 by the L&NWR, which had worked it for 50 per cent of gross receipts, by an Act dated 27 June 1881. Electric working was proposed in 1907, and began on 16 April 1917, with trains of the London Electric Railway (qv – Jt/Ind). The steam service from Uxbridge ceased in 1922, but steam remained on the original section. The line closed to passengers on 3 March 1952, to goods and regular traffic in May 1966, and officially on 2 January 1967.

WEST LANCASHIRE RAILWAY

Incorporated on 14 August 1871 to build a railway along the shore of the Ribble estuary between Preston and Southport, it opened officially from Hesketh Bank to Hesketh Park on 19 February 1878, and

The L&NWR bought the Watford & Rickmansworth Railway in 1881, and shareholders in that company were thereafter beholden to the L&NWR for their dividends. This distribution would have been the last paid by the L&NWR before the LMS took over. (Allan Mott)

London & North Western Railway. (No. 629.)

DIVIDEND STATEMENT.

SECRETARY'S OFFICE, EUSTON STATION,
LONDON, N.W. 1, 28th February, 1923.

Referring to the Resolution passed at the Annual Meeting of the Proprietors held on the 23rd instant declaring Dividends on the several Stocks mentioned below for the Half-year ending 31st December last, I am instructed to send you the following Draft, and to request your particular attention to the notes at the foot of the Draft.

I hereby certify that the amount of Income Tax deducted will be paid by the Company to the proper Officer for the Receipt of Taxes.

Proprietors requiring exemption from Income Tax are informed that the Inland Revenue will receive this Statement as a Voucher in claiming the same.

R. C. IRWIN, *Secretary.*

DIVIDEND—HALF-YEAR ENDING 31st DECEMBER, 1922.

	Per cent.	Amount of Stock. £	Amount of Dividend. £	s.	d.
CONSOLIDATED (ORDINARY) STOCK	*£5:10: 0				
* making with the Interim Dividend already paid a total Dividend for the year of 8½ per cent.					
CONSOLIDATED 4% GUARANTEED STOCK	£2: 0: 0				
CONSOLIDATED 4% PREFERENCE STOCK	£2: 0: 0	5508	110	3	2
4% PREFERENCE STOCK (1902)	£2: 0: 0				
5% REDEEMABLE PREFERENCE STOCK	£2:10: 0				
(To be redeemed on the 30th June, 1926.)					
Less Income Tax:—	s. d.	£ s. d.			
Consolidated (Ordinary) Stock at 5/3 in the £...					
(Being the average rate for the year 1922, viz.:— 3 months at 6/- and 9 months at 5/-.)					
Guaranteed & Preference Stocks at 5/- in the £			24	10	10
		£	82	12	4

Name WILLIAM F. B. WARMAN & ANR.

CHANGE OF POSTAL ADDRESS.
Proprietors should keep the Company informed of the above to prevent loss of Dividend Warrants, &c. Forms for giving orders to the Company to pay Dividends direct to Bankers can be obtained on application to the Secretary, Euston Station, N.W. 1.

No. 52513

This portion of the Sheet to be retained by the Proprietor.

throughout on 16 September 1882 (to the public the next day in each case). Agreement with the MS&LR for a joint station at Fishergate, Preston, was ratified by Parliament on 23 May 1887. Though not wealthy, the company managed to hold off absorption by the L&YR until 1 July 1897 (Act of 15 July). The line lost its passenger service on 7 September 1964.

WEST RIDING UNION RAILWAY

The West Yorkshire (1845) Railway and the Leeds & W Riding Junction Railway (qv) united to form a new company, whose Act (18 August 1846) stipulated amalgamation with the L&YR within three months. This it did wef 17 November 1846, and all openings of the 45.5-mile line were made by the parent company — Bradford to Low Moor on 9 May 1850, Moorfield on 18 July 1848, Halifax on 7 August 1850 and Sowerby Bridge on 1 January 1852.

WHITEHAVEN & FURNESS JUNCTION RAILWAY

This company was incorporated on 21 July 1845 on the advice of George Stephenson, who suggested to Lord Lonsdale a line S from Whitehaven via St Bees and Ravenglass to the FR at Dunnerholme; financial considerations resulted in a junction near Broughton, 33.75 miles. It opened to Ravenglass on 21 July 1849, to Bootle on 8 July 1850 and throughout on 1 November. At Whitehaven the line joined the Whitehaven Junction Railway (qv), and the company was absorbed by the FR wef 1 July 1865, by an Act of 16 July 1866.

WHITEHAVEN, CLEATOR & EGREMONT RAILWAY

This 4.5-mile line between Whitehaven and Egremont was authorized on 16 June 1854, with a 2.25-mile branch to Frizington, on Cleator Moor. The line opened for mineral traffic on 11 January 1856, and to passengers on 1 July 1857, initially running to Whitehaven, but curtailed at Corkickle when, in August 1857, the Whitehaven & Furness Junction Railway (qv) levied a toll through the tunnel. The line was single, on earthworks for double, becoming very busy as ironworks developed. The system grew quickly, but when the company wanted to build S from Egremont to the coast, the W&FJR objected, since it would lose revenue; a joint Agreement was reached. By the time the line was built, the FR had taken over the W&FJR anyway, and trains were worked by the company under arrangement with the FR. The company was vested in the L&NWR wef 1 July 1877, but transferred to the L&NWR/FR jointly by an Act of 17 June 1878, wef 1 July. Passenger traffic ceased on 7 January 1935.

WHITEHAVEN JUNCTION RAILWAY

The Bill for this nominally independent company

was promoted by the Maryport & Carlisle Railway (qv) to link its line with Whitehaven. Receiving Royal Assent on 4 July 1844, George Stephenson was appointed engineer for a line which follows the coast beneath sandstone cliffs, picturesque but at the mercy of storm and rockfall — it has proved difficult to maintain. It opened to Workington on 19 January 1846, to Harrington on 18 May and to Whitehaven on 15 February 1847 (goods), 19 February (passengers), worked by locomotives and stock from the M&CR. Opening of the Whitehaven & Furness Junction Railway (qv) gave the line an outlet S, and the company was absorbed by the L&NWR under an Act of 16 July 1866.

WICK & LYBSTER LIGHT RAILWAY

This 13.75-mile line, authorized by a LRO on 27 November 1899, was funded by a Treasury grant of £25,000 and the HR with local subscriptions (£72,000). It opened on 1 July 1903, the HR working it at cost: the company remained independent until swallowed by the LMS at Grouping. The last train ran on 1 April 1944.

WIGAN BRANCH RAILWAY

This 7-mile line, sanctioned on 29 May 1830, ran from Parkside (L&MR) to Wigan via Golborne, with a 3-mile branch (the Springs branch) which linked it with several collieries. Its Act stipulated that it must be built by the L&MR engineers, and, after opening on 3 September 1832, it was worked by that company, the first example of such an arrangement. On 22 May 1834 the company amalgamated with the Preston & Wigan Railway (qv) to form the NUR.

WIGTOWNSHIRE RAILWAY

Authorized on 18 July 1872 to build 19 miles 10 chains from Newton Stewart to Whithorn, with a branch to Garliestown, it opened to Wigtown on 3 April 1875, Millisle on 2 August and throughout on 9 July 1877. By 1885 the company was in a bad way financially, and amalgamated with the Portpatrick Railway, creating the Portpatrick & Wigtownshire Railway (both qv) from 1 August 1885. The Garliestown branch, opened on 3 August 1876, closed to passengers on 1 March 1903; passenger traffic ceased throughout on 25 September 1950.

WIRRAL RAILWAY

A company was first incorporated in 1883 to build through the Wirral towards the Chester–Connah's Quay line; it opened from Birkenhead Docks to Birkenhead Park on 2 January 1888, where it linked with the Mersey Railway (qv–Jt/Ind). Powers were transferred by an Act of 12 August 1889 to a joint committee of the MS&LR and the WM&CQR. On 1 July 1891 (Act of 11 June) the company was re-incorporated with the Seacombe Hoylake & Deeside

The HR worked the Wick & Lybster Light Railway and this six-wheeler, built at Inverness in 1909 and now restored by the Bo'ness & Kinneil Railway (the No 17 is fictitious), may have been typical of stock used.

Railway (qv) in a new Wirral Railway. The double track between Hoylake and Birkenhead opened the same day as the Seacombe branch (1 June 1895), and was extended to W Kirby (authorized on 6 July 1895) in 1896. Tram competition caused closure of the Seacombe–New Brighton service in 1911. Powers to electrify had been granted on 25 June 1900, but nothing was done until 1935, when a service was inaugurated jointly by the Mersey Railway and the LMS, whose property the company became on 1 July 1923.

Whifflet Junction is still the point at which lines approaching Glasgow converge. The line to Rutherglen crosses in the middle distance, while in the foreground is the route to the north, with a spur towards Rutherglen. In the right background are lines serving steelworks.

WISHAW & COLTNESS RAILWAY

Projected as the Garion & Garturk Railway, but incorporated on 21 June 1829 under its more familiar name, the company built 11.03 miles of line between Chapel (Lanarkshire) and the Monkland & Kirkintilloch Railway (qv – LNER) near Gartsherrie. The single line, laid by Grainger to the 'Scotch' gauge of 4 ft 6 in, was short of funds, but opened partially in 1833, to Jerviston on 21 March 1834, Cleland in 1841, and throughout on 9 March 1844. It was horse-powered until three locomotives by James M. Rowan of Glasgow were delivered, entering service in November/December 1840. The company was vested in the CR by an Act dated 28 July 1849.

WOLVERHAMPTON & WALSALL RAILWAY

This 8-mile line, authorized on 29 June 1865, took seven years and four Acts to complete, opening on 1 November 1872. The L&NWR leased the line on 19 July 1875, but the company was sold by an Act of 11

Stratford Road, Wolverton, in about 1910, the steam tram plying in a busy street. The L&NWR Carriage & Wagon Works lies to the left. (Buckinghamshire County Library/Barry Green)

August 1876 to the MR, which had already absorbed the linking line, the Wolverhampton, Walsall & Midland Junction Railway (qv).

WOLVERHAMPTON, WALSALL & MIDLAND JUNCTION RAILWAY

A great outcry was heard when it was realised that the route of this line, authorized on 6 August 1872, would take it across Sutton Park. However, the protesters changed their tune when they found that household commodities would become cheaper as a result of it! An Agreement in December 1872 with the MR, with which the company had close ties, led to absorption by that company under an Act of 30 July 1874. The line opened for goods on 19 May 1879 and to passengers on 1 July, and was closed to passengers on 18 January 1965. It remains open for goods.

WOLVERTON & STONY STRATFORD TRAMWAY

Incorporated in November 1882, this ill-fated concern had gone into voluntary liquidation by 3 September 1883. A new Tramway Order was obtained on 16 July 1883, renaming the company the Wolverton & Stony Stratford & District Tramway, and authorizing a line from Wolverton to the Barley

Mow Inn, Stony Stratford. Nothing happened until 5 October 1886, when its name changed again, to the Wolverton, Stony Stratford & District LR. Two miles of line were built to 3 ft 6 in gauge and opened on 27 May 1887; in 1888 the line was extended to Deanshanger, but this extension was abandoned within a year! The company again went into voluntary liquidation (4 September 1889), a Receiving Order was dated 17 December, and the line was closed. A syndicate took over, re-opening it on 20 November 1891 – a new company, the Wolverton & Stony Stratford District New Tramway was incorporated on 15 September 1893: this ran until 1919, before a third voluntary liquidation on 17 July. The L&NWR bought the line to take its men to its Wolverton Works, and became responsible for its maintenance. By 1926, however, bus competition had hit – the tramway closed at the beginning of the General Strike and never re-opened.

YORKSHIRE DALES RAILWAY

This 8.75-mile line from the MR at Embsay Junction was meant as the start of a line to Darlington. However, it never went beyond the length authorized on 6 August 1897, between Skipton and Grassington. Though worked by the MR from opening (29 July 1902), the company managed to stay independent until Grouping. The line closed to passengers on 22 September 1930, though a goods service from Swinden Siding to Grassington survived until 11 August 1969. Embsay station is now the home of the Embsay Steam Railway.

PART 3

The London & North Eastern Railway group

The insignia of the London & North Eastern Railway. (Allan Mott)

Overleaf *Mr Nigel Gresley became Chief Mechanical Engineer of the LNER at the Grouping, and his work came to epitomize the company's engines. His unique Class 'A4' 'Pacifics' appeared in 1935, and the 100th, No 4498, was named after its designer.* (Allan Mott)

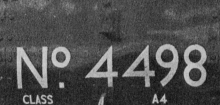

No. 4498
CLASS   A4

LONDON & NORTH EASTERN RAILWAY

Formed under the Railways Act of 19 August 1921, wef 1 January 1923, the LNER had the following constituents: NER, GCR, GER, GNR, H&BR, NBR and GNSR (the H&BR had actually amalgamated with the NER in 1922). Also included were 26 subsidiary companies and committees, giving a total route mileage of 6,590, stretching from Elgin, Mallaig and Wrexham to London, with exclusive areas in the NE, Lincolnshire and E Anglia.

ABERDEEN & TURRIFF RAILWAY

This was the new title, taken on 19 April 1859, of what had been incorporated as the Banff, Macduff & Turriff Junction Railway (qv). Its line opened to Gellymill, a farm 1 mile S of Macduff, on 4 June 1860. The company was consolidated into the GNSR by an Act of 30 July 1866, wef 1 August.

ABERLADY, GULLANE & NORTH BERWICK RAILWAY

Incorporated on 24 August 1893, this line was intended to foster N Berwick as a holiday and golfing resort, but in the event got no further than Gullane (4.75 miles), a railway-owned omnibus covering the last miles. Opened on 1 April 1898, it was taken over by the NBR by an Act of 6 August 1900.

ABOYNE & BRAEMAR RAILWAY

This line was sponsored by the Deeside Railway (qv), authorized on 5 July 1865 and running from Aboyne to Ballater. It opened on 17 October 1866. In 1868, a Col Farquharson agreed to extend it to Bridge of Gairn to carry timber from his estate, but after the railway had been laid, Queen Victoria bought the forest, and the line was removed. The road using part of the route is still known as 'The Track of the Old Line'. The company was absorbed by the GNSR on 31 January 1876, under a retrospective Act of 13 July. On 2 May 1904, a motor omnibus service was introduced between Ballater and Braemar.

ALFORD VALLEY RAILWAY

A railway scheme was authorized along the valley between Kintore and Alford, NW of Aberdeen, in 1846 but collapsed for lack of funds. The idea was revived and a 16.5-mile line re-incorporated on 23 June 1856. The GNSR subscribed £15,000, leased the line before completion and worked it from opening on 21 March 1859 (public), 30 July (official). The company was consolidated with the GNSR on 1 August 1866 under an Act of two days before — the line closed for passengers on 2 January 1950.

The Aberlady, Gullane & N Berwick Railway closed only 34 years after opening, on 12 September 1932. Aberlady station in April 1988, 56 years on, looks forlorn though the platform survives.

ALVA RAILWAY

Incorporated on 22 July 1861, this 3.75-mile line to Cambus (Stirling & Dunfermline Railway, qv) from Alva, E of Stirling, opened on 11 June 1863 and was vested in the E&GR by an Act of 23 June wef 31 July 1864. It closed to passengers on 1 November 1954.

AMBERGATE, NOTTINGHAM & BOSTON & EASTERN JUNCTION RAILWAY

This was formed on 16 July 1846, a union of a Nottingham & Boston scheme, the Nottingham, Erewash Valley & Ambergate Railway, and the Nottingham, Vale of Belvoir & Grantham Railway (both qv). The line opened from Colwick Junction to Grantham on 15 July 1850 and for local goods on 22 July. The GNR coveted the line for access to Nottingham, but the MR was jealous of its monopoly. The GNR made an offer to the Ambergate company, and an Act of 1854 gave authority to work, lease or buy it. The MR replied with an injunction preventing the GNR from working to Ambergate. The first GNR train into Nottingham was surrounded by MR engines — the GN driver set his locomotive in motion and jumped. The engine was locked in a shed for seven months while the MR claimed breach of injunction, the GNR claiming in return that the loco had been hired by the AN&B&EJR! In the end the line was leased to the GNR by an Agreement signed on 30 March 1855, but it had to build its own station in Nottingham. The company changed its name to the Nottingham & Grantham Railway & Canal Company on 15 May 1860, and as such it passed to the LNER in 1923.

ANSTRUTHER & ST ANDREWS RAILWAY

This 15.5-mile line was authorized on 26 August 1880, a further Act of 16 July 1883 sanctioning an extension to the NBR's St Andrews branch. The line opened between Anstruther and Boarhills (9 miles) on 1 September 1883, the rest opening on 1 June 1887. The company was absorbed by the NBR under an Act dated 15 July 1887.

BALLOCHNEY RAILWAY

Incorporated on 19 May 1826, this was an extension from the Kipps branch of the Monkland & Kirkintilloch Railway (qv) to Ballochney and Arbuckle. Engineered by Thomas Grainger at 4 ft 6 in, it opened on 8 August 1828. With branches to Clarkston, New Monkland, Stanrig and Whiterig, Blackrig and Airdrie, its total length was 5 miles. The company merged with the M&KR and the Slamannan Railway to form the Monkland Railways (all qv) on 14 August 1848.

BANFF, MACDUFF & TURRIFF JUNCTION RAILWAY

Nominally independent, the company had GNSR representatives on its Board since that concern had subscribed £40,000. It was incorporated (15 June 1855) to build from Inveramsay (GNSR) to Banff, but later extended towards Macduff by the GNSR-sponsored Banff, Macduff & Turriff Extension Railway (qv). Opened to Turriff on 5 September 1857, the line was not a success. It changed its name to the Aberdeen & Turriff Railway (qv) on 19 April 1859.

BANFF, MACDUFF & TURRIFF EXTENSION RAILWAY

Incorporated on 27 July 1857 to extend the Banff, Macduff & Turriff Junction Railway (qv) towards Macduff, Gellymill (S of Macduff, 11.5 miles) was reached on 4 June 1860, but it was 1 July 1872 before the last short section to Macduff was open. The company was absorbed by the GNSR under its 'blanket' Act of 30 July 1866, wef 1 August 1866.

BANFF, PORTSOY & STRATHISLA RAILWAY

Incorporated on 27 July 1857 for 16.75 miles of railway from Grange (about 5 miles E of Keith) to the named towns, a branch from Tillynaught to Portsoy was also built (both main line and branch opened on 2 August 1859). When powers of 21 July 1863 authorized extension to Portgordon, the company changed its name to the Banffshire Railway (qv).

BANFFSHIRE RAILWAY

This was formed on 21 July 1863 when the Banff, Portsoy & Strathisla Railway (qv) changed its name. The extension authorized with the name-change was dropped, however, until the GNSR built and opened it 1 April 1884, having absorbed the company wef 31 July 1867 under an Act of 12 August.

BARNSLEY COAL RAILWAY

Its down-to-earth title (incorporated on 22 July 1861) hid an important aim, a northward link between the S Yorkshire Railway & River Dun Navigation (qv) at Ardsley (later renamed Stairfoot) and Wakefield. Parliament, however, pruned the scheme so that it ended near Notton, about half-way to its objective, due largely to opposition from the Wooley Estate. Authority for the SYR&RDN to buy the company was ratified by an Act of 13 July 1863, but it was not until 1874 that the MS&LR (which now owned the SYR&RDN) gained powers to complete the link. This opened for goods on 28 January 1870, and to passengers between Stairfoot and Lee Lane on 1 September 1882; the service lasted until 22 September 1930.

BARRINGTON LIGHT RAILWAY

Built under a LRO dated 15 July 1920, this 1.5-mile line, still open, links a cement works with the Royston–Hitchin line between Foxton (Cambs) and Shepreth.

BARTON & IMMINGHAM LIGHT RAILWAY

This scheme, authorized by a LRO on 19 July 1907,

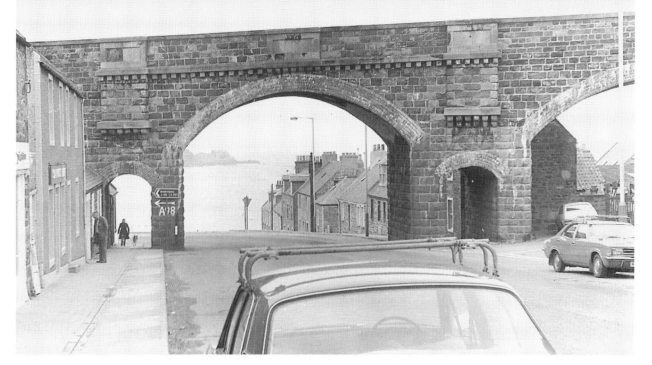

gave Hull direct access to Immingham via New Holland. Its single line, worked on the tablet system, ran from the New Holland–Ulceby line just S of Goxhill for 7.5 miles E to Immingham West, and opened from Immingham to Killingholme on 1 December 1910, to Goxhill on 1 May 1911 (both goods only), and for passengers throughout on the following day. At Immingham it met the Humber Commercial Railway and Dock (qv) in a triangular junction; it was vested in the HCR&D wef 31 December 1912.

BEDALE & LEYBURN RAILWAY

This 11.75-mile line, authorized on 4 August 1853,

ran from an end-on junction with the YN&BR's Bedale branch, along Wensleydale to Leyburn. The line opened for goods on 24 November 1855, and to passengers on 19 May 1856. It was intended that the NER should work the line, formal Agreement with that company resulting in its taking over wef 1 January 1858. The NER extended the line via Aysgarth to Hawes where it met an MR branch from Hawes Junction. The final train along the single line, on 24 April 1954, was hauled by Class 'G5' No 67345.

BERWICKSHIRE RAILWAY

Incorporated on 17 July 1862, the line provided a cross-country route from the Duns branch of the NBR to the Tweed Valley at St Boswells. The first sod was cut by Lady Campbell at Easton Park on 14 October 1862, and though the line opened to Earlston on 16 November 1863, construction of the Leaderfoot viaduct delayed things. St Boswells was reached on 2 October 1865. The company amalgamated with the NBR under an Act of 13 July 1876, wef 1 August. Floods on 12 August 1948 caused so much damage to the line that it closed to passengers between Duns and Earlston immediately.

BISHOP AUCKLAND & WEARDALE RAILWAY

Incorporated on 15 July 1837, this was an extension of the St&DR from Soho (near Shildon), through Shildon tunnel and N towards Crook (see also Shildon Tunnel Railway). The line opened from Soho to South Church on 19 April 1842 and to Crook on 8 November 1843. It was extended by the Weardale Extension Railway and sold to the Wear Valley Railway (both qv) on 22 July 1847.

BISHOP'S STORTFORD, DUNMOW & BRAINTREE RAILWAY

Incorporated on 22 July 1861 to build an 18-mile link between Bishop's Stortford and an end-on junction with the Maldon, Witham & Braintree Railway (qv) at Braintree, it ran into trouble long before completion. The GER had already acquired transfer powers (21 July 1863) and the company was vested by an Act of 29 July 1865, becoming part of its system on opening day, 22 February 1869. The line was closed, apart from some seaside excursions, wef 3 March 1952, but the line was used in June 1960 to test BR's prototype 'Road-Railer'.

BLANE VALLEY RAILWAY

Authorized on 6 August 1861, this extended the E&GR's Campsie branch from Lennoxtown, NW along Strathblane, for 8 miles 29 chains to Killearn (later renamed Drumgoyne). The line was opened on 5 November 1866 (goods), 1 July 1867 (passengers), and worked by the NBR which later absorbed it by an Act of 5 August 1891. A further extension to Gartness was opened on 1 October 1882 (see Strathendrick & Aberfoyle Railway). The last train ran on 29 September 1951.

BLAYDON, GATESHEAD & HEBBURN RAILWAY

Though authorized on 22 May 1834 for 16.5 miles of railway between Blaydon and Hebburn, the line reached only Derwenthaugh (1.75 miles); even its year of opening is uncertain, but is thought to have been 1839, the year in which the N&CR took over. The Brandling Junction Railway (qv) used part of the route for its line.

BLYTH & TYNE RAILWAY

An Act of 30 June 1852 incorporated wagonways between the Rivers Blyth and Tyne into a group — its main constituents were the Seghill Railway (qv), the line linking this with the Tyne, and a branch to Bedlington, later extended to Morpeth under an Act of 4 August 1853. The company's own line ran along the bed of another wagonway, between Whitley and the Tyne. It opened on 31 October 1860, and was a prosperous, well-managed concern, expanding from its wagonway origins into a railway system paying dividends of up to 12.5 per cent. It was bought by the NER on 7 August 1874. The line between Bedlington and Morpeth closed on 3 April 1950, though it was used by excursions until 10 August 1953.

BORDER COUNTIES RAILWAY

Branching from the Border Union (North British) Railway at Riccarton Junction, the line, authorized on 31 July 1854, ran S via Bellingham to join the N&CR (by then part of the NER) at Hexham. The first 5 miles from Hexham to Chollerford opened on 5 April 1858, and the line was open throughout on 24 June 1862 (goods), 1 July (passengers). It was no high-speed route, but did allow the NBR, which had absorbed the company officially by an Act of 13 August 1860, to get RP from Hexham to Newcastle via NER metals. Later, a gun-range brought traffic between Newcastle and the site. The last passenger train to Hexham along this route ran on 15 October 1956.

BORDER UNION (NORTH BRITISH) RAILWAY

Authorized on 21 July 1859 and advertised as the 'Waverley route' by its owners, the NBR, it extended

Left *Takeley, on the Bishop's Stortford, Dunmow & Braintree line, has seen no passengers since 1952, but remains in good condition. The secret is its occupation by a firm of builders, whose activities are screened by the overgrowth on the right.*

Right *A Blyth & Tyne Railway locomotive, seen here in later years as NER No 1336. (K.L. Taylor Collection)*

the Edinburgh & Hawick Railway (qv) to Carlisle, with branches to Langholm and Gretna. The CR and L&NWR tried to blockade this incursion into Carlisle, but the NBR circumvented them by leasing the Carlisle & Silloth Railway & Docks Company (qv). The line opened from Scotsdyke to Carlisle on 12 October 1861 (goods), 28 October (passengers), to Newcastleton on 1 March 1862, to Riccarton on 2 June, and throughout on 24 June (goods), 1 July (passengers). It never really came into its own until the MR opened its Settle–Carlisle line (1 May 1876). The last train along the line was the night sleeper from Edinburgh on 5 January 1969. At Newcastleton, the level crossing gates were locked against it, and the villagers massed in protest. Their only satisfaction, perhaps, was that they halted an important train for an hour, but the line, of course, closed anyway. A privately run operation was proposed, but the price asked by BR was considered too high and the scheme fell through. The line was dismantled with almost indecent haste in 1971.

BOSTON, SLEAFORD & MIDLAND COUNTIES RAILWAY

This line, authorized to a nominally independent company on 20 August 1853, was a GNR project running for 28 miles from Boston to Barkston (Grantham), to join the Ambergate, Nottingham & Boston & Eastern Counties Railway (qv). It opened from Grantham to Sleaford on 13 June 1857 (formally) and 16 June (to the public), and to Boston on 12 April 1859 (formal), 13 June (public). Worked from the start by the GNR, and absorbed under an Act of 25 July 1864, the line became, with the AN&B&ECR, part of the useful cross-country route it still is.

BOURNE & ESSENDINE RAILWAY

Incorporated on 12 August 1857 and opened on 16 June 1860, this short line linked Bourn (Lincs — usually spelt without the 'e' then) with the GNR at Essendine. It was worked by the GNR from the start and absorbed under an Act of 25 July 1864. It closed to passengers on 18 June 1951.

BRACKENHILL LIGHT RAILWAY

A line of less than 3 miles built under a LRO dated 19 March 1901, it ran from a junction with the Swinton & Knottingley Joint Railway (qv — Jt/Ind), S of Ackworth, to Hemsworth Colliery. Though worked from opening on 1 July 1914 by the NER, that company declined a formal WA, with the result

A mile from Manthorpe, Lincs, the Bourne & Essendine Railway crossed a minor road, still marked by a hump in the road and Crossing House to the right. There was a platform once; now the track-bed is used for farm access.

that, nominally at least, it worked the line independently. The company was absorbed by the LNER in 1923, and the line closed to goods traffic on 1 January 1962.

BRADFORD, ECCLESHILL & IDLE RAILWAY

The GNR was empowered to subscribe £30,000 and to work this line, authorized on 28 June 1866, between Laister Dyke and Thackley, and then down to Shipley via the Idle & Shipley Railway (qv). In fact, even the balance of the capital could not be found locally, so the GNR took over under an Act of 24 July 1871. The line opened on 4 May 1874 (goods) and 18 January 1875 (passengers). Limestone for local ironworks used the line, and its 6 miles 7 chains carried heavy freight traffic. It closed to passengers on 2 February 1931, and on 2 November 1964 to goods between Cutlers Junction and Idle, 31 October 1966 between Laister Dyke and Quarry Siding.

BRADFORD & THORNTON RAILWAYS

This was authorized on 24 July 1871 to build 5 miles 49 chains of line between St Dunstans and Thornton, with a short branch to Brick Lane, Bradford, and a linking curve towards Leeds at St Dunstans. It was opened for goods to Claydon in August 1877 and throughout in April 1878; opening to passengers came on 14 October 1878, by the GNR which had taken over on 18 July 1872. An extension to Keighley was authorized on 5 August 1873 (see Halifax, Thornton & Keighley Railway).

BRADFORD, WAKEFIELD & LEEDS RAILWAY

Despite its title, this was actually a direct line between Wakefield and Leeds, joining the Leeds, Bradford & Halifax Junction Railway at Wortley Junction. The Act of 10 July 1854 included powers for the GNR to work the line, which it did from the outset; it opened formally on 3 October 1857, to passengers on 5 October and to goods on 12 November. The GNR took advantage of its powers to become the fourth partner in the new Central station at Leeds. In October 1857 the company gave the GNR notice that it would appoint its own staff. The GNR, possibly in pique, withdrew its engines and wagons, so the company was forced to hire wagons — from the GNR! A plan of 1859 to amalgamate with the LB&HJR collapsed, but a branch to Ossett, authorized in 1860, opened for minerals on 6 January 1862 and general goods on 7 April. By an Act of 21 July 1863, the company was renamed the W Yorkshire Railway (qv — Jt/Ind).

BRAMPTON RAILWAY

From 1799 this line served Naworth Coalfield, in NE Cumbria, originally as a gravity and horse-worked wooden wagonway. Laid out mostly within Lord Carlisle's estate, it needed no Act and is often known as Lord, or the Earl of, Carlisle's Railway. A change

to iron rails had been made by 1809 and its gauge was 4 ft 8 in, a fact which was later to influence the N&CR in its choice. The line was renewed in 1836, and on 15 July James Thompson, Lord Carlisle's agent, hired two locomotives from the N&CR to work the first steam-hauled passenger service in the Lake Counties. Regular services remained horse-drawn, however, until 4 July 1881. In 1837 the colliery concern was leased to Thompson, and his company operated the line for the next 70 years; *Rocket* worked on it between 1837 and 1840. Leased to the NER from 29 October 1912, the line closed as a First World War economy on 1 March 1917, re-opening exactly three years later. It closed finally to passengers on 29 October 1923, the rest surviving under the NCB until March 1953.

BRANDLING JUNCTION RAILWAY

Originally promoted by the Brandling brothers in 1835, and built using wayleaves, a company was incorporated on 7 June 1836; part of the route followed the Blaydon, Gateshead & Hebburn Railway (qv). It opened from Redheugh to Gateshead Quay on 15 January 1839, and to Monkwearmouth and S Shields on 5 September 1839. George Hudson wished to buy the company, and when it demurred, naming a prohibitive sum, he proposed a route of his own, 3 miles shorter. A few days later the company's directors offered him the line at his own price. He bought it in his own name 13 August 1844, transferring it to the Newcastle & Durham Junction Railway (qv) three days later — it took possession on 1 September.

BROXBURN RAILWAY

This short line (1.25 miles) was authorized on 12 August 1867 to run from the E&GR at Broomhouse to Broxburn (Linlithgow). The company was amalgamated with the NBR by an Act of 28 July 1873.

BUCKLEY RAILWAY

This was the title taken by a 5.25-mile horse tramway running from Buckley to the R Dee estuary on authorization (14 June 1860) to convert itself to a proper railway. Opened on 7 June 1862, the line was leased to the WM&CQR by an Act of 5 August 1873, having been worked by it since 1863; the Act also permitted conversion for passenger traffic, but this was never done. The company passed to the GCR wef 1 January 1905, by an Act of 22 July the previous year.

BURY ST EDMUNDS & THETFORD RAILWAY

This 12.5-mile line was authorized on 5 July 1865 to link the two towns, but the company had difficulty raising capital, so the Thetford & Watton Railway (qv) was given operating powers by the Act (7 July 1873) authorizing its own extension to Bury. The line opened on 1 March 1876, and the company was bought by the GER under an Act dated 22 July 1878, ratifying an Agreement of 27 February.

Unusually for a small company, two of the original Brandling Junction Railway stations survive, at Felling and Monkwearmouth. This is the latter: designed by Thomas Moore, it dates from 1848 and is now a Railway Museum. (K.L. Taylor Collection)

CALEDONIAN & DUMBARTONSHIRE RAILWAY

Locally promoted, and authorized on 26 June 1846, capital was hard to find until a lease was taken by a steamer company. The line ran between Glasgow and Bowling, opening from Dumbarton on 15 July 1850 and being the means by which many saw Loch Lomond for the first time. Both CR and E&GR had routes to Dumbarton — this was the E&GR one, but before that it had combined with the Glasgow, Dumbarton & Helensburgh Railway to form the Dumbartonshire Railways (both qv). See also Dumbarton & Balloch Joint Railway (Jt/Ind).

CARLISLE & SILLOTH BAY RAILWAY & DOCK COMPANY

Incorporated on 16 July 1855, 13 miles of almost level track was quickly completed, extending the Port Carlisle Dock & Railway's line to Silloth. The PCD&R agreed to supply the engine if the company provided the rolling-stock. The line opened formally on 28 August 1856, but in 1857 passenger trains reverted to horse-traction, the engine working goods as required. The line did not fulfil its prospects, and an NBR offer to lease was a godsend. This took effect from 3 June 1862 and the NBR absorbed the company wef 1 August 1880, ratified by an Act of 12 August. A modest recovery came when Silloth became known as a resort, and the line became the first branch in the country to have its steam service replaced by diesel on 29 November 1954; it closed finally on 7 September 1964.

CAWOOD, WISTOW & SELBY LIGHT RAILWAY

The first sod of this 4.5-mile line (authorized on 2

July 1896) was cut by the wife of the Chairman, Mrs Henry Liversedge, on 11 July. Single track, the line was almost level across the agricultural land which provided most of its business. Opened on 16 February 1898, it used an independent terminus at Selby, and, at first, its own engine; after purchase by the NER on 3 July 1900, passenger stock became a petrol-electric railcar and a Leyland bus converted to run on rails. The line closed to passengers on 1 January 1930, and completely on 2 May 1960.

CHARLESTOWN RAILWAY & HARBOUR COMPANY

Incorporated on 8 August 1859, this concern was based at a small harbour on the N bank of the Firth of Forth. Amalgamation with the West of Fife Mineral Railway wef 1 August 1861 formed the West of Fife Railway & Harbour (both qv).

CLACTON-ON-SEA RAILWAY

This line of 3 miles 6 furlongs 8 chains from near Thorpe-le-Soken to Great Clacton was an independent extension of the Tendring Hundred Railway (qv). Incorporated on 2 August 1877, it was opened on 4 July 1882 and was worked by the GER for 60 per cent of receipts until it bought the company wef 1 July 1883, by an Act of 29 June.

CLARENCE RAILWAY

Promoted as the Tees & Weardale Railway, its title was changed before incorporation (23 May 1828) to honour the Duke of Clarence, later King William IV. The St&DR saw the company as a threat, and put all it could in the way. The line opened piecemeal for private owners as it was built, the usually accepted dates being between August 1833 and January 1835. Steam was introduced in 1838, mainly for the passenger service. The line was leased to the Stockton & Hartlepool Railway from 22 September 1844 for 21 years, and in perpetuity wef 1 January 1851, but was absorbed by the W Hartlepool Harbour & Railway (both qv) on 30 June 1852. Electrification of the Simpasture–Carlton section was completed on 1 July 1915, but when ole renewals became necessary in 1934 the line reverted to steam traction. It closed for passengers on 31 March 1952 (Stockton–Ferryhill), and 14 June 1954 (Billingham–Port Clarence).

CLEVELAND RAILWAY

A railway was sanctioned on 23 July 1858 between Guisborough (E of Middlesbrough) and Skinningrove to carry iron ore to the Tees. The first section opened in 1861, and by 1863 the line had reached Brotton. In 1865 it was at Skinningrove, and the final section to Loftus was opened in 1867 by the NER, with which the company had amalgamated under an Act of 5 June 1865. Later there was an end-on junction with the W Riding & Middlesbrough Union Railway (qv) at Loftus. In 1911, ore workings threatened the stability of Kilton Valley viaduct (between Skinningrove and Loftus), and it was cased in an embankment. Passenger traffic to Loftus ceased on 2 May 1960, goods on 12 August 1963.

COLCHESTER, STOUR VALLEY, SUDBURY & HALSTEAD RAILWAY

This 34.75-mile line linked Colchester and Cambridge, though authority (26 June 1846) was given only to the Marks Tey–Sudbury section at first, including the 335 yd Chappel viaduct. Extension to Lavenham, Long Melford and Clare, with a branch from Lavenham to Bury St Edmunds, was sanctioned on 8 June 1847 – the Act also authorized the Ipswich & Bury St Edmunds Railway (qv) to lease it. When the EUR amalgamated with the I&BR, it repudiated the lease, but later, reluctantly, honoured it after all. Formal opening of the line to Sudbury was on 2 July 1849, and on to Haverhill in August 1865, where it joined the Cambridge–Haverhill section, open since 1 June. The company amalgamated with the GER by an Act of 1 July 1898. The East Anglian Railway Museum is established in the goods yard at Chappel & Wakes Colne.

COLNE VALLEY & HALSTEAD RAILWAY

The Chappel–Halstead section was authorized by an Act of 30 June 1856, and an extension to Haverhill by another of 13 August 1859. The line from Chappel to Halstead opened on 16 April 1860, to Castle Hedingham on 1 July 1861, to Yeldham on 29 May 1862 and to Haverhill, where the line was to link with the GER, on 10 May 1863. Agreement was made with the GER in 1862 that it should take over if the company asked – it never did, despite the fact that an OR was appointed in 1874, and the line remained in his hands until 1885. The company remained independent until the Grouping, when it passed to the LNER. The Haverhill–Chappel line

Left Chappel station, once belonging to the Colchester, Stour Valley, Sudbury & Halstead Railway, is now the headquarters of the East Anglian Railway Museum. Near the doors of the GER goods shed stands a newly-restored GE four-wheeled carriage, and while weatherproofing the coachbody in the foreground your author was once stranded on its roof when a strong wind removed his ladder.

Right The Dearness Valley Railway's tortuous link with the Stockton & Darlington Railway at Crook included this timber viaduct at Ushaw Moor. (K.L. Taylor)

closed to passengers on 1 January 1962, though Haverhill station had closed from 14 July 1924. The Colne Valley Railway runs an Education Centre and about a mile of relaid track near Castle Hedingham.

COMMERCIAL RAILWAY

This railway of 3.33 miles in 5 ft gauge ran between the Minories and Blackwall, London, and was authorized on 28 July 1836. On 17 August 1839 a 415 yd extension was sanctioned to a new terminus at Fenchurch Street, and the company became the London & Blackwall Railway (qv).

DARLINGTON & BARNARD CASTLE RAILWAY

Sanctioned on 3 July 1854, this line ran from a junction with the St&DR at Hopetown, N of Darlington, to Barnard Castle, in time becoming part of the cross-Pennine route between Durham and the steelworks of Cumbria (see the SD&LUR). Its first sod was cut on 20 July 1854, it opened on 8 July 1856, and the company amalgamated with the St&DR on 23 July 1858.

DEARNESS VALLEY RAILWAY

Authorized on 30 July 1855 and built along the Dearness Valley, W of Darlington, this short line connected Waterhouses with the E Hedleyhope Colliery. A winding link led to the St&DR at Crook, the route including a timber viaduct at Ushaw Moor. Though nominally independent, 20 per cent of company shares was held by the NER, which took over on 13 July 1857, before the line opened in 1858 to goods. Opening to passengers came on 1 November 1877.

DEESIDE RAILWAY

Incorporated on 16 July 1846 to build 29.5 miles of line from Aberdeen to Aboyne, in 1851 it was decided to build only 14.5 miles to Banchory — a first sod was cut at Park, near Mains of Drum, on 5 July 1852. Formal opening to Banchory was on 7 September 1853 (to the public the next day), and extension to Aboyne was re-authorized as the Deeside Extension Railway (qv). In 1861 the GNSR offered to lease the line but the SNER stopped this with an interdict because it wanted RP to link with a proposed line of its own. However, the SNER then became involved in amalgamating with the CR, and the GNSR leased the line for 999 years wef 1 September 1866. The company obtained powers for the Aboyne & Braemar Railway (qv), and amalgamated with the GNSR wef 31 August 1875 by an Act dated 13 July 1876.

DEESIDE EXTENSION RAILWAY

Though nominally independent, the company was promoted by the Deeside Railway (qv) to extend its line from Banchory to Aboyne. It was authorized on 27 July 1857, and its first sod was cut by the Marchioness of Huntly at Rosehall, near Aboyne, on 3 October 1857. Public opening was on 2 December 1859. The line was leased for 999 years wef 1 Septem-

ber 1866 to the GNSR, which absorbed the company on 31 August 1875 (Act of 13 July 1876).

DENBURN VALLEY RAILWAY
Having bought land in 1847, the GNSR shelved this project until 23 June 1864, when a company was incorporated to extend the GNSR line from Kittybrewster for 1.75 miles through Aberdeen to a station shared with the SNER. This station, basically the one still in use today, was only partly completed when the line opened on 4 November 1867, and the company had to wait until 1899 for powers to rebuild; the GNSR part was not finished until 1908, and it was 1921 before it was completed entirely.

DEVON VALLEY RAILWAY
Incorporated on 23 July 1858, this line extended the Stirling & Dunfermline Railway's (qv) Tillicoultry branch to Kinross via Dollar. It opened on 1 May 1871 and passed to the NBR, an Act of 29 June 1875 ratifying an Agreement to vesting dated 21 October 1874.

DOWNHAM & STOKE FERRY RAILWAY
A line in E Norfolk of just over 7 miles authorized on 24 July 1879, it opened on 1 August 1882 under GER operation, and was absorbed by it wef 1 January 1898 under an Act of 6 August 1897. It closed to passengers on 22 September 1930. The Wissington Tramway (qv — Jt/Ind) branched S at Abbey & West Dereham.

DUMBARTONSHIRE RAILWAYS
This was a Joint Maintenance Committee formed to administer the Caledonian & Dumbartonshire and the Glasgow, Dumbarton & Helensburgh Railways (both qv). Both companies were absorbed by the E&GR on 31 July 1862 (Act of 7 July).

DUNFERMLINE & CHARLESTOWN RAILWAY
Developed out of the Elgin Wagonway (qv), its final main line (opened to passengers in 1834) was 6 miles long between Wellwood, Baldridge and Charlestown Harbour on the N bank of the Firth of Forth. In the 1850s a line was built to join a system serving Halbeath collieries. The company was absorbed by the West of Fife Mineral Railway in 1861, with the Charlestown Railway & Harbour, to become the West of Fife Railway & Harbour (all qv).

DURHAM JUNCTION RAILWAY
The line had been intended to run from the Stanhope & Tyne Railway at Washington to the Hartlepool Dock & Railway Company at Moorsley (both qv), but only attained Rainton Meadows (5.5 miles). Authorized on 16 June 1834, it opened for mineral traffic on 24 August 1838, and to passengers

Fencehouses lies SW of Sunderland, on the route of the Durham Junction Railway. Built circa 1897 to an NER design, a track on the nearside of the box, which had necessitated the overhang, had gone by April 1988, though the box remained a working one.

on 9 March 1840. Its main feature was the four-span Victoria Bridge across the Tyne, opened on 29 June 1838, and named because the final stone was laid on the previous day, Queen Victoria's coronation. Designed by the company's Engineer, T. E. Harrison, it is 811 ft long, its spans 135 ft above high water mark. The company was bought by the N&DJR (sale authorized on 23 May 1844); the company asked £100,000, but was in debt and was constrained to accept Hudson's offer of £88,500.

DURHAM & SUNDERLAND RAILWAY

Authorized on 13 August 1834 to build a line between the two towns, with a branch to Haswell (N&DJR), in the event only the branch (from Hendon, Sunderland) was built, opening on 5 July 1836 (mineral), 30 August (formally). Experiments using windpower were made on the line, speeds of 10 mph being reached. The company was more interested in goods traffic than passengers, and had no concern with steam engines either, at least to begin with. When a connection was made at Haswell, a new station was built, and loco-working probably began soon after. The company was bought by the N&DJR wef 1 January 1847 (Act of 27 July 1846). Passenger services between Sunderland and Hartlepool ceased on 9 June 1952.

EARL OF CARLISLE'S RAILWAY

See Brampton Railway.

EAST & WEST YORKSHIRE JUNCTION RAILWAY

This was conceived as a link between the GNER at Poppleton Junction and the Leeds & Thirsk Railway (qv) at Knaresborough, and was authorized on 16 July 1846. It opened from Poppleton Junction to Hay Park Lane (Knaresborough) on 30 October 1848, and throughout on 1 October 1851, worked by the YN&BR. Amalgamation, however, was with the Y&NMR wef 1 July 1851 (Act of 28 May 1852).

EAST & WEST YORKSHIRE UNION RAILWAYS

Incorporated on 2 August 1883, the company's line ran from Drax (H&BR) to a junction with the GNR at Ardsley. It opened on 19 May 1891, and became a local venture run by the Charlesworth family to serve its collieries; with it the company assumed responsibility for working the S Leeds Junction Railway (qv) from July 1895, which it took over on 2 July 1896. In 1898 workmen's services began along a branch between Robin Hood and Royds Green Lower, authorized by a LRO of 1896. A passenger service between Leeds (Wellington) and Robin Hood, opened on 4 January 1904, proved a disaster and ceased on 30 September. All the company's lines went to the LNER in 1923, and all had been closed by 1966.

EAST ANGLIAN RAILWAYS

This was an amalgamation of the Lynn & Dereham, the Lynn & Ely and the Ely & Huntingdon Railways (all qv), on 22 July 1847. By early 1851, however, the company was bankrupt, and in May the GNR agreed to work the lines for 60 per cent of receipts. The ECR contested this, and by blocking the junction between the systems at Wisbech forced the GNR and EAR to accept its own offer. This became operative on 1 January 1852, and lasted until the company was absorbed by the GER in 1862.

EASTERN & MIDLANDS RAILWAY

This was formed wef 1 July 1883 (Act of 18 August 1882) when the Lynn & Fakenham, the Yarmouth Union, and the Yarmouth & N Norfolk Railways (all qv) combined. A railway works had been established at Melton Constable, a line from there to Norwich (City) opening on 2 December 1882, and to Cromer (Beach) on 16 June 1887. The company absorbed the Midland & Eastern and the Peterborough, Wisbech & Sutton Bridge Railways (both qv) from 1 July 1883, and was itself incorporated into the M&GNJR on 1 July 1893.

The Eastern & Midlands' most easterly station was Yarmouth (Beach). The site is now a car park, but monogrammed spandrels from the station canopy have been retained as a feature. Those at the other end carry the initials of the E&MR's successor at Beach, the M&GNR. (Àllan Mott)

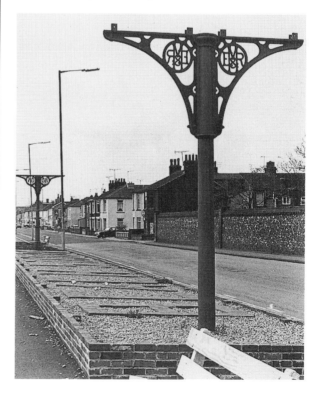

EASTERN COUNTIES RAILWAY

Incorporated on 4 July 1836, it was, at 126 miles between London and Great Yarmouth, the longest line authorized to date, but it built only to Colchester, opening the first section to the public, from Devon Street (Mile End) to Romford, on 20 June 1839. Back to Shoreditch and on to Brentwood were open by 1 July 1840, and the line reached Colchester on 7 March 1843 (goods), 29 March (passengers). Laid to a 5 ft gauge, it was soon converted to standard (September–October 1844), and in that year, wef 1 January, the company leased the Northern & Eastern Railway, extending it to Cambridge. The company took over the Norfolk Railway (both qv) without authority on 8 May 1848, a position not ratified by Parliament until 1849. It absorbed the EAR from 1 January 1852, assumed working of the EUR from 1 January 1854, and absorbed the Newmarket Railway (qv) on 30 March. The company ran these satellites as a single system, earning a reputation for poor and slow service in the process. It was incorporated into the GER on that company's formation in 1862.

EASTERN COUNTIES & THAMES JUNCTION RAILWAY

This was a promotion by G.P. Bidder to link the Eastern Counties Railway with the Thames Docks, and was incorporated on 4 July 1844; it was built by the ECR which had at first scorned the idea! The line opened from Stratford to Thames Wharf on 19 April 1846 and to Canning Town on 29 April, the company being bought by the ECR under an Act dated 9 July 1847. In 1845 the North Woolwich Railway (qv) was authorized to extend this line.

EASTERN UNION RAILWAY

J.C. Cobbold of the Ipswich brewing interest influenced the promotion of this line, and the company was incorporated on 19 July 1844 to build 17 miles of railway between Colchester and Ipswich. This was opened for goods on 1 June 1846, formally on 11 June (a general holiday in Ipswich) and to passengers on 15 June. The company absorbed the Eastern Union & Hadleigh Junction Railway wef 2 January 1847 (Act of 8 June 1847), and the Ipswich & Bury St Edmunds Railway (both qv) by an Act of 9 July. On 12 December 1849 the company gained access to Norwich at Victoria station, and to Bury on 24 December. From 1 January 1854 the ECR took over working without authority, but a WA was ratified on 7 August, and the company was consolidated into the GER in 1862. Norwich (Victoria) closed to passengers on 22 May 1916.

EASTERN UNION & HADLEIGH JUNCTION RAILWAY

This line of 7.5 miles between Bentley and Hadleigh (E of Ipswich), authorized on 18 June 1846, was really an EUR venture to block the ECR route to Norwich. The first sod was cut at Kate's Hill Farm, Hadleigh, on 5 September 1846, and the line opened on 20 August 1847 (formally), 21 August (goods) and 2 September (passengers). A lease by the EUR had been formally agreed before incorporation, but on 26 August 1846 the EUR decided to buy the line outright — this was wef 2 January 1847, and ratified by an Act dated 8 June. The line closed to passengers on 29 February 1932.

Left *Stowmarket station, designed by Frederick Barnes for the Ipswich & Bury St Edmunds Railway, was opened formally on 7 December 1846. It was the Eastern Union Railway which gained, for the companies merged a month later.*

Right *Sibsey (East Lincolnshire Railway) lost its passenger service on 11 September 1961, but the house was still a dwelling in 1987, retaining the characteristic roof and round-topped windows.*

EAST FIFE CENTRAL RAILWAY

Authorized on 24 August 1893, this goods-only line opened from Fife Central Junction (between Cameron Bridge and Leven) to Lochty on 18 August 1898. By then the company had amalgamated with the NBR under an Act of 6 July 1895.

EAST LINCOLNSHIRE RAILWAY

Incorporated on 26 June 1846, this line ran for 47.5 miles from Grimsby to Boston via Louth, opening from Grimsby to Louth on 1 March 1848, to Firsby on 4 September and to Boston on 2 October. To protect its own interests, the Great Grimsby & Sheffield Junction Railway (qv) sought a lease but failed, the lease going to the GNR under an Agreement signed on 2 December 1846, and ratified by Parliament on 9 July 1847. The company retained independence until absorption by the LNER in 1923.

EAST NORFOLK RAILWAY

One of the earliest lines N of Norwich, the original Act (23 June 1864) authorized a line from Whitlingham Junction to N Walsham only; another Act, of 27 June 1872, empowered the 22 miles to Cromer. Whitlingham Junction to N Walsham (14 miles) was opened on 20 October 1874, to Gunton on 29 July 1876 and to Cromer on 26 March 1877. Another extension, 9 miles from Reepham to County School, was authorized on 3 July 1879, and opened on 1 May 1882. An Act of 16 July 1874 gave the GER operating powers between Norwich and N Walsham; the company was absorbed by an Act of 3 June 1881, from 3 August.

EAST OF FIFE RAILWAY

Incorporated on 16 July 1846 for a line from Markinch to Anstruther, it was extended from Leven (Leven Railway, qv) to Kilconquhar, 7 miles away by a further Act of 23 July 1855. It opened on 8 July 1857, the company having TA with the Edinburgh, Perth & Dundee Railway, and merging with the Leven Railway on 22 July 1861 to form the Leven & East Fife Railway (all qv).

EAST SUFFOLK RAILWAY

This was formed from the Halesworth, Beccles & Haddiscoe Railway (qv) on 3 July 1854, when the new company was authorized to take over powers granted on 5 June 1851. The Yarmouth & Haddiscoe and the Lowestoft & Beccles Railways (both qv) were also absorbed under an Act of 23 July 1858. Lines between Saxmundham and Leiston, Wickham Market and Framlingham to Yarmouth (Southtown) and to Snape all opened on 1 June 1859, on which date the ECR took over. An extension from Leiston to Aldeburgh opened on 12 April 1860. The Framlingham branch closed to passengers on 3 November 1952, and the line to Aldeburgh on 12 September 1966, though this remains open for goods to just beyond Leiston.

EDEN VALLEY RAILWAY

This was a link between Kirkby Stephen (SD&LUR) and Clifton (L&CR), S of Penrith. Incorporated on 21 May 1858, the first sod was cut on 4 August at Kirkby Stephen, and the line was opened for minerals on 8 April 1862, and for passengers on 9 June. It was single throughout except at Clifton Junction and for

Halesworth was, until 1859, the terminus of the East Suffolk Railway. In 1922 the platforms were lengthened across a road, and these 'level crossing platforms' were installed. The replacement road bridge, seen beyond, was built in 1958.

a short length between Appleby station and the MR junction. It was worked from the outset by the St&DR, which absorbed it on 1 January 1863 by an Act of 30 June 1862. The line lost its passenger service from 22 January 1962.

EDGEWARE (sic), HIGHGATE & LONDON RAILWAY

Incorporated on 3 June 1862 to build 8.75 miles of single track between Seven Sisters (GNR), Highgate and Edgware, the line was sponsored by the GNR and absorbed on 15 July 1867, just before opening on 22 August. The GNR also supported a project to extend to Watford and link with the L&NWR, but powers obtained in 1864 were allowed to lapse.

EDINBURGH & BATHGATE RAILWAY

Authorized on 3 August 1846, this was the first stage of an alternative route between Edinburgh and Glasgow, from the E&GR's main line near Ratho (Slamannan Railway), and the Wilsontown, Morningside & Coltness Railway (both qv). Opening to Bathgate was on 12 November 1849, and the line, leased to the E&GR for 999 years under the Act of Incorporation, was worked by it from the start. The second stage, to Coatbridge, opened on 11 August 1862 and the line reached Glasgow (College) on 1 April 1871. The company retained its independence, passing to the LNER in 1923.

EDINBURGH & DALKEITH RAILWAY

This line was authorized on 26 May 1826 as a coal-carrying tramway to the 'Scottish' gauge of 4 ft 6 in, linking collieries near Edinburgh with the Firth of Forth at Fisherrow and, later, Leith. Engineered by James Jardine and designed solely for horse traction, except for a gravity-worked incline at St Leonards, it was joined by the Edmonston Waggonway at Newton and opened between St Leonards and Eskbank on 4 July 1831. A branch to Arniston was opened in 1832 and one to Dalkeith in the autumn of 1835 — the line between Niddrie and Leith had opened in March of that year. It was a successful project; the NBR had to pay £113,000 for it, a sale authorized on 21 July 1845 and completed the following October. Horse-drawn until the NBR took over, it was re-gauged and strengthened, re-opening for goods on 7 July 1847 and to passengers on 14 July, though by then merely a branch of the Edinburgh & Hawick Railway (qv). The last passenger train ran on 3 January 1942.

EDINBURGH & GLASGOW RAILWAY

Incorporated on 4 July 1838, this was 46 miles of well-laid-out railway between the cities, though at the approach to Queen Street, Glasgow, it was rope worked at 1 in 42 in order to pass beneath the Forth & Clyde Canal — the notorious Cowlairs incline. The line opened on 21 February 1842, and was extended from Haymarket (Edinburgh) to Waverley Bridge to meet the NBR in a centrally-placed station on 1 August 1846. The company absorbed the Monkland Railways (qv) on 31 July 1865 and was itself absorbed by the NBR next day, both Acts dated 5 July.

EDINBURGH & HAWICK RAILWAY

The NBR at first planned to extend its newly-acquired Edinburgh & Dalkeith Railway to Galashiels, and

An 1842 survival, but not on its original site. This timber and cast-iron trainshed once sheltered E&GR trains at Edinburgh Haymarket, and was moved to Bo'ness, terminus of the Bo'ness & Kinneil Railway, in 1983.

bought out an independent Galashiels Railway project for £1,200 to further this. A few months later the directors decided to head for Hawick — they probably

The loneliness of Falahill, Edinburgh & Hawick Railway. The cottage, still inhabited, marks the summit—to the left of the telegraph pole begins the steep fall towards Edinburgh. To the right, the track-bed (the last train ran on 5 January 1969) climbs from the valley of Gala Water to give access to the cottage.

had Carlisle in mind even then, but funds would not go that far. So the company, incorporated on 31 July 1845, though independent in theory, had £400,000 of its capital supplied by NBR directors in their own names! After authorization, the shares were to carry a 4 per cent guarantee and to be allocated to NBR shareholders. The company was transferred by the NBR (Edinburgh and Dalkeith Purchase) Act of 21 July 1845, ten days before the extension was authorized! The line opened on 1 November 1849.

EDINBURGH & NORTHERN RAILWAY

This was incorporated on 31 July 1845 to build a railway from Burntisland to Perth, but before it opened

the company (which owned the Burntisland–Granton ferries across the Firth of Forth) bought the Edinburgh, Leith & Granton Railway (qv) on 27 July 1847. The company thereupon became the Edinburgh, Perth & Dundee Railway (qv).

EDINBURGH, LEITH & GRANTON RAILWAY

This was authorized on 19 July 1844, when the Edinburgh, Leith & Newhaven Railway (qv) revised its plans and decided to go to Granton instead. Suggestions of a link with the E&GR were greeted with delight, since that concern planned to extend E towards Dunbar and Berwick, and an outlet to Leith without the bother of building it suited the company very well. But the scheme collapsed, and instead the Edinburgh & North Railway (qv), seeking security, bought it by an Act dated 22 July 1847. Trinity to Granton was opened on 19 February 1846, and Scotland Street tunnel on 17 May 1847.

EDINBURGH, LEITH & NEWHAVEN RAILWAY

Authorized on 13 August 1836, this line was to run between the named places but Boardroom battles resulted in a shake-up in 1837. An Act of 1 July 1839 authorized extension to Newhaven and abandonment of the Leith portion, and a line opened from Canonmills to Trinity on 31 August 1842. In 1844, the company was reconstituted as the Edinburgh, Leith & Granton Railway (qv).

EDINBURGH, LOANHEAD & ROSLIN RAILWAY

Incorporated on 20 June 1870, this branch from Millerhill, on the 'Waverley' route, ran 6 miles SW to Roslin. It opened on 23 July 1874 and was extended 2 miles to Glencorse — then known as Glencross — on 2 July 1877. Soon afterwards the NBR, which had worked it from the start, absorbed it wef 1 August 1877, by an Act dated 28 June.

EDINBURGH, PERTH & DUNDEE RAILWAY

Formed on 22 July 1847 by the amalgamation of the Edinburgh, Leith & Granton and the Edinburgh & Northern Railways, (both qv), its line (Burntisland–Cupar opened on 20 September 1847, Leuchars–Ferryport-on-Craig on 17 May 1848) linked the ferries of the Forth and Tay. A new line was opened on 10 June 1861 to avoid the steep route of the Dundee and Newtyle Railway, and the Kinross-shire Railway (both qv) was absorbed on 1 August 1861. The company was itself absorbed by the NBR on 29 July 1862.

EDINBURGH SUBURBAN & SOUTHSIDE RAILWAY

Incorporated on 26 August 1880, its main line ran from St Leonards Junction to Haymarket, and trains could reach Waverley via a spur at Niddrie. Though planned primarily as a goods bypass, it could be, and was, used as a circular passenger route. It opened for goods on 31 October 1884, and to passengers on 1 December, merging with the NBR by an Act of 22 July 1885.

ELGIN WAGONWAY

This 4 ft 3 in gauge wagonway, built on Lord Elgin's land in Fife to link collieries with limeworks, was opened by 1784. Two inclines were engineered by Charles Landale with clever grading of each line between pits and limeworks so that loaded wagons could run downhill in either direction. By the time a Dunfermline branch was added in 1834 the line was already known as the Dunfermline & Charlestown Railway (qv).

ELSENHAM & THAXTED LIGHT RAILWAY

This line, locally promoted and only nominally independent of the GER, was authorized in 1906 by a LRO. Despite a Treasury Grant of £33,000 and the fact that the GER supplied half the capital, it was five years before work began, and even then, at 5 miles 66 chains, it stopped a mile short of Thaxted. The GER worked the line from opening, on 1 April 1913. There was a speed limit of 25 mph, and a rope was carried on the engine for shunting at Sibleys. The line closed to passengers on 15 September 1952, and to goods on 1 June 1953.

ELY & HUNTINGDON RAILWAY

The company had originally applied to build from Ely to Bedford, but on 30 June 1845 Parliament gave powers for a line between the named towns. In effect an extension of the Lynn & Ely Railway, the company, shortly after opening on 17 August 1847, combined with that concern and the Lynn & Dereham Railway (both qv) to form the EAR on 22 July 1847. Since it was isolated from the EAR system, the line was worked at first by the ECR, but when it withdrew, from 1 October 1849, the EAR introduced a horse-drawn tram. The ECR resumed operations on 1 January 1850, and after passing to the GER in 1862, the line became part of the GN&GE Joint system (qv) under an Act of 3 July 1879.

ELY & NEWMARKET RAILWAY

Three schemes failed before this was authorized on 11 August 1875, to run for 12.5 miles between the towns. The line, opened on 1 September 1879, curved N from the Newmarket–Cambridge route at Chippenham Junction; leased by the GER for 999 years at a rent of £5,000 pa wef 1 January 1888 (Agreement of 10 April 1888), it was absorbed under an Act of 1 July 1898.

ELY & ST IVES RAILWAY

Originally the Ely, Haddenham & Sutton Railway

The timber station building at Elsenham (up side). Elsenham & Thaxted trains used the right-hand platform edge, curving sharply past where a parked car may be seen. The Liverpool Street–Cambridge line is on the left.

(qv), the company changed its name when the extension to St Ives opened, on 10 May 1878. It was leased from opening by the GER, which acquired it on 1 July 1898 following an Agreement of 19 July 1897. It closed to passengers on 2 February 1931, except for excursion traffic, which continued until 1957.

ELY, HADDENHAM & SUTTON RAILWAY
The Ely-Sutton section of this line was authorized on 23 June 1864 and opened on 16 April 1866. When an extension to St Ives was authorized on 7 April 1876, the company was also empowered, on opening, to change its title; on 10 May 1878 it did so — see Ely & St Ives Railway.

ESK VALLEY RAILWAY
This short 2.5-mile line, authorized on 21 July 1863, ran from Esk Valley Junction on the Peebles line (NBR) to Lasswade and Polton. The NBR leased the line wef opening (16 July 1867), and absorbed the company by an Act of 13 July 1871, wef 31 July. Passenger traffic ceased on 10 September 1951.

EYEMOUTH RAILWAY
This 3-mile railway from Burnmouth to Eyemouth, authorized by BoT Certificate on 18 August 1884, got off to a slow start — construction finally began in July 1889, and the line opened on 13 April 1891, worked by the NBR. Eyemouth began to develop as a holiday resort, and the company was absorbed by the NBR, under an Act dated 6 August 1900, wef 1 August. Passenger traffic ceased on 5 February 1962.

FELIXSTOWE RAILWAY & DOCK COMPANY
Originally incorporated as the Felixstowe Railway & Pier Company on 19 July 1875, it was renamed on 21 July 1879. The line ran for 13 miles from Felixstowe to Westerfield, W of Ipswich, and opened on 1 May 1877 for goods, and for passengers in June. It was independently worked until 1 September 1879, when the GER took over, finally buying the concern under an Act of 5 July 1887 for £164,000 in shares and £57,000 cash.

FIFE & KINROSS RAILWAY
This 14-mile connection between the EP&DR at Ladybank and Kinross was authorized on 16 July 1855 and opened on 6 June 1857. The company was amalgamated with the EP&DR by an Act of 29 July 1862.

FIRBECK LIGHT RAILWAY
Authorized by a LRO on 22 February 1916, this line ran for 4 miles from Harworth Junction to a colliery at Firbeck, E of Sheffield. Built by the S Yorkshire Joint Line Committee, it opened temporarily in December 1924, and was completed on 1 October 1927.

FORCETT RAILWAY
This short line was authorized on 2 June 1865, and branched S from the Darlington–Barnard Castle line to quarries near Forcett. It was opened in October

1866, worked from the start by the NER, though it retained independence until Grouping. It closed on 2 May 1966.

FORMARTINE & BUCHAN RAILWAY

Authorized on 23 July 1858, the line ran from Dyce (Aberdeen) to Peterhead and Fraserburgh. The GNSR subscribed £50,000 to the project, working the line when it opened to Mintlaw on 18 July 1861, Peterhead on 3 July 1862 and Fraserburgh on 24 April 1865. It duly absorbed it too, by the 'blanket' Act of 30 July 1866.

FORTH BRIDGE RAILWAY

This railway was authorized on 5 August 1873, and was sponsored by the NBR to link their lines on either side of the Firth of Forth. Further powers were granted to the NBR under an Act of 13 July 1876, and although authorized to buy the company (Act of 3 July 1882), it never did so. The bridge was opened ceremonially by the Prince of Wales on 4 March 1890; goods traffic began on that day, passenger the next. Through expresses ran across from 2 June. The company remained technically independent until

A passenger's-eye view of the Forth Bridge from a southbound diesel-hauled train in 1969. (Allan Mott)

Nationalization in 1948, though the line was operated as part of the LNER from 1923.

FORTH & CLYDE JUNCTION RAILWAY

A fairly easily-engineered line of 30 miles 56 chains from Stirling to the Caledonian & Dumbartonshire Railway (qv), it made the first through line between Edinburgh, Glasgow and Loch Lomond. Incorporated on 4 August 1853, it opened between Stirling and Buchlyvie on 18 March 1856, and throughout on 26 May. The company managed its own affairs, but rented space at Stirling from the SCR, which supplied locomotives and men. This arrangement ended on 1 February 1860, and four engines were delivered in 1861. The CR offered terms in 1865, but the company chose independence and, despite a 50-year lease to the NBR wef 1 August 1875, retained it until Grouping. The passenger service ceased between Stirling and Buchlyvie and Gartness and Balloch on 1 October 1934, the remainder on 1 October 1951. Complete closure came wef 5 October 1959.

FRASERBURGH & ST COMBS LIGHT RAILWAY

Authorized under the Light Railways Act on 8 September 1899, this line ran SE along the coast to St Combs from the railhead at Fraserburgh. GNSR-controlled, it opened on 1 July 1903; in 1904 the GNSR ordered two steam railcars for the line, but on delivery one went to the Lossiemouth branch. In October 1910 both were offered for sale, but found no buyer and were broken up. The line closed on 3 May 1965.

FROSTERLEY & STANHOPE RAILWAY

This 2.5-mile line, nominally independent, was sponsored by the St&DR, and was authorized on 28 June 1861, the Act sanctioning WA. An extension of the Wear Valley line, it was transferred to the St&DR on 30 June 1862, having opened for mineral traffic on 30 April. The passenger opening was on 22 October.

GIFFORD & GARVALD LIGHT RAILWAY

A full railway was authorized on 3 July 1891, but in 1898 a LRO was obtained for this 9.25-mile line to Gifford from the NBR's Macmerry branch at Ormiston. Leased by the NBR from opening (14 October 1901), the company remained independent until absorbed by the LNER in 1923. The line closed to passengers on 3 April 1933, and completely on 2 May 1960.

GLASGOW & MILNGAVIE JUNCTION RAILWAY

This was authorized on 1 August 1861 as a nominally independent company, to build from the Glasgow, Dumbarton & Helensburgh Railway (qv) to Milngavie, 3 miles 16 chains away; the Act was actually obtained by the GD&HR. The line opened on 21 May 1863, and the company amalgamated with the NBR under an Act dated 28 July 1873 — it had been worked by that company from the outset.

GLASGOW, BOTHWELL, HAMILTON & COATBRIDGE RAILWAY

Incorporated on 16 July 1874, the line ran from Shettleston, on the NBR's Coatbridge line, to Hamilton, with a branch from Hamilton Castle to the NBR at Whifflet. It opened between Shettleston and Hamilton on 1 November 1877 (goods) and 1 April 1878 (passengers), and the branch opened on 1 November 1878 (goods), 1 May 1879 (passengers); it began operating independently but had to call the NBR to assist by mid-1878. It was absorbed by that company on 2 August 1878, under an Act dated 21 July.

GLASGOW CITY & DISTRICT RAILWAY

Sanctioned on 10 August 1882 as 2.5 miles of NBR-sponsored line linking its routes to E and W of Glasgow via Queen Street (Low Level), it was only the fourth underground line in Britain, and became notorious for its smokiness. The main line opened on 15 March 1886, with a spur to Hyndland, and another joined the Helensburgh line on 1 August making through journeys to the coast possible. It was worked from the start by the NBR, which absorbed it on 1 August 1887 under an Act of 5 July.

GLASGOW, DUMBARTON & HELENSBURGH RAILWAY

Authorized on 14 August 1855, a locally-promoted revival of earlier schemes, this planned to leave the E&GR at Cowlairs, looping via Maryhill to the Caledonian & Dumbartonshire Railway (qv) at Bowling. Just before opening (28 May 1858), however, the company fell out with the E&GR, and the CR offered better terms. This arrangement lasted until 30 June 1858, when the E&GR improved its offer and the company returned to Queen Street, more convenient anyway. A Committee to manage the line was formed with the C&DR, known as the Dumbartonshire Railways (qv). The company was absorbed by the E&GR on 31 July 1862, under an Act dated 7 July.

GLASGOW, YOKER & CLYDEBANK RAILWAY

This short, single-track line, authorized on 4 July 1878, and opened on 1 December 1882, linked the Stobcross branch of the NBR with a new Clydebank shipyard, which later became John Brown's. A new line to the shipyard was authorized on 5 August 1891, and an extension to Dalmuir on 27 July 1893. The company amalgamated with the NBR by an Act dated 15 July 1897.

GREAT CENTRAL RAILWAY

The Act for the MS&LR's London Extension was passed on 28 March 1893, though the company did

The seal of the Great Central Railway—could the thistles imply a hoped-for Scottish extension too? (NRM)

not change its provincial name until 1 August 1897, just before opening, on 26 July 1898 (coal), 9 March 1899 (formal), 15 March (passengers) and 11 April (goods). It ran from Annesley (Nottingham) to the MetR at Quainton Road, but before it got there relations between the companies had soured. However, by a link from Grendon Underwood to Ashendon, the company joined the GWR's route to Birmingham and was able to reach Marylebone via High Wycombe (see Great Western & Great Central Joint Railway — Jt/Ind).

GREAT EASTERN RAILWAY

This was formed on 7 August 1862, its constituents being the ECR, EAR, NR, EUR, Newmarket Railway and ESR, plus several smaller concerns. As successor to the ECR it began expunging that company's bad record, but a difficult inherited situation brought in an OR on 2 July 1867. On the appointment of Lord Cranbourne as Chairman in 1868, things began to improve, and the company never looked back. The GE Metropolitan Station & Railways Company had been formed on 31 December 1863 to extend to a new station at Liverpool Street — this opened for suburban traffic on 2 February 1874 and completely on 1 November 1875, when Bishopsgate, the former terminus, became a goods depot. A joint line to the Nottinghamshire coalfields via March and Spalding was planned with the GNR in 1879 — it opened in 1882, run by the GN&GEJC (qv). A scheme to combine the GER and GNR in 1909 was opposed by anti-monopolists; the Bill was withdrawn, leaving the

Left *Platform furniture was often embellished with a monogram of the owning company. This GER seat sees daily use at Elsenham, Essex.*

Below *Lewis Cubitt's GNR terminus at King's Cross has changed little since its opening in 1852, although the iron and glass canopy has been replaced by a larger (and more practical) modern one. Do the flags flying in opposite directions perhaps symbolize the railways' perennial efforts to satisfy all of the people all of the time?* (Allan Mott)

company to become a constituent of the LNER in 1923.

GREAT GRIMSBY & SHEFFIELD JUNCTION RAILWAY

The company was incorporated on 30 June 1845 with little opposition, largely through Sheffield business interests but also supported by Grimsby Haven Company. The first line ran from Gainsborough to Grimsby via Brigg, the easiest of three routes though not the most populous. On 26 June 1846, branches were authorized to Lincoln, Cleethorpes, Caistor, Newark, Horncastle and Barton-on-Humber. Opening to New Holland was on 1 March 1848, with Ulceby–Brigg and Barnetby–Market Rasen following on 1

November, and Lincoln on 18 December. Barton opened on 1 March 1849, Brigg–Gainsborough on 2 April 1850, Gainsborough–Woodhouse Junction on 16 July and the loop through Lincoln on 7 August. From 1 January 1847 the company amalgamated with the Sheffield & Lincolnshire Junction, the Sheffield & Lincolnshire Extension and the Stalybridge, Ashton-under-Lyne & Manchester Railways (all qv) to form the MS&LR.

GREAT NORTHERN RAILWAY

Incorporated on 26 June 1846, the main constituents were the London & York and the Direct Northern schemes: authorized was a line from London to York via Grantham, Retford and Doncaster, with a loop

from Peterborough to Bawtry via Boston and Lincoln. Total mileage was 285.25 and authorized capital £5,600,000, both figures then a record for a single Railway Act. Peterborough–Lincoln opened on 17 October 1848, and Retford–Doncaster on 4 September 1849, but the Grantham line was delayed in construction. London (Maiden Lane) to Peterborough was opened on 7 August 1850, and Peterborough–Retford for goods on 15 July 1852 and for passengers on 1 August. King's Cross opened on 14 October 1852. George Hudson, having fought the Bill by both fair means and foul, offered part of a Burton Salmon (Y&NMR)–Knottingley (Wakefield, Pontefract & Goole Railway, qv) line to the company as a ready-made link to York. Though impoverished, the company accepted only reluctantly, and an Agreement with the Y&NMR was confirmed on 29 November 1850. Hudson's company could now run through to Doncaster, but perhaps the GNR had the last laugh, for it survived to join the LNER at Grouping.

GREAT NORTHERN & GREAT EASTERN JOINT COMMITTEE

This was formed on 3 July 1879, after incredible wrangling, from the following lines: Huntingdon–St Ives, Needingworth Junction (St Ives)–March, March–Spalding, and Lincoln–Black Carr Junction (Doncaster). The first two were GER-owned, the latter two GNR. A length of new joint railway was built to link Spalding and Lincoln, and this opened for goods on 1 July 1882, and to passengers on 1 August. The Ramsey & Somersham Railway (qv) was bought by an Act of 20 July 1896, and the total mileage controlled in 1903 was 123. All passed to the LNER in 1923.

GREAT NORTH OF ENGLAND RAILWAY

An Act of 4 July 1836 authorized a line only from Newcastle to Croft, 5 miles S of Darlington — a second (12 July 1837) cleared the way to York. The first sod was cut near Croft on 25 November 1837 and in 1839 the Croft branch of the St&DR was bought, though only the N end was used. The line opened on 1 January 1841 (minerals), 30 March (passengers), and its route at the S end is virtually unchanged today. The N end was incomplete when powers were transferred to the N&DJR under an Act of 27 July 1846 — the company itself remained independent until 1850. A branch to Richmond was authorized on 21 July 1845; it opened on 10 September 1846 and closed on 3 March 1969. It was used by Vincent Raven for trials with an electrically-operated fog-signalling system, used by the NER from August 1911.

GREAT NORTH OF ENGLAND, CLARENCE & HARTLEPOOL JUNCTION RAILWAY

This 8.5-mile line was authorized on 3 July 1837 to link the three lines in its title, by building from Wingate (Hartlepool Dock & Railway) to Ferryhill (Clarence Railway), crossing the GNER *en route* (all qv). Unfortunately, the Act omitted to stipulate a crossing of the Clarence line, and that company delayed all it could, even after powers had been obtained. The line opened from Wingate to Kelloe Bank on 18 March 1839, and to Ferryhill in October 1846; it was leased to the YN&BR by an Act of 22 July 1848, the lease being transferred to the NER on its absorption of the smaller concern. The company, however, remained alive until the Grouping.

The GNER station at Richmond, Yorks, dates from the line's opening in 1846, and though it lost its trains in 1969, it is well-preserved, retaining many original features. Instead of passengers it now houses a firm of garden suppliers.

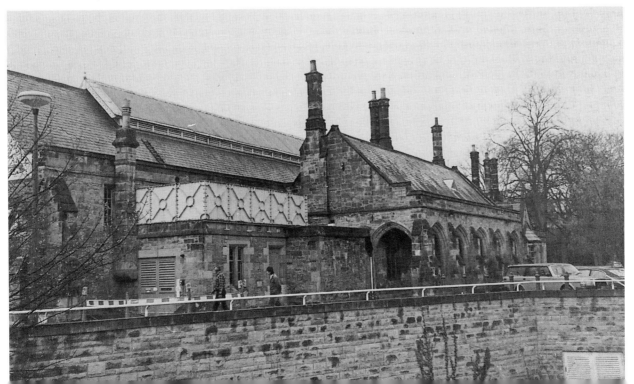

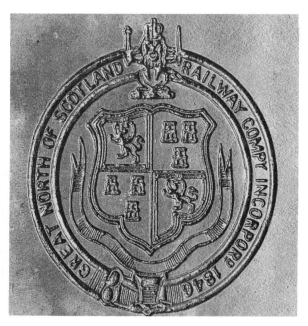

The seal of the Great North of Scotland Railway. (NRM)

GREAT NORTH OF SCOTLAND RAILWAY

Incorporated on 26 June 1846 to build a line from Aberdeen to Huntly, shortage of money meant nothing was done until eventually a first sod was cut by Lady Elphinstone, wife of the Chairman, at Oyne, about 8 miles NW of Inverurie, on 25 November 1852. A line opened from Kittybrewster to Huntly on 12 September 1854 (goods), 19 September (formal), 20 September (public), and a station at Aberdeen (Waterloo) was opened to passengers on 1 April 1856. In July 1855 the company obtained powers to extend to Keith, and a line opened on 11 October 1856. On 30 July 1866 authority to amalgamate its Northern branches was given, and also to lease the Deeside Railway (qv) wef 1 September for 999 years. The Banffshire (1867), the Deeside and the Deeside Extension (1875), and the Aboyne & Braemar Railways (1876) were absorbed, and likewise the Morayshire Railway (all qv) in 1881. A 1906 scheme for amalgamation with the HR was dropped after HR objections, and the company survived to become a constituent of the LNER at the Grouping.

GREAT YARMOUTH & STALHAM LIGHT RAILWAY

This was sanctioned on 26 July 1876 as a LR between the towns, one of the few authorities under the Regulation of Railways Act of 1868. It opened from Yarmouth to Ormesby on 7 August 1877, and to Hemsby on 16 May 1878. An extension from Stalham to N Walsham was authorized on 27 May 1878, when the company was renamed the Yarmouth & N Norfolk Light Railway (qv).

GRIMSBY DISTRICT LIGHT RAILWAY

Authorized on 15 January 1906 and built by the GCR, it was used from May 1906 as a contractor's line, before opening to the public on 3 January 1910 between Grimsby (Pyewipe Road) and Immingham. The line had a triangular connection with the Great Grimsby Street Tramways at Victoria Street and the Great Coates branch at Pyewipe. Used mainly by commuting dockers, the service began with a steam railcar, but this was superseded by electric cars in 1912. The LNER re-christened it the Grimsby & Immingham Electric Railway (qv).

GRIMSBY & IMMINGHAM ELECTRIC RAILWAY

The GCR called it the Grimsby & District Electric Railway in its timetables, but it officially became the above. It was never incorporated, and its line ran parallel with the Grimsby District LR (qv) on its W for 5 miles 50 chains from Corporation Bridge to Immingham, crossing the GCR's Great Coates branch near Cleveland Bridge. When it opened, on 15 May 1912, the steam railcar service on the GDLR ceased. An extension into the dock estate opened on 17 November 1913, but was never regularly used.

HALESWORTH, BECCLES & HADDISCOE RAILWAY

Incorporated on 5 June 1851, this company became the nucleus of the ESR on 3 July 1854. The line, from Beccles to Haddiscoe, opened on 4 December 1854, worked from the start by the ECR.

HALIFAX, THORNTON & KEIGHLEY RAILWAY

Authorized on 5 August 1873, this line extended the Bradford & Thornton Railway (qv), and was built by the firm which had made the high-level section of the Settle & Carlisle line. The HT&KR is probably the most spectacularly engineered route in the W Riding: almost half of it was in tunnel, and it became known as the 'Alpine Route' among GNR enginemen. It opened from Thornton to Denholme on 3 September 1882 (goods) and 1 January 1884 (passengers), and throughout on 1 April 1884 (goods) and 1 November (passengers). Queensbury tunnel was the longest on the GNR until Ponsbourne (Hertford, 2,864 yd) was opened on 4 March 1918, and Queensbury was the only station in England other than Ambergate to have platforms on a triangle, individually connected. Sponsored by the GNR, it controlled the line from the start.

HARTLEPOOL DOCK & RAILWAY

An Act of 1 June 1832 authorized a line from Hartlepool to Moorsley, 14 miles, with branches to Pittington, Thornley and Cassop, but Moorsley, Cassop and Pittington were not attained. What did open, on 1 January 1835, was a line to Thornley Col-

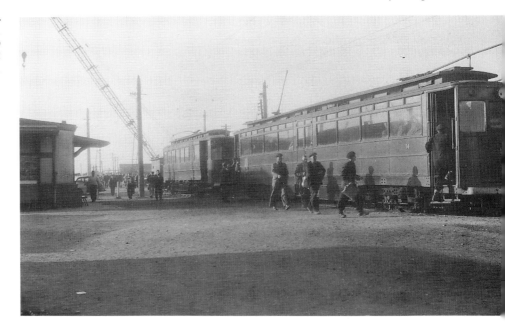

Going-home time on the Grimsby & Immingham Electric Railway— workers hurry from the docks on 29 September 1959 to board Cars 14 (nearest the camera) and 32. (J.H. Price)

liery, followed on 23 November by one between Hartlepool and Haswell. Leased to the YN&BR wef 1 July 1846, the company amalgamated with the NER on 13 July 1857. It closed to the public from 16 June 1947, though a school service ran until 23 March 1964.

HATFIELD & ST ALBANS RAILWAY

This line was incorporated on 30 June 1862, and though supported by the GNR to the tune of £20,000, trouble was experienced raising money for its 5 miles 76 chains, which linked the GNR line at Hatfield with St Albans. It opened on 16 October 1865, however, and in view of the support it is perhaps surprising that the GNR did not take over earlier. Offered the company early in 1882, it declined, but then altered its mind, absorbing it wef 1 November 1883, under an authorizing Act of 16 July. First instalment of the purchase price of £31,500 was paid on 2 November 1883, the balance (£20,000) on 15 February 1884.

HERTFORD & WELWYN JUNCTION RAILWAY

A line of 7 miles 30 chains was authorized between the towns on 3 July 1854; it opened on 1 March 1858, worked jointly by the GNR and ECR. An amalgamation on 28 June 1858 with the Luton, Dunstable & Welwyn Junction Railway formed the Hertford, Luton & Dunstable Railway (both qv).

HERTFORD, LUTON & DUNSTABLE RAILWAY

This was formed on 28 June 1858 by the union of the Luton, Dunstable & Welwyn Junction Railway with the Hertford & Welwyn Junction Railway (both qv),

to give 17 miles of railway between Luton and Hertford. An Agreement was made that the GNR should pay the ECR a proportion of the bookings for London–Hertford journeys, and this remained in force until 1860, when the company requested termination on completion of the Luton–Welwyn section. A connecting line at Welwyn was opened on 1 September 1860; all working was then handed to the GNR, and formal absorption followed on 12 June 1861.

HEXHAM & ALLENDALE RAILWAY

Authorized on 19 June 1865 to build a line 12.25 miles long, the NER and Greenwich Hospital were both permitted to subscribe. It opened for goods on 13 January 1868, and to passengers on 1 March 1869. An extension to Allenheads was authorized but not built, and in fact until 1898 the 'main' line ended at a station known as Catton Road because it was nearer to Catton than Allendale. The company was dissolved and vested in the NER by an Act of 13 July 1876 — the line closed to passengers on 22 September 1930, and to goods in November 1950.

HORNCASTLE RAILWAY

Incorporated as the Horncastle & Kirkstead Railway, the company took its new title on 10 July 1854. It was a 7-mile line between Woodhall Junction and Horncastle which opened for light goods on 11 August 1855 and general traffic (presumably including passengers) on 26 September. It was one of the few Lincolnshire lines which actually paid — investors had a regular 7 or 8 per cent. Although the line was worked by the GNR from the outset, and that company requested a take-over in 1920, the company asked too much, and it remained independent until 1923.

Left *Horncastle station was opened in 1855, but by the 1930s had a very GNR look. The Sheffield Telegraph, advertised on the wall behind the buffers, seems to have had a wider influence than one might expect.* (Douglas Thompson)

Below left *The seal of the Hull & Barnsley Railway.* (NRM)

HULL & BARNSLEY RAILWAY

Incorporated on 26 August 1880 as the Hull, Barnsley & W Riding Junction Railway & Dock Company, the name was changed to the simpler version on 30 June 1905. The company tried to break the area's NER monopoly; docks at Hull opened on 16 July 1885, and the line was open for goods on 20 July, and to passengers on 27 July, but there was soon financial trouble, and amalgamation with either the MR or NER was proposed. The Great War brought more business, but the company joined the NER wef 1 April 1922 as a prelude to the Grouping. The company's shed at Springfield (Hull) did major repairs to its own locomotives until 1923, though they went to Doncaster after that. Light repairs continued into BR days, closure coming on 1 December 1958.

HULL & HOLDERNESS RAILWAY

Incorporated on 8 July 1853, the company formally opened its 17.5-mile line from Withernsea to Hull on 26 June 1854, and to the public the next day. It was allowed to use the Y&NMR station at Victoria Docks, but since that company stopped using it for passengers in November 1854, had sole use thereafter. From 1 January 1860 the line was worked by the NER, being dissolved and vested in it on 7 July 1862. It closed to passengers on 19 October 1964.

HULL & HORNSEA RAILWAY

Nominally independent, this line was authorized on 30 June 1862. It presented no engineering problems, was worked by the NER from opening (28 March 1864) and absorbed under an Act of 16 July 1866. Wassand (known as Goxhill until 1904) was one of the last 'Market Day Only' stations in the NE — it opened in 1865 for one day a week for a single train in each direction until it closed in 1953. The line closed to passenger traffic on 19 October 1964.

HULL & SELBY RAILWAY

When a proposed Leeds & Hull line was curtailed to the Leeds–Selby section (see Leeds & Selby Railway), the people of Hull realized that if they wanted a railway they would have to get it for themselves. Their line, authorized on 21 June 1836, ran for 31 straight, almost level miles along the N bank of the Humber, opening formally on 1 July 1840, and to the public the next day. But it did not have Hull to itself for long — the line was worked by the Y&NMR from 1 July 1845 until 27 July 1846, when the WA became a lease in perpetuity. The lease continued until the NER completed purchase of the line on 1 March 1872 under terms in the same Act.

HULL & SOUTH YORKSHIRE EXTENSION RAILWAY

Like the S Yorkshire Junction Railway (qv), this line, incorporated on 6 August 1897, also began at Wrangbrook Junction (between Upton and Kirk Smeaton, H&BR). It ran 8.5 miles S to Wath, and opened on 31 March 1902 for goods, 23 August for passengers. The company amalgamated with the H&BR on 25 July 1898, and the line closed to passengers on 6 April 1929.

HUMBER COMMERCIAL RAILWAY & DOCK

Incorporated on 22 July 1904, this line ran to Immingham from the New Holland line N of Ulceby, and opened on 29 June 1910 — an Agreement of 15 June 1904 bound the company to lease itself to the Grimsby District LR (qv) for 999 years from completion. Connections with the GDLR meant that the line was the main access to Immingham. It also connected with the Barton & Immingham LR (qv), which it absorbed in 1912. A line to the E jetty was opened on 15 May of that year.

HUNSLET RAILWAY

Incorporated on 27 July 1893, this goods-only line ran from Beeston Junction (GNR) to the Hunslet branch of the NER, 3.75 miles in all. It amalgamated with the GNR on 3 July 1894, exactly five years before it opened. Closure to Hunslet was on 3 January 1966, though the Beeston Junction–Parkside section lasted until 3 July 1967.

HUNSTANTON & WEST NORFOLK RAILWAY

Formed wef 1 July 1874 by an Act of 8 June, this combined the Lynn & Hunstanton and the W Norfolk Junction Railways (both qv). The resulting 33.75-mile line was itself absorbed by the GER, which had worked it from the start, under an Act of 22 May 1890, wef 1 July.

HYLTON, SOUTHWICK & MONKWEARMOUTH RAILWAY

The aim of this 4.5-mile line, incorporated on 25 May 1871, was to develop industry along the N bank of the Wear. It joined the NER at each end and was worked by that company from the start — its first sod was cut in 1872, and it opened on 1 July 1876. Financially, however, it was not a viable concern, and it was vested in the NER from 20 June 1883.

IDLE & SHIPLEY RAILWAY

A line of '. . . about 2 miles and 2.5 furlongs . . .', it was authorized on 12 August 1867 to continue the Bradford, Eccleshill & Idle Railway (qv). The GNR agreed to find most of the capital, in fact finding it all when local efforts failed to raise it. Powers were officially taken over by an Act of 24 July 1871, and the line opened for goods in August 1874, passengers on 15 April 1875. Much Idle Moor stone found its way around the country via the 1 in 60 down to Shipley, some rather more quickly than its proprietors would have wished. The line closed to goods on 7 October 1968, and to passengers on 2 February 1931.

INVERGARRY & FORT AUGUSTUS RAILWAY

There was much wheeling and dealing for the right

Wolferton station was opened in 1862 by the Lynn & Hunstanton Railway, becoming part of the Hunstanton & West Norfolk Railway in 1874. It was used by many visitors, royal and otherwise, to nearby Sandringham House. (Allan Mott)

to make a line along the Great Glen, even the NBR wanting a finger in the pie. In the event, an independent company, incorporated on 14 August 1896, built from Spean Bridge (West Highland Railway, qv) to Fort Augustus, but the line cost so much that no money was left for rolling-stock. The company appealed to the WHR, which offered to work it at cost. It was then offered to the HR, which was authorized to work it for ten years at £4,000 pa; it opened on 22 July 1903, but it was inconveniently separate from the HR system. The HR withdrew on 1 May 1907 in favour of the NBR, which worked the line for four years, closing it on 31 October 1911. Re-opened on 1 August 1913, the NBR finally bought it the following year. The passenger service was suspended wef 1 December 1933, the line closing completely from 1 January 1947.

INVERURIE & OLD MELDRUM RAILWAY
Incorporated on 15 June 1855 as a nominally independent branch of the GNSR, this line ran 4.75 miles between the two towns. The GNSR subscribed £2,000 and worked it at prime cost – the official opening was on 26 June 1856, to the public on 1 July. It did not retain independence long, for it was leased to the GNSR under an Act of 14 June 1858 (wef 1 September 1857), and was absorbed under an Act of 30 July 1866.

IPSWICH & BURY ST EDMUNDS RAILWAY
This 26.25-mile line was incorporated on 21 July 1845 to link the towns with a line running via Stowmarket. The first sod was cut on 1 August 1845, and the line opened from Haughley (EUR) to Bury for goods on 30 November 1846, formally on 7 December and for passengers on Christmas Eve. The company had powers to lease or sell to the EUR, the two lines being worked as one from 1 January 1847. Amalgamation was ratified on 9 July 1847.

JEDBURGH RAILWAY
This 7 miles 10 chains branch from Roxburgh (NBR) was authorized on 25 May 1855, promoted privately and using the E bank of the Teviot and Jed Water. Opened on 17 July 1856, it was worked by the NBR, which absorbed it formally on 31 July 1860 (Act of 3 July). Heavy rain during the week to 12 August 1948 damaged the track so much that it was closed to passengers at once.

KEITH & DUFFTOWN RAILWAY
Incorporated on 27 July 1857, this line (8.5 miles) was backed by the GNSR and built primarily to serve distillers in Strathspey. It opened on 21 February 1862, and the Strathspey Railway (qv), opened the following year, extended it. The line was absorbed by the GNSR under its Act of 30 July 1866.

Much of the station designed by Sancton Wood for the Ipswich & Bury St Edmunds Railway at Bury has survived, though the trainshed was removed in the last quarter of the nineteenth century. It still serves the line between the Midlands and the East Anglian ports. (Allan Mott)

KELVEDON, TIPTREE & TOLLESBURY PIER LIGHT RAILWAY

More familiarly known as the Kelvedon & Tollesbury Railway, or the 'Crab and Winkle' line, it was authorized by a LRO on 29 January 1901, confirmed on 27 February. The line took until 1904 to cover the 8 miles 35 chains to Tollesbury from Kelvedon (GER), opening without ceremony in heavy rain on 1 October. The final 1.5 miles to Tollesbury Pier opened on 15 May 1907. The GER, somewhat reluctantly, agreed to work the line from the start, and thanks to jam from Tiptree and crabs, winkles and oysters (110,000 oysters once left Tollesbury on a single day) achieved a reasonable return. As an economy, passenger services on the Tollesbury Pier section closed on 17 July 1921, and in 1923 the company became part of the LNER.

KELVIN VALLEY RAILWAY

Promoted locally and authorized on 21 July 1873 to run 11.75 miles NE from Maryhill on the outskirts of Glasgow, the NBR built the first section mainly to thwart any CR ideas about encroaching on what it considered its own preserve. It was persuaded into building the next section also, but managed to show that a service was not needed along the whole valley.

Ex-Wisbech & Upwell Tramway carriage, GER No 7, on 13 May 1950 during service as WE 60461 on the Kelvedon & Tollesbury LR. This carriage, the only surviving W&UT vehicle, is now being restored at the Rutland Railway Museum, Cottesmore. (J.H. Aston)

The Glasgow–Kilsyth service via Lenzie opened on 1 June 1878, and the link to Maryhill for goods on 1 June 1879. A connection with the NBR at Maryhill was opened on 1 October 1879, and amalgamation with that company was wef 1 August 1885, by an Act of 22 July. The Maryhill–Kilsyth service ceased on 31 March 1951 and that from Kirkintilloch on 4 August.

KILTONTHORPE RAILWAY

This private, mile-long line was built by J.T. Wharton for mineral traffic, S from the Cleveland Railway (qv) at Kiltonthorpe Junction. It opened on 11 June 1873, and was bought by the NER on 16 July 1874.

KINCARDINE & DUNFERMLINE RAILWAY

This line of 2 miles 10 furlongs was authorized on 12 August 1898 and linked NBR lines at each end, opening on 2 July 1906. The company had but a brief independence, amalgamating with the NBR before Grouping.

KINROSS-SHIRE RAILWAY

Authorized on 10 August 1857, this line ran for 7 miles from the Dunfermline branch of the EP&DR to the Fife & Kinross Railway (qv) at Kinross. It opened on 20 June 1860, and the company was absorbed by the EP&DR by an Act of 1 August 1861.

KIRKCALDY & DISTRICT RAILWAY

Authorized on 16 July 1883 as the Seafield Dock & Railway, this was an 8-mile line from Edinburgh to a

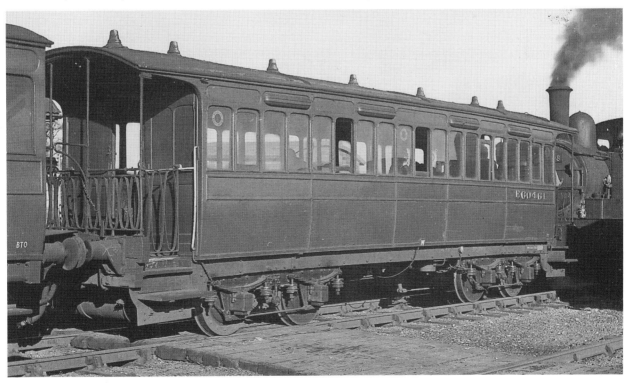

dock at Kirkcaldy. The company changed its title by an Act of 5 July 1888, and an Act of 4 August 1890 authorized eight extensions in Fifeshire. Another, from Kingshorn to Abbotshall, was sanctioned on 5 August 1895 but the company had by then merged with the NBR under an Act of 6 July 1895.

LANCASHIRE, DERBYSHIRE & EAST COAST RAILWAY

The company was incorporated on 5 August 1891 to build 170 miles of railway on which it was empowered to spend £5m, from docks on the Manchester Ship Canal, via Manchester, Buxton, Sheffield and Lincoln, to Sutton-on-Sea, where there was to be a new dock. The only section actually built was from Chesterfield to Lincoln, opened on 8 March 1897, and a branch to Beighton opened for goods on 28 May 1900, and to passengers on 30 May. The GER backed the line as access to the Notts coalfield, subscribing three-quarters of the £320,000 raised in exchange for RP, actually little-used. The W section was abandoned in 1895, but the company kept its title for prestige; railwaymen often referred to it as the 'Clay and Knocker'. Col Yorke of the BoT said it was one of the best-constructed lines he had inspected. It was bought by the GCR wef 1 January 1907, under an Act of 20 July 1906.

LAUDER LIGHT RAILWAY

Confirmation of a LRO was dated 30 June 1898, and resulted in a 10.25-mile line from Fountainhall Junction (Edinburgh & Hawick Railway, qv) to Lauder; it opened 2 July 1901, leased to the NBR from the outset. It retained independence, however, going in 1923 to the LNER. Passenger traffic ceased on 12 September

1932, and serious flood damage on 12 August 1948 caused suspension of goods traffic. It re-opened on 20 November 1950, to close finally on 1 October 1958.

LEADBURN, LINTON & DOLPHINTON RAILWAY

This line, authorized on 3 June 1862, was intended to develop the country E of Leadburn (S of Edinburgh). Running SE for 10 miles from the Peebles Railway (qv), it reached Dolphinton via Linton (later rechristened Broomlee), and opened on 4 July 1864. It merged with the NBR by an Act of 16 July 1866. Passenger services ceased from 1 April 1933.

LEEDS & SELBY RAILWAY

This grew from an 1824 scheme for a line from Hull to Liverpool. A survey was made by James Walker, incorporation was on 1 June 1830, restricted to the Leeds–Selby section, and work began on 1 October. The line opened for passengers on 22 September 1834, to goods on 15 December. At first its 20 miles were isolated, but on 29 May 1839 it joined the Y&NMR at York Junction (Milford), now Gascoigne Road. George Hudson realized that the company could threaten his growing empire, and offered a lease on irresistible terms, £17,000 pa for 31 years, with an option to buy; it was accepted wef 9 November 1840, and confirmed by an Act of 6 April 1841. Hudson later bought the company for £210,000, the transaction being ratified by Parliament on 23 May 1844, wef the date of payment.

LEEDS & THIRSK RAILWAY

By the time its first sod was cut, the company, incorporated in 21 July 1845, was planning to expand N to other lines. Over the next few years it did so, opening

Left Wide eaves characterize many railway buildings, and are well displayed on the original Leeds & Thirsk Railway station house at Thirsk. By 1988, some downstairs windows and the chimneys had been modified, but the house survives, albeit purveying Bed & Breakfast instead of tickets.

Right The line from Harrogate (Starbeck) across Knaresborough viaduct and past this unusual signal box was opened by the Leeds Northern Railway in 1851. The box was still in use on 16 May 1988. (Allan Mott)

between Ripon and Thirsk for minerals on 5 January 1848, formally on 31 May, and to the public the next day. Weeton–Wormald Green opened on 1 September 1848, with the line on to Ripon following on 13 September. Construction of Bramhope tunnel delayed the final section into Leeds, but this was completed on 9 July 1849. On 3 July 1851 the company changed its name to the Leeds Northern Railway (qv).

LEEDS, BRADFORD & HALIFAX JUNCTION RAILWAY

This line, sanctioned on 30 June 1852 initially from Bowling Junction, Bradford (L&YR), to Leeds Junction, formed a useful route by which the GNR could enter Leeds, and that company was duly authorized to work it. The line opened on 1 August 1854 (passengers), 7 August (goods). Another 10.25 miles between Laister Dyke and Ardsley (authorized on 4 August 1853) opened throughout on 10 October 1857, and 3 miles to Batley on 1 November 1864. The company became dissatisfied with the GNR's handling of its service, so it acquired locomotives and took over working from 1 January 1859. On 5 July 1865, however, an Act empowered absorption by the GNR, wef 5 September 1865.

LEEDS, CASTLEFORD & PONTEFRACT JUNCTION RAILWAY

Incorporated on 21 July 1873 for 8.25 miles of railway between the towns, the NER was authorized to subscribe not less than three-quarters of the total capital of £160,000. Powers were transferred to the NER (Act of 13 July 1876), which opened the Garforth–Castleford section (6.5 miles) to passengers on 12 August 1878. It had already been opened for goods.

LEEDS NORTHERN RAILWAY

This was the title taken on 3 July 1851 by the Leeds & Thirsk Railway (qv). The company was short-lived, however, for after opening lines from Starbeck (Harrogate) to Knaresborough on 4 August 1851, and from Melmerby to Stockton on 31 May 1852, it was dissolved by the NER Act of 31 July 1854 and vested in the YN&BR; this then became a constituent of the NER.

LESLIE RAILWAY

Incorporated on 7 July 1857 to build a 4.5-mile line between Markinch (Fife) and Leslie, its total length, with two short branches, was 6.25 miles. Opened on 1 December 1861, and worked by the Edinburgh, Perth & Dundee Railway (qv), it was absorbed under an NBR Act of 18 July 1872.

LEVEN RAILWAY

Incorporated on 17 June 1852 to build a 6-mile line from Markinch (Fife) to Burnmill, it opened on 3 July 1854. On 22 July 1861 the company amalgamated with the East of Fife Railway (qv); both were dissolved and reconstituted as the Leven & East of Fife Railway (qv).

LEVEN & EAST OF FIFE RAILWAY

This was formed on 22 July 1861 by the re-incorporation of the Leven and the East of Fife Railways (both qv). A branch to Wemyss was authorized on 16 July 1866, and another to Anstruther opened on 1 September 1863. The company was absorbed wef 1 August 1877 by the NBR under an Act dated 28 June.

LIVERPOOL, ST HELENS & SOUTH LANCASHIRE RAILWAY

This was created on 26 July 1889 when the St Helens & Wigan Junction Railway changed its name. Before opening (to goods on 1 July 1895 and passengers on 3 January 1900), the new company doubled the previously laid single track. It was absorbed by the GCR wef 1 January 1906 under an Act dated 4 August 1905.

LONDON & BLACKWALL RAILWAY

First incorporated as the Commercial Railway (qv), the company took a new name on 17 August 1839; it was also often known as the Blackwall Railway. Originally worked by cable and gravity, the line was converted for locomotives and to standard gauge as a corollary of a link with the ECR. A new station to replace Minories (near the Tower of London) was opened at Fenchurch Street on 2 August 1841, and an extension to Bow Junction from Stepney, authorized on 27 July 1846, opened on 2 April 1849. The company partially owned the Millwall Extension Railway (qv) and other dock lines. After widening to Stepney, the line was worked by the LT&SR until leased to the GER from 1 January 1866. The L&NWR, GNR and MR were granted RP, but the company remained independent until absorbed by the LNER.

LONDONDERRY RAILWAY

Privately built by the Marquess of Londonderry, this 7-mile line linked his pits at Penshaw (S of Newcastle) with his new harbour at Seaham — the first coal was shipped from there on 25 July 1831, and though the line's date of opening is uncertain it is likely to have been by then. On 8 February 1853 a line was begun N towards docks at Sunderland, and though not officially opened until 3 August 1854, it was ready and in use on 17 January. The Durham & Sunderland Railway (qv) was used for the final stretch, but the company (not incorporated until 8 June 1863) opened its own line on 1 August 1854. Passenger traffic began on 1 July 1855, an Act of 24 July 1894 sanctioning conversion for public services. The Railway (but not the Dock Company) was vested in the NER on 30 July 1900, which bought it for £400,000 wef 30 September; the take-over actually happened at midnight on 6 October.

LORD CARLISLE'S RAILWAY

See Brampton Railway.

LOUTH & EAST COAST RAILWAY

Authorized on 18 July 1872, the company had GNR backing to build a single line from S of Louth to Mablethorpe (11 miles 68 chains) via Saltfleetby,

with a branch to Saltfleet Haven and Cleethorpes. Though intended to be an agricultural line, seaside excursions actually turned out to be more lucrative than farm produce. The line opened on 17 October 1877 — the branch was not built, but a 2 miles 50 chains link with the Sutton & Willoughby Railway (qv) at Sutton-on-Sea was authorized on 25 September 1886, the Act including authority for a TA with the GNR, which then worked the line for 50 per cent of the receipts. The company amalgamated with the GNR for £87,000 by an Act of 1 August 1908.

LOUTH & LINCOLN RAILWAY

This 22-mile line was authorized on 6 August 1866 and aimed to link the towns via Bardney. Hopes that substantial supplies of ironstone could be carried were disappointed when it went to Scunthorpe via the MS&LR. Extra capital was needed before the heavily-graded line could be opened — when it was, on 1 December 1876, it connected with the GNR's Lincoln loop, and the company was vested in the GNR by an Act of 10 August 1882.

LOWESTOFT & BECCLES RAILWAY

This line, sanctioned on 23 June 1856 to link the towns, was backed by the civil engineer Samuel Morton Peto, who then leased it. Before opening (1 June 1859), it joined the ESR by an Act of 23 July 1858.

LOWESTOFT JUNCTION RAILWAY

Incorporated on 6 August 1897, the company's line opened on 13 July 1903 as an off-shoot of the M&GNJR route into Yarmouth (Beach), linking it with the Norfolk & Suffolk Joint (qv) line to Lowestoft. Its 3.75 miles included a substantial steel bridge across the R Bure and Breydon Water. It was operated by the LNER from 1 October 1936, with the rest of the ex-M&GN line. Breydon Bridge closed on 20 September 1953, though parts of the line remained in use until 1959.

LOWESTOFT RAILWAY & HARBOUR

The company was incorporated on 30 June 1845 to build a harbour and dock railway in Lowestoft. A second stage, authorized in 1845, was an 11 miles 30 chains line from Lowestoft to the Yarmouth & Norwich Railway (qv) at Reedham, opened for goods on 3 May 1847, and to passengers on 1 July. Leased by the NR under an Act of 3 July 1846, it passed to the ECR when that company leased the NR in 1848.

LUTON, DUNSTABLE & WELWYN JUNCTION RAILWAY

Incorporated on 16 July 1855, this line of 5 miles 45 chains opened from Luton to Dunstable for goods traffic on 5 April 1858, to passengers on 3 May, and throughout on 1 September 1860. It was operated by the L&NWR for two years, after which the GNR took over, the L&NWR retaining RP to Luton. Amalgamation with the Hertford & Welwyn Junction Railway on 28 June 1858 formed the Hertford, Luton & Dunstable Railway (both qv).

LYNN & DEREHAM RAILWAY

This company, formed on 21 July 1845, had only a brief independence. Its line opened from King's Lynn to Narborough on 27 October 1846, to Swaffham on 11 October 1847, to Sporle on 26 October and throughout on 11 September 1848, linking with the NR at Dereham, the EAR timetable having been used since that company's absorption of the smaller on 22 July 1847. The line closed to goods on 30 June 1966, and to passengers on 9 September 1968, though it remains open between Lynn and Middleton Towers for sand trains.

LYNN & ELY RAILWAY

Incorporated on 30 June 1845 under the influence of a King's Lynn solicitor, J.C. Williams, the line included branches to Wisbech from Watlington (Magdalen Road from 1875) and the harbour at Lynn. Work began in May 1846, and on 22 July 1847 an amalgamation with the Lynn & Dereham and the Ely & Huntingdon Railways (both qv) formed the EAR, as intended from the start. The harbour line opened on 29 October 1846, the main line on 26 October 1847 and the Wisbech branch on 2 February 1848.

LYNN & FAKENHAM RAILWAY

Authorized on 13 July 1876, this 20 miles 65 chains line opened from Lynn to Massingham on 16 August 1879, and on to Fakenham on 16 August 1880. Extension to Melton Constable was authorized on 12 August 1880, opening on 19 January 1882, and a railway works was established there. The company merged with the Yarmouth & N Norfolk and the Yarmouth Union Railways to form the Eastern & Midlands Railway (all qv) wef 1 July 1883. Closure to passengers, and to goods between E Rudham and Melton, was on 2 March 1959. The line closed completely on 1 March 1969.

LYNN & HUNSTANTON RAILWAY

This railway, 15 miles long and authorized on 1 August 1861, opened on 3 October 1862 and was an instant success. It merged with the W Norfolk Junction Railway wef 1 July 1874 to form the Hunstanton & W Norfolk Junction Railway (both qv). Wolferton station was used by many royal visitors to nearby Sandringham House, which may be why the line closed for goods (28 December 1964) earlier than for passengers (5 May 1969).

LYNN & SUTTON BRIDGE RAILWAY

Incorporated in 1860 as the Mid-Eastern & Great Northern Junction Railway, the name was changed on 6 August 1861 when the EAR obtained powers for a nominally independent company to build from S Lynn for 9 miles 51 chains to the Norwich & Spalding Railway (qv) W of Sutton Bridge station. On 28 February 1866, purchase of the company controlling Sutton Bridge was completed, and the railway was combined with the road on a new bridge opened on 18 July 1867. On 23 July 1866, the company had joined the Spalding & Bourn Railway (qv)

Left *The ornate 1847 facade of the Lynn & Ely Railway station at Downham Market. Again, were it not for the cars and the strip light above the entrance, this picture might have been taken at any time in the last century. (K. Ralph/ Andrew C. Ingram)*

Above right *After the Lynn & Sutton Bridge Railway acquired the swing bridge at Sutton Bridge in 1866, the southern (right-hand) span was used by a railway for the next 95 years. On 17 March 1988, work had begun on a by-pass bridge, no doubt affecting usage of the old one in due course.*

to lease the N&SR with powers to amalgamate, taking a new title, the Midland & Eastern Railway (qv). The Act also authorized WA with both the MR and GNR, though the GNR actually worked the line from the outset.

MALDON, WITHAM & BRAINTREE RAILWAY

A link between the towns (12 miles) was authorized on 18 June 1846, and the right to build reputedly cost the promoters £3,000. In September 1846 the ECR offered £6,300 and a promise to open the line within 18 months; the company accepted, and the line opened for goods on 15 August 1848, and to passengers on 2 October. There was no junction between the two halves of the line at Witham and it was worked as two separate 6-mile branches. The last passenger train ran on 6 September 1964, the last goods train on 15 April 1966.

MALTON & DRIFFIELD JUNCTION RAILWAY

Sanctioned on 26 June 1846, this steeply-graded line ran for 19 miles across the NW side of the Yorkshire Wolds. Though independent, the company was closely associated with others preparing to form the NER, and early in 1853 applied for inclusion in any resulting Group, gaining powers to amalgamate within three months of the completion of the NER's Act (31 July 1854). This was duly done on 28 October — the line had been worked from opening (formally on 19 May 1853, to the public on 1 June) by the companies which became the NER. Though never a money-spinner, the line served chalk quarries at Burdale and Wharram and was an invaluable link between local people and the outside world — sometimes, in bad weather, the only link. It closed to passengers on 5 June 1950, and to goods on 20 October 1958.

MANCHESTER & LINCOLN UNION RAILWAY

This 13.5-mile railway was authorized on 7 August 1846 between Staveley (MR, Derbys) and Worksop, where it joined the Chesterfield & Gainsborough Canal, which company it absorbed. Before opening (17 July 1849), however, the company was swallowed under an Act of 9 July 1847 by the rapidly-growing MS&LR, and the route became part of that company's main line.

MANCHESTER, SHEFFIELD & LINCOLNSHIRE RAILWAY

This was the name taken by an amalgamation of the Great Grimsby & Sheffield Junction, the Sheffield, Ashton-under-Lyne & Manchester and the Sheffield & Lincolnshire Junction Railways (all qv) and the group 'began trading' wef 1 January 1847. The constituents were dissolved and consolidated by an Act of 1 August 1849. Never a wealthy concern, it expanded steadily by absorbing smaller companies until its line stretched across the country. In 1889 it obtained powers for an extension S to Annesley, promising the GNR to go no further. However, when the chance came, the company made what many regard as its biggest mistake, deciding to promote a London extension. In accordance with this non-provincial aim, it obtained powers to rename itself the GCR wef 1 August 1897.

MANSFIELD RAILWAY

Authorized on 26 July 1910 and built by local enterprise, this 10 miles 75 chains line joined Kirkby-in-Ashfield (GCR) and Clipstone (LD&ECR). With outlets to five major collieries, it was worked by the GCR from the start, opening from Mansfield Colliery

Worksop West Junction signal box, the last surviving MS&LR Type 1 box. (Robert Humm Collection)

to Clipstone on 16 June 1913, and throughout to goods on 16 September 1916, and to passengers on 2 April 1917. The company was Grouped with the LNER.

MELLIS & EYE RAILWAY

A line of 2 miles 73 chains, it was promoted by local interests and authorized on 5 July 1865 with capital of £20,000. It was opened formally on 1 April 1867 and to traffic the next day, worked by the GER. It soon became obvious that the line would never pay well enough to be worked by the company, and the GER was thus unconcerned to take over officially, although this was finally authorized by an Act of 1 July 1898. It closed to passengers on 2 February 1931, and to goods on 13 July 1964.

MERRYBENT & DARLINGTON RAILWAY

Incorporated on 11 June 1866, this line branched S from the Darlington & Barnard Castle Railway (qv) to serve quarries. It opened on 1 June 1870, but was soon in financial difficulties, being wound up on 17 June 1878. The company's authorizing Act, however, allowed for its purchase by any company '. . . given leave. . .' therein; the NER bought it from Darlington District Bank in 1890, though the purchase was not ratified until 30 July 1900. Traffic ceased after the Second World War, and the track-bed is now part of the Darlington bypass.

MIDDLESBROUGH & GUISBOROUGH RAILWAY

Authorized on 17 June 1852 to connect the named towns, it was joined at Nunthorpe by the N Yorkshire & Cleveland Railway (qv) with its 5.25-mile branch from Battersby, thus forming a link with the Esk Valley line to Whitby and the Rosedale line. Money was scarce, however, until Joseph Pease stepped in with a guaranteed dividend offer. He cut the first sod on 30 October 1852 and the line opened on 11 November 1853 (goods), 25 February 1854 (passengers). The company's independence was short for it amalgamated with the St&DR, which had worked it from the start, on 23 July 1858. Part of the line remains open, giving access to Whitby.

MIDDLESBROUGH & REDCAR RAILWAY

Incorporated on 21 July 1845 to build a 7.75-mile line from Middlesbrough to Saltburn, via Redcar, the line opened on 4 June 1846, and was leased by the St&DR for 999 years wef 1 October 1847. On 8 June 1850, high-quality ironstone was found at Eston, E of Middlesbrough, and a 2-mile branch was built to get it out. The St&DR absorbed the company from 23 July 1858.

MIDLAND & EASTERN RAILWAY

This was formed on 23 July 1866 by the amalgamation of the Spalding & Bourn and the Lynn & Sutton Bridge Railways, which then leased the Norwich & Spalding Railway (all qv), before absorbing it on 12 July 1877. The company had an understanding with the Peterborough, Wisbech & Sutton Bridge Railway (qv), which remained outside the group then but came in when the Eastern & Midlands Railway (qv) was created wef 1 July 1883.

MIDLAND & GREAT NORTHERN JOINT RAILWAY

This company was formed wef 1 July 1893 (Act of 9 June) to take over the Eastern & Midlands Railway (qv) when the Cromer line from Melton Constable was completed and the E&MR had linked with the MR at Saxby. At Grouping, the company owned 182 miles 32 chains of track, of which 109 miles 18 chains was single; MR shares went to the LMS and GNR ones to the LNER, which latter took over sole working from 1 October 1936. The system is closed apart from a section between Sheringham and Holt, run as a preserved steam line by the North Norfolk Railway.

MID-SUFFOLK LIGHT RAILWAY

Incorporated under the Light Railways Act, 28 miles of line were approved in 1901 between Haughley Junction and Halesworth, with a 14-mile branch from Kenton to Westerfield. The Haughley Junction–Laxfield section opened to goods on 20 September 1904 and to passengers on 29 September, but from 1905 money problems had arisen; in May 1907 an OR was appointed and all building ceased. The branch stopped at Debenham (2 miles), and the main line reached only 2.25 miles beyond Laxfield. The company retained independence until absorbed into the LNER in 1924. The last passenger train, hauled by Class 'J15' No 65447, ran on 26 July 1952, the final train of all using the line in June 1953.

MONKLAND RAILWAYS

This company was formed on 14 August 1848 by an amalgamation of the Monkland & Kirkintilloch, the Ballochney and the Slamannan Railways (all qv). It was in its turn absorbed by the E&GR under an Act of 5 July 1865, wef 31 July.

MONKLAND & KIRKINTILLOCH RAILWAY

This was the first railway specifically to be authorized (17 May 1824) to use locomotives. Engineered by

The insignia of the Midland & Great Northern Joint Railway, photographed on a bus-shelter near the site of Melton Constable Works. (Allan Mott)

Grainger and Miller at a gauge of 4 ft 6 in, it ran from Cairnhill Colliery, Monkland, to the Forth & Clyde Canal at Kirkintilloch. It was laid with fishbelly rail on whinstone blocks, single throughout its 10.5 miles, including branches, and there was a junction with the Garnkirk & Glasgow Railway (qv – LMS) near Gartsherrie. Opening on 1 October 1826, and

The Forth & Clyde Canal at Kirkintilloch. Beyond the man walking away from the camera, coal from the Monkland & Kirkintilloch Railway was transferred to barges to continue its journey by water.

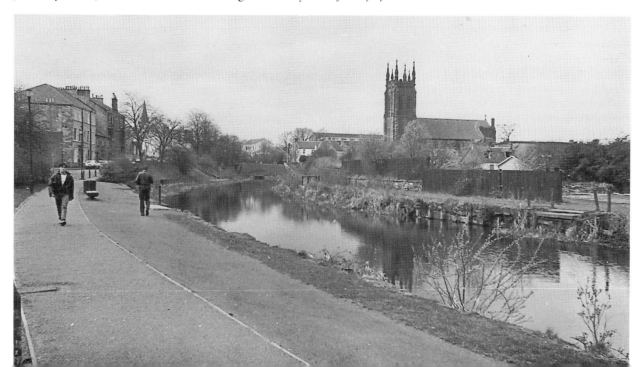

horse-drawn to begin with, it was converted for steam haulage prior to the arrival of two engines, the first ones built in Glasgow, by Murdoch & Aitkin. These entered traffic on 10 September 1831, one on either side of a tunnel with limited clearance, the bore remaining horse-drawn. Through working began in January 1832, by which time the line had been doubled. The company became the first Scottish railway to build its own locomotives, first in a workshop hired from the Ballochney Railway, then in a custom-built factory at Kipps from 1837. Amalgamation with the Ballochney and the Slamannan Railways on 14 August 1848 formed the Monkland Railways (all qv).

MONTROSE & BERVIE RAILWAY

Incorporated on 3 July 1860, this company's line ran for 12 miles from the Montrose branch of the SNER. It was opened on 1 November 1865 by the CR, under whose control it had been, by Agreement, since authorization. When that Agreement expired, however, the company amalgamated with the NBR under an Act dated 18 July 1881 wef 1 August.

MORAYSHIRE RAILWAY

The company's Act of 16 July 1846 authorized lines from Lossiemouth to Elgin, Rothes and Craigellachie, with a branch from Rothes to Orton. The Elgin-Lossiemouth section (5.5 miles) opened formally on 10 August 1852, and to the public the next day. The line from Orton to Craigellachie opened to Rothes on 23 August 1858, and throughout on 23 December; the Orton–Rothes section soon closed, on 1 August 1866, but was not lifted until 1907. At first the company worked its own trains over the Inverness & Aberdeen Junction Railway (qv) between Orton and Elgin. The line from Elgin to Rothes opened on 30 December 1861 (goods), 1 January 1862 (passengers), linking with the Strathspey Railway (qv) at Craigellachie on 1 July 1863. Under the GNSR Act of 30 July 1866, the line was worked by it for 45 per cent of receipts, full amalgamation taking place wef 1 October 1880.

MUSWELL HILL RAILWAY

Authorized on 30 June 1866 to run for ¾ mile from Park Junction, beyond Highgate on the Edgware, Highgate & London Railway (qv) branch to Muswell Hill, its objective being Alexandra Palace. The line was ready for the opening of the Palace on 24 May 1873, but on 9 June it burned down, and the line closed until the Palace re-opened. There were seven further closures in sympathy with the Palace's problems between 1875 and 1898. By an Act of 25 September 1886, the line's owners, Muswell Hill Estates Company, renamed it the Muswell Hill & Palace Railway. The GNR worked it from the start, but did not absorb it until so authorized by an Act of 18

August 1911; it closed to passengers on 5 July 1954, and to goods on 14 June 1956.

NEWBURGH & NORTH FIFE RAILWAY

Incorporated on 6 August 1897, building began in June 1906 (the line single with passing places). The 13.5-mile line from Glenbourne Junction (E&GR) to St Fort and to St Andrews Junction opened to the public on 25 January 1909. The passenger service, after a temporary withdrawal due to staff shortages — nothing is new — was restored on 19 July 1916. The line was to be worked by the NBR in perpetuity, and the company was Grouped with the LNER in 1923.

NEWCASTLE & BERWICK RAILWAY

Authorized on 31 July 1845, the line was to link the towns from a junction with the Brandling Junction Railway (qv) at Gateshead, and, by using the Newcastle and N Shields Railway (qv) to Heaton, to turn N to meet the NBR at Berwick. It opened from Heaton to Morpeth on 1 March 1847, and from Newcastle to Tweedmouth on 1 July. On 9 July 1847 the company merged with the York & Newcastle Railway (qv) to form the YN&BR. Newcastle's Victoria Bridge, designed by John Dobson, was begun in 1847; it cost around £100,000, and was opened on 28 September 1849 by Queen Victoria, who re-visited Newcastle on 29 July 1850 to open the E end of Central station.

NEWCASTLE & CARLISLE RAILWAY

Incorporated on 22 May 1829, this was the first Tyneside line to carry passengers, though not the first public line opened, that distinction belonging to the Stanhope & Tyne Railway (qv). Though the first section opened with great junketings (Blaydon–Hexham, 9 March 1835), the company's problem was an Act forbidding the use of steam locomotives. Because a landowner objected, services were suspended from 28 March to 6 May 1838, when public opinion had persuaded the objector to withdraw. By now almost the whole line was open — Hexham–Haydon Bridge on 28 June 1836, Carlisle (Rome Street)–Greenhead on 19 July, Blaydon–Redheugh on 1 March 1837 (see Blaydon, Gateshead & Hebburn Railway), Carlisle (Canal Basin)–Rome Street on 9 March, and Gateshead–Hay Bridge on 18 June 1838. Redheugh continued in use until 1850, and trains ran into Newcastle Central on 1 January 1851. The company remained independent until 17 July 1862, when it was absorbed by the NER. A branch S from Haltwhistle to Alston, authorized on 26 August 1846 and opened on 17 November 1852, served an isolated community well for many years. The last BR train ran on the branch on 6 May 1976, but a narrow gauge Preservation Society opened 1.5 miles from Alston to Gildersome Halt on 30 July 1983. Progress continues towards Slaggyford.

From railway arches to desirable residence. An imaginative conversion of the Newcastle & Darlington Railway's viaduct at Shincliffe, near Durham (the smoke vent, though seemingly decorative, no doubt has a practical purpose). An embankment survives at either end of the building.

NEWCASTLE & DARLINGTON JUNCTION RAILWAY

Incorporated on 18 June 1842, the company was given a head start when the GNER agreed to abandon its N section to the new concern, matters being ratified by an Act of 11 April 1843. Work went quickly, until the company realized, almost too late, that it had no rolling-stock! The GNER agreed to provide this and locomotives, but not to staff the line. It opened on 18 June 1844, but the company was soon complaining bitterly about the locomotives – the GNER, probably with justification, retaliated by blaming deficiencies on the staff's inexperience. The company planned to run the service from 1 January 1845, but now had no engines. These the GNER agreed to supply, provided that the company paid its debts in full. Despite these setbacks, the company expanded, buying the Durham Junction Railway (1844) and the Brandling Junction Railway (1845). In 1846, the Durham & Sunderland and the Pontop & S Shields Railways (all qv) came into the net with the Wearmouth Dock Company, and, perhaps the unkindest cut of all, the GNER. On 3 August 1846, the company changed its name to the York & Newcastle Railway (qv).

NEWCASTLE & NORTH SHIELDS RAILWAY

This 5-mile line was authorized on 21 June 1836 between N Shields and Newcastle, with a 1-mile extension to Tynemouth. Events overtook the company, however – the main line opened on 19 June 1839, but before its extension to Tynemouth was ready, the company had been bought by the Newcastle & Berwick Railway (qv) on 31 July 1845, which opened it on 31 March 1847.

NEWMARKET RAILWAY

Though its incorporated title (16 July 1846) was the Newmarket & Chesterford Railway, it changed to the shorter version on 8 June 1847. Authorized to build 16.75 miles from Newmarket to Great Chesterford with an 8.5-mile branch to Cambridge from Six Mile Bottom, the main line was leased at opening (3 January 1848 to goods, 4 April 1848 to passengers) by the ECR, a lease repudiated the following February, though it continued to operate the line at exorbitant cost. The company considered working the line itself but could not afford to, and it closed on 30 June 1850, heavily in debt. It re-opened on 9 September, and with ECR help the Cambridge branch was opened on 9 October 1851, when the Six Mile Bottom–Chesterford line closed again. Amalgamation with the ECR was provided for in an Act of 7 August 1854, which ratified current WA until then.

NEWPORT RAILWAY

This Fifeshire line was authorized on 6 August 1866 to run between Tayport and Wormit on the S bank of

The 1887 timber station from Wormit, Newport Railway. It is, however, no longer on its original site, being another rescue by the Bo'ness & Kinneil Railway, which transferred it to Bo'ness in 1981.

the Tay. Powers to extend from the main line to Long Craig were granted on 1 August 1870, and the line between Tayport and Newport opened on 12 May 1879, the section to Wormit following the next day. The NBR leased the line for 999 years wef 1 January 1888, and absorbed the company under an Act of 6 August 1900 from 1 August.

NORFOLK RAILWAY
This was formed on 30 June 1845 by the amalgamation of the Norwich & Brandon and the Yarmouth & Norwich Railways (both qv). Its own line from Wymondham to Dereham opened for goods on 7 December 1846 and to passengers on 15 February 1847, joining the Lynn & Dereham Railway (qv), by now part of the EAR, at Dereham. A link with the Wells & Fakenham Railway (qv) was made at Fakenham when an extension opened on 20 March 1849. The company leased the Lowestoft Railway & Harbour (qv) in 1846, and in May 1847 an Agreement was made to amalgamate with the EUR. When this was not proceeded with, the ECR stepped in, leasing the company's 94 miles of track and four locomotives wef 8 May 1848.

NORFOLK & SUFFOLK JOINT RAILWAY
This joint venture was created on 25 July 1898 following an Agreement dated 18 March 1897 between the GER and the M&GNJR. It covered the lines from W Runton to N Walsham via Mundesley

— opened between N Walsham and Mundesley in July 1898 and to Cromer on 3 August 1906 — and the line from Yarmouth to Lowestoft via Gorleston, opened on 13 July 1903 (see also Lowestoft Junction Railway). Though these lines remained technically independent until Nationalization, they were worked as part of the M&GNJR system.

NORTH BRITISH RAILWAY
Incorporated on 4 July 1844 after a surprisingly easy journey through Parliament, owing partly to a degree of confusion in the rival Caledonian ranks, the line was authorized to run from Berwick to Edinburgh (57 miles 3 furlongs), with a 4 miles 5 furlongs branch to Haddington. The main line opened officially on 18 June 1846, and to the public on 22 June, but trouble came in September, when heavy rain washed away a length of embankment, causing three bridges to collapse and damaging six others. The Haddington branch was singled on 7 October 1856, the Edinburgh & Dalkeith Railway (qv) was acquired and refurbished, and other branches built. On 1 August 1865 the E&GR was absorbed, the Tay Bridge opened on 1 June 1878, and expansion by amalgamation added more than 50 subsidiaries before Grouping, when the company became an LNER constituent.

NORTH BRITISH, ARBROATH & MONTROSE RAILWAY
This was incorporated on 13 July 1871 as an NBR promotion, '. . . to secure, in the interest of the NB Company, that important link in the chain of direct railway communication . . . between the Tay Bridge

The Tay Bridge was not something which the NBR was anxious to remember, though the fact that the company had the courage to rebuild it counts to its credit. The bases of the old bridge piers can be seen close beside the new ones. (Allan Mott)

at Dundee, and Aberdeen'. It opened from Arbroath to Letham Grange on 1 October 1880, and throughout, including a link between Montrose and Kinnaber Junction, on 1 March 1881. An Act of 12 August 1880 amalgamated the company with the NBR from 1 August.

NORTH EASTERN RAILWAY

This company was formed on 31 July 1854 by the consolidation of the Y&NMR, the YN&BR and the Leeds Northern Railway (qv). They were joined by the Malton & Driffield Junction Railway (qv) three months later. The Act encompassed 720 miles of railway — more than any other company in the UK at the time — 26 miles of waterway and 44 acres of dock. The company's own line to the GNR at Shaftholme Junction opened on 2 January 1871, and the terminus at York was replaced by a through station on 25 June 1877. The company had its difficult times, but grew steadily, until it became a constituent of the LNER at the Grouping.

NORTHERN & EASTERN RAILWAY

Authority was given on 4 July 1836 for 53 miles of railway from Islington to Cambridge. Laid to 5 ft gauge, progress was slow and financial problems soon coerced the company to an Agreement with the ECR

to join its line at Stratford and use the station at Shoreditch; this was ratified by an Act of 19 July 1839. The line opened between Stratford and Broxbourne on 15 September 1840, to Harlow on 9 August 1841, Spelbrook on 22 November and Bishop's Stortford on 16 May 1842. A branch to Hertford from Broxbourne, also at 5 ft gauge, was authorized on 21 June 1841 and opened on 31 Oct-

The seal of the NER combining the arms of York (top), with those of the Leeds Northern Railway (left), and the YN&BR.

Left *Roydon station was opened by the Northern & Eastern Railway in 1841, but was built earlier and rather elaborately for a (then) country station. In fact, it was at first the headquarters of the line's engineer; now it is a wine bar, though its present name seems not inappropriate.*

Right *The present North Woolwich station, opened in 1854, won an award as the best renovated station in 1985. The main building now houses the GER Museum, while behind, and perhaps more importantly, the station still operates.* (Allan Mott)

ober 1843. From 1 January 1844 the ECR took the line on a 999-year lease, converting it to standard gauge in September/October that year. The line was extended to Cambridge in 1845 and to Brandon on 29 July 1845, public services beginning the next day. Though the ECR (and lease) passed to the GER on its formation in 1862, the company was not formally dissolved until 1 July 1902, by an Act of 23 June.

NORTH LINDSEY LIGHT RAILWAY

The company was incorporated on 19 September 1900 and was promoted by the S Yorkshire LR Syndicate to build a line running N from Scunthorpe towards the Humber. The company was encouraged by the GCR, which hoped to keep at bay the L&YR, already in Axholme. Opening from Frodingham to W Halton on 3 September 1906 and to Winteringham on 15 July 1907, the line was worked by the GCR for 60 per cent of gross receipts, an arrangement ratified by Parliament on 26 July 1907. A branch to W Haven was opened on 15 July 1907, and though further branches were planned only one was built, to Whitton, opening on 1 December 1910. The company retained independence until allotted to the LNER in 1923. Passenger traffic between Scunthorpe and Whitton ceased on 13 July 1925.

NORTH MONKLAND RAILWAY

A line from Red Bridge (Ballochney Railway, qv) to Southfield Row (Slamannan Railway, qv), with branches to Nettlehole and Cullochrigg, was sanctioned on 18 July 1872. It opened on 18 February 1878 and was absorbed by the NBR, which paid £6 for every £10 share, wef 31 July 1888 under an act dated 7 August.

NORTHUMBERLAND CENTRAL RAILWAY

The company was authorized on 28 July 1863 to build from the Wansbeck Railway (qv) at Scotsgap to Cornhill (Coldstream, NER). The line opened from Scotsgap to Rothbury on 1 November 1870, but got no further — the N section was never built and the NER filled the gap by building S to Wooler and Alnmouth. What there was of the company's line was absorbed by the NBR under an Act of 18 July 1872, wef previous 1 February.

NORTH WOOLWICH RAILWAY

Empowered on 21 July 1845 to extend the Eastern Counties & Thames Junction Railway (qv) for 2.75 miles from Barking Creek to the N Woolwich ferry, the line opened on 14 June 1847 and soon after was bought by the ECR under an Act of 9 July. G.P. Bidder ran an hourly service until 1854, when the ECR was persuaded to start a service from Fenchurch Street via Stratford. Between 1854 and 1866 the NLR worked the trains, but from then until 1874 they were worked by the NLR and GER in alternate years. The GER took over sole working thereafter.

NORTH YORKSHIRE & CLEVELAND RAILWAY

This was a line authorized on 10 July 1854 from Picton (Leeds Northern Railway, qv, between Northallerton and Eaglescliffe) to Grosmont along the Esk Valley. Early financial problems were eased by an Agreement with the NER of 23 July 1858, when authority was given for a mineral branch to Rosedale, deep in the N Yorkshire Moors — it was opened on 27 March 1861 and extended to E Rosedale on 18 August 1865. It included the self-acting Ingleby

incline — in June 1869 working was suspended when friction on the brake drum set fire to the drum-house and burned it out. The company was vested in the NER on 8 August 1859. After working profitably for many years, the final train ran on 11 January 1929 — Hutton-le-Hole village hall is built of stones from Rosedale engine shed, demolished and transported in 1937. The Esk Valley line, opened on 2 October 1865, remains open.

NORWICH & BRANDON RAILWAY

Incorporated on 10 May 1844 to build 36.75 miles of railway between the towns, on the opening day (30 July 1845) the company amalgamated with the

The first station at Thetford (nearest camera), built by the Norwich & Brandon Railway, was supplemented by a later building (beyond the cars) in 1889, simpler but with a semicircle of steps to the entrance. (Allan Mott)

Yarmouth & Norwich Railway (qv), which had antici-pated the event by changing its name to the NR. Trowse Bridge, and the extension to Thorpe Junction, Norwich, were opened on 15 December 1845 — the engineer for the bridge, a balanced cantilever swinging span of 107 ft, was G.P. Bidder, the contractor S.M. Peto.

NORWICH & SPALDING RAILWAY

An EUR-backed scheme to thwart the ECR, its Act of 4 August 1853 authorized a line from Spalding to Sutton Bridge, with a link to the ECR at Wisbech. Money was hard to find, and only the Spalding–Holbeach section was built at first, opening on 9 August 1858 (goods), 15 November 1858 (passen-gers). The line was worked by the GNR, under an Agreement of 2 September 1858, for three years, and then for a further ten. Opening to Sutton Bridge was on 1 July 1862, but the Wisbech line was abandoned. A lease to the Lynn & Sutton Bridge Railway (qv) was authorized on 23 July 1866, and the company was vested in the Midland & Eastern Railway by an Act of 12 July 1877.

NOTTINGHAM & GRANTHAM RAILWAY & CANAL COMPANY

See Ambergate, Nottingham & Boston & Eastern Junction Railway.

NOTTINGHAM, EREWASH VALLEY & AMBERGATE RAILWAY

This line was authorized on 4 August 1845 to run between Nottingham and Ambergate, where it was planned to link with the Manchester, Buxton & Matlock Railway (qv). The two projects combined with two others on 16 July 1846 to form the Ambergate, Nottingham & Boston & Erewash Valley Railway (qv).

NOTTINGHAM SUBURBAN RAILWAY

Formed by local businessmen and authorized on 25 June 1886 to open up the residential areas in the NE of Nottingham, it ran for 3 miles 47 chains from Trent Lane Junction N to Daybrook. Building took two years, and the tunnel at Sherwood had to be 10 yd longer than planned to avoid disturbing a farmer's stackyard. The GNR worked the line from opening on 2 December 1889, with an option to purchase; this was never exercised, and it passed to the LNER in 1923. Electric trams affected traffic, and the line closed for passengers on 14 September 1931, and completely on 1 August 1951.

NOTTINGHAM, VALE OF BELVOIR & GRANTHAM RAILWAY

A scheme to link Nottingham and Grantham, the company amalgamated with the Nottingham, Erewash Valley & Ambergate Railway and others on 16 July 1846 to form the Ambergate, Nottingham & Boston & Eastern Junction Railway (both qv).

PEAK FOREST TRAMWAY

Incorporated on 28 March 1794, this plateway brought limestone from quarries at Dove Holes, Derby-shire, to the Peak Forest Canal at Bugsworth (now Buxworth). Engineered by Benjamin Outram to a gauge of 4 ft 2 in, the line was 6 miles long, and worked by gravity. It opened from Bugsworth to Marple on 31 August 1796, and was completed on 1 May 1800 — the incline at Chapel-en-le-Frith had a rise of 209 ft in 512 yd, and in its heyday the line carried 600 tons of stone a day. It survived until 1820, and under an Act of 27 July 1846 both tram-

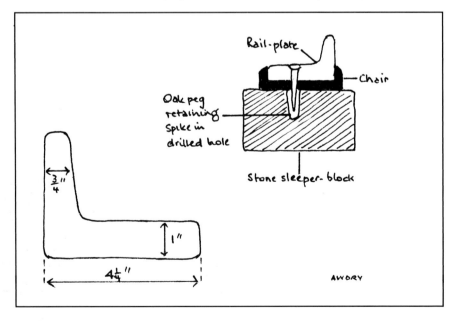

Left *Diagram showing the type of plate and method of laying used by Benjamin Outram on the Peak Forest Tramway.*

Right *Ramsey North (Ramsey Rail-way) looking west on a wet day in 1969. The line's only gradients in its 5.5 miles to Holme (GNR) were to bridges across drainage dykes. (Allan Mott)*

way and canal came into the control of the Stalybridge, Ashton-under-Lyne & Manchester Railway (qv) — soon to become the MS&LR — to which it passed on 2 August 1863. The LNER closed the Dove Holes–Chapel Milton section in 1924 and throughout in 1926 — it was lifted ten years later.

PEEBLES RAILWAY

Authorized (to the NBR) on 8 July 1853, this line was built in a wide southward loop from Eskbank (Edinburgh) to Peebles via Leadburn and Innerleithen. It opened on 4 July 1855, and until the NBR took over working on 1 February 1861, the company differed from most NBR sponsorships in that it ran its own traffic and affairs with four engines, one an old Bury bought for £800 from the L&NWR. The NBR leased the line on 11 July 1861, and its 18.75 miles were vested in it wef 1 August 1876. The passenger service ceased on 5 February 1962.

PENICUIK RAILWAY

This branch was authorized on 20 June 1870 to run from Hawthornden on the Peebles Railway (qv) to Roslyn Castle and Penicuik, a distance of '. . . 4 miles 3 furlongs 3 chains or thereabouts'. The line opened on 2 September 1872, and the company was amalgamated with the NBR by an Act of 13 July 1876, wef 1 August.

PETERBOROUGH, WISBEACH (sic) & SUTTON BRIDGE RAILWAY

Authorization was given on 28 July 1863 for a railway across N Cambridgeshire from Peterborough to Sutton Bridge, near the mouth of the R Nene. Its 26.75 miles were opened, after three BoT refusals, for goods on 1 June 1866 and for passengers on 1 August, worked by the MR for 50 per cent of receipts. The company was absorbed by the E&MR from 1 July 1883.

PONTOP & SOUTH SHIELDS RAILWAY

Incorporated on 23 May 1842, the company was to take over the 24.5-mile section of the Stanhope & Tyne Railway (qv) between Leadgate and S Shields. The company opened the curve between Boldon and Brockley Whins in conjunction with the Brandling Junction Railway (qv) on 19 August 1844, but was bought by the N&DJR on 3 August 1846.

PORT CARLISLE DOCK & RAILWAY

When the Carlisle Canal Company was re-incorporated on 4 August 1853, the Act authorized the conversion of the canal to a railway. The 11-mile line was almost entirely in cutting, and level except where the locks had been. It opened for goods on 22 May 1854, and for passengers a month later, using engines and rolling-stock hired from the N&CR, until the company's own engine was delivered in 1855. A 12.75-mile extension to Silloth Bay was opened on 2 June 1856, and the company was leased by the NBR for 999 years wef 1 August 1862, to be absorbed under an Act of 1 August 1880. The horse-drawn passenger service ceased on 4 April 1914, and its replacement closed from 1 January 1917 to 1 February 1919. Attempts to delay closure of the Drumburgh–Port Carlisle section involved a steam railcar, but passenger traffic succumbed on 1 June 1932. Dandy No 1, a horse-drawn carriage once used at a bowls club, is now at the NRM. The whole line closed on 7 September 1964.

RAMSEY RAILWAY

Incorporated on 22 July 1861 to build a 5 miles 58 chains single line from Holme (GNR) to Ramsey in

Left *In the car park of Audley End station, and now used for the storage of bicycles, the branch platform and small shelter of the Saffron Walden Railway remain. The last train called in 1964.*

Right *From the track-bed of the old Wylam Wagonway, later the Scotswood, Newburn & Wylam Railway and now a footpath and cycle-track, may be seen the cottage in which George Stephenson spent his youth.*

N Cambridgeshire, it was worked at first (the line opened on 1 August 1863) by the GNR. The company was acquired under an Act of 19 July 1875 by the GER, which planned to link it with a line from Somersham — see Ramsey & Somersham Railway. The scheme collapsed, and the line was leased to the GNR at 2 per cent on capital of £43,000 for 21 years by an Agreement of 15 December 1874, wef 1 July 1875. This was renewed for a further period by an Act of 20 July 1896. The line closed to passengers on 6 October 1947, and to goods in December 1973.

RAMSEY & SOMERSHAM RAILWAY
This 7-mile line authorized on 2 June 1865 to link the named towns via Warboys opened on 16 September 1889. A scheme authorized in 1875 to link with the Ramsey Railway (qv) at Ramsey came to nothing, and the line became part of the GN&GEJR from 1 January 1897. It closed to passengers on 22 September 1930, and to goods (Warboys–Ramsey) in September 1956, (Somersham–Warboys) 13 July 1964.

ROYSTON & HITCHIN RAILWAY
Parliament restricted a 73-mile proposal for a line between Oxford and Cambridge via Dunstable and Hitchin to a 12.75-mile Royston-Hitchin link. Authorized on 16 July 1846, it was leased under a 6 per cent guarantee to the GNR by an Act of 9 July 1847, and although another of 22 July had authorized lease or sale to the GNR on completion (21 October 1850), it was the ECR which took a 14-year lease wef 1 April 1852. An extension to Shepreth was authorized on 14 August 1848 and opened on 3 August 1851, but a further extension to Cambridge was rejected. The GNR resumed control (in a very run-down state) in 1866, under a perpetual lease at £16,000 pa. Agree-

ment to work and maintain the line to Shelford was made with the GER on 15 December 1874, wef 1 July. The company was vested in the GNR wef 1 January 1898.

SAFFRON WALDEN RAILWAY
An Act of 22 July 1861 authorized only 2 miles between Audley End and Saffron Walden, but another (22 June 1863) sanctioned a further 6.25 miles to Bartlow. It opened to Saffron Walden on 23 November 1865 and to Bartlow on 22 October 1866, but soon fell on hard times and petitioned for an OR. The GER was authorized to buy the company on 12 July 1877, wef previous 1 January. The line closed to passengers on 7 September 1964, and to goods on 28 December.

ST ANDREWS RAILWAY
Incorporated on 3 July 1851 to build from Milton Junction (Leuchars, EP&DR) to St Andrews, 4.75 miles, the line was opened on 1 July 1852. The company was absorbed by the NBR under an Act of 28 June 1877, wef 1 August.

ST HELENS & WIGAN JUNCTION RAILWAY
Incorporated on 22 July 1885 for a line between St Helens and Lowton St Mary, WA with the Wigan Junction Railway (qv) or the MS&LR were also authorized. The MS&LR was permitted to subscribe (and did so) though its colleagues on the CLC were not interested. The company renamed itself the Liverpool, St Helens & S Lancashire Railway (qv) on 26 July 1889.

SCARBOROUGH & WHITBY RAILWAY
A line along the N Yorkshire coast was suggested as early as 1848, but not until 29 June 1871 was an Act passed; a first sod was cut on 3 June 1872, but money

ran short and only private finance saved the 20.5-mile line. Opened on 16 July 1885, it was a spectacular route, with gradients up to Ravenscar of 1 in 41 (S) and 1 in 39 (N), and a 915 ft viaduct across the Esk near Whitby. The NER worked the line from the start for 50 per cent of the receipts, absorbing it wef 1 July 1898. On either side of the Second World War it was used for scenic excursions. The last train ran on 6 March 1965.

SCARBOROUGH, BRIDLINGTON & WEST RIDING JUNCTION RAILWAY

Powers in the authorizing Act (6 August 1885) covered two lines — Seamer (Scarborough) to Nafferton (Driffield), 16.5 miles, and Market Weighton to Driffield, 13.25 miles. Only the latter was built, double track throughout, opening on 18 April 1890 (goods), 1 May (passengers). It joined the NER at both ends; that company worked it from the outset under TA included in the Act, absorbing it wef 1 July 1914 by a retrospective Act of 31 July. Passenger traffic ceased on 14 June 1965, and goods in 1964.

SCOTSWOOD, NEWBURN & WYLAM RAILWAY & DOCK COMPANY

Incorporated on 16 June 1871, lack of river access had made the 'dock' in the title useless by 1876, and the company was allowed to drop it by an Act of 7 April. The line's first sod was cut on 17 May 1872 and it opened to Newburn on 12 July 1875, to Wylam on 13 May 1876 and throughout on 24 August. It was partly laid along the bed of the old Wylam Wagonway, passing George Stephenson's boyhood home at Wylam. There were WA with the NER from the outset, the concern being bought by that company for £155,746 under an Act of 29 June 1883.

SEGHILL RAILWAY

Built using wayleaves (and not therefore incorporated) by the owners of Seghill Colliery who were dissatisfied with the service offered by the Cramlington Wagonway, it ran for 4.5 miles between Seghill and Blyth, and opened on 1 June 1840 (minerals) and 28 August 1841 (passengers), but water at Blyth was too shallow for larger vessels, and in 1843 it was decided to build S towards the Tyne. The Newcastle & N Shields Railway (qv) worked the line from 25 June 1844, and a connecting line from Blyth was opened for mineral traffic in 1846, and to passengers on 3 March 1847. In 1850 the line was joined at Newsham by a branch from Bedlington, and the company became a major part of the Blyth & Tyne Railway (qv) when that company was incorporated in 1852.

SELKIRK & GALASHIELS RAILWAY

Incorporated on 31 July 1854 as a 6.25-mile line linking the towns, it was opened on 5 April 1856. Worked from the start by the NBR, that company duly absorbed it on 21 July 1859.

SHEFFIELD & LINCOLNSHIRE EXTENSION RAILWAY

Planned from Clarborough Junction (NW of Retford) to Lincoln, it joined there the Great Grimsby & Sheffield Junction Railway (qv) branch from Market Rasen. Its 8.75-mile route avoided a detour through Gainsborough, following the GNR Lincoln–Gainsborough line from Sykes Junction into Lincoln; perhaps because of this the GNR was authorized (3 August 1846) to build it. The MS&LR was given RP into Lincoln in exchange for powers from Retford to Sheffield. The company had little life of its own; on incorporation it was amalgamated with the MS&LR, which opened the line on 7 August 1850.

SHEFFIELD & LINCOLNSHIRE JUNCTION RAILWAY

This company had little independent life, amalgamating with the MS&LR on its date of incorporation, 3 August 1846, along with the Sheffield & Lincolnshire Extension Railway (qv). A line from Sheffield to Beighton was opened on 12 February 1849, and to Gainsborough on 17 July 1849. MS&LR trains used it as a through route to Eckington (between Sheffield and Chesterfield) until the Staveley line opened in 1892.

SHEFFIELD, ASHTON-UNDER-LYNE & MANCHESTER RAILWAY

This line began in 1813 as an idea for a railway from Sheffield to Manchester using six inclines and a 2.75-mile water tunnel. In 1831, a Sheffield & Manchester Railway was authorized — it died, and this company, incorporated on 5 May 1837, replaced it. Money was short and it was a difficult line to build — it opened from Manchester to Woodhead on 8 August 1844 and from Sheffield to Dunford Bridge on 14 July 1845. Woodhead tunnel at opening on 23 December 1845 was the longest in the country (3 miles 22 yards). Within a year it was realized that a second bore was needed — before this opened (3 miles 66 yards) on 2 February 1852, the company had joined the Sheffield & Lincolnshire Junction, the Sheffield & Lincolnshire Extension and the Great Grimsby & Sheffield Junction Railways (all qv) to form the MS&LR wef 1 January 1847 (Act of 27 July 1846).

SHEFFIELD DISTRICT RAILWAY

Incorporated on 14 August 1896, this line between Treeton and Brightside was intended as an extension of the LD&ECR line to Beighton, and though nomi-

nally independent, its two sponsors, the GER and the LD&ECR, had RP over it — the latter leased it from 1898. When the MR sponsored a similar line, it was agreed that the schemes should combine. An Act of 6 August 1897 ratified this, the line opening for goods on 28 May 1900 and to passengers on 30 May. The MR used its RP considerably in later years, and, when the line was absorbed by the GCR on 20 July 1906, retained them.

SHEFFIELD, ROTHERHAM, BARNSLEY, WAKEFIELD, HUDDERSFIELD & GOOLE RAILWAY

Incorporated on 7 August 1846, the S section of line built by this company with the longest title ran a mere 11.25 miles, though even that exceeded the N section. It had a short independence too, being transferred to the S Yorkshire, Doncaster & Goole Railway (qv) by an Act of 22 July 1847. The line opened on 4 September 1854 (see also LMS section).

SHILDON TUNNEL RAILWAY

This company was promoted to finance a railway through the 1,225 yd Shildon Tunnel, connecting the Bishop Auckland & Weardale Railway (qv) at South Church with the St&DR at Shildon. It was built without the blessing of Parliament, was opened on 19 April 1842 and sold to the Wear Valley Railway (qv) on 22 July 1847. It remains in daily use.

SLAMANNAN RAILWAY

A line of 12.5 miles was authorized on 3 July 1835

In the cutting lies the Stockton & Darlington Railway's outlet to Bishop Auckland, via Shildon Tunnel, burrowing beneath a housing estate. The estate George Stephenson would not recognize, but he would have no difficulty with the tunnel mouth.

Right *Totally unexpectedly, the author found this Slamannan Railway stone sleeper-block on 20 April 1988, dislodged from the wall behind, which is apparently built of them.*

Below *The western outpost of the South Durham & Lancashire Union Railway at Kirkby Stephen. This view, looking east, was taken in September 1963.* (H.P. White)

between Airdriehill (Ballochney Railway, qv) and the Union Canal at Causewayend, thus bypassing a lock-ladder at Falkirk. The main line opened on 31 August 1840, but was successful only briefly as the shortest route between Glasgow and Edinburgh — the E&GR's opening put paid to that. The company amalgamated with the Ballochney and the Monkland & Kirkintilloch Railways on 14 August 1848 to form the Monkland Railways (all qv). An extension to Bo'ness (authorized on 26 June 1846, 4.5 miles) was opened on 17 March 1851, the Act also sanctioning lease of the harbour — the railway was built but the

harbour was not leased. The CR was given RP to the harbour, but ran a passenger service only in 1899. Passenger services on the main line ceased on 1 May 1930, but part of the harbour section is preserved as the Bo'ness & Kinneil Railway.

SOUTH DURHAM & LANCASHIRE UNION RAILWAY

A creation of the St&DR, this was an ambitious scheme to link coke from Durham with the haematite and ironworks of Cumbria. Authority was given on 17 July 1857 for a line from Spring Gardens Junction,

near W Auckland, to Tebay via Barnard Castle. The first sod of the Pennine section was cut by the Duke of Cleveland on 25 August 1857; the Darlington & Barnard Castle Railway (qv) was used to link with the St&DR. The engineer was Thomas Bouch, brother of the designer of the Tay Bridge, and the line was noted for several viaducts. It opened for minerals on 4 July 1861, formally on 7 August and to the public the next day. Stainmore summit (1,370 ft) was bleak, bad weather frequently stranding trains for days at a time. The final section was opened on 1 August 1863, after the company joined the St&DR on 1 January (Act of 30 June 1862). It became a heavily-used route, mainly for mineral traffic as intended. It closed in stages, but finally to passengers on 30 November 1964 and to goods on 5 March 1965.

SOUTH LEEDS JUNCTION RAILWAY

Incorporated on 24 August 1893, this 2.25-mile line joined the Leeds–Pontefract line with the E & W Yorkshire Union Railway (qv), which worked it, absorbing it on 2 July 1896. It opened for goods on 6 April 1895, and a link with the MR at Stourton was added on 1 November 1903.

SOUTH YORKSHIRE, DONCASTER & GOOLE RAILWAY

Authorized on 22 July 1847, the plan was to link Barnsley and Doncaster; the line opened on 10 November 1849 between Swinton and Doncaster, and from Aldam Junction to Barnsley on 1 July 1851, the MR working the service and the GNR supplying the coal wagons. The incorporation Act stipulated that an amalgamation with the Don Navigation, also sought by the company, should not happen until half the authorized capital had been raised. When this occurred (19 April 1850), the company name was changed to the S Yorkshire Railway & River Dun Navigation (qv).

SOUTH YORKSHIRE JUNCTION RAILWAY

Authorized on 14 August 1890, the line was promoted by the Denaby & Cadeby Colliery Company to link its pit with the H&BR at Wrangbrook Junction, between Upton and Kirksmeaton. On 28 July 1891, the H&BR was empowered to work its 11.5 miles from opening, on 1 September 1894 (goods), 1 December (passengers). The passenger service ceased from 2 February 1903, and though the company passed to the LNER at Grouping, legal difficulties prevented transfer until 2 July 1924. Final closure came on 7 August 1967.

SOUTH YORKSHIRE RAILWAY & RIVER DUN NAVIGATION

'Dun' is not a misprint, but an old spelling of Don which for legal reasons was used in the Incorporation Act of 19 April 1850, when the S Yorkshire, Doncaster & Goole Railway (qv) changed its name.

The line opened from Aldam Junction (Wombwell) to Moor End (Barnsley) on 1 July 1851, and to Sheffield (Wincobank) on 4 September 1854. The GNR bought 17,000 shares at £20 apiece, and when the line was transferred to the MS&LR it agreed in early February 1861 that the GNR should lease the line. This was ratified by an Act of 23 June 1864, and the line was ultimately vested in the MS&LR by an Act of 16 July 1874.

SPALDING & BOURN (sic) RAILWAY

Incorporated on 29 July 1862, before the line's 9 miles 30 chains opened on 1 August 1866 it had amalgamated with the Lynn & Sutton Bridge Railway to form the Midland & Eastern Railway (both qv) on the previous 23 July. The line met the Bourne & Essendine Railway (qv) end-on at Bourne, and was worked jointly, under Agreement, by the GNR and MR.

SPILSBY & FIRSBY RAILWAY

Authorized on 5 June 1865, this was a lightly-built line of 4 miles 14 chains from the E Lincolnshire Railway near Firsby to a terminus at Spilsby. Money was slow, but the first sod was cut by the Rev Edward Rawnsley, the scheme's instigator, at Spilsby on 14 March 1867, and a commemoration ball was held in the Town Hall that evening. The single line opened on 1 May 1868, worked by the GNR under an Agreement finalized in April 1865, and was bought by it for £20,000 wef 1 January 1891.

STAFFORD & UTTOXETER RAILWAY

This was incorporated on 29 July 1862 to build 13.5 miles of railway with a 2-mile branch to Weston on the NSR, with RP on that line. It was an extension of the GNR's Derbyshire line, and that company also had RP from opening (23 December 1867), and was authorized to work it on 11 August 1879. The NSR, however, had a low opinion of the service provided, a footnote to its timetable tartly observing: 'The times of these trains are given for information only'. Wishing to reach N Wales, the GNR bought the line for £100,000 wef 1 August 1881 (Act of 18 July), beginning a through service between Burton and Stafford. Although closed to passengers on 4 December 1939, a service continued to the RAF Camp at Stafford Common.

STAMFORD & ESSENDINE RAILWAY

The Marquis of Burghley began to regret the stand which had caused the GNR to avoid Stamford, and built a branch (authorized on 15 August 1853) N from Stamford for 3 miles 67 chains to the GNR at Essendine. Opened on 1 November 1856, the line was worked by the GNR at first, then the company from 1 January 1865 until 1 February 1872, when the GNR took over once more. Meanwhile, an 8 miles 22 chains branch S to the L&NWR at Wansford had

The only raised land visible from Twenty station contains a drainage dyke, and there were few engineering problems for the Spalding & Bourn's engineers. The station buildings, seen looking west in M&GNR days, are little changed today, despite railway disuse since 1965. (Douglas Thompson)

Spilsby station from the buffer stops—the passenger service was suspended during the Second World War and did not resume. Now, on 9 July 1954, the goods service had only a little over four years left, the last train running on 30 November 1958. (Douglas Thompson)

been authorized on 25 July 1864 and opened on 9 August 1867. By an Agreement of 15 December 1893, the company was leased to the GNR in perpetuity wef 31 December 1892 (Act of 3 July 1894), but retained independence until the LNER swallowed it in 1923. The Wansford branch closed to passengers on 1 July 1929, the Essendine line on 15 June 1959, though the company's station at Stamford E had closed on 4 March 1957.

STANHOPE & TYNE RAILWAY

Authorized by a Deed of Settlement dated 3 February 1834, and built under the wayleave system, the line opened from Stanhope to Annfield on 15 May 1834, and to S Shields on 10 September. The company became insolvent and was dissolved on 5 February 1841; the E section (Leadgate–S Shields, 24.5 miles) was incorporated into the Pontop & S Shields Rail-

way (qv) on 23 May 1842, and the W end was sold to the Derwent Iron Company, who used it to carry limestone from quarries at Stanhope to works at Consett. Leased by the St&DR wef 1 January 1845, this section was later sold to the Wear Valley Railway, becoming known as the Wear & Derwent Junction Railway (both qv).

STIRLING & DUNFERMLINE RAILWAY

Authorized on 16 July 1846 to link the towns, there were also branches NW to Tillicoultry and to Alloa Harbour. Opening between Dunfermline and Alloa was on 28 August 1850; the harbour and Tillicoultry branches opened on 3 June 1851, and the Alloa–Stirling line on 1 July 1852. The Tillicoultry branch was extended to Kinross — see Devon Valley Railway — after the company's vesting in the E&GR by an Act of 28 June 1858.

North Road station, Darlington, once perhaps the most important station on the Stockton & Darlington Railway. Initiative from Darlington has restored it to a museum of railways in the NE, and more development is planned.

STIRLINGSHIRE MIDLAND JUNCTION RAILWAY

Authorized on 16 July 1846 to build a 5-mile line from Polmont (E&GR) to a point near Larbert (SCR), via Grahamston, the E&GR was hoping to gain traffic from the N. It was to 'requisition' for transfer of the company should it so wish — this was done before opening, which was on 1 October 1850.

STOCKTON & DARLINGTON RAILWAY

Communication between Darlington and the pithead was first mooted as early as 1768, but by canal. The railway scheme did not really surface until 13 November 1818 — a company was incorporated on 19 April 1821, and its line opened to the public on 27 September 1825. The initial concern was coal rather than passengers, who were carried in horsedrawn vehicles until 1833. An extension to Middlesbrough was authorised on 23 May 1828, and opened on 27 December 1830. The system expanded by take-overs and amalgamations until the company was itself absorbed by the NER on 13 July 1863. Timothy Hackworth, appointed foreman of the line in May 1825, also ran his own business from Soho Works, Shildon. The house in which he lived is now a museum.

STOCKTON & HARTLEPOOL RAILWAY

This line, in essence an extension of the Clarence

Railway (qv) from Billingham to Hartlepool, was opened for goods on 12 November 1840 and for passengers on 9 February 1841. It was built without Parliamentary sanction, though the position was later regularized (30 June 1842). The company floated a Dock Company, the Hartlepool W Harbour & Dock (23 May 1844), amalgamating with it on 30 June 1852, and changing its name to the W Hartlepool Harbour & Railway (qv). A 21-year lease of the Clarence Railway (qv) was acquired on 2 September 1844, and a perpetual one wef 1 January 1851; the amalgamation Act with the HWH&DC authorized purchase, lease or amalgamation of the CR — the latter took place wef 17 May 1853.

STRATHENDRICK & ABERFOYLE RAILWAY

Authorized on 12 August 1880 to extend the Blane Valley Railway to Aberfoyle, it used the line of the Forth & Clyde Junction Railway (both qv) between Gartness Junction and Buchlyvie Junction. The line opened on 1 August 1882, worked by the NBR, which absorbed it under an Act of 5 August 1891.

STRATHSPEY RAILWAY

A line from Dufftown to Craigellachie was authorized on 17 May 1861 and opened to Abernethy on 1 July

Old stations are converted to a remarkable variety of uses. Knockando on the erstwhile Strathspey Railway is now a Visitor Centre for a firm of whisky distillers. (Allan Mott)

1863; an extension to the HR 2 miles S of Boat of Garten (authorized on 5 July 1865) was opened on 1 August 1866. Heavily backed by the GNSR, the line was not one of its more successful bargains, being costly to build and unremunerative to run. But the HR also ran through Strathspey, and so . . . The company was absorbed by the GNSR under its enveloping Act of 30 July 1866. The Boat of Garten–Craigellachie section closed to passengers on 18 October 1965.

SUTTON & WILLOUGHBY RAILWAY
Incorporated on 28 July 1884, this line developed out of the Alford & Sutton Tramway (qv — Jt/Ind) into a 7 miles 13 chains line between Louth & Willoughby via Mablethorpe. The aim was to link the E Lincolnshire Railway (qv) with docks at Sutton-on-Sea; the GNR was unwilling to work the line until the docks opened, since its subsidiary Lincolnshire & E Coast Railway (qv) saw the company's line as a threat to its own traffic. The company maintained that it could not build the docks unless it had a railway! However, an Act of 25 September 1886 authorized TA with the GNR, which agreed to work the line for 21 years at 50 per cent of receipts — the Act

also authorized a 2 miles 47 chains extension from Sutton to the L&ECR at Mablethorpe. The line opened formally on 23 September 1886 and to the public on 4 October, and the Mablethorpe extension opened on 14 July 1888. The company amalgamated with the GNR by an Agreement of March 1902.

TANFIELD WAGONWAY
The line developed from a wagonway at Ravensworth, opened, it is believed, about 1632. In June 1726, a group extended it and made branches. Causey Arch was built across Beckley Burn gorge in 1727 and, beautifully restored, is scheduled as an Ancient Monument. In 1820 the route was revised, and in the 1840s relaid with iron edge-rails. Locomotives were introduced in 1881, by which time the company had passed first to the N&DJR and then the NER. The S section continued in use until August 1962, and closed finally on 18 May 1964 — a Preservation group has made a headquarters at Sunniside, near Gateshead.

TEES VALLEY RAILWAY
Incorporated on 19 June 1865 as an independent concern after the NER had absorbed the SD&LUR, it ran for 7.75 miles to Middleton-in-Teesdale from a junction W of Barnard Castle, and served large quarries at Middleton. The line opened on 12 May 1868, and though not officially vested in it until 19 June 1882, was worked by the NER from the start. It

The Tendring Hundred Railway opened its station at Thorpe-le-Soken in 1867, and the company's directors would probably recognize it still. The footbridge is more recent, and what they would make of the overhead line equipment is perhaps best left to the imagination. (Allan Mott)

closed to passengers on 30 November 1964, and to goods wef 5 April 1965.

TENDRING HUNDRED RAILWAY
Authorized on 13 August 1859, the line ran to Wivenhoe (2.5 miles) from the Hythe branch of the Colchester, Stour Valley, Sudbury & Halstead Railway (qv). It opened on 6 May 1863, and on 13 July an extension to Walton-on-the-Naze was authorized, even though the Wivenhoe & Brightlingsea Railway (qv) was already in the area — wrangling with it lasted ten years! A station at Colchester St Botolph's was opened on 1 March 1866, and Walton was reached on 17 May 1867. The GER funded £28,000 of the £33,000 capital required by the 1863 Act, and worked the line from opening for 70 per cent of receipts — 60 per cent after 1882. The company was vested in GER wef 1 July 1883, by an Act of 29 June (see also Clacton-on-Sea Railway).

THETFORD & WATTON RAILWAY
This Norfolk line, authorized on 16 July 1866,

opened from Roudham Junction to Watton on 26 January 1869. On 7 July 1873 the company gained powers to work the Bury & Thetford Railway and the Watton & Swaffham Railway (both qv) on completion. A Bill for amalgamation with the W&SR was rejected in 1878, and from 1 August 1879 the company handed working to the GER. A formal lease followed, wef 1 January 1880, with sale and dissolution on 1 July 1897 by an Act dated a fortnight later.

TICKHILL LIGHT RAILWAY
This was an 8-mile line linking Bawtry and Haxey, built by a LRO of 7 August 1901. There were to be no junctions with the GNR, GCR or L&YR, but powers were transferred to the GNR in 1907, which opened the line for goods on 26 August 1912.

TRANENT & COCKENZIE WAGONWAY
Worked by gravity and horses, this wooden plateway opened in 1722 between pits at Tranent and the Firth of Forth at Cockenzie (Port Seton). It was about 2.5 miles long, with a gauge of 3 ft 3 in, and carried coal and salt. In 1815 it was converted to edge-rails, and in 1846 the NBR took over the Tranent–Meadowmill section — it re-opened the line from Tranent pits to Tranent (later Prestonpans) on 11 December 1849, doubling the main line. Re-singled in April 1853, the rest was abandoned.

TRENT, ANCHOLME & GRIMSBY LIGHT RAILWAY

This was a small private railway between the River Trent and Ancholme, in which both the S Yorkshire Railway (qv) and the MS&LR became interested. A joint promotion was arranged and a 14-mile line between Keadby and Barnetby via Scunthorpe was authorized on 22 July 1861. Though ready by 1864, the BoT would not pass it for traffic until certain improvements had been made. It opened for goods on 1 May 1866, passengers on 1 October. In 1910 the bridge across the Trent needed renewal – this was done with a 160 ft single-span lifting Scherzer, with two 135 ft fixed spans. A road was included, and it opened on 21 May 1916. The company was dissolved and vested in the MS&LR on 12 July 1882.

WAINFLEET & FIRSBY RAILWAY

This 4 miles 22 chains line was authorized on 13 May 1869 – the company was planning a Skegness extension before opening, and its 5 miles 2 chains were sanctioned on 18 July 1872. The line opened on 24 October 1871 (to Skegness on 28 July 1873), and was worked by the GNR from the start. Through running via Firsby S curve was possible from 1881, and the GNR, which had bought the company for £76,500 wef 1 January 1896 (Act of 30 May 1895),

doubled the line in 1900. Sunday excursions were run as Skegness developed, despite criticism from evangelical churches; the famous 'Jolly Sailor' poster appeared in this connection in 1908. Firsby closed to passengers on 5 October 1970, but the line to Skegness, via the curve, remains.

WANSBECK RAILWAY

This was formed on 8 August 1859 as an NBR sponsorship between the Border Counties Railway and the Blyth & Tyne Railway (both qv), with a short branch to the NER, and obviously (at least to NE eyes) a ploy by the NBR to tap its preserves. It opened from Morpeth (NER) to Scotsgap on 23 July 1862, to Reedmouth (NBR) on 1 May 1865, and its 28 miles were duly absorbed by their patron by an Act of 21 July 1863. The last train, hauled by Class 'J27' No 65882, passed on 6 October 1966 – the final passenger train had run four days before.

WARE, HADHAM & BUNTINGFORD RAILWAY

Despite its name, this line never went to Ware – had

Little remains of the Ware, Hadham & Buntingford Railway, but a prospective passenger at Buntingford might have seen something like this (caravan excepted) as he approached to buy his ticket. The building is now privately owned. (Allan Mott)

it not been for help from the ECR in 1861 and later from the GER, it would never have gone anywhere. Authorized on 12 July 1858, it joined the Broxbourne–Hertford branch near St Margarets and was opened on 3 July 1863 under GER operation. The GER bought the line on 1 September 1868; provision had been made for this in the GER Incorporation Act. The line closed to passengers on 16 November 1964 and to goods on 20 September 1965.

WATTON & SWAFFHAM RAILWAY

Incorporated on 20 July 1869, this line was a 9 miles 2 furlongs 8 chains extension of the Thetford & Watton Railway, linking Watton with the Lynn & Dereham Railway (both qv) at Swaffham. It was opened on 20 September 1875, leased by the GER with the T&WR in 1879, dissolved and vested by an Act of 15 July 1897, wef 1 July.

WAVENEY VALLEY RAILWAY

Powers for 13 miles from Tivetshall to Bungay were given to the EUR on 3 July 1851, and authority to extend to Beccles was granted on 4 August 1853. Opening from Tivetshall to Harleston was on 1 December 1855, to Bungay on 2 November 1860, and to Beccles on 2 March 1863; the line was worked at first by the ECR, but after disputes the company operated traffic itself. Nothing came of several grandiose E–W schemes, and by the time the ESR arrived at Beccles, the GER had agreed to incorporate the whole line. The absorption Act gained Royal Assent on 21 July 1863.

WEAR & DERWENT RAILWAY

This was the name by which the W section of the erstwhile Stanhope & Tyne Railway (qv) became known. It was leased by the St&DR from the Derwent Iron Company wef 1 January 1845, and was sold to the Wear Valley Railway on 22 July 1847. With the Weardale Extension Railway (both qv), this line became unofficially known as the Wear & Derwent Junction Railway.

WEARDALE EXTENSION RAILWAY

Built for the Derwent Iron Company by the St&DR, and opened on 14 May 1845, this ran from the Bishop Auckland & Weardale Railway at Crook to the Wear & Derwent Railway (both qv) at Waskerley. The line had no Parliamentary sanction, and was bought by a consortium of St&DR businessmen, probably early in 1845. It was resold to the Wear Valley Railway on 22 July 1847, after which it became (unofficially) known as the Wear & Derwent Junction Railway.

WEAR VALLEY RAILWAY

Authorized independently on 31 July 1845, this was a 10.75-mile branch from the Bishop Auckland & Weardale Railway (qv) to Frosterley, with a branch to Bishopley Crag from Broad Wood. Opening day was 3 August 1847. Purchase of the Bishop Auckland & Weardale, the Shildon Tunnel, the Wear & Derwent and the Weardale Extension Railways (all qv) was confirmed by an Act of 22 July 1847, and the company was itself leased by the St&DR in September 1847 and absorbed on 23 July 1858. The Frosterley & Stanhope Railway (qv) extended it to Stanhope in 1862. Stanhope shed was a temporary refuge for *Locomotion No 1* and *Derwent* when they were evacuated from Darlington Bank Top during the Second World War. The line's passenger service closed on 29 June 1953.

WEAR VALLEY EXTENSION RAILWAY

This was incorporated on 20 June 1892 after pressure to build along the Wear Valley to Wearhead, but before the 9.25-mile line was complete the minerals boom had passed its peak. The company had little independence — its powers were transferred to the NER on 31 July 1894, and the line was opened on 21 October 1895. A self-acting incline at Heights was closed in 1922.

WELLS & FAKENHAM RAILWAY

This 9.5-mile line was promoted by the Earl of Leicester, landowners and a group of NR directors. It was authorized on 24 July 1854, and was opened on 1 December 1857, worked by the ECR. A harbour branch at Wells was sanctioned on 13 August 1859, the Act authorizing the NR to subscribe and hold shares. The company remained independent until absorbed by the GER in 1862. Never a busy route, it closed to passengers on 5 October 1964, and to goods on 31 October; the Wells & Walsingham LR, a 12.75 in gauge pleasure line, now uses the track-bed between Wells and Walsingham.

WEMYSS & BUCKHAVEN RAILWAY

Built under a BoT certificate of 1879, this line belonged to a coal-owner, R.E. Wemyss, and opened to Buckhaven on 1 August 1881 and to Methil on 5 May 1887. By an Act of 26 July 1889, Wemyss sold the line to the NBR (which had worked it), and got a seat on the NBR Board, having undertaken that coal-owners would not support any new coal railways in Fife, unless projected by the NBR, for 21 years, and would build none themselves. When, in 1897, Wemyss announced that he was planning a new line to Methil in opposition to the one he had sold, he sparked off a row which brought the NBR into much disrepute.

WEST DURHAM RAILWAY

This line ran from an end-on junction with the Clarence Railway (qv) 2 miles W of Spennymoor, and was built without benefit of Parliament by promoters hoping to be able to rely on wayleaves. There

Not many stations can have been converted into churches. Walsingham station (Wells & Fakenham Railway) is now the church of the Greek Orthodox community in the town. Even old platforms can be useful . . . (Allan Mott)

was much opposition from the St&DR which viewed askance interlopers in 'its' territory, so that when construction was well advanced an Act was sought; passed on 4 July 1839, it made the acquisition of land easier. The line, opened from Willington to Byers Green on 12 June 1840 and throughout on 19 October, was later extended to Whitemee Colliery, N of Crook, almost 5.5 miles, including a notable bridge across the Wear. Though successful at first (dividends of 10 per cent were paid), it did not last. After absorption of the St&DR by the NER, the company could no longer compete, and WA with the NER in 1866 led to absorption on 4 July 1870.

WEST HARTLEPOOL HARBOUR & RAILWAY

This was formed on 30 June 1852 when the Hartlepool W Harbour and Dock Company merged with the Stockton & Hartlepool and Clarence Railways (all qv). The company competed successfully with the St&DR and NER in the fight for ironstone from Cleveland, but succumbed to absorption by the NER wef 5 July 1865.

WEST HIGHLAND RAILWAY

Incorporated on 12 August 1889, this was an NBR effort to counter the Callander & Oban Railway (qv — LMS) and reach the Scottish W coast. It climbed from the Clyde at Craigendoran, alongside Loch Lomond to Crainlarich, reaching 1,350 ft on Rannoch Moor. It then descended to Tulloch and Fort William, reached first by passengers on 7 August 1894 — an official opening was held on 11 August. On 31 July that year an extension to Mallaig was authorized, opening on 1 April 1901. This stretch includes Glenfinnan viaduct, and has been a route for steam specials in recent years. The company was absorbed by the NBR on 21 December 1908.

WEST NORFOLK JUNCTION RAILWAY

Incorporated on 23 June 1864, this was 18.75 miles of railway between Heacham and Wells, opened on 17 August 1866 and operated from the start by the GER. The company merged with the Lynn & Hunstanton Railway wef 1 July 1874 (Act of 8 June) to form the Hunstanton & W Norfolk Railway (both qv). Passenger services were withdrawn from 2 June 1952.

WEST OF FIFE MINERAL RAILWAY

Authorized on 14 July 1856 between Dunfermline and Killairnie, with a branch to Kingseat, this was

Glenfinnan Viaduct (West Highland Railway), the first viaduct in which concrete was extensively used, is 100 ft high, with 21 spans of 50 ft. Here Steamtown's Stanier Class '5' No 5407 with the Fort William–Mallaig 'West Highlander' in August 1984, eases the train across in compliance with the speed restriction. (J.M. Webber)

extended to Beath (see Kinross-shire Railway) by an Act of 23 July 1860. On 1 August 1861 the company joined the Charlestown Railway & Harbour to form the W of Fife Railway and Harbour Company (both qv).

WEST OF FIFE RAILWAY & HARBOUR COMPANY

This was formed on 1 August 1861 by the merging of the W of Fife Mineral Railway and the Charlestown Railway & Harbour. The company's independence was short, for by an Act of 29 July 1862 it was vested in the NBR.

WEST RIDING & GRIMSBY JOINT RAILWAY

The company was sponsored by the S Yorkshire & River Dun Navigation as the W Riding, Hull & Grantham Railway to run from Wakefield to Stainforth, with a branch to Doncaster. Also backed by the MS&LR, it was incorporated on 7 August 1862, but the GNR saw the line as a threat and tried to buy it. After argument, a joint purchase with the MS&LR was authorized on 28 June 1866, wef opening day,

1 February 1866. The company was absorbed by the GCR and GNR jointly from 1 August 1897, passing to the LNER at Grouping.

WHITBY & PICKERING RAILWAY

This 24-mile line was surveyed by George Stephenson and authorized on 6 May 1833. It opened between Whitby and Grosmont on 8 June 1835 and to Pickering on 26 May 1836, using a rope-worked incline to rise from the Esk Valley; this was superseded by an ascent suitable for steam engines on 1 July 1865, though these had been used between Pickering and the head of the incline since 1847. The company was bought by the Y&NMR on 30 June 1845. The line closed on 8 March 1965, and the stretch between Grosmont and Pickering is now run by the North Yorkshire Moors Railway as a preserved line. BR retains services along the Esk valley to Whitby. Both the incline and the original tunnel at Grosmont, built for horse-worked days, are now used as footpaths, the latter for access to the NYMR loco shed.

WHITBY, REDCAR & MIDDLESBROUGH UNION RAILWAY

Incorporated on 16 July 1866, the company was soon in financial trouble and asked the NER to finish its line. It had made a poor job of the work so far, a part between Sandsend and Kettleness having already fallen into the sea! There were five major viaducts, and a zigzag to mines at Loftus and Skinningrove Gasworks. The line, leased to the NER from 1 July 1875 (Act of 19 July) opened on 5 December 1883, and was absorbed by an Act of 5 July 1889. It closed S of Skinningrove on 5 May 1958, but part has been reinstated as far as Boulby for freight only.

WHITEINCH RAILWAY

Authorized on 1 July 1872, this was a short branch from the Stobcross branch of the NBR near Crow Road to the Glasgow–Dumbarton trunk road. The NBR worked it from opening in September 1874, and, having coveted it for some time, bought it under an Authority dated 5 August 1891. See also Whiteinch Tramway.

WHITEINCH TRAMWAY

Authorized on 1 July 1872 and opened in September 1874, this horse-worked line continued the Whiteinch Railway (qv) from the Glasgow–Dumbarton trunk road to the Clyde. In 1875 an engine was bought, and in 1878 and 1891 the NBR tried, in vain, to oust the proprietors. The opening of the Lanarkshire & Dumbartonshire Railway (qv) put the company into voluntary liquidation; a firm of coalmasters took over management, the NBR supplying an engine and track maintenance — it was given rights to work the line in perpetuity in 1916.

WIGAN JUNCTION RAILWAY

Authorized on 16 July 1874 to build from Glazebrook to Wigan, the first sod was cut in October 1876. Help came from the MS&LR, which worked it from the start — opening (goods) between Glazebrook and Strangeways was on 16 October 1879, (passengers) 1 April 1884, when the line opened through to Wigan also. Wigan Central opened on 3 October 1892. The GCR absorbed the company wef 1 January 1906 by an Act dated 4 August 1905.

WILSONTOWN, MORNINGSIDE & COLTNESS RAILWAY

This line of 8.65 miles authorized on 21 June 1841 ran from Chapel (Wishaw & Coltness Railway, qv) via Morningside and Wilsontown to Longridge, near Whitburn. Though primarily a coal railway, it also served an ironworks at Wilsontown, and was opened on 2 June 1845. Not one of the better-made lines, it survived to be vested in the E&GR on 28 July 1849.

WISBECH, ST IVES & CAMBRIDGE JUNCTION RAILWAY

The ECR was to help build this line, authorized on 7 August 1846, the Act also sanctioning sale of the company to it. Since the company was part of the ECR before it came into the GER (1862), the ECR appears to have exercised its powers without troubling Parliament further. The line opened from Wisbech to

March on 3 March 1847 and through to St Ives on 1 February next year. The latter section became part of the GN&GEJR from 1882, closing on 18 April 1966 (goods), 6 March 1967 (passengers). The March–Wisbech section survives for goods, and at the time of writing representations are being made for a re-opening to passengers.

WIVENHOE & BRIGHTLINGSEA RAILWAY

This 5 miles 4 chains line, authorized on 11 July 1861, ran beside an Essex tidal creek, and yielded good oyster and fish traffic. The GER worked it from opening (18 April 1866) for 40 per cent of receipts, before buying it outright for £31,000 by an Act of 12 May 1893 — it was reckoned to have made a bargain.

WREXHAM, MOLD & CONNAH'S QUAY RAILWAY

This was incorporated on 7 August 1862 to build to the Buckley Railway (qv) from Wrexham, agreeing in 1863 to work the BR as its own line. The major engineering work was a five-arch viaduct across the River Alyn at Caergwrle, and the line opened, single track, for goods on 1 January 1866, but for passengers on 1 May only after a second inspection. Working or purchase of the line by the L&NWR was sought in 1866, but objections were raised by the GWR and the matter was dropped. Extension across the Dee to Hawarden and new docks at Connah's Quay were authorized on 18 August 1882. On 26 July 1889 the

Buckley Junction signal box, where the WM&CQR joined the Buckley Railway, which it worked from 1863 – the Buckley line here diverges towards the camera, the WM&CQR continuing to Hawarden and Connah's Quay. (Robert Humm)

MS&LR bought a majority shareholding, having paid in 1884 for the Chester–Hawarden link (opened on 31 March 1890) to be built. In 1897 the GCR forced the company into the hands of an OR from where official take-over was but a short step; the company was vested in the GCR wef 1 January 1905, by an Act of 22 July 1904.

YARMOUTH & HADDISCOE RAILWAY

Another of Peto's projects, this was authorized on 7 July 1856, including dock branches at Yarmouth (Southtown). Independence was brief, and on 23 July 1858 the company amalgamated with the ESR, which opened the line on 1 June 1859.

YARMOUTH & NORTH NORFOLK RAILWAY

This was the title taken by the Yarmouth & N Norfolk LR when authorized (11 August 1881) to extend to the Lynn & Fakenham Railway (qv). It amalgamated with the L&FR before either line was open, and in combination with the Yarmouth Union and the Lynn & Fakenham Railways (both qv) formed the E&MR from 1 July 1883.

YARMOUTH & NORTH NORFOLK (LIGHT) RAILWAY

This was the title (from 27 May 1878) of the company incorporated as the Great Yarmouth & Stalham LR (qv). The Hemsby–Martham section was opened on 15 July 1878, and an extension to the Lynn & Fakenham Railway at Pudding Norton was authorized on 11 August 1881. This prompted another name-change, to the Yarmouth & N Norfolk Railway (qv).

YARMOUTH & NORWICH RAILWAY

Incorporated on 18 June 1842, this was planned as the first part of a cross-country trunk route. Backed and surveyed by the Stephensons, the contractors were Grissell & Peto, Peto acting as resident engineer. It opened on 1 May 1844. A brewery contribution was part of a deal to provide a public house near most stations, and prohibited a refreshment room at Yarmouth (Vauxhall). It may have been the basis of a lawsuit at Berney Arms; the station was built as a condition of the sale of land, but stops at the station were not specified in the bill of sale. When the company failed to halt its trains there, the landlord of the hostelry sued, and ten years of litigation ended in 1860 with the plaintiff's victory. Following an amalgamation Agreement with the Norwich & Brandon Railway (qv), the company became the NR under an Act of 30 June 1845, the N&BR joining it on its own opening a month later.

YARMOUTH UNION RAILWAY

Incorporated on 26 August 1880, this was a link between Yarmouth's quayside tramways and Yarmouth (Beach) station. It opened on 15 May 1882, and after a brief independent life amalgamated with the Yarmouth & N Norfolk, and the Lynn & Fakenham Railways (both qv) by an Act of 18 August 1882 to form the E&MR wef 1 July 1883.

YORK & NEWCASTLE RAILWAY

An Act of 3 August 1846 authorized purchase of the Pontop & S Shields Railway by the N&DJR and sanctioned a name-change. But it did not last long —

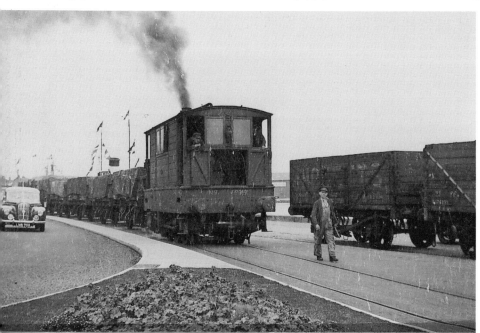

Left *The GER 'tram' engines (Classes 'Y6' and 'J70') were built to work the dock lines of East Anglia. Here 'J70' No 68919 uses the one-time Yarmouth Union line to return to Yarmouth (Vauxhall) with a train from the harbour one evening in August 1951. (Rev W. Awdry)*

Above right *Less well-known than his bridges at Conwy or Menai was Robert Stephenson's tubular bridge across the River Aire at Brotherton, Yorks, for the Y&NMR. The tube was replaced by a girder in 1903, but the stonework is original.*

amalgamation on 9 July 1847 with the Newcastle & Berwick Railway (qv) formed the YN&BR.

YORK & NORTH MIDLAND RAILWAY

This line, authorized on 21 June 1836, went S from an end-on junction with the GNER at York to link with the Leeds & Selby Railway (qv) at York Junction and later with the NMR at Altofts; it opened to York Junction on 29 May 1839, to Burton Salmon on 11 May 1840 and to Altofts on 1 July. Having leased the L&SR and then bought it (23 May 1844), the company bought the Whitby & Pickering Railway (qv) on 30 June 1845. It leased the Hull & Selby Railway wef 27 July 1846 and absorbed the E & W Yorkshire Junction Railway (both qv) on 28 May 1852. Powers to extend to Harrogate (opened on 20 July 1848) were given in 1845, and the next year branches to Knottingley, Boroughbridge via Knaresborough, and Hull were authorized. The company became a constituent of the NER on 31 July 1854.

YORK, NEWCASTLE & BERWICK RAILWAY

This was formed on 9 July 1847 when the York & Newcastle and Newcastle & Berwick Railways (both qv) amalgamated. The line from Northallerton to Leeming Bar was opened on 6 March 1848, and on 30 June authority was given for a railway along the Team Valley. It opened on 1 April 1857, but by then the company had been part of the NER since 31 July 1854.

PART 4

The Southern Railway group

The insignia of the Southern Railway. (Allan Mott)

Overleaf *The companies making up the SR all had outlets to the continent, and made much of them. These 'destination bricks' can still be seen at Blackfriars, though the station itself has now been incorporated into office blocks.* (Allan Mott)

ANTWERP ASHFORD GRAVESEND DARMSTADT

BALE BADEN BADEN BECKENHAM HERNE BAY FLORENCE NICE

BERLIN BICKLEY MAIDSTONE FRANKFORT

GENOA BOULOGNE BROADSTAIRS MARGATE GENEVA PARIS

BREMEN BROMLEY RAMSGATE LAUSANNE

MILAN BRINDISI CANTERBURY ROCHESTER LEIPSIC ROME

BRUSSELS CHATHAM SEVENOAKS LUCERNE

LYONS CALAIS CRYSTAL PALACE SITTINGBOURNE MARSEILLES TURIN

CANNES DEAL SHEERNESS VIENNA

NAPLES COLOGNE DOVER ST LEONARDS ST PETERSBURG VENICE

DRESDEN WIESBADEN

SOUTHERN RAILWAY

Formed wef 1 January 1923, this was an amalgamation of the L&SWR, LB&SCR, LC&DR and SER, with several smaller concerns. Most of the new company's activities went on between Hampshire and Kent, though the L&SWR influence gave it tentacles into Dorset, Devon and as far W as Padstow, in Cornwall.

ALTON, ALRESFORD & WINCHESTER RAILWAY

This was an independent company incorporated on 28 June 1861 to extend the Alton branch of the L&SWR for 17 miles to Winchester. Before the line opened, the company changed its name to the Mid Hants (Alton Lines) Railway (qv).

ANDOVER & REDBRIDGE RAILWAY

Incorporated on 12 July 1858, the company had GWR support to build a broad gauge line along the course of the Andover Canal. When the company went bankrupt, both GWR and L&SWR tried to gain control. In 1863 it was agreed that the L&SWR should do so, by an Act backdated to 14 November 1862 — it opened the line 6 March 1865. Another Act authorized extension to the L&SWR main line, and the company was absorbed into the L&SWR, an Act of 29 June 1863 confirming an Agreement of 12 December 1862, with amalgamation authorized on 25 July 1864. In 1885, the line's severe curves were eased and the track doubled — it became known as the 'Sprat and Winkle' line.

AXMINSTER & LYME REGIS LIGHT RAILWAY

The first of several abortive attempts to build a railway to Lyme Regis was made in 1845. Then, after an Act of 14 August 1871, a first sod was cut on 29 September 1874; 24 years later people were still arguing about where the line should start! Finally, a LRO was obtained on 15 June 1899, and the line opened four years later on 24 August 1903. Though well-used, traffic fell short of hopes and there were always financial problems. The L&SWR was asked to take over, which it did wef 1 January 1907 by an Act of 20 July 1906. The line closed on 29 November 1965 — in 1970 a miniature railway was projected at Combpyne, but was abandoned for financial reasons.

BANSTEAD & EPSOM DOWNS RAILWAY

Incorporated on 17 July 1862, this was a 4-mile branch from Sutton (LB&SCR) to Epsom Downs promoted by local businessmen to exploit traffic to the racecourse. Dissension among the Directors almost wrecked the venture, and it was perhaps a relief when the company amalgamated with the LB&SCR on 29 July 1864 — the line opened on 22 May 1865.

The Axminster & Lyme Regis Light Railway station at Lyme was above the town, the road falling steeply beyond the station. The train, leaving in July 1960, includes through carriages to London, and is hauled by Nos 30582 and 30583, two of the Adams 4-4-2 tank engines that were the mainstay of the line. No 30583 is now preserved as L&SWR No 488 on the Bluebell Railway. (MWK/Andrew Ingram)

BARNSTAPLE & ILFRACOMBE RAILWAY

Incorporated as a LR on 4 July 1870, this spectacular but heavily-graded line of 14 miles 6 furlongs was run by the L&SWR from its opening on 20 July 1874. Amalgamated with the working company under an Act of 16 July 1874, the track was doubled in 1889–91, and closed to passengers on 5 October 1970.

BASINGSTOKE & ALTON LIGHT RAILWAY

This line, running between Butts Junction, S of Alton, and Basingstoke, was a retaliation by the L&SWR to a GWR threat to build a direct line to Portsmouth. The first sod was cut in 1898 and the line opened on 1 June 1901, but it was never a paying proposition; it was closed on 1 January 1917 and the rails were taken to France. The SR sought an abandonment order in 1923, but were compelled to re-open on 18 August 1924. Final closure came for passengers on 12 September 1932, and for goods on 1 June 1936. During the summer of 1937, the Will Hay feature film *Oh, Mr Porter!* was shot on the line. Demolition was simultaneous, the rails being removed to the new steelworks at Corby, Northants.

BASINGSTOKE & SALISBURY RAILWAY

This line was authorized on 13 August 1846, but work was soon suspended. Powers to acquire land and complete the line were transferred to the L&SWR by an Act of 26 June 1849, and work began again in 1851. Opening to Andover was on 3 July 1854, and to Milford, just outside Salisbury, on 1 May 1857.

BERE ALSTON & CALSTOCK RAILWAY

Authorized by LRO on 12 July 1900 as an independent company within the PD&SWJR, this 3 ft 6 in gauge line linked Bere Alston and the E Cornwall Mineral Railway (qv) at Calstock, with a substantial viaduct across the Tamar — the direct distance between the places is somewhat less than the 4.5 miles of the railway! An Order of 12 October 1905 authorized conversion to standard gauge. The line opened on 2 March 1908, and in July 1908, the L&SWR was asked to take over, but advised the PD&SWJR to run the line itself, which it did until Grouping. The last passenger train above Gunnislake ran on 5 November 1966, but the rest survives as BR's Gunnislake branch.

BEXLEYHEATH RAILWAY

Authorized on 20 August 1883, this was a branch from the North Kent line (SER) at Blackheath to a second junction E of Slade Green. Money was short and progress consequently slow, but with grudging approval from the SER the line was opened on 1 May 1895. When bankruptcy loomed, the SER, hearing of building developments in the area, stepped in and bought the line cheaply on 10 July 1900.

BIDEFORD EXTENSION RAILWAY

Authorized on 4 August 1853 as a 6.5-mile extension of the NDR&DC from Fremington to Bideford, it was leased from opening on 2 November 1855 by Thomas Brassey, who worked it as one with the N Devon Railway (qv). The L&SWR took over the lease from 1 August 1862, absorbing the company

Left *The Banstead & Epsom Downs Railway acquired a second rival for the Epsom race traffic when the SER opened its line to Tattenham Corner from Purley—the Chipstead Valley Railway. Kingswood was the terminus of the line between November 1897 and July 1900.* (Allan Mott)

Right *Bishop's Waltham from the buffer stops in May 1953. It was a large building, albeit a terminus, for a short line.* (Douglas Thompson)

wef 1 January 1865 (Act of 25 July 1864). Powers to remove the broad gauge rails were obtained on 13 July 1876, a Torrington extension having opened on 18 July 1872. Passenger traffic ceased on 4 October 1965.

BISHOP'S WALTHAM RAILWAY

The company was incorporated on 17 July 1862 to connect Bishop's Waltham with Botley (3.75 miles), between Eastleigh and Fareham. The line opened on 1 June 1863, worked by the L&SWR from the outset; an Act authorizing permanent lease or absorption received Royal Assent on 22 June 1863. The last passenger train ran on 31 December 1932.

BODMIN & WADEBRIDGE RAILWAY

Incorporated on 23 May 1832, Cornwall's first locomotive railway ran from Wadebridge to Wenford Bridge, with branches to Bodmin and Ruthern Bridge. Built to carry ore for shipment, it was laid with edge-rails on granite blocks, and was subscribed almost entirely by local people; its 22.5 miles cost only £35,498 2s 9d (£35,498.14p). It opened between Wadebridge and Dunmere on 4 July 1934, and throughout on 30 September. It was 'acquired' by the L&SWR in 1847, remaining in its hands until the situation was legalized by an Act of 25 June 1886. It was not connected with the L&SWR system until the North Cornwall Railway (qv) opened to Wadebridge in 1895. A feeder from Bodmin to Bodmin Road (GWR) opened on 27 May 1887, and an extension to Boscarne Road on 3 September 1888. The last train to Ruthern Bridge ran on 29 November 1933, though the official closure date was 30 December; the

last BR train on the Bodmin–Wenford Bridge section ran on 26 September 1983. Bodmin (General) station is now the headquarters of the Bodmin Steam Railway.

BOGNOR RAILWAY

Sanction to build to Bognor Regis from the Brighton-Portsmouth (LB&SCR) line was given to a nominally independent company on 11 July 1861, after powers granted in 1853 had lapsed. The LB&SCR opened the line on 1 June 1864 and was authorized to absorb its protégé by an Act of 29 July that year.

BRADING HARBOUR IMPROVEMENT & RAILWAY

This was incorporated on 7 August 1874 to build a line from Bembridge, on the E coast of the Isle of Wight, to St Helens, where it joined an Isle of Wight (E Section) Railway (qv) branch from Brading. The 2.75-mile line was worked by the IOW(ES)R from opening (27 May 1882) and bought on 2 August 1898 for £17,000; an Act of 14 August 1896 had redefined the Harbour limits and changed the undertaking's name to the Brading Harbour & Railway Company.

BRIDGEWATER (sic) RAILWAY

The Incorporation Act (18 August 1882) of this 7.5-mile line from Edington to Bridgwater (Somerset) included authority for WA with the L&SWR. Earthworks were built for double track, though the line remained single — opened on 21 July 1890, it was worked by an S&DR committee by Agreement with the L&SWR. It passed to the SR at Grouping, and closed on 1 October 1954.

BRIGHTON & CHICHESTER RAILWAY

Powers stipulated at Incorporation (4 July 1844) enabled the London & Brighton Railway to buy the company under a further Act of 27 July 1846, the same Act which combined the L&BR and the London & Croydon Railway as the LB&SCR. The line had opened to Worthing on 24 November 1845, to Lyminster (Littlehampton) on 16 March 1846 and to Chichester on 8 June. Extension to Portsmouth was authorized on 8 August 1845, and agreement between the LB&SCR and L&SWR made this section (opened 14 June 1847) a joint line.

BRIGHTON & DYKE RAILWAY

Authorized on 2 August 1877, this 3.5-mile line ran from Dyke Junction along the South Downs to the Devils Dyke. Opened on 1 September 1887 and always worked by the LB&SCR, it retained independence until reluctantly absorbed by the SR in 1923. It was closed between 1 January 1917 and 26 July 1920 as a wartime economy, closing finally to goods from 2 January 1933, and to passengers from 1 January 1939.

BRIGHTON, LEWES & HASTINGS RAILWAY

Powers for this line, 32.5 miles long, were granted to the London & Brighton Railway on 29 July 1844. Selfishly, perhaps, it left the building to the independent company before absorbing it on 27 July 1846, under powers in the Incorporation Act. The LB&SCR realized that the decaying port of Newhaven had possibilities, and obtained powers for a 6-mile extension there on 18 June 1846. The line from Brighton to Lewes opened on 8 June 1846, to Bulverhythe on 27 June, to St Leonards on 7 November, and to Hastings on 13 February 1851.

BRIGHTON, UCKFIELD & TUNBRIDGE WELLS RAILWAY

A line between these towns, 15.5 miles long, was authorized on 22 July 1861; before opening (to goods in 1867, and to passengers on 3 August 1868), the company was absorbed by the LB&SCR (29 July 1864). It joined the East Grinstead, Groombridge & Tunbridge Wells Railway (qv) at Groombridge, and its main engineering feature was Crowborough Tunnel, 1,020 yds long, through clay.

BROMLEY DIRECT RAILWAY

A short, locally-promoted line of 1 mile 50 chains between Bromley and Grove Park, its Act (16 July 1874) including powers to make WA with the SER. The line opened on 1 January 1878, and the next year (21 July) the company was absorbed by the SER, which wanted to break the LC&DR monopoly in the area. Bromley was renamed Bromley North by the SER on 1 June 1899, and the line closed for goods traffic on 20 May 1968.

BUDLEIGH SALTERTON RAILWAY

Not the first scheme of its kind (the other, of 28 July 1863, failed), this locally-sponsored line gained Royal Assent on 20 July 1894. It used the Otter Valley from a junction with the Sidmouth Railway (qv) at Tipton St Johns, and was opened on 15 May 1897. Powers were given for WA with the L&SWR, which built an extension to Exmouth, opened on 1 June 1903, and absorbed the company by an Act of 18 August 1911.

CALLINGTON & CALSTOCK RAILWAY

The company was authorized on 9 August 1869 to

The Brighton, Lewes & Hastings Railway enjoyed no real independence, as is perhaps indicated by this fine 'Brighton' insignia adorning the station at Lewes. (Allan Mott)

The locomotive Invicta *(the motto of the County of Kent) was built at Robert Stephenson's Newcastle works for the Canterbury & Whitstable Railway. Edward Fletcher drove it on the opening day, later becoming Locomotive Superintendent on the NER.* (Canterbury Heritage–Time-walk Museum)

build a railway, at any gauge between 3 ft and standard, for almost 8 miles between the towns, using the earthworks of the Tamar, Kit Hill and Callington Railway (qv). A gauge of 3 ft 6 in was chosen, but before the line was finished the company changed its name to the East Cornwall Mineral Railway (qv) on 25 May 1871.

CANTERBURY & WHITSTABLE RAILWAY

Authorized on 10 June 1825, this was the first steam-powered railway in southern England, the first to haul passengers by steam and to issue season tickets (in 1834). It was built by Joseph Locke, one of George Stephenson's assistants, and opened on 3 May 1830 with great rejoicing. The line was single, 6 miles long, and included a 1,012 yd tunnel. An extension to Whitstable harbour was opened on 19 March 1832. The line was leased by the Contractor in 1838, but he went bankrupt three years later and the line was worked by stationary engines. The SER came to the rescue, working the line from 29

September 1844 and absorbing it under an Act dated 4 August 1853. It closed to passengers from 1 January 1931, and to goods on 1 December 1952, though it re-opened for a few weeks after the floods of 1953.

CATERHAM RAILWAY

This company, incorporated on 16 June 1854, built a branch from the SER at Purley, 4 miles 50 chains of line, which was to become a bone of contention between the SER and the LB&SCR, neither being prepared to let the other work it. Opening was delayed until 5 August 1856, and rolling-stock hired from the LB&SCR was used. The company then sued the LB&SCR over the delay; it countered in regard to the hire of the stock, at which point the company went bankrupt! The LB&SCR continued to cause trouble over traffic and connections, and when negotiations finally broke down the company was bought by the SER on 7 July 1859; £14,000 was paid for a railway that had cost £40,000 to build. The single track was doubled at the end of 1899.

CENTRAL CORNWALL RAILWAY

Incorporated as the Launceston, Bodmin & Wadebridge Junction Railway (qv), the company's title was changed on 6 July 1865 when an extension from Ruthern Bridge was authorized. Powers lapsed, however, to be revived on 18 August 1882 as the North Cornwall Railway (qv).

CHARD RAILWAY

This 3-mile line was authorized on 25 May 1860 to link Chard with the L&SWR — powers were also granted to build a tramway to the Chard Canal. Opened on 8 May 1863, the company was absorbed by the L&SWR under an Act of 22 June 1863.

CHARING CROSS RAILWAY

Incorporated on 8 August 1859, this 1.9-mile extension ran from the SER at London Bridge to the site of Hungerford Market, duly renamed. The station was designed by the company's engineer, N. Hawkshaw, and, with the extension, cost £4 million. London & Greenwich and Mid-Kent trains used it from 11 January 1864, and North Kent traffic from 1 April; the main line was opened on 1 May. The SER absorbed the company by an Act of 13 July 1863, wef 1 August 1864. A spur to Cannon Street was authorized, and opened on 1 September 1866; a spur into Waterloo was stipulated, but, though built, was used only for specials and exchange of vehicles — it

Charing Cross station in 1863, just before opening. The photograph was taken by Saxby & Farmer, the engineers installing the signalling equipment. (Westinghouse Signals Ltd/Rev W. Awdry Collection)

opened on 11 January 1864 and was last used on 25 March 1911.

CHICHESTER & MIDHURST RAILWAY

Incorporated on 23 June 1864, the company collapsed before the completion of its 12-mile single line. Its powers, including an authorization to extend to Haslemere, were transferred by an Act of 13 July 1876 to the LB&SCR, which finished and opened the line on 11 July 1881. The final passenger train ran on 5 July 1935; the line closed to goods between Lavant and Midhurst in 1953, and throughout in 1972.

CHIPSTEAD VALLEY RAILWAY

Incorporated on 27 July 1893, this line, like the Caterham Railway (qv), was a sore point between the SER and LB&SCR. It opened between Purley and Kingswood on 2 November 1897, to Tadworth on 1 July 1900, and to Tattenham Corner on 4 June 1901. Authorized in 1898 to subscribe up to £200,000, the SER formally absorbed the company on 13 July 1899, and doubled the track on 2 July 1900.

The Cranbrook & Paddock Wood Railway six years before the end—ex-SE&CR Wainwright 0-4-4T No 31516 prepares to propel its ex-L&SWR bogies towards Paddock Wood on a warm summer day in 1955. (H.P. White)

COWES & NEWPORT RAILWAY

The first railway on the Isle of Wight was incorporated on 8 August 1859. Opening on 16 June 1862, it was worked under contract by one H.D. Martin until the Ryde & Newport Railway (qv) opened, a joint committee then being formed to operate both. On 25 August 1877, powers were obtained to build a wharf on the River Medina, 1.5 miles upstream from Cowes, which opened in November 1878. Amalgamation with the R&NR and the Isle of Wight (Newport Junction) Railway (qv) was made wef 1 July 1887 (Act of 19 July) to form the IoWCR.

CRANBROOK & PADDOCK WOOD RAILWAY

Incorporated on 2 August 1877, progress was slow, and when extension to Hawkhurst was authorized on 12 July 1882, powers were allowed to lapse because of financial problems. Revived by the SER (Act of 12 July 1887), the line was opened to Hope Mill (Goudhurst) on 1 October 1892, and throughout on 4 September 1893, the SER working it from the outset and absorbing the company on 10 July 1900.

The line closed on 12 June 1961.

CROWHURST, SIDLEY & BEXHILL RAILWAY

This branch, 4.3 miles long, from Crowhurst (SER), was authorized on 15 July 1897. It was worked by the SER from opening (1 June 1902), becoming vested in it under an Act of 4 August 1906, wef 1 January 1907. Closed as a Great War economy — 1 January 1917 to 1 March 1919 — it closed finally to goods on 9 September 1963, and to passengers on 15 June 1964.

CROYDON & EPSOM RAILWAY

Authorized on 29 July 1844 and opened between W Croydon and Epsom Town on 10 May 1847, its independence was shortlived, for it was bought by the London & Croydon Railway (qv), before opening, for £200,000.

CROYDON, MERSTHAM & GODSTONE IRON RAILWAY

This line was incorporated on 17 May 1803 to extend the Surrey Iron Railway (qv — Jt/Ind) towards Portsmouth. Engineered by William Jessop, the cost of construction was high, and though the railway opened on 24 July 1805, it got no further than Merstham where it ended in the Godstone lime works. The London & Brighton's Act of 15 July

1837 required it to buy the company; the line closed in 1838, the company was dissolved in 1839, and 8.5 miles of the track-bed were used for the L&BR route. When the M25 was being built in 1972, several rough-cut stone sleeper blocks, about 15 in square, were unearthed from the old line.

CRYSTAL PALACE & SOUTH LONDON JUNCTION RAILWAY

Much of it graded at 1 in 78, this line between Peckham Rye and Crystal Palace (High Level), authorized on 17 July 1862, was backed by the LC&DR. An Act (23 June 1864) sanctioned letting or transfer to the LC&DR, and the line opened on 1 August 1865. Transfer was wef 1 July 1875, and the company was dissolved by an Act of 27 June 1876. The Crystal Palace–Nunhead section was closed temporarily during both World Wars (1 January 1917–1 March 1919, and 22 May 1944–4 March 1946), and the line closed completely on 20 September 1954.

DEVON & CORNWALL RAILWAY

Incorporated as the Okehampton Railway (qv), it changed its title on 26 July 1870. The project was backed by the L&SWR, which acquired it wef 1 January 1872, after an Agreement to purchase for £105,000 had been signed on 17 March 1871 and ratified by Parliament on the following 24 July. The line was opened from N Tawton to Okehampton on 3 October 1871 and to Lydford (then Lidford) on 12 October 1874. Its course, single track at first but doubled by the end of 1879, included Meldon Viaduct, 120 ft high and on a 30-chain radius curve.

DEVON & CORNWALL CENTRAL RAILWAY

This was incorporated on 18 August 1882 to make a link between the L&SWR-worked Devon & Cornwall Railway at Lydford, and Callington via the East Cornwall Mineral Railway (both qv). The Act included an Agreement to buy the ECMR and re-equip it as a main line, but capital was hard to raise and eventually powers given to the PD&SWJR by an Act of 7 August 1884 allowed that company to assume the D&CR's obligations.

DOVER & DEAL JOINT RAILWAY

Notable as being the only joint enterprise between the SER and the LC&DR, the line was incorporated on 30 June 1874, and vested jointly in the two companies. The line ran for 8.5 miles from Buckland Junction (a mile N of Dover Priory) to an end-on connection with the SER line from Minster at Deal. The first sod was cut by Lord Granville on 29 June 1878, and the line was opened on 15 June 1881.

EAST CORNWALL MINERAL RAILWAY

Incorporated as the Callington & Calstock Railway (qv) and renamed on 25 May 1871, this line linked mines in the Gunnislake area and quarries at Kit Hill with quays on the River Tamar, where there was a cable-worked incline; the upper level was loco-worked. Opening on 8 May 1872, it did well at first, but harder times came and the company was bought by the PD&SWJR by an Act of 19 July 1887 wef 1 June 1891, though the actual purchase (for £62,500) was not completed until 4 January 1894. The line was converted to standard gauge under a LRO in 1900 and 1905, and extended to Bere Alston, becoming part of the Bere Alston & Calstock Railway (qv).

EAST GRINSTEAD RAILWAY

A line from Three Bridges (LB&SCR) to East Grinstead, authorized on 8 July 1853, it had its first

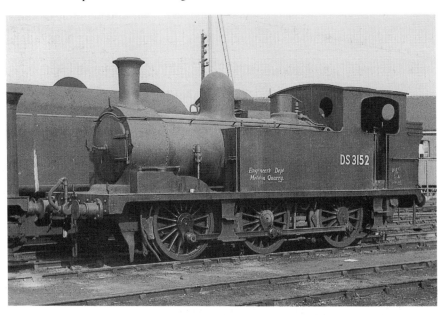

Left *'Engineer's Dept, Meldon Quarry' it says on the sidetank. The engine, one of 34 Class 'G6' 0-6-0Ts built for the L&SWR in the final years of the nineteen century, was away from quarry duty for overhaul at Eastleigh Works when this picture was taken.* (MWK/Andrew Ingram)

Right *The Thames Tunnel, the first tunnel beneath a river, was built by Marc Brunel, and opened on 25 March 1843. In 1866 it was bought by the East London Railway, which opened it in 1869—it now forms part of the LTE route between Wapping and New Cross.* (Allan Mott)

sod cut on 22 November 1853. It was worked by the LB&SCR, to which the company obtained authority to lease, sell or transfer itself by an Act of 28 June 1858; it exercised these powers wef 1 January 1865. Rowfant, the only intermediate station at the opening on 9 July 1855, was reputed to be the only LB&SCR station to boast a Stationmistress. The line closed to passengers on 1 January 1967.

EAST GRINSTEAD, GROOMBRIDGE & TUNBRIDGE WELLS RAILWAY

Incorporated on 7 August 1862, this line was promoted to link Tunbridge Wells with E Grinstead; in fact, it joined the Brighton, Uckfield and Tunbridge Wells Railway (qv) at Groombridge, continuing to Tunbridge Wells as part of that line. The single track was absorbed by the LB&SCR on 29 July 1864, more than two years before opening on 1 October 1866.

EAST KENT RAILWAY

Proposed as a 48.5-mile line between Strood and Canterbury, with two short branches, powers were also granted, on 4 August 1853, to use the SER station at Strood. Opening from Chatham to Faversham took place on 25 January 1858, with Chatham–Strood on 29 March, but the Canterbury section was short of funds — it eventually opened as a single track, using engines borrowed from the GNR. On 30 July 1855, powers were obtained for extension to Dover, and the company then sought a link with the West End of London & Crystal Palace Railway (qv). When this was sanctioned, a line between London and Dover had been arranged piecemeal, and on 1 August 1859 it became the LC&DR.

EAST LONDON RAILWAY

A company was incorporated on 26 May 1865 to take over Marc Brunel's Thames Tunnel and form a rail link between the GER and the LB&SCR and SER at New Cross. An Agreement of 17 November 1869 (ratified by Parliament on 20 June 1870) permitted the LB&SCR to work, use and manage the line wef 1 January 1870, and gave it RP to Liverpool Street or the '. . . Metropolitan station of the Great Eastern Railway'. It was connected with the M/DR by an Act of 1879. From 1892 the line was worked jointly by the LB&SCR, GER and M/DR. Electrification came, the last steam train running on 30 March 1913; thereafter the MetR ran the line, which was acquired by the SR wef 1 January 1925 and transferred to the LTE in 1948.

ELHAM VALLEY LIGHT RAILWAY

This independent company, authorized on 18 July 1881 to build just over 16.25 miles of railway between Shorncliffe (near Folkestone) and Canterbury, was quickly taken over by the SER under an Act of 28 July 1884. The line opened from Shorncliffe to Barham on 4 July 1887 and through to Canterbury on 1 July 1889. The double track was singled during the Great War and the Lyminge–Canterbury section closed to passengers on 2 December 1940; the rest remained open until 3 May 1943 for use by the Army. The closed length re-opened on 7 October 1946, closing finally on 16 June 1947.

EPSOM & LEATHERHEAD RAILWAY

Incorporated on 14 July 1856 and opened on 1 February 1859, the line ran 3 miles 54 chains from Epsom Town. A link with the Horsham, Dorking & Leatherhead Railway (qv) was authorized on 13 July 1863 and opened on 23 December 1866. The line

was worked by the L&SWR under lease (ratified by Parliament on 6 August 1860) until an Agreement with the LB&SCR of 29 July 1859 resulted in joint working. Another (1 January 1862, ratified on 25 July 1864), established an Epsom & Leatherhead Joint Committee, which administered the line thereafter.

EXETER & CREDITON RAILWAY

This line was incorporated on 1 July 1845 after a scheme of 23 June 1832 came to nothing. Laid to the broad gauge (although the L&SWR held most of the shares) and double track, the 5.75-mile line was then 'standardized' and almost ready when a row about the gauge caused delay. The line finally opened (broad gauge) on 12 May 1851 on lease to the B&ER. The L&SWR took leases on 25 February 1864 and 21 January 1869, and bought the line in 1879, having gained powers to do this and to remove the broad gauge rails on 13 July 1876.

EXETER & EXMOUTH RAILWAY

Incorporated on 2 July 1855, this was the second

such company, the first (3 July 1846) having proved abortive; it was to build a broad gauge line from Exmouth Junction, a canal branch also being included. The L&SWR persuaded the company to build standard gauge in exchange for a share in its Queen St Station at Exeter, and gained authority to lease the line on 6 August 1860. Formal absorption followed by an Act of 5 July 1865, wef 1 January 1866.

FRESHWATER, YARMOUTH & NEWPORT RAILWAY

First authorized on 7 July 1873 and dissolved on 23 July 1877, the company was re-incorporated on 26 July 1880 to build a 12-mile railway W from Newport. There was good support from locals and the L&SWR, which wanted to develop boat services between Lymington and Yarmouth. The line opened, worked by the IoWCR, on 10 September 1888 (goods), 20 July 1889 (passengers), but connection with the line at Newport was awkward, involving reversal — although the IoWCR promised to adjust this, it did nothing. From 1 January 1913, the

Exeter Queen Street, in which the Exeter & Exmouth Railway was offered a share by the L&SWR, was rebuilt and reopened as Exeter Central on 1 July 1933. It appears, from this 1988 picture, to have sustained further additions. (Allan Mott)

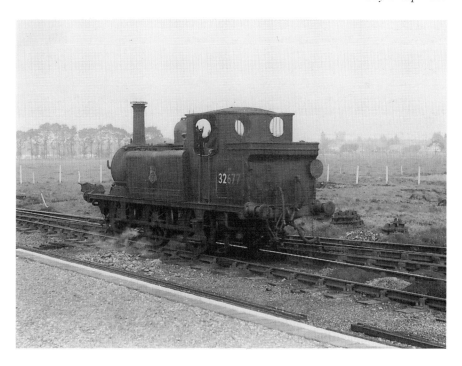

An ex-LB&SCR 'Terrier' No 32677 awaits its next duty at Hayling Island on Sunday 16 September 1956, sporting a multiplicity of pipework on its rear bufferbeam. The levels of the Island stretch, apparently limitless, beyond. (J.H. Price)

company took over working; it bankrupted itself in the process, but remained independent until reluctantly absorbed by the SR wef 1 September 1923.

GRAVESEND RAILWAY
Backed by the LC&DR, this nominally independent company was incorporated on 18 July 1881 to build 4 miles 70 chains of line between Fawkham Junction and Gravesend. Double track, with an extension to West St Pier, Gravesend (Act of 24 July 1882), the line opened to the public on 10 May 1886, but was never a financial success; it had been vested in the LC&DR on 29 June 1883. It closed between Fawkham and Gravesend W (passengers) on 17 April 1953, and from Southfleet to Gravesend W (goods) on 24 March 1968.

GRAVESEND & ROCHESTER RAILWAY
This single line, authorized on 31 July 1845, was laid by the Thames & Medway Canal Company along the towpath of its canal, to link the Thames at Gravesend with the Medway opposite Rochester (Strood). The line opened on 10 February 1845, and an Act of 3 August 1846 authorized purchase by the SER, which closed it in November that year so that the canal in the tunnel near Strood could be filled in and converted to double track railway — it re-opened on 23 August 1847. This route became known as the North Kent line.

GUILDFORD JUNCTION RAILWAY
The first extension of the embryo L&SWR, this line from Woking to Guildford, authorized on 10 May 1844, opened officially on 1 May 1845 as a single line, though it was not really ready until 5 May. It was doubled in 1847. The company was independent only in name — the L&SWR was granted powers, built the line and absorbed the company under an Act of 4 August 1845.

HAYLING RAILWAY
Sanctioned on 23 July 1860, the first sod was cut on 20 July 1863, and 4 miles 45 chains of single line railway were built from Havant (LB&SCR) to Langstone (the 'e' was dropped in 1873) on Hayling Island. Financial problems became acute, but the line eventually opened for goods to Langston on 19 January 1865, and throughout to the public on 17 July 1867, with a service operated by the Contractor, Frederick Furniss, using four-wheelers hired from the L&SWR; he worked the line until 31 December 1871. The LB&SCR took control then, by a temporary arrangement converted to a £2,000 pa lease from mid-1874. The company remained independent until absorbed by the SR at Grouping. The last public train ran on 2 November 1963.

HERNE BAY & FAVERSHAM RAILWAY
This line between the two towns via Whitstable, proposed in defiance of SER opposition, was authorized on 17 August 1857. In 1859 powers were obtained to extend to Margate, and the company's title was changed to the Margate Railway (qv).

HORSHAM & GUILDFORD DIRECT RAILWAY
Incorporated on 6 August 1860, the company's 15.5 miles of single line linked Stammerham Junction

(Horsham, LB&SCR) with Peasmarsh Junction (L&SWR) near Guildford. The uncompleted works were sold to the LB&SCR under an Act dated 29 July 1864; that company finished and opened the line on 2 October 1865.

HORSHAM, DORKING & LEATHERHEAD RAILWAY

Incorporated on 17 July 1862 to link Boxhill and Dorking, the LB&SCR obtained powers for the 4.5 miles to Leatherhead on 13 July 1863, and absorbed the company on 29 July 1864. The line was opened from Boxhill to Dorking on 11 March 1867, and entered Horsham on 1 May.

HUNDRED OF HOO RAILWAY

Though nominally independent, this railway, authorized on 21 July 1879, was backed by the SER, retaliating against the LC&DR for opening a port at Queenborough on Sheppey. Opened to Sharnal Street on 1 April 1882, and throughout on 11 September, its single track crossed the Hoo peninsula from Shorne to Stoke, where, later, an SR branch diverged to Allhallows-on-Sea. Powers for a pier at Port Victoria were granted on 2 August 1880, the company being vested in the SER on 11 August 1881. The pier closed in 1916, but industrial activity after the First War revived it, and the line now serves the refinery. Grain to Port Victoria closed for passengers on 4 September 1951, and from Hoo Junction on 4 December 1961.

ISLE OF WIGHT CENTRAL RAILWAY

This was formed wef 1 July 1887 (Act of 19 July) by the amalgamation of the Ryde & Newport, the Cowes & Newport, and the Isle of Wight (Newport Junction) Railways (all qv). It worked the Newport, Godshill & St Lawrence Railway (qv) from opening, and when that company went bankrupt, absorbed it. It was itself absorbed by the SR in 1923, when its route mileage of 28.5 miles was substantially the greatest on the Island.

ISLE OF WIGHT (EASTERN SECTION) RAILWAY

This company was incorporated on 23 July 1860 to build 11.25 miles of railway from Ryde (St Johns Road) to Ventnor. It opened to Shanklin on 23 August 1864, but the Earl of Yarborough forced a diversion through the ¾-mile Boniface Down tunnel, and opening to Ventnor was delayed until 10 September 1866. By an Act of 28 July 1863, the words 'Eastern Section' were dropped from the title, and the company took over the working of the Brading Harbour Improvement & Railway (qv) under contract wef 27 May 1882, purchasing it in 1898. The company was absorbed by the SR at Grouping, and though the Shanklin to Ventnor section closed on 18 April 1966, the remainder is now the only section of line on the Island still run by BR.

ISLE OF WIGHT (NEWPORT JUNCTION) RAILWAY

This was incorporated on 31 July 1868 for a 9.5-mile link between Sandown and Newport via Merstone. Money troubles from the start delayed opening (Sandown–Shide on 1 February 1875, to Newport on 6 October 1875), and the short viaduct at Newport (opened on 1 June 1879), linking with the Ryde & Newport Railway, finally bankrupted the company. The line was run by a joint C&NR/R&NR com-mittee under the OR. Amalgamation with these two companies formed the IoWCR.

Another Wainwright 0-4-4T, this time No 31517, on its push-pull set at Allhallows-on-Sea, the terminus of the branch from Stoke Junction on the Hundred of Hoo Railway. Sometimes known as the 'Dead Sea' resort, some of its bleakness is captured here. (J.H. Price)

Blackwater, on the one-time Isle of Wight (Newport Junction) Railway, as a Newport train pulls in on a summer evening in the 1930s. Note the tall 'repeater' home signal, duplicated for visibility above the station canopy. (Douglas Thompson)

KENT COAST RAILWAY

When the Margate Railway (qv) obtained powers to extend to Ramsgate on 6 August 1861, it took a new title. The line was opened on 5 October 1863, worked by the LC&DR under lease, authorized on 7 August 1862, wef 1 September 1863. Amalgamation with that company was authorized by an Act dated 31 July 1871, wef 1 July.

LAUNCESTON, BODMIN & WADEBRIDGE JUNCTION RAILWAY

Incorporated on 29 July 1864 to build a railway from Launceston to the Bodmin & Wadebridge Railway (qv), in 1865 a further Act empowered an extension of the B&WR's Ruthern Bridge branch to Truro (not built), and the company changed its title to the Central Cornwall Railway (qv).

LEE-ON-THE-SOLENT LIGHT RAILWAY

This 3.5-mile line from Fort Brockhurst to Lee-on-the-Solent was built by a Certificate dated 11 July 1893, under the Regulation of Railways Act (1868). It was opened on 12 May 1894 by Lady Clanwilliam, and was worked by its Contractor until WA were made with the L&SWR on 16 August 1909. It lost money steadily, and because of accumulated debts the SR absorbed it only very reluctantly in 1923, closing it to passengers wef 1 January 1931. The last goods train ran on 28 September 1935.

LEWES & EAST GRINSTEAD RAILWAY

This line was authorized on 10 August 1877 in three sections — N and S from E Grinstead, and a branch from Horsted Keynes to Copyhold Junction (LB&SCR). Capital was hard to find, and the company

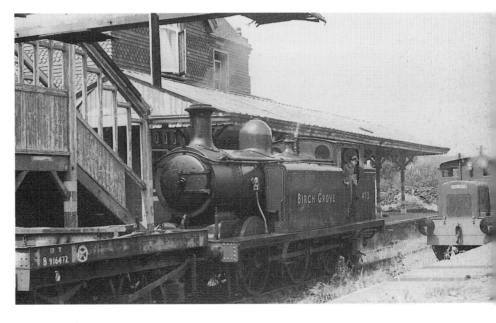

Preserved ex-'Brighton' engine Birch Grove, on loan from the Bluebell Railway, assisting in dismantling the Lewes & East Grinstead Railway at West Hoathly, 29 June 1964. Now the trend has reversed, and track is being relaid towards this point. (K.D. Chown, Bluebell RPS Archives)

turned to the LB&SCR for help; Parliament ratified (17 June 1878) an Agreement that the LB&SCR should back and build the line, and though the company retained nominal independence until completion, it was then dissolved. The main line was opened on 1 August 1882, the branch on 3 September 1883. Scheduled for closure on 13 June 1955, an ASLEF strike caused the 'final' train to run on 28 May 1955 – until a clause was noticed in the Agreement between the company and LB&SCR which guaranteed certain stations four trains a day! BR had to re-open (7 August 1956) until further powers had been obtained – closure came finally on 17 March 1958. The line between Sheffield Park and Horsted Keynes is now well-known as the Bluebell Railway, and this concern has ambitions towards E Grinstead also . . .

LEWES & UCKFIELD RAILWAY

Incorporated on 27 July 1857 to build between the named towns, the line opened officially on 11 October 1858, and to the public a week later. Amalgamation or lease to the LB&SCR was authorized on 1 August 1859; it wasted no time, absorbing the company wef 31 May 1860. A new section to avoid Lewes tunnel was opened on 1 October 1868. The last train ran on 23 February 1969, when buses

were substituted until the official closure date, 6 May. A preservation site has been established around Isfield station.

LONDON & BRIGHTON RAILWAY

This project emerged from the plans of six contenders and obtained powers on 15 July 1837 to build a line from the London & Croydon Railway (qv) '. . . at or near Selhurst Farm' (S of Norwood Junction). The company was compelled to buy the defunct Croydon, Merstham & Godstone Railway (qv), whose route it would partly use. The first sod was cut at Merstham in July 1838, and work began on 4 February 1839, to a gauge of 4 ft 9 in. A line from Brighton to Shoreham was opened on 12 May 1840; the main line from Norwood Junction to Haywards Heath followed on 12 July 1841, reaching Brighton on 21 September. The company bought the Brighton & Chichester and the Brighton, Lewes & Hastings Railways (both qv) in 1845 and 1846 respectively. The Act for the latter authorized amalgamation with the L&CR and a name-change to the LB&SCR.

Brighton station on a wet day in 1988. The canopy is a later addition, and though impressive (and practical on a day like this) it does rather obscure the original facade of Mocatta's terminus. (Allan Mott)

Above *Anerley, an original London & Croydon station, in April 1987. The canopy is a later addition, hiding original facilities rudimentary by today's standards, the only waiting area probably being within the arches midway along the building.* (Allan Mott)

Below *Sir John Betjeman described this London & Greenwich Railway column at London Bridge, with its colleagues, as '. . . joyous undisciplined ornamentation running riot through the station'. A perfect summary.* (Allan Mott)

LONDON & CROYDON RAILWAY

The company's Act of 12 June 1835 empowered purchase of the Croydon Canal between Croydon and New Cross, with RP along the London & Greenwich Railway for a further 1.75 miles to London Bridge, where another Act authorized a station on the N side. The line, 8.75 miles long, opened formally between Corbett's Lane and W Croydon on 1 June 1839, and to the public on 5 June, the Company making good business from tolls of 1 shilling (5p) per passenger received from the SER and L&BR. Semaphore signalling, invented in France for telegraphy, was used here in 1841–2. In 1844 the company obtained powers to lay an extra line, atmospherically-worked, between New Cross and Croydon — this opened in January 1847, but was abolished in May of that year, after amalgamation with the L&BR.

LONDON & GREENWICH RAILWAY

Incorporated on 17 May 1833, this was the first railway to enter London. Only 3.75 miles between London Bridge and Greenwich were authorized at first (the company had designs on Dover); the line opened formally on 14 December 1836, and to the public ten days later. Traffic was disappointing at first, though the company made a good income from

tolls paid by others for use of the line. The world's first signal box opened at Corbett's Lane in 1839. The line was leased to the SER for 999 years under an Act of 21 July 1845, for a rent of £36,000, increased by £1,000 pa to £45,000, the company remaining independent until dissolved and amalgamated with the SR in 1923.

LONDON & SOUTHAMPTON RAILWAY

Authorized on 25 July 1834, progress was slow until Joseph Locke took over in 1837. After the initial opening (Nine Elms–Woking, formally on 19 May 1838, and to the public on 21 May), the line was extended to Shapley Heath (38.5 miles) on 24 September 1838 and to Basingstoke on 10 June 1839, the same day as the Southampton–Winchester section opened. When, on 4 June 1839, the company obtained powers to build to Portsmouth, it also changed its title to the L&SWR.

LONDON & SOUTH WESTERN RAILWAY

This was incorporated on 4 June 1839 when the London & Southampton Railway (qv) obtained authority to extend to Portsmouth. That branch closed four days after opening (29 November 1841) while a tunnel at Fareham was made safe; it re-opened on 7 February 1842. The main line to Southampton opened on 11 May 1840, and on 31 July 1845 powers were obtained for a 2-mile extension to Waterloo. The inspiration came from a company planning a railway to Richmond; the L&SWR persuaded it to build to what later became Clapham Junction and leave the rest to the L&SWR. Waterloo

was designed by Sir Francis Tite. Extension to Southwark was also planned and sanctioned, but not built. On 1 November 1892 the company bought the Southampton Docks for £1,360,000, to prove invaluable to the SR in due course. By Grouping, the L&SWR had one of the longest lines in S England (966 miles), with a high density of traffic.

LONDON, BRIGHTON & SOUTH COAST RAILWAY

When the London & Brighton and London & Croydon Railways (both qv) combined on 27 July 1846, this became the new company's title. A branch to Brighton, Kemptown, was authorized on 13 May 1864 and opened on 2 August 1869, and the company entered Victoria in 1860 (see Victoria Station & Pimlico Railway). Newhaven harbour was created, the Harbour Company being vested in the SR in 1926 — the steamers had become Railway property in 1867. The company had continuous trouble with the SER around Coulsdon and Redhill, and while the company's engines gave a feeling of opulence, this was often belied by the quality of the service. The line was electrified (using ole) between Victoria and London Bridge on 9 December 1909, and to Selhurst in 1910, but was converted to third-rail between 1925 and 1930. The company became a constituent of the SR at Grouping.

LONDON, CHATHAM & DOVER RAILWAY

Born on 1 August 1859 out of the East Kent Railway

The seal of the London & South Western Railway. (NRM)

The superb confidence of the early railways is shown in the ironwork of this LB&SCR clock amid the roofbeams at Brighton station. (Allan Mott)

The seal of the London, Chatham & Dover Railway. The company's East Kent origins no doubt justified use of the horse motif and motto. (NRM)

(qv), by 1866 the company was in serious financial difficulties, and offered to lease itself to the SER, which refused to have anything to do with it. Perhaps it hoped the upstart would collapse and come to them for nothing! But an OR was appointed, and by 1871 the company was solvent again. It absorbed the Kent Coast Railway (qv) and several others; more attempts were made to amalgamate with the SER, but it was not until 1899 that the two settled their differences and came together under the SE&CRCJMC.

LONDON, DEPTFORD & DOVER RAILWAY

This was the title by which the undertaking later to become the SER was incorporated on 21 June 1836.

LONDON NECROPOLIS RAILWAY

Incorporated on 30 June 1852 to serve Brookwood Cemetery, the Act stipulated a contract with the L&SWR; it always worked the .75-mile line, which opened in December 1854. A station at Brookwood was opened in 1864. The special platform at Waterloo, from which the trains ran, was bombed during the Second World War, but services continued from the main station.

LYDD RAILWAY

Incorporated on 8 April 1881, this was a nominally independent company which superseded an earlier Rye & Dungeness Pier Company scheme of 1873, and had powers to build from Appledore (SER) to

Dungeness. On 24 July 1882, authority was given for a 3 miles 24 yds extension to New Romney. This opened on 19 June 1884 — the earlier line had opened for goods to Dungeness and passengers to Lydd on 7 December 1881, and for passengers to Dungeness on 1 April 1883. The line was absorbed by the SER on 20 September 1895. Closure to passengers between Romney Junction and Dungeness came on 4 July 1937, and to goods in May 1953. All services ceased on 6 March 1967.

LYMINGTON RAILWAY

The company was incorporated on 7 July 1856 to build from Brockenhurst (L&SWR) to Lymington, 4 miles of single line, and to acquire the ferry between Lymington and the Isle of Wight. Hopes that traffic to Wight would develop failed, partly perhaps because the L&SWR tended to concentrate on Portsmouth. Though authorized to lease the company on 6 August 1860, the L&SWR did not agree transfer until 31 October 1878 — the Conveyance was dated 21 March 1879.

LYNTON & BARNSTAPLE RAILWAY

The only 1 ft 11.5 in gauge line in the W Country, it was sponsored locally after several other schemes had failed to link Lynton and Lynmouth with the outside world. Authorized on 27 June 1895, it cost twice as much to build as predicted, and because litigation bankrupted the contractor, the company had to pay the expenses! The line opened a year late, formally on 11 May 1898 and to the public on 16 May. Traffic was well short of hopes, but the first loss was not made until 1922. During that year negotiations for a take-over began with the L&SWR — the SR Act (1923) gave acquisition powers, final agreement being reached in March. The company actually lost its independence on 1 July 1923, though the SR had had control since 1 January. The SR kept the 19.75-mile line going until 29 September 1935; at the subsequent auction, five locomotives fetched only £236.

MAIDSTONE & ASHFORD RAILWAY

Another satellite of the LC&DR, this company was authorized on 12 August 1880 to build an 8.75-mile link from an end-on junction with the Sevenoaks, Maidstone & Tunbridge Railway (qv) at Maidstone E. An Act of 29 June 1883 authorized purchase by the LC&DR from the date of completion — the line opened on 1 July 1884. It did not join the SER at Ashford, but had its own terminus on the edge of the town; the company had RP into Ashford station but preferred not to use them. Closure of this station was one of the first acts of the SE&CRCJMC in 1899, and the buildings and site were put to use as Ashford's goods yard.

MARGATE RAILWAY
This was the title taken by the Herne Bay & Faversham Railway (qv) when it obtained powers on 13 August 1859 to extend to Margate. Opening between Faversham and Whitstable was on 1 August 1860, and to Herne Bay on 13 July 1861, though the latter was delayed by an SER claim that a bridge under the Canterbury & Whitstable Railway (qv) was unsafe. The line was worked from the outset by the LC&DR under lease. In 1861 the company obtained authority for an extension to Ramsgate, and changed its name again, to the Kent Coast Railway (qv).

MID-HANTS (ALTON LINES) RAILWAY
This was the title taken on 1 January 1865 by the Alton, Alresford & Winchester Railway (qv). The line opened on 2 October 1865, and the L&SWR took a 999-year lease wef August 1880, under Authority of 26 August 1880, with an option to buy, which it did in June 1884. During both World Wars the line was a valuable route from Aldershot to the ports, being more direct than others. The last BR train ran on 4 February 1973, but trains do still run — steam ones of the Mid-Hants Railway, which re-opened the line from Ropley to Four Marks on 28 May 1983, and through to Alton on 25 May 1985.

MID-KENT (BROMLEY to ST MARY CRAY) RAILWAY
Originally authorized at 2.5 miles on 21 July 1856,

Above *A few traces of the Lynton & Barnstaple Railway remain, the most substantial, perhaps, being Chelfham viaduct, looking as solid in August 1987 as when it was last used, in September 1935.*

Left *Alton, looking east in the 1930s, as a Maunsell 'Mogul' prepares to leave with a down train. Then it was still part of a through route to Southampton.* (Douglas Thompson)

this line eventually continued the route of the West End of London & Crystal Palace Railway (qv). It opened between Southborough Row (now Bickley) and Bromley on 5 July 1858, joining the LC&DR line from Rochester on 3 December 1860. The LC&DR leased it for 999 years wef September 1863 by an Act of 7 August 1862, but the company retained independence until Grouping.

MID-KENT & NORTH KENT RAILWAY

Another extension of the West End of London & Crystal Palace Railway (qv), this time 4.75 miles from Lewisham to Beckenham, it was authorized on 23 July 1855 and opened on 1 January 1857. Further extension, to Addiscombe Road, was empowered on 17 July 1862 — it opened on 1 April 1864, and the company was merged with the SER by two Acts, one of 29 July 1864 and another of 16 July 1866, because of doubts about the validity of the first.

MID-SUSSEX RAILWAY

The company was authorized on 10 August 1857 to build 17.5 miles of line between Horsham and a point near Petworth, via Pulborough. The LB&SCR was authorized to lease its single track by an Act of 1 August 1859 — it had opened on 10 October 1859 — and absorbed it by an Act of 29 July 1864.

MID-SUSSEX & MIDHURST JUNCTION RAILWAY

Incorporated on 13 August 1859 to complete the Mid-Sussex Railway (qv) from Petworth to Petersfield, it opened on 15 October 1866. In June 1874 the company was sold to the LB&SCR, which, wishing to fulfil a territorial agreement, left completion to the L&SWR. The LB&SCR worked it from the start (see also Petersfield Railway).

NEWPORT, GODSHILL & ST LAWRENCE RAILWAY

Incorporated (14 August 1885) as the Shanklin & Chale Railway, the line was to run for 6 miles between the towns. Abandoned, the scheme resurfaced as a 6.75-mile route between Merstone and Ventnor, authorized on 12 August 1889, with a change of name. The luck did not change, however — the line opened from Merstone to St Lawrence on 20 July 1897 and to Ventnor West on 1 June 1900, and the company went bankrupt in 1913. It was absorbed by the IoWCR, which had worked it from the start, on 8 April 1913.

NORTH CORNWALL RAILWAY

Created on 18 August 1882 from the defunct Central Cornwall Railway (qv), whose powers had lapsed 12 years earlier, it was a nominally independent L&SWR subsidiary. Progress was slow, but the line opened in stages after the Halwill Junction–Launceston section on 21 July 1886 — to Tresmeer on 28 July 1892,

Camelford on 14 August 1893, Delabole on 18 October 1893, and Wadebridge on 1 June 1895. The Padstow section was added on 27 March 1899. Traffic was sparse, though the line greatly helped the Delabole slate quarry, the largest in the world. The L&SWR worked it throughout its life — it passed to the SR in 1923. Since closure on 3 October 1966, 2 miles of track-bed W of Launceston have been taken over by the Launceston Steam Railway, which now runs trains using locos from the Dinorwic and Penrhyn quarries of North Wales.

NORTH DEVON RAILWAY & DOCK COMPANY

The company (previously the Taw Vale Railway & Dock Company, qv) took a new name on the last day of the Parliamentary Session in which it was authorized on 24 July 1851, opening the works done by its predecessor on 12 July 1854, though regular services did not begin until 1 August. The line was worked for a year by the B&ER and was then leased by Thomas Brassey, who also had the Bideford Extension Railway (qv). The L&SWR took over the lease wef 1 January 1863, absorbing the company under an Act dated 25 July 1864, wef 1 January 1865. It obtained authority to remove the broad gauge rails on 13 July 1876. The concern became known as the N Devon Railway.

OKEHAMPTON RAILWAY

Originally incorporated on 17 July 1862 to build from Coleford Junction (NDR&DC) to Okehampton, an Act of 13 July 1863 gave powers to extend to the Launceston & S Devon Railway at Lidford (now Lydford). On 29 June 1865 a further 41 miles were authorized, from Meldon Junction to Bude, with a branch to Torrington. The Coleford Junction–N Tawton section was opened on 1 November 1865, and on 26 July 1870 the company changed its name to the Devon & Cornwall Railway (qv).

OXTED & GROOMBRIDGE RAILWAY

The company was authorized on 11 August 1881 to build 12 miles 10 chains of line along part of the Surrey & Sussex Railway's abandoned works. Though nominally independent, the company was supported by the LB&SCR, which formally absorbed it by an Act of 3 July 1884. It opened between Hurst Green and Edenbridge on 2 January 1888, and to Ashurst Junction on 1 October.

PETERSFIELD RAILWAY

Although authorized (23 July 1860) to build a line between Midhurst and the Portsmouth line at Petersfield, 9.5 miles away, because of friction between the company and the Mid-Sussex Railway (qv) a clause in the Act forbade a junction at Midhurst. The company was acquired by the L&SWR

on 22 June 1863; single track throughout, it opened on 1 September 1864 and closed to passengers on 5 February 1955.

PLYMOUTH & DARTMOOR RAILWAY

The idea for a railway from Plymouth to Princetown came from Thomas Tyrwhitt, later knighted, a politician and diplomat. It took three Acts — the first (2 July 1819) authorized the main route, and the second an extension to Sutton Pool, with a branch to Cattewater. The single line, 23 miles long, opened from Sutton Pool to King Tor on 26 September 1823. The third Act (19 June 1865) authorized the issue of preference shares in exchange for a mortgage, and relaying was begun. Later, the route above Yelverton was taken over by the Princetown Railway (qv — GWR), and the Marsh Mills–Laira section passed to the SDR. Only occasional traffic used the lower end, and the rails were removed in 1916, some going to the Lee Moor Tramway (qv — Jt/Ind). The Company passed to the SR in 1923.

PLYMOUTH, DEVONPORT & SOUTH WESTERN JUNCTION RAILWAY

A company with grand ideas, it was incorporated on 25 August 1883 to build an expensive line from Lydford (L&SWR) to Devonport. The 22.5 miles of double track were L&SWR-worked from the opening on 2 June 1890. It was a reasonably prosperous company; it took over the East Cornwall Mineral Railway (qv) on 1 June 1891 and obtained powers in 1900 to convert and equip the line for passenger traffic, completing this for an opening on 2 March 1908 as part of the Bere Alston & Calstock Railway

(qv). This it worked for itself, remaining independent until absorbed by the L&SWR in 1922. The main line between Bere Alston and Lydford closed on 6 May 1968, the last train having run the previous day.

POOLE & BOURNEMOUTH RAILWAY

Authorized on 26 May 1865, this line was mainly an S&DR project, but that company's impecuniousness led to assistance being sought from the L&SWR wef 16 July 1866. The line opened from Broadstone to Poole on 2 December 1872, and to Bournemouth on 15 June 1874. Authority for sale to the L&SWR was granted on 24 July 1871, which company worked it until absorption from 31 October 1882; the S&DR retained RP. The single line was doubled in 1883.

PORTSMOUTH RAILWAY

From an abortive scheme (authorized in July 1846 but wound up in 1854) for a direct London–Portsmouth line, this company was incorporated on 8 July 1853 to build from the L&SWR at Godalming to the LB&SCR at Havant via Haslemere and Petersfield. It was hoped to open on 1 January 1859, but though the line had been ready for a year the company owned no rolling-stock. When the inaugural train (L&SWR-worked) reached Havant, rails had been removed and an engine chained to the track. After a skirmish here and another further on, the matter went to law, which found for the L&SWR. The first train actually to reach Portsmouth arrived on 24 January 1859. Authority for lease or sale to the L&SWR was granted on 21 July 1859 — it opted for a lease at £18,000 pa. The company was dissolved by an Act of 12 August 1861.

READING, GUILDFORD & REIGATE RAILWAY

This was incorporated on 16 July 1846 for 45.75 miles of line from Reading to the London & Brighton Railway at Reigate (Redhill). The Redhill–Dorking and Reading–Farnborough sections opened on 4 July 1849, and the line was opened throughout on 15 October. The company, supported by the SER, was authorized to lease the line to it — the SER worked the line from the outset, the company being vested in it from 17 June 1852.

RICHMOND RAILWAY

Authorized on 21 July 1845, the company's 6 miles of railway between Clapham Junction and Richmond (see L&SWR) opened on 27 July 1846 and were bought by the L&SWR, wef 31 December 1846.

RINGWOOD, CHRISTCHURCH & BOURNEMOUTH RAILWAY

Authorized on 8 August 1859 to build 7.75 miles of single line along the Avon valley from Ringwood to Christchurch, it opened on 13 November 1862. In 1863 a 3.5-mile extension to Bournemouth was authorized, opening 14 March 1870. The line was worked by the L&SWR from the outset, and amalgamated with it by an Act dated 16 June 1873, wef 1 January 1874.

RYDE & NEWPORT RAILWAY

The company was authorized on 25 July 1872 to build a line from Smallbrook Junction (1.5 miles S of Ryde St Johns) to Newport. An Agreement was made with the Cowes & Newport Railway (qv) for the line to be jointly worked. It was opened on 20 December

1875, the company amalgamating with the C&NR and the Isle of Wight (Newport Junction) Railway (qv) to form the IoWCR wef 1 July 1887.

RYDE PIER & TRAMWAY COMPANY

A pier was built at Ryde under powers of 1812. On 29 August 1864, a tramway opened along the E side; this was horse-drawn at first, and though one or two steam experiments were made, regular steam workings did not begin until the LB&SCR and L&SWR obtained authority on 23 July 1877 to lengthen the pier and build a double-track link with Ryde St Johns. This opened on 5 April 1880 from St Johns to Esplanade, and to the Pierhead on 12 July. After only five years, horse-power returned until 14 March 1886, when there was a partial re-opening as an electrified line — it was fully opened the following summer. The railway passed to the SR in 1923, but the Pier Company was not absorbed until the next year, by an Act of 1 August 1924, wef previous 1 January. The line closed on 27 January 1969.

SALISBURY & DORSET JUNCTION RAILWAY

Incorporated on 22 July 1861, this was a nominally independent concern to link the Salisbury–Romsey line with the Southampton & Dorchester Railway (qv), and to run from Adderbury Junction to West Moors via Fordingbridge. Its 19 miles of single track opened on 20 December 1866, worked by the L&SWR, which leased it for £1,000 pa (authorized on 16 June 1873) and absorbed it wef 1 January 1883, under an Agreement dated 6 December 1882.

Left *One of the two engines built by Hawthorn, Leslie for the Plymouth, Devonport & South Western Junction Railway in 1907. Named* Earl of Mount Edgcumbe *and numbered 4, it then carried its SR number (757) until BR renumbered it 30757. It was moved to Eastleigh Works in 1957, and used (as seen here) on pilot duties before scrapping that year.* (MWK/Andrew Ingram)

Right *Breamore, on the Salisbury & Dorset Junction Railway, on a wet day, 17 March 1964. The station has timber buildings and no footbridge, but crossings at either end of the platform. It also retains its L&SWR nameboard, despite 16 years of Nationalization.* (Douglas Thompson)

SALISBURY & YEOVIL RAILWAY

This was incorporated on 22 July 1848 as an L&SWR project, but when it collapsed six years of argument followed. Finally the company was re-incorporated on 7 August 1854 as an independent body with L&SWR support. After more argument, work eventually began in 1856, and on 21 July 1856 the L&SWR obtained powers for a Yeovil–Exeter line, to assure the future of the company as a link. A new station at Salisbury was sanctioned, next to that of the WS&WR, and an end-on junction was made with the line from Basingstoke. The station and first section of line (Salisbury–Gillingham) were opened on 2 May 1859, and to Sherborne on 1 June 1860. Doubling began in 1861 and share prices rose to 12.5 per cent, the highest dividend paid by any English railway. The L&SWR agreed to work the line, and by 1872 was moving towards a take-over, Agreement for lease or sale having been ratified by an Act of 5 July 1865. Despite resistance, it bought the company under an Act dated 4 July 1878 for 260 stock per 100.

SEATON & BEER RAILWAY

Incorporated 13 July 1863 to build from Colyton to Seaton in S Devon, this line managed in the process to deprive Axmouth harbour of what business it had. The L&SWR worked the line from opening (16 March 1868), but in February 1879 the company sought terms from both L&SWR and GWR. It agreed to those of the L&SWR, and under its management concentrated on visitors, doing extremely well. The L&SWR absorbed the Company wef 1 January 1888 under an Act of 16 August 1880.

SEVENOAKS RAILWAY

Though nominally independent, this company's 1 August 1859 authorization was for a 6-mile branch from the LC&DR to Sevenoaks. Built from Swanley and opened on 2 June 1862, powers for extension to Maidstone East were obtained on 17 July 1862, with authority to rename the company the Sevenoaks, Maidstone & Tunbridge Railway (qv).

SEVENOAKS, MAIDSTONE & TUNBRIDGE (sic) RAILWAY

This was the title taken on 17 July 1862 by the Sevenoaks Railway following authority for its Maidstone Extension. That line, opened on 1 June 1874 and backed, as its predecessor had been, by the LC&DR, was vested in it by an Act of 30 June 1879.

SHEPPEY LIGHT RAILWAY

This 8.75-mile line was authorized on 3 April 1899 to run from Queenborough to Leysdown, on the E coast of Sheppey. Laid out by Col Stephens, it opened on 1 August 1901 and was always worked by the SE&CR, though purchased (for £65,000, 31 October 1905) by the LC&DR since the SE&

CRCJMC was merely a controlling and operating Committee. Leysdown developed as a holiday resort between the wars, but insufficiently, and the last train ran on 2 December 1950.

SHORTLANDS & NUNHEAD RAILWAY

Nominally independent, this company, authorized on 12 August 1889, was backed by the LC&DR for 4.75 miles of railway between the towns. It opened on 1 July 1892, worked by the LC&DR from the start, to be absorbed by it under an Act of 7 August 1896.

SIDMOUTH RAILWAY

A scheme for a line to Sidmouth from the L&SWR originated in 1862 but collapsed. Revived and re-incorporated on 29 June 1871, its steeply-graded, 8.25-mile route opened on 6 July 1874 and carried a steady tourist traffic. Attempts at amalgamation with the L&SWR were made, but the company remained independent until absorption by the SR in 1923.

SITTINGBOURNE & SHEERNESS RAILWAY

Incorporated on 7 July 1856 to build a branch from Sittingbourne to Queenborough (Sheppey) and Sheerness, its 7 miles of single track opened on 19 July 1860. It included a lifting bridge across the Swale, and was worked by the LC&DR to which powers were transferred by an Act dated 30 July 1866 (wef 19 July 1865). The company was wound up on 13 July 1876. A ½-mile extension from the dockyard to Sheerness on Sea was opened on 1 June 1883, and in time the original station became a goods depot. An extension to Queenborough Pier, opened on 15 May 1876, closed to passengers in October 1914, though it re-opened briefly between 27 December 1922 and 1 March 1923.

SOUTHAMPTON & DORCHESTER RAILWAY

Incorporated on 21 July 1845, it was promoted by A.L.Castleman, a Wimborne solicitor, the line's winding course earning it the nickname of 'Castleman's Corkscrew'. Castleman knew that the line could not pay on its own, so sought help from first the L&SWR, then the GWR. The L&SWR agreed to lease the line at £20,000 plus half the profits; construction began on 21 July 1845, light gradients making the 60.5-mile route easy to build. Though the official opening was 1 June 1847, normal services did not begin until 6 August because a tunnel near Southampton was considered unsafe. The company amalgamated with the L&SWR by an Act of 22 July 1848, with Castleman on the Board, and the line was doubled between 1857–63. A branch to Hamworthy (Poole) became redundant after the Poole & Bournemouth Railway (qv) had opened, and it was closed to

A 1930s summer evening at Beaulieu Road, on 'Castleman's Corkscrew' (Southampton & Dorchester Railway) as a down express pulled by an unidentified 'King Arthur' (Class 'N15') 4-6-0 hurries through. (Douglas Thompson)

passengers on 1 July 1896. A single-track branch to Swanage, opened on 20 May 1885, was absorbed by the L&SWR, which had always worked it, under an Act of 25 June 1886. It closed to passengers on 3 January 1972, but a preservation scheme is now working towards Worgret Junction.

SOUTHAMPTON & NETLEY RAILWAY

Incorporated on 1 August 1861, this was a line from Portswood (St Denys after 1876, between Southampton and Eastleigh) to the Netley Military Hospital. The company amalgamated with the L&SWR before it opened (5 March 1866), under Acts of 14 July and 25 July 1864, wef the previous 1 January. The line was extended to Fareham, opening on 2 September 1889.

SOUTH EASTERN RAILWAY

Incorporated as the London, Deptford & Dover Railway, this concern soon became known as the South Eastern, and was usually referred to as the 'Dover Railway', even in documents — a timesheet of 1 February 1843 is headed 'London & Dover Railway'! After various changes of plan, the junction with the LB&SCR was located at Redhill, though its passage there used the lines of the 'Brighton', the London & Croydon and the London & Greenwich Railways. Progress was slow, but opening from Redhill to Headcorn was on 31 August 1842, to Ashford on 1 December, to Folkestone on 18 December 1843 and to Dover on 7 February 1844. Bricklayers Arms opened in 1845, and authority for Ashford Works was given in 1846. In 1899 a WA with the LC&DR resulted in the formation of the SE&CRCJMC. The company became a constituent of the SR in 1923.

SOUTH EASTERN & CHATHAM RAILWAY COMPANIES JOINT MANAGEMENT COMMITTEE

This was formed on 1 August 1899 to manage and operate the SER and LC&DR lines, though the companies retained their identities. The Committee set about making a cohesive whole of competing systems, and much was achieved before the Great

The seal of the South Eastern Railway. This company, like the LC&DR, also used the Kentish horse, twice, since it appears in the crest also. (NRM)

The seal of the South Eastern & Chatham Railway Companies Joint Managing Committee. The insignia of the two companies are the same depth and exactly side by side, no doubt to forestall any suggestions of inequality. (NRM)

War intervened. The incomplete work passed to the SR on 1 January 1923.

SOUTHSEA RAILWAY

The second such scheme (the other dated from 1867), this was only 1 mile 30 chains long. Authorized on 26 August 1880, it was worked by the L&SWR from opening on 1 July 1885. By an Agreement of 18 November 1882, ratified by an Act of 20 August 1883 (wef that date), the line was bought jointly by the L&SWR and LB&SCR, though the 'Brighton' probably came to think it would have been better off without it; electrification of the local tramways soon sealed its fate. It closed on 6 August 1914, the outbreak of war being used as an excuse to abandon it — Parliament ratified this in 1923.

STAINES, WOKINGHAM & WOKING RAILWAY

Incorporated on 8 July 1853 to build from Staines (SER) to Wokingham via Virginia Water, with a branch to Woking, it opened between Staines and Ascot on 4 June 1856, and to Wokingham on 9 July. It was worked from the outset by the L&SWR, which leased it under an Act of 28 August 1858 and absorbed the company on 1 July 1878 (Act of 4 July).

STOKES BAY RAILWAY & PIER COMPANY

The company was incorporated on 14 August 1855 to build a 1.5-mile line from Gosport to Stokes Bay, and a pier for steamer connections to Ryde. Ferries, pier and railway were leased to the L&SWR under an Act of 6 August 1860, and services began on 6 April 1863; it bought them outright on 17 June 1875. Custom fell away, however, steamers stopped calling at the outbreak of war, and the last train ran on 31 October 1915. The line S of Gosport was sold to the Admiralty on 3 March 1922 — the link with the pier was cut, and the pier was served by a narrow gauge line from the RN depot.

TAMAR, KIT HILL & CALLINGTON RAILWAY

Formed under the Companies Act of 1862, the first sod was cut at Callington on 26 November 1863; after difficulties, an Incorporation Act was obtained on 29 July 1864. The 7-mile line linked Callington and Calstock, and included an incline to quays at Calstock. Originally authorized in standard gauge, a further Act was obtained (30 July 1866) to allow broad gauge. Work was suspended in the financial crisis of 1866, and the unfinished works were taken over by the Callington & Calstock Railway (qv).

TAW VALE RAILWAY & DOCK COMPANY

Authorized on 11 June 1838 to build railways around Barnstaple and a dock at Fremington Pill on the R Taw, the company then obtained powers (21 July 1845) for a broad gauge line from Barnstaple to Crediton. However, before building was completed the company became the NDR&DC in 1851.

THAMES VALLEY RAILWAY

Incorporated on 17 July 1862 to build 6.5 miles of line from Strawberry Hill, on the Kingston loop, to Shepperton, it opened on 1 November 1864, and transfer or sale to the L&SWR was granted by an Act of 5 July 1865. The line carries its heaviest traffic when there is a race meeting at Kempton Park.

TOOTING, MERTON & WIMBLEDON RAILWAY

This was authorized on 29 July 1864 to connect Streatham Junction, on the LB&SCR's Peckham–Sutton line, and the L&SWR at Wimbledon, with a loop to Merton Park. The 6-mile line passed to the two companies, jointly, wef 5 July 1865, and was opened on 1 October 1868. In 1878 the LB&SCR bought out the L&SWR's holding for £28,000.

TOTTON, HYTHE & FAWLEY LIGHT RAILWAY

Powers obtained on 10 November 1903 by the L&SWR for a line serving the W shore of Southampton Water remained unused. A separate company obtained LROs in 1921 and 1923, and the 9.5-mile line was taken over by the SR in 1923. It opened on 25 July 1925, and closed to passengers on 14 February 1964.

Right *The Totton, Hythe & Fawley Light Railway—Hythe station on 24 July 1961, three years before the line closed to passengers.* (Douglas Thompson)

Below *Mixed gauge track leading to the LC&DR/GWR side of Victoria station—a Saxby & Farmer official photograph of 1860. Note the curious signals with disc spectacles; how they worked is at present shrouded in mystery, as is the cause of the strange 'jigsaw' effect on this old print.* (Westinghouse Signals Ltd/Rev W. Awdry Collection)

TUNBRIDGE WELLS & EASTBOURNE RAILWAY

A line between Polegate and Hailsham was authorized in 1846, but what really led to this one was a 3 ft gauge line authorized on 5 August 1873. The scheme expanded, but little money was forthcoming and the LB&SCR stepped in; the company was vested in it by an Act of 27 June 1876 for £8,534. The line opened from Polegate to Hailsham on 14 May 1879, to Heathfield on 5 April 1880 and to Eridge on 1 September, where it joined the Brighton, Uckfield and Tunbridge Wells Railway (qv). The line was closed to passengers between Eridge and Heathfield on 14 June 1965, for goods from Hailsham to Heathfield on 26 April 1968, and throughout on 9 September 1968.

VICTORIA STATION & PIMLICO RAILWAY

This company was incorporated on 23 July 1858 to build 73 chains from the West End of London & Crystal Palace Railway (qv) terminus at Stewarts Lane to a new station on the site of the disused Grosvenor Canal basin. The LB&SCR subscribed half the cost and so was entitled to half the station; its section

opened on 1 October 1860. The other half opened on 25 August 1862, leased to the LC&DR and GWR — the GWR service (see W London Extension Railway) ceased from 22 March 1915, but it remained a lessee until 1933. The company passed to the SR in 1923.

WATERLOO & CITY RAILWAY

This scheme was authorized on 27 July 1893 and backed by the L&SWR for an underground link between Waterloo and the City of London. The Duke of Cambridge opened it officially on 11 July 1898 (public services began on 8 August), and it was absorbed by its sponsor in 1907 under an Act dated 20 July 1906.

WEST END of LONDON & CRYSTAL PALACE RAILWAY

This was a 5.75-mile link authorized on 4 August 1853 between the L&SWR at Wandsworth Common and the LB&SCR at Sydenham. It opened to Sydenham on 1 December 1856, to Norwood on 1 October 1857 and to Pimlico formally on 27 March 1858 and to the public on 29 March, worked by the LB&SCR which absorbed it by an Act of 23 July 1860.

WESTERHAM VALLEY RAILWAY

These 5 miles of single track, authorized on 24 July 1876, linked Westerham with the SER at Dunton Green. Opened on 7 July 1881, it was vested in the SER by an Act of 11 August 1881.

WEST WICKHAM & HAYES RAILWAY

This was incorporated on 9 July 1880 for slightly over 3 miles of line from Elmers End (Mid-Kent Railway) to Hayes. Several schemes sought to exploit the area between the Chatham and Mid-Kent lines, and this was the successful one. The company was bought on 11 August 1881 by the SER, which opened the line on 29 May 1882.

WIMBLEDON & CROYDON RAILWAY

Incorporated on 8 July 1853, this railway was promoted by a local Contractor, G.P. Bidder, and was built for 5.75 miles along the bed of the Surrey Iron Railway (qv). Bidder worked it at first (it opened on 22 October 1855), but the LB&SCR took a 21-year lease wef 1 July 1856, ratified by Parliament on 21 July. The Company was authorized to sell or transfer itself on 28 June 1858, the LB&SCR taking over wef 1 January 1866.

WIMBLEDON & DORKING RAILWAY

This 5.75-mile branch between Epsom Junction (later Raynes Park) and Wimbledon was authorized on 27 July 1857 against much Parliamentary opposition. The L&SWR bought 1,500 shares and nominated two Directors; an Agreement that it should work the line was sealed on 16 March 1859 (the line opened on 4 April), and confirmed by the L&SWR Act of 6 August 1860. Official transfer was ratified by an Act dated 3 June 1862. The company then quarrelled with the L&SWR over joint ownership of the Epsom & Leatherhead Railway (qv), resolved when the L&SWR agreed to take over that concern's assets and debts.

WIMBLEDON & SUTTON RAILWAY

Authorized on 26 July 1910 to build 4.75 miles of line between the two towns, the project lay dormant until 1922, when a link with the Morden extension of the City & S London Railway (qv — Jt/Ind) was suggested. The SR opposed this, and took over the concern itself by an Act of 1 August 1924, wef the previous 1 January. The line opened to S Merton on 7 July 1929, and throughout on 5 January 1930.

WINDSOR, STAINES & SOUTH WESTERN RAILWAY

Incorporated on 25 June 1847 to extend the Richmond Railway (qv) to Windsor, it was soon swallowed by its backer, the L&SWR, as provided for in its Act. The line opened to Datchet on 22 August 1848, and to Windsor on 1 December 1849.

WOODSIDE & SOUTH CROYDON RAILWAY

This 2.5-mile line between the Mid-Kent Railway (qv) at Woodside and the Oxted line at Selsdon Road was authorized on 6 August 1880. Transferred jointly to the SER and LB&SCR on 10 August 1882, it opened as part of the Oxted/Croydon joint scheme exactly three years later. It was closed to passengers on 1 January 1917, but re-opened on 30 September 1935.

PART 5

Independent and Joint railways, and London Passenger Transport Board constituents

Overleaf *Col Holman F. Stephens was associated with numerous independent light railways in various parts of England and Wales. The upper picture was taken in 1924 during the construction of Hole Bridge, on the North Devon & Cornwall Junction Railway. Col Stephens himself is the tall figure in the pale cap, standing in front of the FWD lorry. The lower picture dates from 1932. The Kent & East Sussex Railway was one of Col Stephens' main interests, and here No 2 Northiam waits to leave Tenterden with a single-coach train for Robertsbridge (Both pictures, Col Stephens Museum Collection, Tenterden, K&ESR)*

ABERFORD RAILWAY
Built about 1845, this line, owned by Garforth Colliery, ran N from the Leeds & Selby Railway (qv – LNER) to Aberford. From opening until about 1875, the 2.75 miles were worked by horses towards Aberford and gravity back, the horses travelling in dandy-carts. After 1875, the colliery worked the line with steam, until road competition after the Great War led to the line's dismantling about 1924.

ALFORD & SUTTON TRAMWAY
A scheme for a winding connection with the Louth & E Coast Railway (qv – LNER) was rejected by Parliament, but Sutton still wanted a railway, and this 2 ft 6 in gauge tramway was the result. Incorporated on 12 August 1880 and opened on 2 April 1884, it succeeded at first, and a third steam tram was bought to augment the original pair. The opening of the Sutton & Willoughby Railway (qv–LNER) in 1886 proved its undoing, however, and it closed in December 1889.

ASHOVER LIGHT RAILWAY
Authorized on 4 December 1919, this 2 ft gauge Derbyshire line used rails and equipment reclaimed from the battlefields of France. It ran for 7.25 miles from Clay Cross (where there was an LMS interchange) to stone quarries between Stretton and Ashover, opening formally on 6 April 1925, and to the public the next day; it carried 5,000 passengers in the first week. It became popular with hikers, but the motor car killed it – passenger services became 'summer only' from 1931 until final withdrawal on 14 September 1936, though the goods service lasted until 31 March 1950.

AVONMOUTH LIGHT RAILWAY
Privately promoted, this line, authorized on 12 December 1893, was planned to leave the GWR's Avonmouth line at Holesworth Junction and run to local works. Nothing much was done until a LRO of 1 December 1903 revived it, though it remained incomplete, and was still less than half its authorized length when the GWR and LMS bought it jointly in 1926.

AXHOLME JOINT RAILWAY
This was formed on 1 October 1902 when, by an Act dated 31 July 1902 (Agreement of 14 June), the NER and L&YR bought, jointly, the Goole & Marshland LR and the Isle of Axholme LR (both qv). The Reedness Junction–Crowle and Eastoft–Fockerby sections (5.75 miles) opened for goods on 10 August 1903, Crowle–Haxey Junction on 4 November 1904 (goods), and for passengers throughout on 2 January 1905, forming a link between the NER and L&YR systems. A goods extension to Hatfield Moor opened in 1909, its main traffic being peat. The lines closed to passengers on 17 July 1933, having been vested jointly in the LNER and LMS at Grouping.

Epworth station on the Axholme Joint Railway served passengers only until 2 February 1959, nine months after this picture was taken. Buffer stops in the cutting indicate that, contrary to appearances of double-track busyness, the far line is merely a siding. (Douglas Thompson)

AYLESBURY & BUCKINGHAM RAILWAY

The initiative for this line (authorized on 6 August 1860) came from local landowners who wanted to link the Buckinghamshire Railway (qv – LMS) at Claydon – renamed Verney Junction after the company's Deputy Chairman – with Aylesbury; the junction with the Aylesbury Railway (qv – LMS) was not built. The line opened on 23 September 1868, and the GWR, approached to work it, was happy to gain a foothold in L&NWR territory; however, it missed a chance to absorb the company when given authority on 30 June 1874, and was superseded by the MetR, under an Act of 25 July 1890, wef 1 July 1891. The line was doubled, and running was taken over in 1907 by a joint MetR/GCR committee. The LPTB withdrew passenger services between Aylesbury and Verney Junction wef 6 July 1936 as an economy measure. The goods service survived until 8 September 1947.

AYLESBURY & RICKMANSWORTH RAILWAY

Projected as a London & Aylesbury Railway and so incorporated (1871), the plan was dropped in 1878. The MetR then promoted its own scheme, authorized on 18 July 1881, which ran for 21.5 miles from Rickmansworth to the Aylesbury & Buckingham Railway (qv) at Aylesbury. It opened to Chalfont Road on 8 July 1889 – a 2.5-mile branch from Chalfont Road to Chesham (authorized on 16 July 1885) was opened the same day. The Amersham branch opened on 2 September 1892, and was closed for passengers on 10 September 1961, and to goods on 3 April 1967. The Chesham line closed to goods on 4 July 1966.

BAKER STREET & WATERLOO RAILWAY

Incorporated on 28 March 1893, this was the forerunner of the present-day Bakerloo line, linking the named places. It opened on 10 March 1906, and by an Act of 26 July 1910 (wef 1 July) the company was absorbed by the London Electric Railway (qv).

BANGOUR RAILWAY

Authorized on 30 July 1900 as a private railway, this 1.5-mile line served the Bangour Mental Hospital, W of Edinburgh, branching from the Edinburgh–Bathgate line between Livingston and Uphall. It opened on 19 June 1905 and was worked by the NBR mainly for the use of patients, passengers and staff, though a siding at the intermediate station, Dechmont, took public traffic. The line was abandoned after the Great War.

BELVOIR CASTLE RAILWAY

Owned by the Duke of Rutland, this 2-mile horse-drawn tramway was engineered by William Jessop and built by the Butterley Ironworks Company, with fishbellied rails spiked to stone sleepers to a gauge of 4 ft 4.5 in. It opened from the Grantham Canal to the Peacock Inn in June 1815, and to the Castle in September, worked with four-wheeled flanged wagons, which used two horses per loaded wagon. The final consignment of coal was carried on 17 October 1916, and though the line was repaired in 1917 it remained in use only until the following May. Various relics survive, *in situ*, on display at the Castle, and at the NRM.

BIDEFORD, WESTWARD HO! & APPLEDORE RAILWAY

This, the second scheme promoted in this area of N Devon, was incorporated on 21 May 1896, the company becoming, in 1900, a subsidiary of the British Electric Traction Company. Almost from opening to Northam on 24 April 1901 and to Appledore on 1 May 1908, a series of petty injunctions was brought by Bideford Town Council, draining the company's financial resources and leading to its early demise. The last train ran on 28 March 1917 (the locomotives had been requisitioned by the Government) and no attempt was made to re-open the line after the war. Stock and rails were sold, one of the engines surviving in private use until 1937.

BIRKENHEAD RAILWAY

This title was taken by the Birkenhead, Lancashire & Cheshire Junction Railway (qv) on re-incorporation on 1 August 1859. The company's independence was short, for it was taken over jointly by the GWR and L&NWR wef 1 January 1860, by an Act of 11 July 1861, the GWR thus getting its access to Birkenhead. A service to Paddington was introduced on 1 October 1861.

BIRKENHEAD, LANCASHIRE & CHESHIRE JUNCTION RAILWAY

Incorporated on 26 June 1846, the first sod of this 38.5-mile railway was cut by Sir Richard Brooke near Preston Brook on 14 November 1846; less than a year later, on 22 July 1847, the company absorbed the Chester & Birkenhead Railway (qv), promptly doubling its single line. The first section opened was Chester W loop, on 1 August 1848, with the Chester–Warrington section opening formally on 31 October 1850, and to the public on 18 December. The company became the Birkenhead Railway (qv) from 1 August 1859.

BIRMINGHAM, BRISTOL & THAMES JUNCTION RAILWAY

This was incorporated on 21 June 1836 to connect the navigable Thames with both the GWR (at Wormwood Scrubs) and the L&BR at W London Junction. Powers were given to convert the Kensington Canal in order to achieve this, the line

Above *Partners in Chester Joint station were the Chester & Birkenhead and the C&HR, later joined by the L&NWR, the SUR&CC, the Birkenhead, Lancashire & Cheshire Junction, and the Shrewsbury & Chester. It was built under the direction of George Grove, who later left engineering to become the first director of the Royal College of Music and to compile a well-known music dictionary.*

Right *Blackpool tramcar No 709 leaves Sandcastle for Starr Gate in September 1987.* (Allan Mott)

terminating initially at the basin of the Canal. In 1840 the company changed its name to the West London Railway (qv).

BISHOPS CASTLE RAILWAY

This 9.75-mile line, authorized on 28 June 1861, ran from Stretford Bridge (Craven Arms, S&HR) to a junction with the Oswestry & Newtown Railway (qv – GWR) near Montgomery. Short of money from the start, the line opened to Lydham Heath on 1 February 1866, and an OR was appointed the next year. The line re-opened on 2 July 1877, and even as late as 1920 attempts were being made to reach Montgomery. Excluded from Grouping, the line closed on 21 April 1935.

BLACKPOOL & FLEETWOOD TRAMWAY

Authorized on 20 July 1896 to build a standard gauge electric line between Blackpool and Fleetwood, it opened on 14 July 1898, and was taken over by Blackpool Corporation wef 31 December 1919.

A L&YR/L&NWR consortium planned to build a traffic interchange to Cleveleys, but a connection was made at Fleet instead, and wagons were worked that way, an arrangement which lasted until 1949.

BOWES RAILWAY
See Pontop & Jarrow Wagonway.

BREAKWATER RAILWAY
The line at Portland was Admiralty property, opened on 29 May 1874 and worked jointly by the GWR and L&SWR. The stretch between Portland and Church Hope was leased by the Admiralty.

BRIGHTON, ROTTINGDEAN & SEASHORE ELECTRIC TRAMWAY
In essence a continuation of the Volks Electric Tramway (qv) beyond Black Rock, it was authorized in July 1893 and opened on 1 September 1897. Its rails were under water at high tide, and the conveyance looked not unlike a length of mobile pier. Soon after opening, storm damage caused temporary closure, but it re-opened the same year, to close finally on 17 January 1901. When the new Marina was built, some remains were concealed, though further E it is still possible to trace the course in places.

BRISTOL PORT, RAILWAY & PIER
This was incorporated on 17 July 1862 to make a railway from the port of Bristol to the old channel at the mouth of the Avon, and to build a pier there. The line was mixed gauge, and the company had WA with the Bristol & S Wales Union Railway (qv — GWR) from the outset — the railway opened on 6 March 1865, the pier on 3 June. A 4-mile 'Clifton' extension to the B&SWUR and the Bristol–Birmingham line (MR), was authorized on 15 August 1867 and opened in 1874. The company was purchased by the GWR and MR jointly under an Act of 25 July 1890 for £97,500.

BRYNMAWR & WESTERN VALLEYS RAILWAY
A line sanctioned on 13 July 1899, it ran 1.5 miles SW from Brynmawr (Merthyr, Tredegar & Abergavenny Railway, qv — LMS) to the GWR at Nantyglo. The company was vested jointly in the L&NWR/GWR on 31 July 1902 and, worked by the GWR, opened for goods on 12 July 1905 and to passengers on 28 May 1906. It closed in 1962.

CAMPBELTOWN & MACHRIHANISH LIGHT RAILWAY
This line in Kintyre, between a colliery at Machrihanish and Campbeltown harbour, was converted to a 2 ft 3 in gauge line by a LRO of 8 May 1905. The line began earning at once by carrying coal along the old line, but hopes of a quick passenger opening were disappointed. A test run on 4 August 1906 had, fortunately, invited miners on board, who were several times called upon to lift the engine back on to the rails! Opening came on 18 August (public), 25 August (official), a confirmatory LRO following on 30 May 1908. Bus competition and a need for heavy repairs to the locomotives caused closure, and in 1932 passenger rights were sold to a bus company. A liquidator was appointed on 21 November 1933, and the line was dismantled the next year.

CANNOCK CHASE & WOLVERHAMPTON RAILWAY
Financed by John Robinson McClean (see S Staffordshire Railway, LMS), this line linked the Cannock Chase Railway, the SSR, the MR and the L&NWR, opening on 1 February 1858. A company was

Abersychan & Talywain on the Brynmawr & Western Valleys Railway was GWR/L&NWR joint despite claims at the foot of this undated picture. Churns and platform accessories suggest a pre-1930 period, but the dress of the gentleman on the near platform is distinctly later.

incorporated on 29 July 1864, and an extension to Hednesford authorized on 16 July 1866. Part of the route now forms a section of the Chasewater LR.

CENTRAL LONDON RAILWAY

This was incorporated on 5 August 1891 out of several competing ideas to build a line from Wood Lane, E of Shepherds Bush, to Bank. A short extension to Liverpool Street was also authorized on 28 June 1892, though the powers lapsed and it did not open until 28 July 1912. Shepherds Bush–Bank opened on 30 July 1900, and a short extension to Wood Lane on 14 May 1908. Electric locomotives were used at first, but vibration prompted a change to emus, and the line became the original 'Tuppeny Tube', by virtue of its flat-rate fare. A further extension from Wood Lane to Ealing Broadway opened on 3 August 1920, and the company was vested in the LPTB wef 1 July 1933.

CHARING CROSS, EUSTON & HAMPSTEAD RAILWAY

The company was incorporated on 24 August 1893 to build a railway between Charing Cross and Hampstead. In 1902 it made an Agreement with the newly-formed Underground Electric Railways Company of London for that company to build and equip its line. The UERCL leased the line under an Act of 21 July 1903, and opened it on 22 June 1907; the company was absorbed by the London Electric Railway wef 1 July 1910 (Act of 27 July). On 20 April 1924, an extension opened to the District and Circle lines at what is now Embankment, and on 13 September 1926 another joined the City & S London Railway (qv) at Kennington, forming what is today the LTE's Northern Line.

CHARLESWORTH'S RAILWAY

See Lake Lock Rail Road.

CHATTENDEN NAVAL TRAMWAY

Built under a LRO of 24 July 1901, this was a standard gauge single line linking Lodge Hill, Chattenden, with the Hundred of Hoo Railway (qv – SR) at Sharnal Street. A further double-track section was authorized to Kingsnorth, but was never built. The line, worked by the Kingsnorth LR (qv) from 24 July 1926 under an Agreement of 14 August 1924, was transferred to that company by an Order dated 25 July 1929.

CHATTENDEN & UPNOR RAILWAY

Originally built to standard gauge in the 1870s, a 2 ft 6 in gauge line was laid out by the Royal Engineers shortly before the Boer War, for training. When the RE moved to Longmoor, the line was taken over by the Admiralty from 1 April 1906. By the Second World War it was very run down, but new stock was provided, and, after the War, the line was dieselized.

As might be expected, the devices of the three owning companies, GNR (top), MR (bottom right) and MS&LR, make up the seal of the Cheshire Lines Committee. (NRM)

It closed on 31 December 1961, though some rolling-stock survives on the Welshpool & Llanfair LR (qv – GWR) and the Sittingbourne & Kemsley LR.

CHESHIRE LINES COMMITTEE

This was formed on 5 July 1865, when the constituents were vested in the GNR and MS&LR; they were joined in 1866 by the MR, and given a corporate identity by an Act of 15 August 1867. The system covered: Stockport–Timperley–Altrincham, 8 miles 8 chains; Stockport–Woodley, 2.75 miles; Garston–Liverpool, 3 miles 73 chains; Cheshire Midland Railway, 12.75 miles; West Cheshire Railway (both qv), 22.75 miles; Liverpool Central station. The owning companies supplied motive power, though GCR engines later hauled most trains. The company promoted a link between Glazebrook Junction (MS&LR) and Skelton Junction (Stockport, Timperley & Altrincham Railway, qv), which opened on 1 March 1873 for goods and 1 August for passengers. The company also opened a direct line into Chester Northgate on 2 November 1874 (goods), 1 May 1875 (passengers), as inheritors of powers granted in 1865 to the Chester & W Cheshire Junction Railway (qv). The Committee remained independent until Nationalization.

CHESTER & BIRKENHEAD RAILWAY

Authorised on 12 July 1837, this 14.5-mile line joined the Chester & Crewe Railway (qv – LMS) at Chester with Birkenhead (Grange Lane). Opened formally on 23 September 1840 and to the public on 23 December, the line was extended to Monks Ferry on 23 October 1844 — it closed to passengers the day after a new terminus at Woodside opened on 31 March 1878. By then the company had been merged with the Birkenhead, Lancashire & Cheshire Junction Railway (qv) for many years, under an Act of 22 July 1847. Green Lane closed on 7 May 1945 and Woodside on 6 November 1967, Rock Ferry becoming the terminus for Chester trains.

CHESHIRE MIDLAND RAILWAY

Promoted by landowners who were supported by the MS&LR, and incorporated on 14 June 1860, the company had powers to build from the Manchester, South Junction & Altrincham Railway (qv) at Altrincham, 12.75 miles to Northwich. The L&NWR was given leave to subscribe, but left it to the MS&LR, which got help from the GNR. The line opened for passengers to Knutsford on 12 May 1862, to Northwich on 1 January 1863, and throughout for goods on 1 May 1863, the company becoming part of the CLC on 15 August 1867.

CHESTER & WEST CHESHIRE JUNCTION RAILWAY

This company, incorporated on 5 July 1865, had but a brief independent life, its powers being transferred to the CLC on 10 August 1866. Building began on 7 miles 35 chains of line between Mouldsworth Junction (W Cheshire Railway, qv) and Chester Northgate in 1871, which opened for goods on 2 November 1874 and to passengers on 1 May 1875.

CITY & SOUTH LONDON RAILWAY

Originally incorporated as the City of London &

Southwark Subway Company (28 July 1884), the company was renamed by an Act of 25 July 1890, and opened between King William Street (now Borough) and Stockwell on 18 December 1890. Extensions were opened to Moorgate (25 February 1900), Clapham Common (3 June 1900) and Euston (12 May 1907), giving a line of 7.25 miles. The company remained independent until amalgamation with the LPTB wef 1 July 1933, and the line now forms part of the Northern (City) Line.

CORRINGHAM LIGHT RAILWAY

Built under a LRO confirmed on 1 July 1899, the first sod was cut by Miss Kate Chamberlain, a relative of Neville Chamberlain. It opened 1 January 1901 (goods), 29 June (passengers) and ran from Corringham, Essex, to Shell Haven on the N bank of the Thames estuary, upstream from Canvey Island, with a branch to Kynoch Explosive Works and its narrow gauge system. The Corringham section closed on 1 March 1952, the company having remained independent through Grouping and Nationalization. In 1962 it passed to the Mobil Oil Company and was wound up by a LRO of 6 September 1971.

CROESOR & PORTMADOC RAILWAY

This company was formed on 5 July 1865 to maintain and extend the Croesor Tramway, opened in 1864. The gauge was officially 2 ft, the line running 4.5 miles N from the harbour at Portmadoc to Croesor, where an incline led to 4 miles of track serving slate workings in the Croesor Valley. The company changed its name by an Act of 21 July 1879 to the Portmadoc, Croesor & Beddgelert Tram Railway (qv).

Latter days on the Corringham Light Railway—the Avonside 0-6-OST and LT&SR four-wheeler wait at Corringham one sunny afternoon, before leaving with what appears to be an enthusiasts' special.

Another enthusiasts' special, this time on the Derwent Valley Railway. In NER livery, 'J72' Joem waits at Dunnington on a summer afternoon in 1976. (Allan Mott)

DERWENT VALLEY LIGHT RAILWAY

A LRO made on 29 September 1899 and confirmed in 1902 was allowed to lapse, but another company was formed and a second Order (19 December 1905) confirmed in 1907; building began in 1911, and the line opened officially on 19 July 1913 and to the public on 21 July. The single line, 16.5 miles long plus sidings, ran from Cliff Common, on the Selby–Market Weighton line, along the Derwent valley to Layerthorpe, York. At first engines were hired from the NER, but the company bought two buses on rail-wheels for passenger traffic, and a Sentinel steam locomotive for goods. Passenger services ceased from 1 September 1926, and, still independent, the line was cut to the 4 miles between York and Dunnington on 30 September 1972, though the last train to Elvington had run on 22 June. It closed completely on 25 November 1980.

DORSET CENTRAL RAILWAY

This company arose from an abortive scheme of 1852, and was incorporated on 29 July 1856. Worked by the L&SWR with stock provided by the Somerset Central Railway (qv), its line opened from Wimborne to Blandford on 1 November 1860 (formally on 31 October), and from Templecombe

to Cole on 18 January 1862 (formally), 3 February (to the public). At Cole it joined the SCR, with which it amalgamated under an Act of 7 August 1862 to form the Somerset & Dorset Railway (qv) wef 1 September.

DOWLAIS RAILWAY

This line, owned by the Dowlais Iron Company, the largest in the world at the time, was built under powers granted to the TVR on 28 July 1849 to link the Ironworks with its own system. A public goods and passenger service opened on 21 August 1851 in conjunction with the TVR, though the passenger service ceased in May 1854 after an accident on the 1 in 12 double-track, rope-worked incline. Public goods traffic ceased in 1876, and the line closed completely in October 1930.

DUMBARTON & BALLOCH JOINT RAILWAY

This was formed by an Agreement between the CR and the NBR of 31 October 1891 (ratified on 27 June 1892), in which the Lanarkshire & Dumbarton-shire Railway (qv – LMS) was also involved, to run the line between Balloch and Dumbarton E, terminus of the L&DR. It had 6 miles of track and a fleet of steamers on Loch Lomond. Because the CR pre-cipitated the opening of the L&DR before it was ready, the company was unprepared for its own opening on 1 October 1896, but despite this in-auspicious beginning the line did well. It was vested

jointly in the CR and NBR from 1 August 1909, and worked as a joint LMS/LNER line from Grouping until 1948.

DUNDEE & ARBROATH RAILWAY

Incorporated on 19 May 1836, this 5 ft 6 in gauge line, with a branch to Almericloss, was 16.75 miles long; its drawback was competition from both a thriving waterborne coastal trade and a good road between the towns. The line opened from a temporary station at Craigie (Dundee) in October 1838, and throughout in April 1840. A junction with the Arbroath & Forfar Railway (qv – LMS) was never built, and the line was isolated until the arrival of the Dundee & Perth Railway (qv – LMS), which was authorized to lease the line by an Act of 31 August 1848. The company was absorbed by the

SNER in 1862, passed to the CR by virtue of this under an Act of 26 June 1846, and was later leased to the Aberdeen Railway (qv – LMS). From 1 February 1880 (Act of 21 July 1879) it passed jointly to the CR and NBR, and, at Grouping to the LNER/LMS.

EALING & SOUTH HARROW RAILWAY

A 5-mile line, authorized on 25 August 1894, from Hanger Lane to S Harrow, it was actually ready in 1901 but used as a test track for electric trains before being opened to the public. A service was provided for the Royal Show at Park Royal from 23–27 June 1903, and a full service opened immediately thereafter. An Agreement of 26 March 1897 had provided for working by the DR but the company was vested in the M/DR wef 1 July 1900, ratified by an Act of 6 August.

Above The lower length of the Dowlais incline has been landscaped, but the upper section can be found, climbing from the van body (right) to the gap in the hedge and beyond. But it is steeper than this picture indicates!

Left A joint LNER/LMS 'Trespassers' notice for the Dundee & Arbroath Joint Railway, one of the collection at Winchcombe Railway Museum.

EASINGWOLD RAILWAY

It cost £17,000 to build this 2.5-mile line from the NER at Alne; authorized on 23 August 1887, it opened on 27 July 1891, and became the Easingwold Light Railway in 1928. It owned two engines — replacements for any under repair were hired from the NER, which, in the end, worked the line entirely. The coaches, vintage four- or six-wheelers, came from the NER, NLR and GCR, but a passenger service survived until 29 November 1948. The company remained independent, and the last train, worked by Class 'J72' No 68698, ran on 27 December 1957.

EAST KENT LIGHT RAILWAY

Built under a LRO of 19 June 1911 to link pits in the Kent coalfield, the line opened for goods in November 1912 and to passengers on 16 October 1916. Gradual extension reached Sandwich by 1925, but closed on 31 October 1928, the rest closing completely to passengers on 31 October 1948, and to goods on 1 July 1951, except for the Shepherds Well–Tilmanstone section. Traffic on this length was killed by the miners' strike in 1984, the last train running on 1 March of that year; official closure came on 31 December 1987. The company had retained independence until Nationalization. A Preservation Society was formed in 1985, and has now leased the platforms at Shepherds Well.

EASTON & CHURCH HOPE RAILWAY

An 1867 scheme linking quarries at Easton (Portland) with Church Hope Cove was abandoned in 1874, but fresh powers on 14 August 1884 for 3.5 miles between Easton and Portland enabled work to re-start. The heavily-graded line joined the Breakwater Railway (qv), and was worked jointly by the GWR and L&SWR as an extension of the Portland branch. It opened to goods on 1 October 1900, and to passengers on 1 September 1902, but was in the hands of an OR later that month. Landslips caused the suspension of services in 1907 and 1935.

EDENHAM & LITTLE BYTHAM RAILWAY

No Act was necessary for this 4 miles 12 chains line, built by Lord Willoughby de Eresby on his own land, E of Little Bytham on the ECML, and opened on 1 November 1856. Both Daniel Gooch and William Stroudley were friends of Lord Willoughby, and visited the estate and advised him. Single throughout, the line ended in the goods yard at Little Bytham station — buildings at Edenham survive. Three BoT inspections were needed to pass an intended passenger service, which opened on 8 December 1857 and was discontinued on 17 October 1871 because of the state of the last remaining locomotive (out of three). Horse-drawn for a while, the line was abandoned after, it has been suggested, wagons overtook the horses and killed them. The line was offered to the GNR, which declined, and the rails were lifted in 1883.

EDGE HILL LIGHT RAILWAY

Built under a LRO of 28 January 1919 in association with the S&MJR (qv — LMS) to tap ironstone deposits on Edge Hill, NW of Banbury, the line ran for just over 2 miles S from Burton Dassett siding.

No-one would think from this 1939 picture that the Edge Hill Light Railway had been abandoned for 14 years. The two ex-LB&SCR engines (the other stood just off camera, right) languished for another seven before they were scrapped. (H.P. White)

Opened in 1920, it was partly rope-worked, but an extension was never completed, and the line was abandoned after the last load on 27 January 1925. After closure, the layout lay derelict until 1946. The company went into voluntary liquidation on 25 November 1957.

EDGWARE & HAMPSTEAD RAILWAY

When nothing had happened ten years after this company's incorporation on 18 November 1902, powers were transferred, by an Act dated 7 August 1912, to the London Electric Railway (qv), which opened the line on 19 November 1923.

ELAN VALLEY RAILWAY

A privately-built line, authorized on 27 June 1892, it was 33 miles long at its busiest period. The first section opened in the summer of 1894 (throughout in 1896), serving construction works on reservoirs for Birmingham Corporation, and joining the Mid-Wales Railway (qv – GWR) S of Rhayader. Traffic was handled by the Corporation's own engines, though from 1895 the CambR worked goods up to Caban Coch, where the Waterworks were officially opened by King Edward VII on 21 July 1904. The branches were mostly lifted by 1912, but the main line lasted until October 1916, the Noyadd–Elan Valley Junction section closing on 23 February 1917. A scheme for a miniature tourist line on the track-bed was mooted in 1987.

ELSECAR & THORNCLIFFE WAGGONWAY

Built about 1837, this wagonway served the Milton Ironworks at Hoyland, Yorkshire. Laid on stone sleepers and worked by horses combined with stationary engines, it ran from the Dearne & Dove Canal at Elsecar to collieries and ironstone pits, as well as the Thorncliffe Ironworks at Chapeltown. The W section closed in 1879, but in 1886 the rest was relaid as a standard gauge colliery line, remaining in use until 1911.

FAIRBOURNE RAILWAY

Originally a 2 ft gauge horse-tramway, it opened in 1890 to carry materials to the site of speculative building at Penrhyn Point, on the S side of the Mawddach estuary. It began to carry the public, and in 1916 the gauge was converted to 15 in. Though extensively damaged during the Second World War, it was repaired and partially re-opened in 1947, the whole line coming back into use in due course, from a point near Fairbourne station to Barmouth Ferry. There has been another gauge change in recent years.

FESTINIOG RAILWAY

Incorporated on 23 May 1832 to build a line of 1 ft 11.5 in gauge from slate quarries at Blaenau Ffestiniog in N Wales to a harbour at Portmadoc, 13.25 miles away, it opened on 20 April 1836. An incline near Tan-y-Grisiau was superseded when the line changed from horse to steam haulage in 1863 (goods only) and a deviation was made through Moelwyn Tunnel. Steam-hauled passenger services began in January 1865, and in 1869 the first of the double-ended Fairlie engines was delivered and bogie carriages were introduced. After a long and prosperous career the line closed in 1946 (passenger traffic had been suspended in 1939), to be revived as a tourist line

Festiniog Railway No 10 Merddin Emrys, *newly restored and minus cab, stands at Portmadoc on a dull morning in 1959.*

from 1954, a role in which it has now found a second period of prosperity. A large-scale deviation through a new tunnel and round a reservoir was opened on 24 June 1978, and the line re-opened to Blaenau on 25 May 1982.

FISHGUARD BAY RAILWAY & PIER

The company was incorporated on 29 June 1893 to build a harbour and breakwater in Fishguard Bay, and a mile of railway linking them with the approaching N Pembroke & Fishguard Railway (qv – GWR). The company ended up not only completing the NP&FR but also the Maenclochog line too. The original opening date (4 January 1895) was postponed because of snow; it was 14 March before it opened for goods, and 11 April for passengers. The company's name was changed to the Fishguard & Rosslare Railways & Harbours Company on 31 July 1894 – it remained independent, and is now jointly owned by BRB and Coras Iompair Eireann.

FURZEBROOK TRAMWAY

This was perhaps the best-known (and more correctly called Pike's Tramway) of a group of clay-carrying lines in Purbeck, linking pits near Furzebrook first with the R Frome and later with the railway at Furzebrook. The gauge was 2 ft 8.5 in, and it opened in about 1840 – the first steam locomotive arrived in 1866. The line closed in 1956, but at the time of writing a scheme for a narrow gauge tourist line is proposed for the nearby Fayle's Tramway, closed in the early 1970s.

GARSTON & LIVERPOOL RAILWAY

Authorized on 17 May 1861, this railway was promoted jointly by the MS&LR and GNR, later to form the CLC. In 1862 the company was authorized to build a terminus at Brunswick Dock, a curtailment of the original plan and disappointing to the company, which had been aiming at Queens Dock. The 3 miles 73 chains of double track opened on 1 June 1864 and, after the company's amalgamation into the CLC (15 August 1867), became that company's route to Liverpool.

GLYN VALLEY TRAMWAY

An Ellesmere & Glyn Valley Railway scheme had been authorized on 6 August 1866, but the Ellesmere section was abandoned in 1869, the line changed to narrow gauge, and the company re-incorporated on 10 August 1870. Work began in June 1872, to a gauge of 2 ft 4.5 in – the line opened between Chirk and Glyn Ceiriog for goods in April 1873, and to passengers on 1 April 1874. Extensions to quarries at Pandy were authorized in 1878. Horses were used until steam was authorized in 1885, and the Snailbeach District Railways (qv) locomotives ran a goods service from mid-1885. A passenger service,

The life of the Glyn Valley Tramway was short, but one of the nameplates from the eponymous locomotive has survived in the Narrow Gauge Railway Museum at Tywyn.

with GVT engines, began on 15 March 1891. Road competition forced closure to passengers wef 6 April 1933, and to all traffic from 6 July 1935.

GOOLE & MARSHLAND LIGHT RAILWAY

Built under a LRO dated 16 August 1898 to run between Marshland Junction and Fockerby, the first section, between Reedness and Goole opened on 8 January 1900. The company was bought for £73,500 jointly by the NER and L&YR wef 2 October 1901 (Act of 31 July 1902); combination with the Isle of Axholme LR under an Agreement of 14 June 1902 formed the Axholme LR (both qv) wef 1 October 1902.

GORSEDDAU TRAMWAY

Opened between 1856–7, this 3 ft gauge horse-drawn tramway was built to move slates from the slopes of Moel Hebog, S of Snowdon, to Portmadoc, using part of an even earlier Tremadoc Tramway. On 25 July 1872, the Gorseddau Junction & Portmadoc Railway (qv) was incorporated to take it over.

GORSEDDAU JUNCTION & PORTMADOC RAILWAY

This was incorporated on 25 July 1872 to take over the Gorseddau Tramway (qv). It converted the gauge to 1 ft 11.5 in before re-opening on 2 September 1875, but the Gorseddau Quarry branch closed about then, the section between Cwm Trwgl and Cwm Dwyfor by 1884, and the rest by 1892. The total length, including branches, was 13 miles 2 furlongs 3 chains.

GOWDALL & BRAITHWELL RAILWAY

Authorized on 16 August 1909,. this 21.25-mile line ran from Aire Junction (H&BR) to Braithwell Junction, where it joined the Rotherham, Maltby & Laughton Railway (qv). It was jointly owned by the H&BR and the GCR; the GNR had RP which it did not use. The line opened on 1 May 1916, but by 1942 was being used only for wagon stabling — it was officially closed between Aire Junction and Bullcroft Junction on 20 October 1958, though the section to Thorpe Marsh power station was re-opened from about 1961 to 6 September 1970, after which the line was dismantled.

GREAT NORTHERN & CITY RAILWAY

Incorporated on 28 June 1892, this was an attempt by the GNR to emulate the L&SWR's Waterloo & City Railway (qv — SR), and was planned to run from the Canonbury curve to Moorgate. There were disagreements, however, about through running, so the GNR built its own terminus under Finsbury Park, leasing it to the company; it opened on 14 February 1904, and the MetR took control under an Act of 15 August 1913, wef 1 July. This line was the scene of the worst ever LTE accident, when, on 28 February 1975, a train ran into the dead-end tunnel at Moorgate. BR took the line over, linking it with the ex-GNR network on 8 November 1976, a mere 84 years late!

GREAT NORTHERN, PICCADILLY & BROMPTON RAILWAY

This was formed on 18 November 1902 when the Brompton & Piccadilly Circus Railway (incorporated on 6 August 1897) changed its name. The line opened between Finsbury Park and Hammersmith on 15 December 1906, and the S Kensington–Earls Court section eventually became part of the present Piccadilly line. On its name-change, the company absorbed the unbuilt GN & Strand Railway, and changed its own title yet again, becoming the London Electric Railway (qv) by an Act of 26 July 1910.

GREAT WESTERN & GREAT CENTRAL JOINT COMMITTEE

This was formed on 1 August 1899 to administer a line from Old Oak Common through the Chilterns to High Wycombe, and beyond to Aylesbury. The line was joint from Northolt Junction, and GWR from Old Oak Common to there. The line's 'main' status has disappeared over the years, but a frequent dmu service to High Wycombe runs from Marylebone: the line is now regularly used for steam excursions, also from Marylebone.

HAFAN & TALYBONT TRAMWAY

See Plynlimon & Hafan Tramway.

HALESOWEN RAILWAY

This was the title assumed on 13 July 1876 by the Halesowen & Bromsgrove Branch Railway (qv). A joint WA had been made between the GWR and MR before the line opened on 10 September 1883, and the company was vested in its operators by an Act of 20 July 1906. The line serves the Austin (Longbridge) factory, established only four years before the line lost its regular passenger service in April 1919; it became joint LMS/GWR at Grouping, and workmen's trains continued until 1958 to Old Hill, and until 1964 between Halesowen and Northfields.

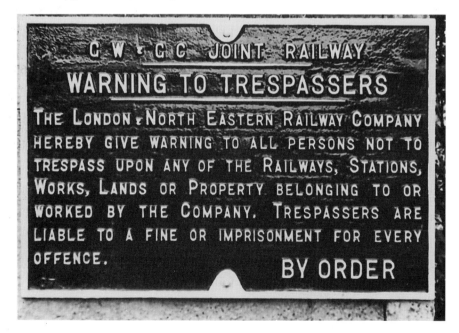

Another 'Trespassers' notice, this time issued by the LNER as the GCR's successor. Note that here the LNER assumes sole working, whereas the Dundee Joint line (see picture on page 212) was clearly a joint affair.

HALESOWEN & BROMSGROVE BRANCH RAILWAY

Incorporated on 5 July 1865 to make a line 6 miles long between Halesowen Junction, on the ex-B&GR, and Old Hill (Stourbridge Railway, qv – GWR). It opened on 1 March 1872 and the company changed its name to the Halesowen Railway (qv) on 13 July 1876.

HALIFAX HIGH LEVEL & NORTH & SOUTH JUNCTION RAILWAY

This was conceived as a grandiose scheme foreseeing Scottish expresses using its line to link the GNR and MR. When reality broke the rose-coloured spectacles, only 3 miles of the line authorized on 7 August 1884 had actually been built. It opened for goods between Holmfield (GNR) and Pellon on 1 August 1890, and to Halifax St Pauls (goods) and passengers throughout on 5 September. The company was vested jointly in the GNR and L&YR wef 1 October 1894 (Act of 3 July) and closed to passengers 1 January 1917; the goods service lasted until 27 July 1960.

HALIFAX & OVENDEN JUNCTION RAILWAY

Incorporated on 30 June 1864, this project was supported by the GNR and L&YR, which subscribed £30,000 each. It grew from a plan for a line between Halifax and Keighley, and building began soon after authorization. However, lack of capital caused a halt, and work was not resumed until amalgamation as a joint GNR/L&YR concern on 1 August 1870. Further delay was then caused by a landslip at Wade Street, Halifax. The 2.75-mile line opened for goods between Halifax and N Bridge on 17 August 1874, to Holmfield on 1 September 1874 and to passengers throughout on 1 December 1879. Heavily graded, the line climbed at 1 in 45 from N Bridge to Holmfield. It closed to passengers on 23 May 1955, and to goods on 27 July 1960.

HAMMERSMITH & CITY RAILWAY

Authorized on 22 July 1861, this was 2.5 miles of double track, broad gauge and GWR-worked, from Green Lane Junction (Westbourne Park) to Hammersmith via Notting Hill and Shepherds Bush. The line opened on 13 June 1864, and the company was dissolved and vested jointly in the GWR and MetR on 15 July 1867 (Act of 19 June 1865), after which the MetR worked it. An electrified service began in November 1906, the line closing for goods on 1 February 1960.

HAMMERSMITH EXTENSION RAILWAY

Incorporated on 7 July 1873 to extend the DR from Earls Court to Hammersmith Broadway, further extensions were abandoned when the L&SWR gave the company RP to Richmond. The line opened on 9 September 1874, and a connection with Studland Junction was opened on 1 June 1877; the independent company had been absorbed by the DR wef opening date.

HARRINGTON & LOWCA LIGHT RAILWAY

This 3.25-mile private line opened in 1858 for mineral traffic from Rosehill colliery (Cleator & Workington Junction Railway, qv – LMS) to Lowca and Harrington Ironworks. It was converted to a LR by an Order confirmed on 16 May 1913, and re-opened on 2 June, using basic 'bus-shelter' stations. The line included the steepest adhesion climb on which passengers were taken in the British Isles, 13 chains at 1 in 17. The Furness Railway (qv) provided and worked the engine and coach, though the line was controlled by the Workington Iron & Steel Company. The public service closed on 31 May 1926, but workmen's trains continued until 1 April 1929. The line closed finally on 29 May 1973.

HARROW & RICKMANSWORTH RAILWAY

A line authorized on 7 August 1874 was abandoned by an Act of 14 August 1877 – at which point the MetR stepped in to further its interests to the N, and built it under revived powers of 6 August 1880. It opened to Pinner on 25 May 1885, Rickmansworth on 1 September 1887, Chesham on 8 July 1889 and Aylesbury on 1 September 1892. It remains open for passengers, though the goods service ceased on 3 April 1967.

HARROW & UXBRIDGE RAILWAY

This was incorporated on 6 August 1897 to extend the DR's S Harrow line (see Ealing & S Harrow Railway). Capital could not be raised, and the MetR was persuaded to work the line (opened ceremonially on 30 June 1904, and to the public on 4 July), an action authorized on 9 August 1899. The DR was granted RP from S Harrow, for which it was to pay £2,000 pa, keeping its own traffic receipts above this sum. The MetR assumed financial responsibility on 25 February 1904, the company being vested in it wef 1 July 1905 (Act of 30 June). The line was electrified in 1905, and lost its goods service on 10 August 1964.

HAYTOR TRAMWAY

Built as a feeder for the Stover Canal, which ran along the Teign valley, this line, its rails made of L-shaped granite blocks laid lengthwise, carried that commodity 6 miles from Dartmoor down to Ventiford Wharf, Teigngrace, in horse-drawn wagons – stone for the National Gallery and London Bridge came this way. The line, opened on 16 September 1820, rose 1,200 ft, mostly in the first 4 miles. Though it lapsed into disuse in 1858, much of its course and the track can still be seen.

Left *Piccadilly Line services were extended to Uxbridge in 1933—this undated picture shows a train running into Uxbridge Old station (replaced in 1938) during the interim period.*

Right *The view SW from the summit of the Warden Law incline of the Hetton Colliery Railway. At the incline foot, the line swung to the left and continued to fall. Both stretches are now public footpaths.*

Left *High on Dartmoor, the main line of the Haytor Tramway continues straight and more or less level. The stone 'pointwork' begins a branch to a granite quarry to the left and at a lower level.*

HECK BRIDGE & WENTBRIDGE RAILWAY

Incorporated on 5 May 1826, this early plateway was built to a gauge of around 3 ft 6 in for carrying stone along a 7.5-mile route between Wentbridge and the Knottingley & Goole Canal near Heck. It was never finished, and its sale was authorized in 1833, but 50 years later part of the route, between Kirksmeaton and Heck, was used by the H&BR.

HENDRE DDU TRAMWAY

Built to link slate mines with the Mawddwy Railway (qv – GWR), it was opened soon after that line to a new station at Aberangell. The system had several branches, and carried slate, timber and the occasional tourist special until lifted early in the Second World War.

HETTON COLLIERY RAILWAY

Opened on 18 November 1822, this private railway was built to carry coal from Hetton Lyons colliery to staiths on the Wear at Sunderland. The company pioneered the use of steam, though only a quarter of its 8-mile route was locomotive-worked; it was engineered by George Stephenson, who used it to try out his engines. It closed on 9 September 1959, and has now been lifted. An 0-4-0 of 1822 by Stephenson

and Nicholas Wade, rebuilt twice, remained in use until the present century and led the 1925 St&DR Centenary Cavalcade at Darlington under its own steam. It now belongs to the NRM.

HOUNSLOW & METROPOLITAN RAILWAY

Incorporated on 26 August 1880, this was promoted by local landowners who hoped to increase property values in the area by building a branch from the DR at Mill Hill Park to Hounslow Barracks. The line opened to Hounslow on 1 May 1883 and to the Barracks on 21 July 1884, worked by the DR from opening, and vested in it from 21 July 1903. Hounslow station became Hounslow Town on 2 May 1909, and survives, but Hounslow Barracks lost its service on 12 July 1975.

HUNDRED of MANHOOD & SELSEY RAILWAY

Authorized on 29 April 1896, this line ran 7.75 miles from Chichester (LB&SCR) to Selsey at a cost of £21,000. It opened on 27 August 1897, and was extended to Selsey Beach on 1 August 1898, but the extension fell out of use about 1904. Somewhat primitive, it became part of Col Stephens' 'empire', changing its name to the W Sussex Railway (Selsey Tramway Section) in January 1924. Its last train ran on 19 January 1935, and the company was wound up in 1938.

ISLE of AXHOLME LIGHT RAILWAY

Authorized under a LRO of 11 March 1899, the first sod of this N Lincolnshire line was cut by Miss Bletcher, daughter of the Chairman, on 20 July 1899. It linked Reedness Junction with Haxey, and was bought, jointly, for £27,500 by the NER and L&YR, which combined it with the Goole & Marshland LR to form the Axholme LR (both qv)

wef 1 October 1902. Sanction for this, following an Agreement dated 14 June 1902, was by an Act of 31 July.

KENT & EAST SUSSEX LIGHT RAILWAY

This was the new title taken on 1 June 1904 by the Rother Valley LR (qv). Managed by Col Stephens, the line was run with his usual variety of other people's 'offcuts'. The Maidstone line which spurred the name-change was never built, but the line opened from Tenterden to Headcorn on 15 May 1905. On Col Stephens' death in 1931, the company went into liquidation (15 March 1932), to be managed by W.T. Austen; it remained independent until vested in BR in 1948. The line was closed to passengers on 4 January 1954 — though hop-pickers' specials ran to Bodiam until 1959 — and to goods on 12 June 1961. The Tenterden–Headcorn section was dismantled in 1956, but the section along the Rother valley from Tenterden survives as a preserved steam line, working its way towards Bodiam.

KEPWICK TRAMWAY

Thought to be only the second railway in the N Riding, this 3-mile tramway was built to carry limestone from quarries above Kepwick (6 miles NE of Thirsk) to kilns near Leake church, by the Thirsk–Stockton road. Opened in the early 1830s, the lower part was horse-worked and the upper section included an incline, probably self-acting. The line appears to have closed about 1890.

KILSYTH & BONNYBRIDGE RAILWAY

Originally promoted in 1862, revised powers were obtained on 10 August 1882, the line opening between the Kelvin Valley Railway (qv – LNER) at Kilsyth and the CR at Bonnybridge on 2 August 1886. Though a NBR/CR scheme, it was never a

joint railway — each company paid its own expenses and provided its own staff and trains. After passing to the LMS/LNER at Grouping, the 8-mile line closed on 1 February 1935.

KINGSBURY & HARROW RAILWAY

This was authorized on 16 July 1874 to extend the Metropolitan & St Johns Wood Railway (qv) by 5.5 miles to Harrow — there was a link with the MR at Finchley Road. The line was owned jointly by the MetR and the M&SJWR, but an Agreement of 1 May 1878 (Act of 22 July) authorized the MetR to 'exercise powers'. It did so, working the line from opening on 2 August 1880.

KINGS LYNN DOCK & RAILWAY

Authorized on 19 June 1865 to build railways in and around the docks at Kings Lynn, the Lynn & Sutton Bridge, the Peterborough, Wisbeach & Sutton Bridge Railways (both qv — LNER) and Lynn Corporation being empowered to subscribe £15,000 apiece. An Act of 24 June 1869 gave RP to the GER and the Midland & Eastern Railway (qv — LNER), and the company changed its title to the Kings Lynn Dock Company. The system opened in 1870, the concern retaining independence until Nationalization.

KINGSNORTH LIGHT RAILWAY

A 2-mile extension of the Chattenden Naval Tramway (qv), and opened to Admiralty traffic in 1915, it ran between Sharnal Street and Kingsnorth Pier on the Medway estuary. After a LRO was obtained permitting passenger traffic, the line was rebuilt as a LR, and powers to transfer the CNT to the company were given by an Order dated 25 July 1929. The line closed between 1945 and 1957, while the CNT section is thought to have lasted until about 1961.

LAKE LOCK RAIL ROAD

Built under the Wakefield Inclosure Act of 1793, which permitted any owners of 'waggons with suitable wheels' to use it, its gauge was 3 ft 4 in and claims have been made in its favour as the first public railway in precedence to the more usually accepted Surrey Iron Railway. It was opened to Lofthouse Gate in 1796, its E terminus being at Lake Lock (on the R Calder) by 1800 — by 1804 the line had been extended to a new one at Bottom Boat. It was used for carrying coal, lime and roadstone, but had mostly been abandoned by 1840. A ½-mile extension, known as Charlesworth's Railway, opened to E Ardsley in 1805 and closed in 1836.

LAMBTON WAGONWAY

This line, opened by 1770, linked pits at Fencehouses (S of Newcastle) with the R Wear near Penshaw, and trials with an 0-8-0 locomotive built by Phineas Crowther of Newcastle were being made along it as early as 21 December 1814. In 1822 the company bought the Newbottle Wagonway (opened in 1813), and extended it SW to join its own system. Part of this purchase fell into disuse, however, after an Agreement with the NER in 1864, which allowed coal trains to use that company's main line to reach Sunderland.

LEE MOOR TRAMWAY

On 24 July 1854 authority was granted to the S Devon & Tavistock Railway (qv – GWR) to build a broad gauge branch to china clay workings at Lee Moor, on the SW edge of Dartmoor. The SD&TR duly built it, but may have been relieved when, before opening, it passed to Lord Morley, on whose land much of it was laid. It was badly done, many improvements being needed before opening on 24 September 1858. The line included two gravity-worked inclines, at Torycombe and Cann. Loco-motives were introduced on the stretch between the inclines in 1899, and both survive, one at Saltram House and the other at the Wheal Martyn China Clay Museum near St Austell, with other relics of the line. It crossed the GWR near Laira, Plymouth, on the level, and this section was the last to remain open. The final train, horse-drawn, ran on 26 August 1960.

LIVERPOOL OVERHEAD RAILWAY

Incorporated on 24 July 1888 to assume powers granted by the Mersey Docks & Harbour Board (Overhead Railways) Acts, 1882 and 1887, it was the first electrically-worked, elevated line in the world, the first to use an escalator (at Seaforth Sands), the first to use automatic signalling and the first to use a colour-light system, in 1921. It opened between Herculaneum and Alexandra Dock on 6 March 1893, to Seaforth Sands on 30 September 1894 and to Dingle on 21 December 1896. A great success at first, traffic fell away over the years until, when renewals costing £2 million became necessary in the mid-1950s, the expense was felt not to be justified. The

In 1896, when this view of Liverpool Pierhead station was taken, a train standing at the platform, the Liverpool Overhead Railway was only three years old and had just embarked on a period of prosperity. 'Electric Railway' truthfully boasts the legend on the bridge, 'Trains Every Five Minutes'. (Liverpool Museum)

6.5-mile line closed on 31 December 1956, having remained independent all its life, escaping even Nationalization.

LONDON ELECTRIC RAILWAY

From 26 July 1910 this was the new name of the GN, Piccadilly & Brompton Railway (qv), which from 1 July had absorbed the Charing Cross, Euston & Hampstead and the Baker Street & Waterloo Railways (both qv). Powers of the Edgware & Hampstead Railway (qv) were vested by an Act of 7 August 1912, and the company was absorbed by the LPTB from 1 July 1933.

LONGMOOR MILITARY RAILWAY

Authorised by a LRO in 1902 as the Woolmer Instructional Military Railway, the line was built by the Royal Engineers during 1906–7, and opened as a training school for railway troops; it changed its name when it was extended to Liss in 1933. The passenger service was withdrawn on 16 September 1957, and the line closed completely on 31 October 1969. Its best-known locomotive, *Gordon* (named after the hero of Khartoum), is now on the Severn Valley Railway.

LUDLOW & CLEE HILL RAILWAY

This 6-mile quarry system, authorized on 27 July 1861, included a 1.25-mile rope-worked incline, and

The top quarter-mile of the Ludlow & Clee Hill Railway's incline to its stone quarries. Another steep mile lies behind the camera, and the levels at the summit were loco-worked.

was a prosperous private concern. It opened on 24 August 1864, and at its peak sent out about 6,000 tons of roadstone per week. Its owners made WA with the GWR and L&NWR jointly on 1 June 1867, and these two absorbed the line wef 1 January 1893, by an Act of 28 June 1892.

MACCLESFIELD, BOLLINGTON & MARPLE RAILWAY

Incorporated on 14 July 1864, this 10.5-mile line was opened between Marple and Bollington for passengers on 2 August 1869, to goods on 1 March 1870, and on to Macclesfield on 3 April 1871 (goods), 1 July 1873 (passengers). Soon after linking with the NSR at Macclesfield, the company was vested jointly in the MS&LR and NSR wef 25 May 1871, surviving as GCR/NSR to Grouping, when it became LNER/LMS.

MANCHESTER SHIP CANAL COMPANY (RAILWAYS)

Incorporated on 6 August 1885, both Canal and railways opened on 1 January 1894. The company owned several branch railways serving its docks; most were vested in other companies, including the L&NWR, the CLC, and the L&NWR/GWR jointly, but the system was worked independently until Nationalization.

MANCHESTER SOUTH DISTRICT RAILWAY

This line grew from an abortive Manchester & Cheadle idea, and was sanctioned on 5 August 1873 to serve the residential area of Alderley. It never got there, merely linking two CLC lines by one 6 miles 18 chains long. Powers were transferred to the Manchester & Stockport Railway (qv) in 1876, and the company was vested in a Sheffield & Midland Committee by an Act of 11 August 1876. Powers were given on 12 July 1877 for the GNR to have part control, but the company was transferred to the MR by an Act of 11 August 1877. The line opened on 1 January 1880, the section from Throstle's Nest Junction to Chorlton-cum-Hardy subsequently passing to the CLC wef 1 October 1891 (Act of 28 April 1887).

MANCHESTER SOUTH JUNCTION & ALTRINCHAM RAILWAY

This company was incorporated on 21 July 1845, most of its capital subscribed by the M&BR and the MS&LR, which bought off the opposing interests of Lord Egerton (Bridgewater Trustees) with £50,000-worth of shares. By an Act of 2 July 1847, the L&NWR re-purchased them, and Lord Egerton removed his directors from the Board, leaving the L&NWR and MS&LR in joint command. The line opened from Altrincham to Manchester, Oxford Lane, on 20 July 1849, and to London Road on 1 August. The company owned its own carriages, but MS&LR engines worked the line until 1899, after which the L&NWR shared working. The line was electrified in 1928, using an overhead 1,500-volt dc

system, at an estimated cost of £500,000; electric services began on 11 May 1931.

MANCHESTER & STOCKPORT RAILWAY

This was promoted by the MS&LR (which, under the Act of 16 July 1866, was permitted to subscribe and make WA) to improve the MR approach to Manchester, and it was perhaps because of this that the MR was admitted to the CLC on 18 July 1866. The line was not built, however, until an Act of 24 June 1869 authorized a joint MS&LR/MR take-over of powers, and gave RP over parts of the MS&LR to the MR. The line opened between Romiley and Stockport on 15 February 1875 (goods), 1 April (passengers), and on to Ashburys for goods on 17 May and passengers on 2 August.

MARLAND LIGHT RAILWAY

This private 3 ft gauge line along the Torridge valley ran S from Torrington (Bideford Extension Railway, qv – SR) to the N Devon Clay Company's workings at Peter's Marland. The line opened in 1880, and in 1922–25 the track-bed between Torrington and Dunsbear was used by Agreement in construction of the N Devon & Cornwall Junction LR (qv). A replica of one of the four-wheeled tramcars used on the line can be seen on the nearby Launceston Steam Railway.

MARPLE, NEW MILLS & HAYFIELD JUNCTION RAILWAY

Incorporated on 15 May 1860, it was an extension of the MS&LR branch to Hyde and Marple, to serve

The first coach in the short train is a replica, built at the Launceston Steam Railway, of one of the Marland Light Railway vehicles. The original builder was probably the Lancaster Wagon Company.

mill towns higher up the valley. The line opened from Marple to New Mills on 1 July 1865 for goods, and 1 February 1867 for passengers. The MR came to an Agreement with the MS&LR to extend its Miller's Dale line to connect at New Mills, and this was opened on 1 October 1866. The line to Hayfield was single and 3 miles long, but before opening on 1 March 1868 the company's entire 6 miles had been vested first in the MS&LR on 5 July 1865, and then jointly with the MR on 24 June 1869.

MERCHANTS RAILWAY

See Portland Railway.

MERSEY DOCKS & HARBOUR BOARD

The company operated a large system of lines around the docks of Birkenhead and Liverpool, and by the 1920s owned about 60 miles of railway. The L&NWR had access to the docks over its lines, and in 1907 the GCR gained access also. Rail working in the N Docks at Liverpool ceased on 11 September 1973.

MERSEY RAILWAY

Originally incorporated on 28 June 1866 as the Mersey Pneumatic Railway, this idea was abandoned for steam working on 31 July 1868, but work on the line, between Birkenhead and Liverpool, did not begin until 1879. It was ceremonially opened on 20 January 1886, and to the public on 1 February; an extension to Rock Ferry opened on 15 June 1891,

The seal of the Mersey Railway. (NRM)

with a branch to Birkenhead on 2 January 1888, where it joined the newly-formed Wirral Railway (qv — LMS). The line from St James to Liverpool Central opened on 11 January 1892. Steep gradients and foul air caused operating difficulties, and an Act of 2 July 1896, renewed on 30 July 1900, authorized use of electricity — when the service began on 3 May 1903, the line was the first steam-worked underground railway to have been so converted. Independent until Nationalization, it continues to develop, forming a vital part of Liverpool's traffic system.

METHLEY JOINT RAILWAY

A joint GNR, NER and L&YR Committee was set up on 23 June 1864 to work a line between the Bradford, Wakefield & Leeds Railway (qv — LNER) and the Methley branch of the L&YR, authorized by powers to the BW&LR on 21 July 1863. The GNR built most of it and was to become the main user — after taking over the WYR in 1865, a one-third share in the Methley line became GNR property, a very handy link between the WYR and its own system. The line opened for goods in June 1865; passed for passengers that year, it did not carry any until June 1869. There was trouble with flooding (at its E end the line crosses the floodplain of the R Calder) and, later, mining subsidence. The line became joint LNER/LMS property in 1923.

METROPOLITAN RAILWAY

The company reached its well-known title via the North Metropolitan Railway (qv). It was incorporated on 7 August 1854, but building was slow, and the GWR, a backer, became impatient — it would have preferred the company to use broad gauge, but agreed to mixed. The GWR worked the line from opening on 10 January 1863, but relations with the company cooled and the GWR gave notice to cease working after 30 September 1863. On 1 August it advanced this date to 10 August! The company hired stock from the GNR and opened a King's Cross connection. Steady expansion followed, the line eventually reaching Aylesbury via the Metropolitan

The Metropolitan Railway built a large headquarters at Baker Street, and made quite sure that the public was aware of it. Presumably the company was confident that at this remove from St Pancras, no one would mistake its initials for anyone else's . . . (Allan Mott)

& St Johns Wood, the Kingsbury & Harrow, the Harrow & Rickmansworth and the Aylesbury & Buckingham Railways (all qv) to join the GCR at Quainton Road. Electric workings began on 1 January 1905, and the LNER took over goods working in 1937. By then, though, the company had been part of the LPTB since 1 July 1933.

South Kensington station retains evidence of its past at both entrances—this is the one in Thurloe Street. However, re-development was taking place as this picture was taken, on 7 March 1988, and how long the ironwork will remain is a matter for conjecture.

METROPOLITAN DISTRICT RAILWAY

The company was a fusion of two schemes, the Metropolitan Grand Union and the M/DR; after incorporation on 29 July 1864, it was usually known as the 'District' to distinguish it from the MetR, which it joined, end-on, just E of S Kensington station. The line opened from S Kensington to Westminster Bridge on 24 December 1868, to W Brompton on 12 April 1869, Blackfriars on 30 May 1870, and Mansion House on 3 July 1871. In 1866 the MetR had agreed to work the line for 45 per cent of the gross takings, but the company gave a year's notice on 1 January 1871; the MetR ceased working on 3 July. The company passed to the LPTB wef 1 July 1933.

METROPOLITAN & ST JOHNS WOOD RAILWAY

Incorporated on 29 July 1864 as a single line from St Johns Wood to Swiss Cottage, it was mostly in tunnel. A MetR 'creature', it was worked by that company from opening (13 April 1868). A double-track extension from Swiss Cottage to the R Brent was sanctioned on 5 August 1873, and new lines were opened to W Hampstead (opened 30 June 1879) and Willesden Green (24 November 1879). The 1873 Act included powers to double the original line, but this was not done until 1882, in which year,

on 3 July, the company was absorbed by the MetR. A goods service began on 1 November 1909, and ceased on 1 July 1936.

METROPOLITAN INNER CIRCLE COMPLETION RAILWAY

Incorporated on 7 August 1874 to do what its title proclaimed, the company's independence was short-lived, for it was taken over jointly by the MetR and the M/DR under an Act of 11 August 1879. The line was completed on 6 October 1884.

MIDDLETON RAILWAY

A wagonway built by Charles Brandling existed by 1755 from Middleton (Leeds) down to the R Aire. When Brandling was granted his Act on 9 June 1758 it was the first railway so authorized. Its gauge was 4 ft 1 in and its track was double from Middleton to Casson Close, near Leeds Bridge. By 1808 the system was complete at about 4.25 miles, and from 1809 the timber rails had cast-iron plates fixed on top of them. Steam traction was inaugurated on 12 August 1812, with a rack engine built by Matthew Murray, called *Prince Regent*, the first locomotive to be used commercially on rails. In 1835, however, when renewals to the railway were necessary, the collieries had passed to Trustees, and horse-power was restored. The line was converted to standard gauge in 1881, and ran until 1958. When closure threatened, the Middleton RPS became the first for a standard gauge line, and ran its first train on 20 June 1960. The main section, from Hunslet Moor to Middleton Park, re-opened on 30 June 1969.

MILFORD HAVEN DOCKS & RAILWAY

Authorized on 23 July 1860 to build 1.75 miles of railway from the SWR Milford Haven branch to docks at Noyes Point, the line was leased to the contractor (Samuel Lake & Company) on 3 June 1881. It was opened on 19 January 1882, and was then sub-let to the Milford Haven Railway Estate. In 1921 it became privately controlled, as it still is.

MILLWALL EXTENSION RAILWAY

Though built under powers granted to the London & Blackwall Railway (qv — LNER) on 19 June 1865,

and actually owned by the Port of London Authority, the line was in fact shared by several dock companies and the GER. The first 5 chains from Millwall Junction were GER, then came 41 chains acquired from the London & E India Dock Company by the E & W India Dock Company. Either side of S Dock station were 52 chains owned by the Millwall Dock Company, and the final 31 chains to N Greenwich were GER. The line closed to passengers on 4 May 1926, and to goods between Millwall Junction and Millwall Docks in 1966. Part of its course has recently been revived to accommodate the Docklands LR.

NEWARK & LEICESTER RAILWAY

This was a scheme adopted by the GNR late in 1871

The Millwall Extension Railway has a new lease of life, much of its course having been taken over by the Docklands Light Railway. It was opened formally by the Queen on 30 July 1987, and to the public on 31 August. Here one of the two-coach sets enters Island Gardens on 8 September. (Allan Mott)

Before the Great War, 'hunting' specials were a feature of traffic, particularly on the Newark & Leicester Joint Railway. John o'Gaunt, here seen on 18 July 1953, was originally Barrow & Twyford—in 1883 its name was changed to that of a nearby fox covert. (Douglas Thompson)

on hearing that the Duke of Rutland agreed with it, but the House of Lords threw out all except the Newark–Melton Mowbray section, on the grounds that it would interfere with fox-hunting. What was left gained Royal Assent on 6 August 1872, and opened from Newark to Bottesford on 1 April 1878 (goods), 1 July (passengers), and to Melton on 30 June 1879 (goods), 1 September (passengers). Encouraged by the MS&LR, which no doubt had its reasons, the GNR suggested a line on to Market Harborough — Parliament agreed, the line to be jointly built by the GNR and L&NWR. At the Grouping it became joint LMS/LNER.

NEWBOTTLE WAGONWAY
See Lambton Wagonway.

NIDD VALLEY LIGHT RAILWAY
Authorized on 30 March 1901, this was an independent, 5.75-mile extension from the NER at Pateley Bridge to Lofthouse-in-Nidderdale. It opened on 11 September 1907, and from 1921 the company used an ex-GWR steam railcar for its passenger service — this was sold for scrap after the last passenger train ran on 31 December 1929, the line closing completely in 1936. Another 6.5 miles of railway beyond Lofthouse belonged to Bradford Corporation, and was built to convey personnel and materials to reservoir works at Scar House and Angram.

NORTH DEVON & CORNWALL JUNCTION LIGHT RAILWAY
Though incorporated on 28 August 1914, the Great War delayed work, and powers were re-granted on 22 April 1922. The course of the Marland LR (qv) was used for the first 5.5 miles, the line being built by Col Stephens with financial aid from the Government and from Town Councils along the route. The first sod was cut by Mr A. Neal of the MoT on 30 June 1922, and the 20.5-mile line opened from Torrington

to Halwill Junction on 27 July 1925; it carried considerable clay and livestock, but passenger traffic was always light. The line was worked by the SR from opening, but the company remained independent until Nationalization. Officially closed to passengers on 1 March 1965, the last train ran on 27 February, though a goods service survived until 1970.

NORTH METROPOLITAN RAILWAY
Authorized on 15 August 1853, this undertaking was instigated by a London solicitor, Charles Pearson, who had fingers in several good causes of the day. To stifle opposition, the company had to reduce its aims to a 3.5-mile line between Paddington and Farringdon; the GWR and the City Corporation then subscribed substantially, and the company was re-incorporated on 7 August 1854, dropping the 'North' from the title.

NORTH SUNDERLAND RAILWAY
Incorporated on 27 June 1892, this was a privately-built line of 4 miles 6 chains between Chathill and Seahouses. Opened on 1 August 1898 (goods), 14 December (passengers), it was managed by the LNER from Newcastle after 1939, without being part of its system or that of BR. The last train ran on 27 October 1951.

NORTH WALES NARROW GAUGE RAILWAY
This line was authorized on 6 August 1872 to carry slate, goods and passengers on a 1 ft 11.5 in gauge line between Dinas Junction, near Caernarfon, and Rhyd Ddu, on the S slopes of Snowdon. The Act also embraced other lines too, but this was the only one built; it opened in stages from May 1877, and throughout for both passengers and goods on 14 May 1881. A 4.5-mile extension to Beddgelert was authorized on 3 November 1900, and built, though not by this company. An Agreement with the Portmadoc, Beddgelert & S Snowdon Railway (qv)

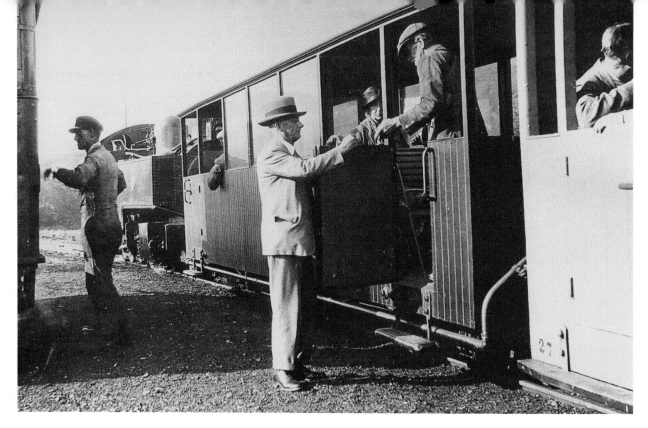

The North Wales Narrow Gauge Railway never reached Beddgelert, the scene of this picture, but both vehicles shown belonged to the company. The carriage was its observation saloon, nicknamed the 'Gladstone' car because it was once used by that gentleman, while 2-6-2T Russell is now enjoying a restored lease of life on the Welsh Highland Railway at Portmadoc. (Gwynedd Archives Service)

took effect from 26 August 1904, and powers to work the line as a LR were given by a LRO of 6 June 1905. Passenger traffic to Bryngwyn ceased on 31 December 1913, and to S Snowdon (Rhyd Ddu) on 31 October 1916. The company was bought by the Welsh Highland (Light Railway, qv) on 1 January 1922, as part of a new system.

OLDHAM, ASHTON-under-LYNE & GUIDE BRIDGE JUNCTION RAILWAY

The line was authorized on 10 August 1857 to link Mumps (Oldham, L&NWR) with Guide Bridge (L&YR). The formal opening was on 31 July 1861, the public opening on 26 August, and goods traffic began on 1 February 1863. It was worked jointly from the outset by the MS&LR and L&NWR, which absorbed the company on 30 June 1862.

OTLEY & ILKLEY JOINT RAILWAY

After several abortive schemes, it was agreed that the NER should build a line from Arthington to Otley, that Otley–Ilkley would be built jointly with the MR, and that the MR would make a connection with the Leeds & Bradford Railway (qv – LMS) at Apperley. Authorized on 11 July 1861, the line opened for passengers from Arthington to Otley on 1 February 1865, to Ilkley on 1 August, and for goods

throughout on 1 October 1866 — Wharfedale was transformed. At the Grouping the line became joint LNER/LMS.

OXFORD & AYLESBURY TRAMROAD

Incorporated on 7 August 1888 to build a line between Brill and Oxford, it never did so, but by an Agreement of 17 July 1888 it rented the Wotton Tramway (qv) and took over working; an Act of 24 July 1888 authorized steam power for this. The line was leased to the MetR wef 1 December 1899, and the Metropolitan & GC Joint Committee assumed responsibility from 2 April 1906. The LPTB closed the line completely wef 1 December 1935.

OYSTERMOUTH RAILWAY

This was incorporated on 29 June 1804 to build 6 miles of line between Swansea and Oystermouth. The original gauge was about 4 ft, and when the line opened for goods in April 1806, and to passengers on 25 March 1807, it was laid with plate rail. Passengers travelled in horse-drawn coaches similar to stage-coaches — the service lasted until 1827. Between 1855 and 1860 the line was relaid to standard gauge, using edge-rails, and passenger traffic resumed. The Swansea Improvements & Tramways Company worked the line between 1884 and 1 April 1886, and ran a steam service with a Hughes tram-engine for a short while in 1877. The company was reconstituted as the Swansea & Mumbles Railway (qv) by an Act of 26 July 1893.

PADARN RAILWAY

Built apparently without Parliamentary sanction, this was a 4 ft gauge line running for 6 miles 50 chains

Right *The Padarn Railway was not far from Beddgelert, serving the slate quarries at Dinorwic (Llanberis). This dual-language notice from the quarries, however, is a long way from home, in the Buckinghamshire Railway Museum.*

Below right George Henry, *a vertical-boilered locomotive built by de Wintons of Caernarfon in 1877 for the Penrhyn Railway, is now an exhibit in Tywyn's Narrow Gauge Railway Museum.*

from slate quarries at Dinorwic (Llanberis) to a harbour at Port Dinorwic. It opened on 3 March 1843, replacing a 2 ft gauge tramway built in 1824. Steam supplanted horses in November 1848, and an early locomotive, *Fire Queen*, can be seen at nearby Penrhyn Castle. Also surviving is a 'host' wagon, on which four narrow gauge slate wagons could travel. The line closed on 3 November 1961, but the trackbed beside Llyn Padarn is used by the Llanberis Lake Railway.

PARK PREWETT HOSPITAL RAILWAY

Built privately to link the Hospital site and the L&SWR, the line was almost complete by the end of 1913. The railway was opened shortly after, and was used to bring materials to the building site. The line remained private, worked by the L&SWR until 1923, then by the SR. It fell into disuse after the Second World War and closed on 21 May 1954.

PENRHYN RAILWAY

One of the first narrow gauge lines in Caernarfonshire, it was laid with oval rails, and linked slate quarries at Bethesda with the sea at Port Penrhyn. It was horse-worked at opening in July 1801, and used inclines, but by 1877 the route had been realigned to avoid these and to allow steam working. By 1951 Penrhyn Estates was owned by the National Trust — traffic had declined and closure followed on 24 July 1962. Two of the locomotives have found employment on the Festiniog Railway (qv), and a third, a vertical-boilered de Winton built in Caernarfon, is in the Narrow Gauge Railway Museum at Tywyn. Other relics of the line are on display at Penrhyn Castle.

PENSNETT RAILWAY

Also known as the Shut End Railway, this private line, opened in 1829, linked Lord Dudley's colliery at Shut End with the Ashwood basin of the Staffordshire & Worcestershire Canal, 3 miles away. During the 1850s it stretched rapid tentacles towards sources of coal, limestone, sand and iron ore.

PENTEWAN RAILWAY

This was a 2 ft 6 in gauge tramway connecting St Austell and quarries in the Pentewan valley with a harbour at the outfall of the St Austell river at Pentewan. It was only the third railway built in Cornwall, and the only true narrow gauge one. Laid with edge-rail, and engineered by Richard Carveth, it opened in June 1829, worked by gravity and horses. On 7 August 1874 the St Austell & Pentewan Railway, Harbour & Dock Company was formed to convert the tramway to a railway. Silting in the harbour entrance, and the development of Par and Fowey as china clay ports led to the death of the company — the last train ran on 29 January 1918, and stock and materials were requisitioned for the War Effort.

The bridge carrying the road to Merthyr Tydfil contrasts with the course of perhaps the best-known early tramway—the Pen-y-darren. Trevithick's locomotive (he described it as a 'tramwaggon') used this ledge—seen above the site of the Canal basin at Abercynon on 8 May 1988—in 1804 to prove that steam power could haul loads on rails.

PEN-Y-DARREN TRAMWAY

Built under powers given to the Glamorganshire Canal Company by an Act of 1796, this plateway ran 9.5 miles from Plymouth Colliery, Pen-y-darren, to a basin on the Glamorganshire Canal at Abercynon, with extensions to Dowlais and Morlais quarries. It was laid out by George Overton to a gauge of 4 ft 2 in on stone blocks, to a ruling gradient of 1 in 36. Opened in about 1802, it became notable as the line which carried the first steam locomotive hauling a load, when Richard Trevithick's engine made a successful trial on 21 February 1804. The line never became a true railway, but did not fall into disuse until 1880–90 — a stretch in Merthyr Tydfil remained in use until the 1920s.

PIKE'S TRAMWAY

See Furzebrook Tramway.

PLYNLIMON & HAFAN TRAMWAY

Also known as the Hafan & Talybont Tramway, this was first proposed in 1892 to link the Hafan lead and granite quarries with the sea. Since the CambR blocked the way, the company settled for 7 miles 26 chains to Llanvihangel (now Llandre) instead — there were no statutory powers. The first sod was cut at Talybont on 11 January 1896, and construction to a gauge of 2 ft 3 in began two days later. On 12 May 1897 the first locomotive arrived, and a passenger service began from Llanvihangel to Talybont (2.25 miles) on 28 March 1898 — it was 'curtailed' on 12 August, and never ran again. Beset by money problems, the concern went into voluntary liquidation on 19 December 1899. A replica of one of the carriages is planned for the Launceston Steam Railway.

POLDICE TRAMWAY

This, the earliest line in Cornwall, was built to connect mines with the harbour at Portreath, 3 miles N of Camborne. Work began on the 5-mile route in 1809, and the line was open by 1812, but the Poldice copper mine was exhausted by 1856. There was traffic from others, but the line appears to have become disused by 1865; even so, it was not dismantled until early this century.

PONTOP & JARROW WAGONWAY

This early wooden wagonway, opened about 1729, was converted in time for a re-opening to Kibblesworth in 1842. It formed extensions of the Springwell Wagonway, which linked Springwell colliery with the R Tyne at Jarrow. Another extension to Marley Hill, opened in 1854, joined the Tanfield Wagonway (qv). The line, later known as the Bowes Railway, worked until 1887, when the service was suspended because the electrical system had become dangerous and was condemned.

PORTLAND RAILWAY

This line, authorized in 1825 and opened in October 1826, was also known as the Merchants Railway, running from the W side of Portland and down an incline to Castletown Pier. Its traffic was stone, together with visitors to the prison during part of the nineteenth century. The line closed in 1939.

PORTMADOC, BEDDGELERT & SOUTH SNOWDON RAILWAY

Incorporated on 17 August 1901 to build a line from Porthmadoc to Caernarfon, part used earthworks of the N Wales Narrow Gauge Railway and the Croesor Tramway (both qv). Powers for the NWNGR's Beddgelert–S Snowdon section were taken over too, but only 4 miles 60 chains of line were built; though used for timber traffic before 1911, it never officially opened. Wef 1 January 1922, the company was acquired, with the NWNGR, by the newly-formed Welsh Highland Railway (qv).

PORTMADOC, CROESOR & BEDDGELERT TRAM RAILWAY

Promoted to absorb the Croesor & Portmadoc Railway (qv), the company was authorized on 21 May 1879 to build branches to Llanfrothen and Beddgelert — nothing came of either. The company went into Receivership in 1882; powers were sold to the Portmadoc, Beddgelert & S Snowdon Railway (qv) by an Act of 17 August 1901. The line was horse-worked, and can still be traced, particularly above Parc — this section was out of use by about 1936. The lower length was incorporated into the Welsh Highland Railway (qv).

POTTERIES, SHREWSBURY & NORTH WALES RAILWAY

This was formed on 16 July 1866 by the merging of two companies having difficulty getting their respective schemes off the ground — the Shrewsbury & Potteries Junction and the Shrewsbury & N Wales Railways. The S&NWR began at Llanymynech and ran roughly SE for 14.25 miles to an end-on junction with the S&PJR at Redhill, which covered the final 3.25 miles to Shrewsbury (Abbey). The line opened on 13 August 1866, its greatest engineering feature being a viaduct across the R Severn at Shrawardine, and there were goods branches to Criggion and from Llanymynech to Nantmawr quarries. Traffic ceased on 21 December 1866, but re-opened after a sale of stock in December 1868. An OR was appointed in 1877 and the company was wound up on 18 July 1881, though the Nantmawr branch remained in use, worked by the CambR. The works were taken over by the Shropshire & Montgomeryshire LR (qv) on its formation in 1909.

RADSTOCK TRAMWAY

Built along the disused Radstock arm of the Somerset Coal Canal to link collieries at Radstock with the canal basin at Midford, 7 miles away, it was laid with edge-rail on stone blocks to a gauge of 3 ft 5.5 in, single track with passing places. Opened by 20 July 1815, power was by horse at first; a steam engine was introduced in August 1827, but even at 2 tons 3 cwt was too heavy for the track! It was withdrawn and used for stationary haulage at Clandown. The line was sold to the S&DR by an Act of 21 August 1871 (Agreement of 1 February) for £15,000 cash and £5,000 paid-up shares, with a stipulation that sale must be within six months of the date of the Act. The new owner narrowed the lines around Radstock to 3 ft 2 in.

RAVENGLASS & ESKDALE RAILWAY

This 7-mile line was incorporated on 26 May 1873 in 2 ft 9 in gauge, but this was later changed to 3 ft, at which gauge it opened for goods on 25 May 1875, and to passengers on 20 November 1876. Its main purpose was to bring haematite from quarries at Boot to the coast at Ravenglass, but it was soon in financial trouble; an OR was appointed, and on 30 November 1908 it closed. In 1915, Bassett-Lowke's acquired it and converted the gauge to 15 in — it had moderate success as a feeder for a granite quarry, but in 1958 was again for sale. A Preservation Society, backed by Colin Gilbert, stepped in, bought the line at auction in 1960, and it is now a thriving tourist attraction. The pioneer of radio traffic control in the UK, the company has also built a steam locomotive of its own at Ravenglass, and plans two more.

REDLAKE TRAMWAY

Built to link china clay workings on the SW edge of Dartmoor with the GWR main line at Ivybridge, it opened on 11 September 1911. Its 7.5 miles were gauged at 3 ft, an incline taking the rails from 400 ft above sea level at Ivybridge to 1,400 ft. Locomotives worked the line above the incline until the clay company failed in 1932.

REDRUTH & CHASEWATER (sic) RAILWAY

Though not the first (incorporated on 17 June 1824, and opened on 30 January 1826), this was perhaps the most important mineral line in Cornwall, doing good business until the copper boom collapsed. The main line authorized was from Pool Quay, on the Deveron, to Redruth (9.33 miles), and there came to be 5 miles of branches. The first railway in Cornwall to use wrought-iron edge-rails and flanged wheels, it was single throughout, with many loops or 'turn-outs'. An amalgamation approach by the Hayle Railway (qv — GWR) in 1844 was not proceeded with, and an Act to permit steam haulage was obtained on 9 May 1853. After mines closed and

Ravenglass & Eskdale Railway locomotive Northern Rock, *built in the company's workshops in 1976, pauses at Irton Road with a down train.* (P. van Zeller)

business dwindled, an OR was appointed on 19 July 1879; working continued, and the last train ran on 25 September 1915. An Act of Abandonment was obtained on 19 April 1918, the effects were sold in May/July that year, and the company was wound up on 23 February 1920.

Redruth & Chasewater Railway locomotive Miner *with her crew and other staff at Devoran. The young man standing on the buffer is brakeman Stephen Gay, who was killed, aged 35, in an accident at Higher Carnon Bridge on 16 March 1899.* (Royal Institution of Cornwall)

ROMNEY, HYTHE & DYMCHURCH RAILWAY

This 15 in gauge line along the Kent coast from Hythe to Dungeness was founded in the early 1920s by two racing-drivers — Captain J.E.P. Howey and Count Zbrowski — who were also railway enthusiasts. Built by Henry Greenly, the line opened officially on 16 July 1927, though it was not open throughout until 1928–9. The line assisted in the War Effort, carrying equipment for the undersea pipeline between England and France, and is today a popular tourist line.

ROSSENDALE VALLEY TRAMWAYS

Incorporated on 24 July 1888, this steam tramway

ran between Rawtenstall and Bacup, in competition with the Bacup branch of the ELR. When it closed in 1909 it was the last steam-worked street tramway in the country.

ROTHERHAM, MALTBY & LAUGHTON RAILWAY

Authorized on 4 August 1905, this line ran to Silverwood colliery from junctions with both the GCR and MR by way of part of the private Roundwood & Dalton line. It continued to Braithwell and Laughton to join the Shireoaks, Laughton & Maltby Railway (qv) at Anston Junction, S of Dinnington. An Agreement of 20 July 1906 transferred powers to the GCR, the duplicated portion (Braithwell–Laughton) becoming joint GCR/H&BR. The MR came in as a partner on 9 August 1907, and the line opened for goods on 1 October 1909.

ROTHER VALLEY LIGHT RAILWAY

This 12-mile line between Robertsbridge and Rolvenden (then Tenterden) was the first to be authorized (2 July 1896) under the Light Railways Act of 1896. The official opening took place on 26 March 1900, and the line opened to the public on 2 April. Tenterden station was renamed Rolvenden when the present station opened on 16 March 1903, and extension to Headcorn was authorized that year. With an ambitious plan to extend to Maidstone, the company changed its name to the less limiting Kent & E Sussex Railway (qv) on 1 June 1904.

ROWRAH & KELTON FELL (MINERAL) RAILWAY

Authorized on 16 July 1874, the line was built by William Baird & Company to extract haematite in the Skiddaw area near Knockmurton, engines and rolling-

stock being provided by Baird's. The 3-mile line opened on 1 January 1877, and the company then persuaded the Cleator & Workington Junction Railway (qv – LMS) to build a 6.5-mile branch from Distington to an end-on junction at Rowrah, this link being authorized on 4 July 1878 and opened on 1 May 1882. The C&WJR worked its own line, and from 1889 its engines appeared on the mineral line too. The company was bought by the Salter Quarry Company; the line was disused by 1927, lifted in 1934.

RYE & CAMBER RAILWAY

Proposed in 1894, and built on private land, the line ran for 2 miles from a station just outside Rye to Camber Golf Links. It opened on 13 July 1895 and a ½-mile extension to Camber Sands was added on 13 July 1908. The line was still operated independently at the outbreak of the Second World War, when it was requisitioned by the Admiralty. Public services did not resume.

SALISBURY RAILWAY & MARKET HOUSE

Authorized on 14 July 1856 to build a short branch to serve Salisbury's Market House, from a junction with the Salisbury & Yeovil Railway (qv – SR), it opened in May 1859, and an increase in capital (1864) seems to indicate that it had the favourable effect on trade which had been intended. The line remained independent, though worked in due course by SR and BR. It closed on 1 July 1964, and few traces remain – the site of the Market House is now partly occupied by Salisbury's Public Library.

SAND HUTTON RAILWAY

This opened in 1910 as a private 15 in gauge railway

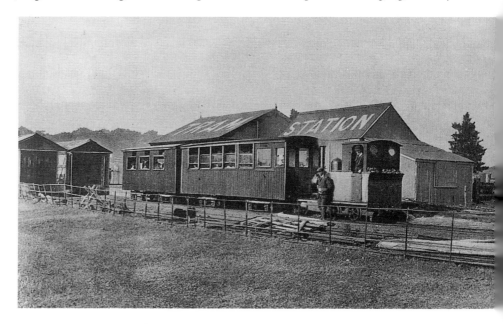

Rye & Camber 2-4-0T Camber with both coaches at Rye station in about 1922. This is a reproduction of a postcard posted on 7 August 1924. (Col Stephens Museum Collection/Kent & East Sussex Railway)

Above Synolda, *built for the Sand Hutton Railway in 1912, is now part of the Ravenglass & Eskdale Railway's Museum at Ravenglass. But she is no stuffed exhibit, as can be seen from this picture, taken during a visit to the oldest miniature railway in the world at Southport during 1983.* (P. van Zeller)

Below *The Severn & Wye Railway began life as a narrow gauge line, which is how this cast-iron milepost qualifies as an exhibit in the Narrow Gauge Railway Museum at Tywyn.*

in the grounds of Sand Hutton Hall, near York, but in May 1920 a LRO was obtained for extensions to farms on the Estate. When a quantity of 18 in gauge War Surplus equipment was bought soon after, the line was converted; 4.5 miles long, it carried passengers from 4 October 1924 until 7 July 1930, a goods service continuing until 1932.

SAUNDERSFOOT RAILWAY & HARBOUR

Incorporated on 1 June 1829 and opened in 1832, it linked collieries with a harbour at Saundersfoot, near Tenby. Officially the gauge was 4 ft, though in practice it was variable. The main line used a self-acting 1 in 5 incline to go inland to St Thomas Chapel and Reynalton, and there was a coastal line to Wisemans Bridge and then inland to Stepaside. Steam superseded horse-working in 1874, the track having been entirely relaid. Closure came in 1939, and the coastal section, tunnels and all, has been converted into part of the Pembrokeshire Coast Path. At the time of writing there is a proposal to use part of the track-bed for a miniature railway.

SEAHAM & SUNDERLAND RAILWAY

Demand for coal prompted the building of this private 9-mile line between Seaham and Sunderland. Work began on 8 February 1853, and the first coal from Hetton ran on 17 January 1854, though only to Ryhope, using the Durham & Sunderland Railway to Hendon Dock. The Londonderry Railway (both qv – LNER) continued the line to Hendon, opening it on 3 August 1854.

SEVERN & WYE RAILWAY & CANAL

Incorporated on 10 June 1809 as the Lydney & Lidbrook (sic) Railway, it was re-authorized as above

Ludlow station, looking south along the joint L&NWR/GWR Shrewsbury & Hereford Railway, on 7 May 1988. Bus-shelters and other station furniture are in the modern style, but the tunnel is original, and the worn footbridge steps look as if much history has passed over them.

on 12 June 1810. It was opened as a plateway in 1813; there were several branches but the line made little development other than by 1-in widenings of the 3 ft 6 in gauge in both 1840 and 1843. In 1847 the SWR agreed to control the line and in 1853 obtained powers to supply motive power and become carriers. The line was converted from a tramway to a broad gauge railway on 19 April 1869, and was re-converted to standard gauge in May 1872. The company was rescued from financial trouble by the MR and GWR under an Act of 17 August 1894 (wef 1 July). The passenger service (opened in 1875) ceased on 8 July 1929. The line from Lydney Town to Parkend has been acquired by the Forest of Dean RPS, which has established its headquarters at Norchard, N of Lydney.

SEVERN & WYE & SEVERN BRIDGE JOINT RAILWAY

This was formed by an Act of 21 July 1879, when the Severn & Wye Railway & Canal Co and the Severn Bridge Railway (both qv) merged. The companies were not fully united, however, until 1885, and in 1886 the Severn Tunnel was opened, causing a loss of business to the bridge. After struggling for some years, the company approached the MR to take over — it declined, but agreed with the GWR for a joint purchase, for £477,300, by an Act of 17 August 1894, wef 1 July.

SEVERN BRIDGE RAILWAY

Incorporated on 18 July 1872 to bridge the Severn estuary from Sharpness, the company was backed by the MR and the SWR. Building began in 1875, on a bridge 4,162 ft long, 70 ft above high water, and costing £200,000. When the company fell into

financial problems, the line was bought jointly by the MR and GWR for £477,300, and opened on 17 October 1879. On 25 October 1960, one of the supports was hit by drifting oil barges, and, after more damage in February 1961, no viable scheme could be found for the bridge's restoration. In 1965 the MoT gave permission for its demolition.

SHIREOAKS, LAUGHTON & MALTBY RAILWAY

Powers were granted to the GCR on 9 August 1901 for a 3.25-mile line from the MR at Brantcliffe, a mile from Shireoaks, to Dinnington and Laughton. A GCR Act of 31 July 1902 dissolved the company and placed its assets under the control of a joint GCR/ MR Committee, while the part N of Rotherham Lane, opened in 1905, passed to the S Yorkshire Joint Railway (qv). Opened for goods on 2 October 1905, and to passengers on 1 December 1910, the line closed to passengers in April 1926; it re-opened on 25 July 1927 but closed finally on 2 December 1929. Goods traffic ceased in April 1914.

SHREWSBURY & HEREFORD RAILWAY

Though authorized on 3 August 1846, work on this 51-mile line began only in 1850, when Thomas Brassey took the contract and offered to run the line on lease. It opened for goods on 30 July 1852 and to passengers on 6 December 1853, and in the summer of 1854 Brassey began his lease, paying 3.5 per cent of the cost. Six years later the company paid a dividend of 6 per cent on its income from Brassey! From 1 July 1862 (Act of 29 July), the line was leased jointly to the L&NWR, GWR and WMR, re-arranged as a joint L&NWR/GWR vesting under an Act dated 12 July 1870 – it became an LMS/GWR joint line at the Grouping.

SHREWSBURY & WELSHPOOL RAILWAY
This was incorporated on 29 July 1856, with a 9.25-mile branch from Hanwood (L&NWR) to Minsterley. The branch was the first part opened, on 14 February 1861, the main line, running from Hanwood to the Oswestry & Newtown Railway (qv – GWR) near Butting-ton, being opened on 27 January 1862. The line was L&NWR-worked, an Act of 14 July 1864 providing for transfer or lease of the company; the GWR and L&NWR took this up jointly under a further Act of 5 July 1865. The Minsterley branch closed to passengers on 5 February 1951 and to goods in 1965, but the line to Welshpool is still in use, albeit without intermediate stations.

SHROPSHIRE & MONTGOMERYSHIRE LIGHT RAILWAY
This was promoted by Col Stephens to take over the moribund Potteries, Shrewsbury & N Wales Railway (qv); reconditioning began from the Llanymynech end on confirmation of the LRO on 11 February 1909. It opened formally on 13 April 1911 (the Criggion branch on 22 February 1912) and for passengers in August 1912. After the Great War, traffic declined, and the Criggion branch closed beyond Melverley in September 1932, passenger services ceasing completely on 1 November 1933, though the line was still used for excursion and goods

traffic from Criggion. During the Second World War, the line (except the Criggion branch) was requisitioned by the War Department, and in 1947 passed into joint GWR/WD control before reverting to BR, which dismantled it.

SHUT END RAILWAY
See Pensnett Railway.

SILKSTONE RAILWAY
This plateway was built by the Barnsley Canal Company, and opened in 1809 from its terminal basin at Barnby Bridge, NW of the town, to Silkstone Colliery, two miles to the S. Laid to a gauge of 4 ft 2 in with double-flanged plates of a square 'U' section, its heavy stone sleeper-blocks were, unusually, laid diagonally in an attempt to give extra support to the plates. The line was abandoned about 1860, but many of the sleeper-blocks can still be seen.

SNAILBEACH DISTRICT RAILWAYS
Authorized on 5 August 1873 to get lead from quarries in the Stiperstones Hills SW of Shrewsbury, the line opened throughout in 1877. Other minerals were obtained too, and though loadings were good, the line never stretched beyond a 3.75-mile line from Pontesbury to Slipstone mines, with a branch to Snailbeach, laid to the unusual gauge of 2 ft 3.75 in. The line, closed in 1915, re-opened when Col Stephens took over in 1923; granite was now being carried from Callow Hill. In 1947, Shropshire County Council, the lessees of the Callow Hill quarry, bought the line, having worked it previously with a tractor. This method prevailed until 1959, when the line closed completely.

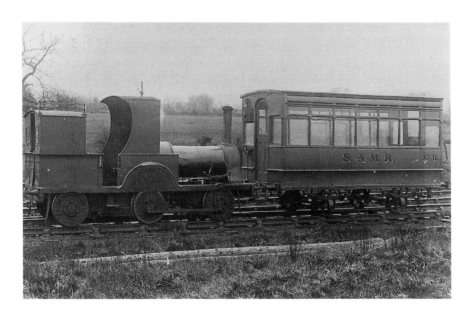

The Shropshire & Montgomeryshire Light Railway's No 1 Gazelle, *seen here with the converted LCC tram-car in about 1920. This set was used for the service on the Criggion branch.* (Col Stephens Museum Collection/Kent & East Sussex Railway)

SNOWDON MOUNTAIN RAILWAY

Laid to a gauge of 2 ft 7.5 in and worked on the Abt rack system, this is the only such line in the UK. It runs for 5 miles from Llanberis to a station near the summit of Wales's highest peak. Opened on 6 April 1896, an accident on opening day caused temporary closure, but the line re-opened the following April, and is still going strong.

SOMERSET & DORSET RAILWAY

Operation as a joint concern began wef 1 September 1862, by an Act of 7 August, being a combination of the Somerset Central and the Dorset Central Railways (both qv). The 16-mile link between Blandford and Templecombe opened officially on 31 August 1863, and to traffic on 14 September. A financial crisis in 1866 resulted in the appointment of an OR, but on his discharge in 1870 plans were made to extend 26 miles from Evercreech to Bath. Authorized on 21 August 1871, work began the next year, and the line opened on 20 July 1874. Profits, however, were not as expected, and more financial trouble resulted in bankruptcy. The GWR, when approached, suggested that the L&SWR might take the line S of Templecombe. The L&SWR told the MR, which arranged an Agreement for a joint MR/L&SWR lease of the line for 999 years wef 1 November 1875, an Act of 13 July 1876 creating the Somerset & Dorset Joint Railway. This company was vested in the SR/LMS wef 1 July 1923, but remained outside the Grouping arrangements.

SOMERSET CENTRAL RAILWAY

Though nominally an independent company, incorporated on 17 June 1852 to build from Highbridge to Glastonbury, it was fostered by the B&ER, and laid to broad gauge along the line of the Glastonbury Canal. It opened on 28 August 1854, with extensions to Burnham Pier (3 May 1858) and Wells (15 March 1859), worked by the B&ER until 1861 for a

Sheep graze unconcernedly as a Snowdon Mountain Railway train heads upwards on 26 September 1987. The train is powered by one of the newly-acquired diesel locomotives. (Diana Awdry)

guaranteed 4 per cent. A plan to exploit coastal traffic from the pier at Burnham was not a success, and a scheme to amalgamate with the WS&WR also collapsed. Leave was sought for conversion to standard gauge so that a junction could be made with the Dorset Central Railway (qv) at Glastonbury. Amalgamation as the S&DR followed wef 1 September 1862.

The seal of the Somerset & Dorset Railway, a splendid combination of the counties' devices: Dorset on the right and Somerset, including Glastonbury Tor, on the left. (NRM)

SOUTHPORT & CHESHIRE LINES EXTENSION RAILWAY

Promoted by the CLC, the 14 miles of line were authorized on 11 August 1881 to link Aintree and Birkdale Palace. An Act of 13 August 1882 sanctioned another mile into Southport, the line opening throughout on 1 September 1884, worked by the CLC, though an Act of 12 August 1889 ratified WA with other companies. The line closed from 1 January 1917 to 1 April 1919; passenger services ceased again on 1 July 1951 and all traffic was withdrawn on 7 July. The company remained independent until 1948.

SOUTH SHIELDS, MARSDEN & WHITBURN COLLIERY RAILWAY

This private line was owned by the Harton Coal Company and built primarily to serve Whitburn colliery, but because it was conveniently placed near Marsden Bay, it did a good trade with passengers and excursionists too. It ran from Westoe Lane, S Shields, where there was an interchange with the NER, for about 3 miles to Whitburn Colliery. In 1920 a LRO enabled a diversion to be brought into use, and the line's title became the S Shields LR. Its elderly stock came from various corners of England, and because the line was colliery-owned it was Nationalized into the NCB in 1947. The passenger service lasted until 20 November 1953, the line S along the coast to Whitburn closing completely in 1968.

SOUTH YORKSHIRE JOINT RAILWAY

This single line, authorized on 14 August 1903, was used by the GCR, GNR L&YR, MR and NER, and connected the Don valley line with the GNR. It opened for minerals on 1 January 1909 and to passengers on 1 December 1910; the passenger

A bridge-plate from the South Yorkshire Joint Railway, one of the collection at Winchcombe Railway Museum.

service was run by the GCR and GNR at first, but the GNR withdrew on 2 October 1911, and the GCR carried on alone. The passenger service ceased in April 1926, but re-opened on 25 July 1927, closing finally on 8 July 1929 between Potteric Carr Junction and Maltby, the Maltby–Dinnington section surviving until 2 December 1929. Additions were authorized from Tickhill to Harworth colliery and to Firbeck colliery on 31 July 1914, opening on 15 October 1929 and 1 October 1927 respectively (see Firbeck LR, LNER). At the Grouping the line became joint LMS/LNER.

STOCKPORT, TIMPERLEY & ALTRINCHAM JUNCTION RAILWAY

This line was sanctioned on 22 July 1861, being an 8 miles 8 chains extension from the Stockport & Woodley Junction Railway at Portwood to the Manchester S Junction & Altrincham Railway (both qv) at Deansgate (Altrincham). The GNR and MS&LR subscribed equally, though it was primarily a locally-supported line — it opened on 1 December 1865, and a Skelton–Broadheath (L&NWR) connection was opened on 1 February 1866. By then, however, the company had amalgamated with the S&WJR, the Cheshire Midland, the W Cheshire and the Garston & Liverpool Railways (all qv) to form the CLC on 15 August 1867.

STOCKPORT & WOODLEY JUNCTION RAILWAY

This line was promoted by landowners and backed by the MS&LR, which, with the GNR, was permitted to subscribe. Incorporated on 15 May 1860, this 2.75-mile line opened on 12 January 1863 between the places named, and, by amalgamating with the Cheshire Midland, the W Cheshire, the Stockport, Timperley & Altrincham, and the Garston & Liverpool Railways (all qv), the company became part of the CLC on 15 August 1867.

STOCKSBRIDGE RAILWAY

This private railway, authorised on 30 June 1874, ran from Deepcar (MS&LR), NW of Sheffield, for 1 mile 7 furlongs to serve Samuel Fox's ironworks at Stocksbridge. Fox sought help from the MS&LR, but it was not interested and Fox built the line himself. It opened on 14 April 1877, and Sheffield Corporation completed a 3-mile extension in September 1898 to assist in the construction of Langsett Reservoir. The work was finished in 1904, but the track remained until 1912. A passenger service ran until 1931 along the rest, passengers being carried free but at their own risk.

STORETON TRAMWAY

Probably the first railway in the Wirral, it was built in 1837 and opened on 14 August 1838, to connect

Rail-plates and sleeper-blocks from the Surrey Iron Railway have been preserved, and are on display in Rotary Field, Purley. The spikes would have been retained in an oak plug rather than cement, as here. (Allan Mott)

sandstone quarries, worked since AD 44, with a tidal creek at Bromborough. It was standard gauge and single throughout, using second-hand rail lifted from the L&MR in 1835. When William Lever arrived to cut the first sod of his new Port Sunlight soap factory on 3 March 1888, he was not impressed. For many years he contested the line's right of way, but not until 1905 did the quarry company give him best and return to road transport. Various relics of the line still exist *in situ*.

SURREY IRON RAILWAY

Incorporated on 21 May 1801, this is generally regarded as the world's first public railway; it grew from a wish to link Portsmouth with London, through a system part-rail and part-canal. It was engineered by William Jessop, using 4 in plates laid on stone blocks to a gauge of about 4 ft 2 in. The line was double, about 9.5 miles long, with a branch of 1.25 miles to Hackbridge. Never financially successful, traffic ceased on 31 August 1846 and the track was lifted in 1848 — the Wimbledon & Croydon Railway (qv — SR) was later built on part of its course.

SWANSEA & MUMBLES RAILWAY

This was the title taken on 26 July 1893 by the Oystermouth Railway (qv); an extension to Mumbles Pier was opened on 10 May 1898. The company was leased to Swansea Improvements & Tramways Ltd by an Act of 9 August 1899; it was by then under the control of the British Electric Traction Company, which had electrified the street tramways in Swansea. Electrification was tried in 1902, but abandoned — it eventually came about (overhead) in 1929. A section of line E of Rutland Street, leased to the Swansea Harbour Trust in 1897, passed to the GWR in 1923. The rest closed completely on 5 January 1960.

SWINTON & KNOTTINGLEY JOINT RAILWAY

Authorized on 16 July 1874, this ran from Swinton to a point near Knottingley (it did not actually enter the town), and was used by far more than its joint proprietors, the MR and NER. The line opened on 19 May 1879 (goods), 1 July (passengers), both the GNR and MS&LR having RP. The latter made most use of them, and the L&YR used the line for access to collieries. The company became joint LNER/LMS at Grouping.

TALYLLYN RAILWAY

Incorporated on 5 July 1865 to build a line from slate

Above *Centenary year for the Talyllyn Railway was 1965; locomotive No 1 Talyllyn also celebrated her hundredth birthday, and is seen during May of that year at Wharf station, Tywyn, with the four original carriages. Centenary or not, work went on: standard gauge sleepers in the foreground were being halved to provide narrow gauge replacements up the line.*

Below *Car No 8 of Volks Electric Railway at Marina station, Brighton, on a windy day in August 1988. Some cars have been repainted in the original livery.* (Allan Mott)

quarries at Bryn Eglwys, in the parish of Talyllyn, Mid-Wales, to the coast at Tywyn, it opened to regular passenger traffic on 1 October 1866. In 1911 the line and quarries were sold to Sir Henry Haydn Jones who undertook to keep the line running during his lifetime. When he died in 1950 the line was run down, but was taken over by the Talyllyn RPS, the first Society of its kind. The line, just over 7 miles long, has been run as a preserved tourist railway since 1951, and original locomotives and rolling-stock, supplied for the opening, are in regular use.

TENBURY RAILWAY

Incorporated on 21 July 1859, this was a 5.25-mile line from Woofferton (S&HR) to Tenbury Wells, where it joined the Tenbury & Bewdley Railway (qv – GWR) end-on. The S&HR provided land (an old canal, surplus to requirements) and worked the line for its first years. It opened on 1 August 1861, and was vested jointly in the GWR and L&NWR wef 1 January 1869 by an Act of 1 July 1871, having been jointly leased by those companies since 30 July 1866.

TOTTENHAM & HAMPSTEAD JUNCTION RAILWAY

This short line of 5.75 miles was authorized on 29 July 1862 – WA had been made with the GER on 3 June 1862, and though the GNR expressed interest, this waned when the GER and MR were authorized to contribute. The line opened from Highgate Road to Fenchurch Street on 21 July 1868, and the company was vested jointly in the GER and MR by an Act of 31 July 1902, wef 1 July.

VALE OF TOWY RAILWAY

Incorporated on 10 July 1854 to build a single line of mixed gauge from Llanelly to Llandovery, 11.25 miles away, it opened 1 April 1858, meeting the

This timber building, a store and office in a scrapyard when this picture was taken in 1977, served as stables for the Wantage Tramway in its horse-drawn days. Entrance to the hayloft can be seen in the gable, and the doors at the right-hand end of the building still opened in two halves.

Central Wales Extension Railway end-on at Carmarthen. From 1 April 1868 it was leased jointly by the CWER, the Knighton, the Central Wales and the Llanelly Railways (all qv). The company was vested in the GWR and L&NWR jointly by an Act of 28 July 1884.

VOLKS ELECTRIC RAILWAY

This, the first electric railway in the UK, was built to a gauge of 2 ft, opened on 3 August 1883, and extended to Parton Place on 4 April 1884. It was rebuilt soon after to what is described as 'nominally 2 ft 9 in'; two-rail electric at first, an off-centre three-rail system was adopted within a few years. It runs for about 1.25 miles from the Aquarium, Brighton, to Black Rock. Ownership passed to Brighton Corporation wef 1 April 1940. (See also Brighton, Rottingdean & Seashore Electric Tramway.)

WANTAGE TRAMWAY

Authorized in 1873, opened for goods on 1 October 1875 and to passengers on 10 October, this was a 2.5-mile roadside tramway from the town to Wantage Road station (GWR). Traffic was horse-drawn at first, but an Act passed on 27 June 1876 confirmed a provisional Order of 1870 which authorized '. . . the use of steam or other than animal power', steam working beginning soon after. Passenger services ceased on 1 August 1925, but goods traffic continued until 19 December 1945. The Sandy & Potton Railway (qv – LMS) locomotive *Shannon* worked on the line from 1878 until closure, and after preservation on Wantage Road station, is now at the Great Western Society centre, Didcot.

WELSH HIGHLAND RAILWAY

This was authorized by a LRO of 30 March 1922, having acquired the N Wales Narrow Gauge and the Portmadoc, Beddgelert & S Snowdon Railways (both qv) wef 1 January 1922. Despite scenic grandeurs, the scheme was not a success — the line opened between Porthmadoc (New) and Beddgelert on 1 June 1923, extending to Porthmadoc Harbour on 8 June, but traffic ceased on 31 December 1931. The Festiniog Railway leased the line from 9 July 1934, closing it to passengers on 26 September 1936. The official closure date for goods is given as 31 May 1937, though the final train actually ran on 1 June. The company was wound up on 7 February 1944. There is a scheme to rebuild part of the line, which has progressed a short distance N from Porthmadoc.

WEST CHESHIRE RAILWAY

Incorporated on 11 July 1861, this was 14 miles 48 chains of line running W from the Cheshire Midland Railway at Northwich to join the Birkenhead Railway (both qv) at Helsby. On 15 August 1867 the company became a constituent of the CLC, and its line opened for goods on 1 September 1869, and to passengers on 22 June 1870. The passenger service lasted only until 1 May 1875, though a 'summer only' Birkenhead to Northwich service ran between 1934 and 1938. The line was also used by workmen's trains until 1944.

WEST LONDON RAILWAY

Incorporated as the Birmingham, Bristol & Thames Junction Railway (qv), the company was re-incorporated on 23 July 1840 and, on 27 May 1844, 2.5 miles of single mixed-gauge line opened from W London Junction (Willesden, L&BR) to the Kensington Canal at Kensington Basin, via the GWR at Wormwood Scrubs. The passenger service lasted only until 30 November, however, and the line was little used until the advent of the W London Extension Railway (qv). The boost which this gave to traffic encouraged the L&NWR and GWR to lease the line jointly under an Act dated 31 July 1854, and the track was doubled. Kensington, as Addison Road, became a goods interchange, and as Kensington (Olympia) now has a very different role from that envisaged in 1836! The company retained independence until 1948.

WEST LONDON EXTENSION RAILWAY

This was authorized on 13 August 1859 for 4 miles 6 chains of mixed-gauge double line linking Kensington (W London Railway, qv) with Clapham Junction. It opened on 2 March 1863, jointly owned by the L&NWR and GWR (one-third each), and the L&SWR and LB&SCR (one-sixth each). The fillip to traffic which this line gave encouraged the GWR and L&NWR to lease, jointly, the W London Railway. The broad gauge rail was removed in 1890, the broad gauge service to Victoria having ceased by the autumn of 1866, and to Chelsea Basin by 1875. The passenger service from Ludgate Junction to Richmond via Kensington closed on 21 October 1940, but the line is still used for goods.

WESTON-SUPER-MARE, CLEVEDON & PORTISHEAD RAILWAY

Authorized on 6 August 1885, this line opened on 1 December 1897 between Weston and Clevedon as a 'proper' railway, with a WA with the GWR and authority to carry mails, but an Act of 9 August 1899 decreed it could become a LR. Another company took over the original line in 1904, and the railway was extended to Portishead on 7 August 1907 to give a total length of 14 miles. Then both holding companies went into voluntary liquidation, and the line was taken over by Col Stephens. The final train ran on 19 May 1940 — the sole creditor sold the line to the GWR, which dismantled it.

WEST SOMERSET MINERAL RAILWAY

This was authorized on 16 July 1855 to link workings on Brendon Hill with the harbour at Watchet. Construction began in 1856, and next year ore workings began — a 1,100 yd incline at 1 in 4 joined the line to the workings on the Hill. The incline was opened officially on 28 September 1859; it was self-acting at first, but a stationary engine was installed in 1883. A passenger service to Comberow, at the foot of the incline, began on 4 September 1865. The line was leased to the Ebbw Vale Company of S Wales for 55.25 years at £5,595 pa from 24 September 1865, and its successor, the Ebbw Vale Steel, Iron & Coal Company, took over for 51.5 years wef 25 March 1868 (Act of 24 June 1869), committing itself to keep the line in good order until 1919. Foreign ore became cheaper and the mines closed in 1883, but the rental was still paid and the passenger service continued until 7 November 1898. The mines re-opened in 1907, the line on 4 July, but it was finally abandoned in 1910, the rails being commandeered in 1917.

WEST YORKSHIRE RAILWAY

This was the title taken on 21 July 1863 by the Bradford, Wakefield & Leeds Railway (qv — LNER). An Act of 23 June 1864 permitted the NER and L&YR to subscribe £25,000 each, equalizing the sum already put in by the GNR. Lofthouse N Junction–Methley (5.25 miles) became part of the Methley joint line (see Methley Joint Railway) and was opened in June 1865 (goods), 1 May 1869 (passengers). The company was absorbed by the GNR under an Act of 5 July 1865 — it had taken over working wef 1 January — but at the Grouping was shared by the LNER and LMS.

WEYMOUTH & PORTLAND RAILWAY

Incorporated on 30 June 1862, it was a mixed gauge

Weston, Clevedon & Portishead Railway No 5 (previously named Hecate) at Weston in July 1933. No 5, an 0-6-OST, was built by Manning Wardle in 1919, working exclusively on the WC&P until the sale in 1940. (Rev W. Awdry)

line extending the WS&WR to Portland. It opened to the public on 16 October 1865 (officially on 9 October), and was leased jointly, in perpetuity, by the GWR and L&SWR – the latter worked it. The broad gauge rail was removed in 1874. An extension to Easton (4 miles) opened on 1 October 1900 (goods), 1 August 1902 (passengers), and was worked by the owning companies for alternate periods, the GWR being responsible for maintenance.

WHITECHAPEL & BOW RAILWAY
Authorized on 6 August 1897 to extend the M/DR from Whitechapel to join the LT&SR at Campbell Road Junction, the line opened on 2 June 1902, worked by the M/DR which, with the LT&SR, owned it jointly. It served as a useful relief line for the LT&SR, since Fenchurch Street was becoming congested, the company passing into MR control wef 1 January 1912. It retained its independence, however, until Nationalization.

WHITTINGHAM RAILWAY
This was a private railway, opened in June 1888, built to serve a mental hospital at Grimsargh, near Preston, to and from which staff, stores and visitors were carried. Owned by Lancashire County Council, the line closed on 30 June 1957.

WIDNES RAILWAY
A BoT certificate of 1873 was ratified by an Act of 7 July, and though this stipulated that the MS&LR could subscribe, the line was a local project. It joined the CLC at Hough, but because the GNR had refused to allow the company into the CLC, it became jointly owned by the MS&LR and MR from 29 June 1875. The line opened from Widnes E Junction to Widnes on 3 April 1877 (goods), to Hough on 1 July 1879, and throughout to passengers on 1 August, passing to joint LMS/LNER ownership after 1923.

WISSINGTON TRAMWAY
Opened about 1905, this line was built by A.J. Keeble and ran S from Abbey & W Dereham (see Downham & Stoke Ferry Railway, LNER) for land reclamation and to develop his estate. When Wissington sugar-beet factory opened in 1924, it served that also. In 1941 the estate was taken over by the Ministry of Agriculture; the sugar company leased

the line, and maintained the service on a system of 18 miles, including sidings. Most of it closed in 1957, but for a while the British Sugar Corporation worked about 2 miles serving its factory.

WORSBOROUGH RAILWAY
A plateway opened in about 1820 to a gauge of 4 ft 3 in, running SW from Worsborough Basin, on the Dearne & Dove Canal, for 3.25 miles to pits at Ratten Row, E of Thurgoland. Another branch, 1.5 miles long, came into use around 1832 from a junction at Rockley Abbey to Pilley. In about 1851 the line came into the possession of the S Yorkshire Railway (qv – LNER); it was abandoned shortly after the Great War.

WOTTON TRAMWAY
This private railway on the estate of the Duke of Buckingham and Chandos opened for goods on 1 April 1871; horse-drawn, the traffic was mainly agricultural, but in January 1872 passengers began to be carried, and the line was extended 2 miles to Brill. Under an Agreement of 17 July 1888, it was rented by the Oxford & Aylesbury Tramway (qv), passing to the Metropolitan/GCR Joint Committee wef 2 April 1906.

WREXHAM & MINERA JOINT RAILWAY
This was incorporated on 11 June 1866 when part of the Wrexham & Minera Railway (qv – GWR) was leased jointly to the GWR and L&NWR. Opened for goods on 27 January 1872, it consisted of that part of Railway No 1, authorized by 28/29 Victoria c260, which ran from a junction with the Minera branch of the GWR at Broughton to the '. . . branch railway of the Mold branch of the Chester & Holyhead Railway in the parish of Treidden'. The passenger service, when it began on 2 May 1898, was worked by the L&NWR from Mold. It ceased on 27 March 1950.

WRINGTON VALE LIGHT RAILWAY
Authorized by a LRO of 18 March 1897, this line was locally promoted and ran from Congresbury (on the GWR Cheddar–Wells branch) to Blagdon – 6.5 miles; it was supported by Bristol Corporation, then building the reservoir at Yeo. The line opened on 4 December 1901, the GWR agreeing to work it, and a passenger service continued until 14 September 1931.

APPENDIX

'Family tree' charts of constituent companies

NOTES FOR USING THE CHARTS

It has been the intention in preparing these 'genealogical' charts to try to show as simply as possible how each of the major railway companies built and expanded itself during its lifetime, before finally succumbing to the Grouping in 1923. Vertical columns divide each chart into periods of years. Within each period are shown the companies authorized during that period, with the year of incorporation (or, in some cases, of opening). By following the line leading from each company's name, its progress can be traced through other groupings or changes of name to amalgamation with a major company, the year of amalgamation being shown where the course of the companies' lines intersect. A broken line between two companies indicates joint ownership by the companies thus linked, unless otherwise stated. It should also be mentioned that many of the major companies often leased a line, sometimes for a very lengthy period, before actually absorbing it; since this detail would congest the chart unreasonably, this information should be found in the main text of the book, in the section dealing with the company concerned. In the extreme right-hand column of Charts 2, 9, 15 and 16 are lists of companies which remained independent until the Grouping or after, with a note indicating which of the 'Big Four' each then joined.

1 GWR: North of the Thames

To 1845	1846–1855	1856–1860	1861–1870

Wye Valley Railway *1866* —

Nantwich & Market Drayton Railway *1861*

Kington Tramway *1818* —

Kington & Eardisley Rly *186*

E. Gloucestershire Railway *1*

Witney Railway *1859* —
Faringdon Railway *1860* —

Watlington & Princes Risborough Railway *1869*
Wallingford & Watlington Railway *1864*

Severn Valley Railway *1853* —

Stourbridge Railway *1860* —
Tenbury & Bewdley Rly *1860* —

Wellington & Drayton Railway *1862*

Wycombe Railway *1846* —
N. Wales Mineral Railway *1844*
Hereford, Ross & Gloucester Railway *1851*

Shrewsbury, Oswestry & Chester Junc. Railway *1845*
Shrewsbury & Chester Railway *1846*

Oxford Railway *1843* —
Shrewsbury & Birmingham Railway *1846*

Cheltenham & G. Western Union Railway *1836*
GW & Uxbridge Rly *1846*

GREAT WESTERN RAILWAY *1835* 44
46 | 48
47   54
62   63   67 68 69

Oxford & Rugby Railway *1845*

Birmingham & Oxford Junction Railway *1846*
B'ham, W'hampton & Dudley Railway *1846*

Llanvihangel Railway *1811* —
Chipping Norton Rly *1854* —
Grosmont Railway *1812* —
Newport, Abergavenny & Hereford Railway *1846*

Hereford Railway *1826* —
Worcester & Hereford Rly *1853*

Stratford & Moreton Railway *1821*

Oxford, Worcester & Wolverhampton Railway *1845*
West Midland Railway *1860* —

47
52

South Wales Railway *1845* —
Forest of Dean Railway *1826*
Bristol & South Wales Union Railway *1857*

Bullo Pill Railway *1809*

Wrexham & Minera Railway

Gloucester & Dean Forest Railway *1846*

Bourton-on-the-Water Rly *1860* —
Stratford-upon-Avon Rly *1857* —

Worcester, Bromyard & Leominster Railway *1861*

Wellington & Severn Junction Railway *1853*

Wenlock Railway *1861* —

Much Wenlock & Severn Junction Railway *1859*

Leominster & Kington Railway *1854*
Abingdon Railway *1855* —

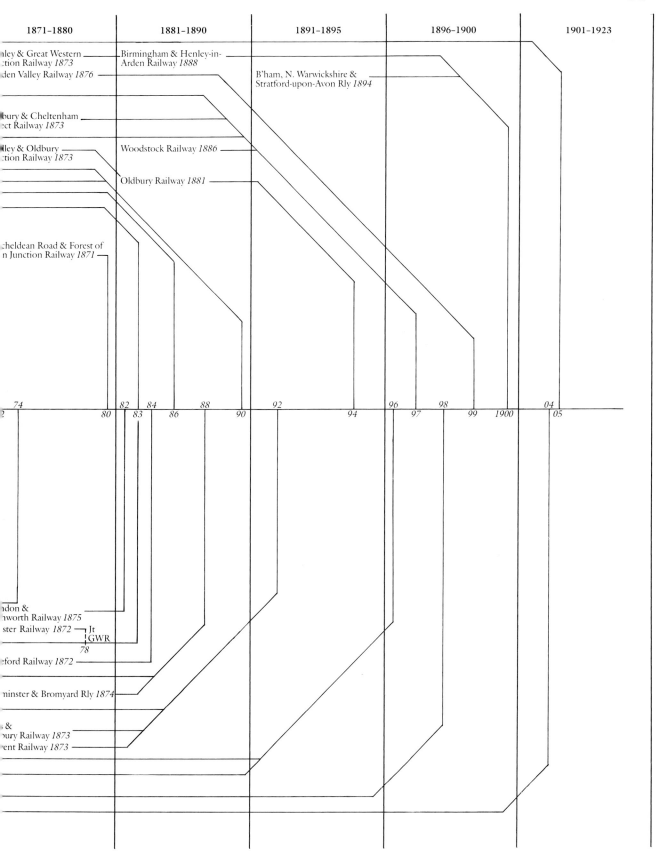

| 1871–1880 | 1881–1890 | 1891–1895 | 1896–1900 | 1901–1923 |

nley & Great Western
ction Railway 1873

Birmingham & Henley-in-
Arden Railway 1888

den Valley Railway 1876

B'ham, N. Warwickshire &
Stratford-upon-Avon Rly 1894

bury & Cheltenham
ect Railway 1873

lley & Oldbury
ction Railway 1873

Woodstock Railway 1886

Oldbury Railway 1881

cheldean Road & Forest of
n Junction Railway 1871

74   80 82 84   88   92   94   96   98   04
2   83 86   90   97 99 1900 05
          78

ndon &
nworth Railway 1875
ster Railway 1872   Jt
                     GWR

eford Railway 1872

minster & Bromyard Rly 1874

s &
bury Railway 1873
rent Railway 1873

2 GWR: South and West England

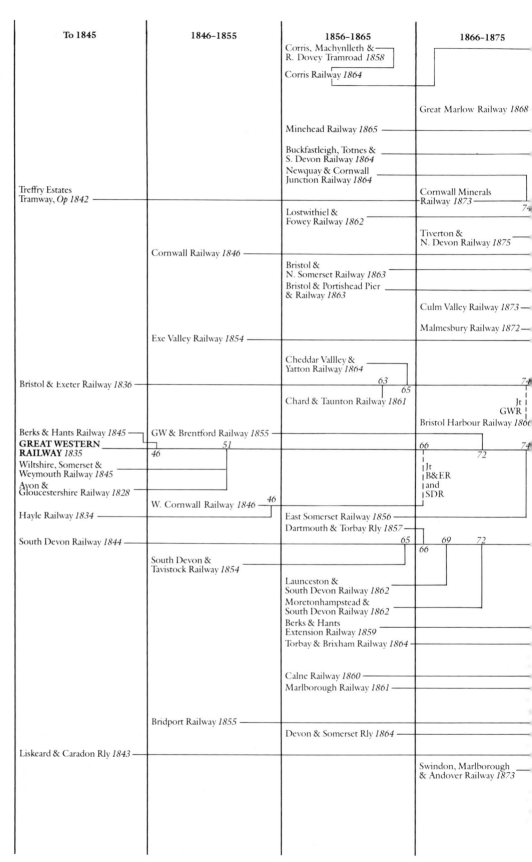

To 1845	1846–1855	1856–1865	1866–1875
		Corris, Machynlleth & R. Dovey Tramroad 1858	
		Corris Railway 1864	
			Great Marlow Railway 1868
		Minehead Railway 1865	
		Buckfastleigh, Totnes & S. Devon Railway 1864	
		Newquay & Cornwall Junction Railway 1864	
Treffry Estates Tramway, Op 1842			Cornwall Minerals Railway 1873 74
		Lostwithiel & Fowey Railway 1862	
			Tiverton & N. Devon Railway 1875
	Cornwall Railway 1846		
		Bristol & N. Somerset Railway 1863	
		Bristol & Portishead Pier & Railway 1863	
			Culm Valley Railway 1873
			Malmesbury Railway 1872
	Exe Valley Railway 1854		
		Cheddar Vallley & Yatton Railway 1864	
Bristol & Exeter Railway 1836		63 65	74
		Chard & Taunton Railway 1861	Jt GWR
			Bristol Harbour Railway 1866
Berks & Hants Railway 1845	GW & Brentford Railway 1855		
GREAT WESTERN RAILWAY 1835	51		66 72 74
	46		
Wiltshire, Somerset & Weymouth Railway 1845			Jt B&ER and SDR
Avon & Gloucestershire Railway 1828			
	W. Cornwall Railway 1846 46		
Hayle Railway 1834		East Somerset Railway 1856	
		Dartmouth & Torbay Rly 1857	
South Devon Railway 1844		65	69 72
	South Devon & Tavistock Railway 1854	66	
		Launceston & South Devon Railway 1862	
		Moretonhampstead & South Devon Railway 1862	
		Berks & Hants Extension Railway 1859	
		Torbay & Brixham Railway 1864	
		Calne Railway 1860	
		Marlborough Railway 1861	
	Bridport Railway 1855		
		Devon & Somerset Rly 1864	
Liskeard & Caradon Rly 1843			
			Swindon, Marlborough & Andover Railway 1873

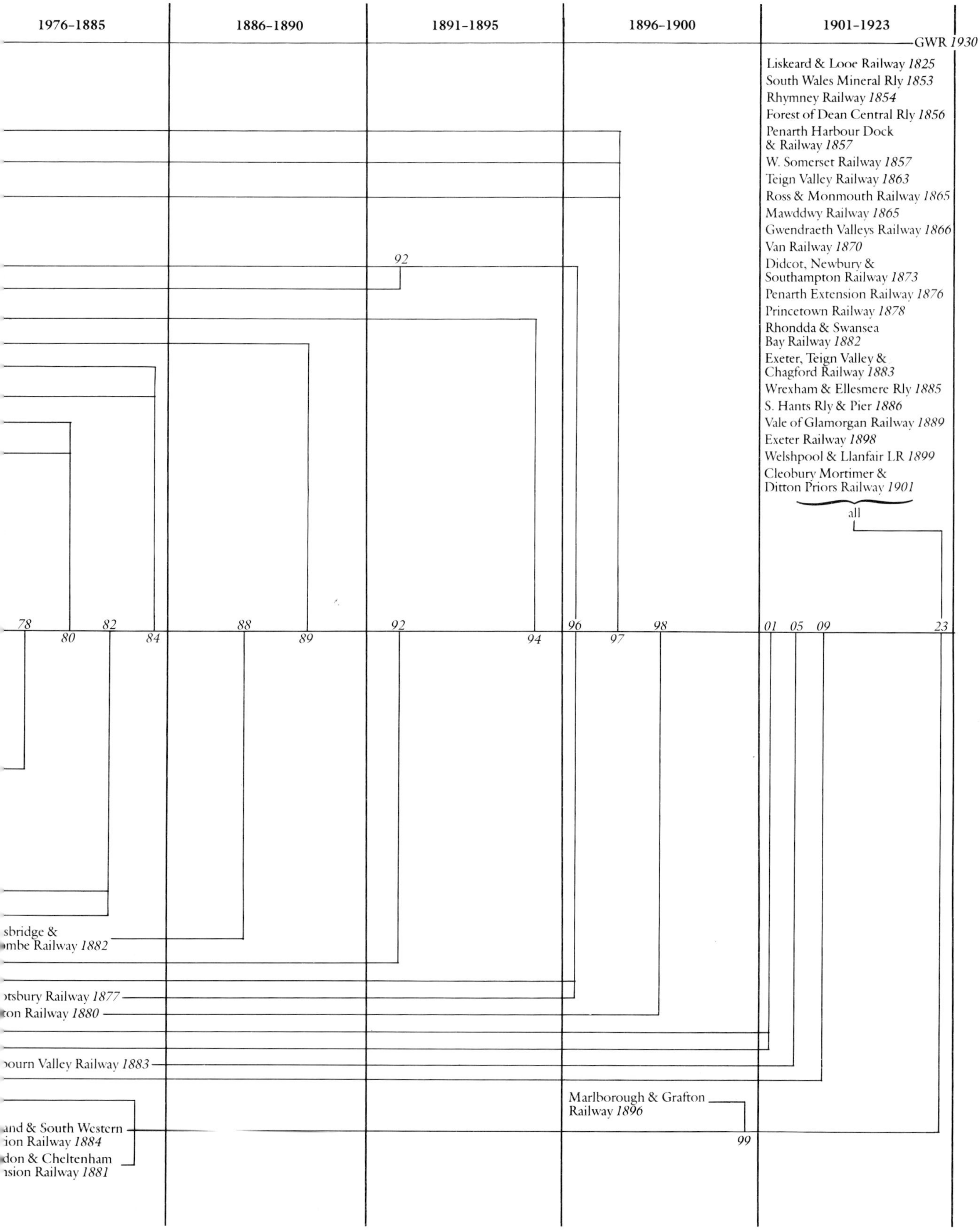

1976–1885	1886–1890	1891–1895	1896–1900	1901–1923

GWR *1930*

Liskeard & Looe Railway *1825*
South Wales Mineral Rly *1853*
Rhymney Railway *1854*
Forest of Dean Central Rly *1856*
Penarth Harbour Dock
& Railway *1857*
W. Somerset Railway *1857*
Teign Valley Railway *1863*
Ross & Monmouth Railway *1865*
Mawddwy Railway *1865*
Gwendraeth Valleys Railway *1866*
Van Railway *1870*
Didcot, Newbury &
Southampton Railway *1873*
Penarth Extension Railway *1876*
Princetown Railway *1878*
Rhondda & Swansea
Bay Railway *1882*
Exeter, Teign Valley &
Chagford Railway *1883*
Wrexham & Ellesmere Rly *1885*
S. Hants Rly & Pier *1886*
Vale of Glamorgan Railway *1889*
Exeter Railway *1898*
Welshpool & Llanfair LR *1899*
Cleobury Mortimer &
Ditton Priors Railway *1901*

all

92

78   *82*   *88*   *92*   *96*   *98*   *01* *05* *09*   *23*
  80   *84*   *89*   *94*   *97*

sbridge &
ombe Railway *1882*

otsbury Railway *1877*
ton Railway *1880*

ourn Valley Railway *1883*

Marlborough & Grafton
Railway *1896*

and & South Western
ion Railway *1884*
don & Cheltenham
nsion Railway *1881*

99

3 GWR: South Wales

	To 1840	1841–1850	1851–1860	1861–1865
	Cefn & Pyle Railway, *Op 1798*			
				Alexandra (Newport Dock) Company *1865*
				Kidwelly & Burry Port Rly *18*
				Burry Port & Gwendreath Valley Railway *1865*
	Carmarthenshire Railway *1802*			
			Ely Valley Railway *1857*	
	Dyffryn Llynfi & Porthcawl Railway *1825*		Milford Railway *1856*	
		Llynfi Valley Railway *1846* 47	55	
	Bridgend Railway *1828*			Ogmort Valley Railways *186*
				Ely Valley Extension Railway *1863*
	Blaenavon Tramroad *1792*	Monmouthshire Railway & Canal Company *1845*		
				Pontypool, Caerleon & Newport Railway *1865*
			Briton Ferry & Floating Dock Company *1851*	
	GREAT WESTERN RAILWAY *1835*			63
		S. Wales Railway *1845*		
			Aberdare Valley Railway *1855*	
		Vale of Neath Railway *1846*		63
				64
				Swansea & Neath Railway *18*
	Monmouth Railway *1810*			
			Coleford, Monmouth, Usk & Pontypool Railway *1853* 53	
			Carmarthen & Cardigan Rly *1854*	
	Llanelly Railway & Dock Company *1828*			
			Pembroke & Tenby Railway *1859*	
	Taff Vale Railway *1836*	Aberdare Railway *1845*		
				Cowbridge Railway *1862*
				Dare Valley Railway *1863*
				Llantrisant & Taff Vale Railway *1861*
	Rumney Railway *1825*			
			Brecon & Merthyr Tydfil Junction Railway *1859*	63
				Neath & Brecon Railway *186*
				Dulas Valley Mineral Railway *1862*
				Swansea Vale & Neath & Brecon Junc Railway *1864*

| 1866–1870 | 1871–1880 | 1881–1890 | 1891–1900 | 1901–1923 |

Barry Dock & Railway *1884* —— The Barry Railway *1891* —
Port Talbot
Railway & Docks Co. *1894*
96

Pontypridd, Caerphilly &
Newport Railway *1878*

Alexandra (Newport & S. Wales)
Docks & Railway *1882*
97
Bute Docks Company *1886* —— Cardiff Railway *1897* —

Llanelly &
Mynydd Mawr Railway *1875*

Narberth Road & — N. Pembroke &
Maenclochog Railway *1872* — Fishguard Railway *1884*
Rosebush & Fishguard Rly *1878*⌐

...land & Taf Vale Rly *1869* —— Whitland & Cardigan Rly *1877* —
Llynfi & 76
Ogmore Railway *1866*

Cardiff & Ogmore Railway *1873*

Ely & Clydach
Valleys Railway *1873*

81   89   92   97
73   76   80   83   90   96   98   03   22 23

East Usk Railway *1885* —

89   94
02

...dda Vale &
...ain Junc. Rly *1867*

Treferig Valley Railway *1879* —
Cowbridge &
Aberthaw Railway *1889*

69

4 GWR: North and Mid-Wales

	To 1845	1846–1850	1851–1860	1861–1865
			Mid-Wales Railway *1859*	
				Oswestry, Ellesmere & Whitchurch Rly *1861*
			Newtown & Machynlleth Railway *1857*	
				Cambrian Railways *1864*
			Oswestry & Newtown Railway *1855*	
			Llanidloes & Newtown Railway *1853*	Aberystwith & Welsh Coast Railway *1861*
				Bala & Dolgelly Railway *1862*
	GREAT WESTERN RAILWAY *1835*			
	Pontcysyllte Railway, *pre 1846*			Festiniog & Blaenau Rly *186_*
			Vale of Llangollen Rly *1859*	
			Llangollen & Corwen Railway *1860*	
				Corwen & Bala Railway *1862*
			Manchester & Milford Railway *1860*	

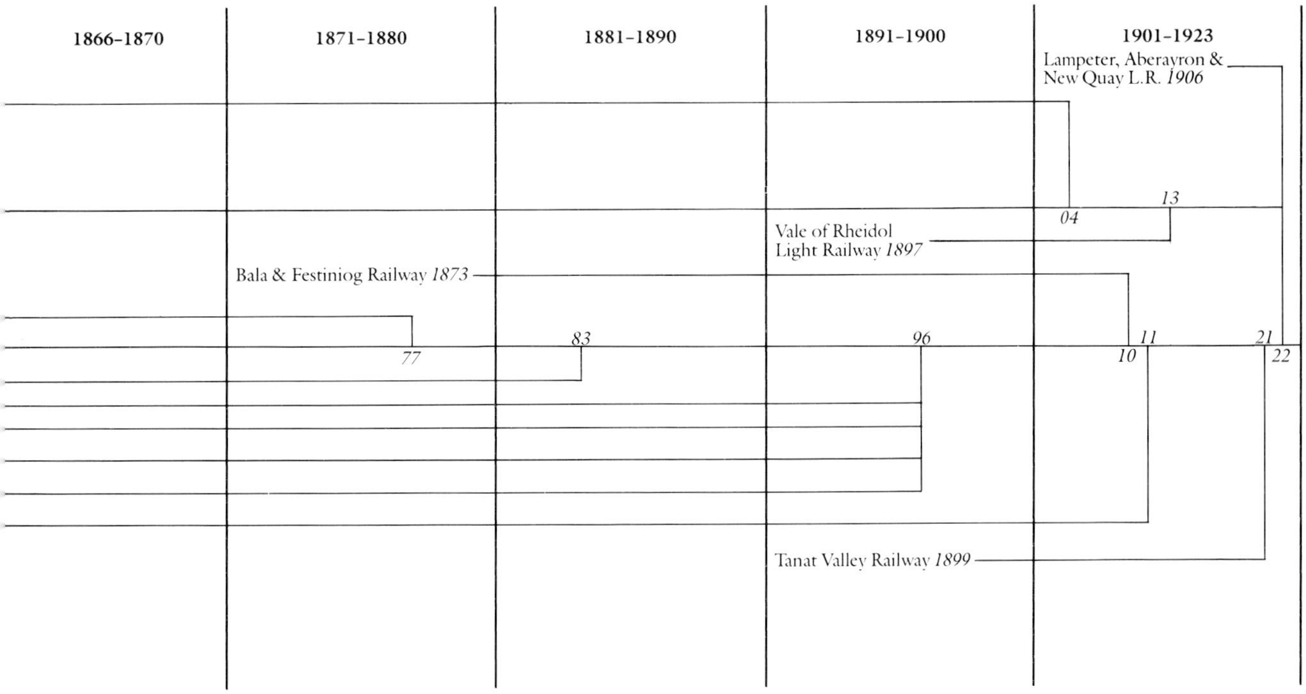

1866–1870	1871–1880	1881–1890	1891–1900	1901–1923

Lampeter, Aberayron & New Quay L.R. *1906*

04 *13*

Vale of Rheidol Light Railway *1897*

Bala & Festiniog Railway *1873*

77 *83* *96* *11* *21*

10 *22*

Tanat Valley Railway *1899*

5 LMS: Caledonian Railway and Glasgow & South Western Railway

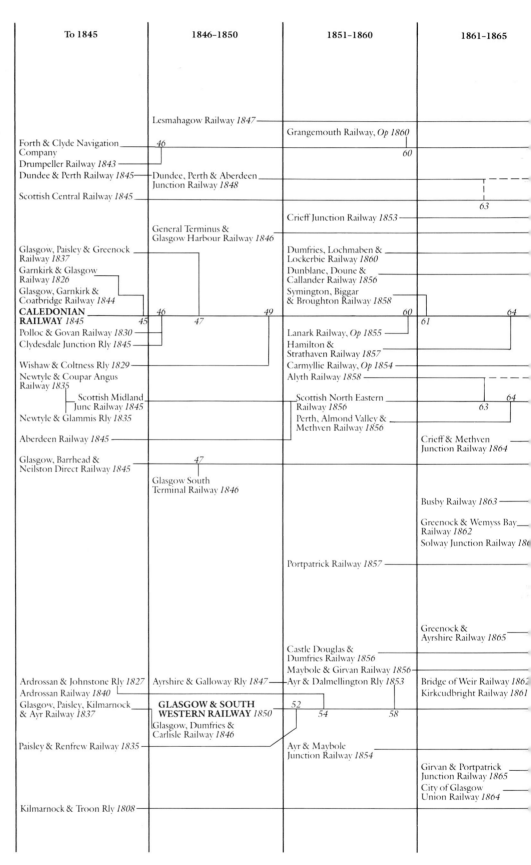

To 1845	1846–1850	1851–1860	1861–1865
	Lesmahagow Railway 1847		
		Grangemouth Railway, Op 1860	
Forth & Clyde Navigation Company	46	60	
Drumpeller Railway 1843			
Dundee & Perth Railway 1845	Dundee, Perth & Aberdeen Junction Railway 1848		
Scottish Central Railway 1845			63
		Crieff Junction Railway 1853	
	General Terminus & Glasgow Harbour Railway 1846		
Glasgow, Paisley & Greenock Railway 1837		Dumfries, Lochmaben & Lockerbie Railway 1860	
Garnkirk & Glasgow Railway 1826		Dunblane, Doune & Callander Railway 1856	
Glasgow, Garnkirk & Coatbridge Railway 1844		Symington, Biggar & Broughton Railway 1858	
CALEDONIAN RAILWAY 1845 45	46 47 49	60	61 64
Polloc & Govan Railway 1830		Lanark Railway, Op 1855	
Clydesdale Junction Rly 1845		Hamilton & Strathaven Railway 1857	
Wishaw & Coltness Rly 1829		Carmyllie Railway, Op 1854	
Newtyle & Coupar Angus Railway 1835		Alyth Railway 1858	
Scottish Midland Junc Railway 1845		Scottish North Eastern Railway 1856	64
Newtyle & Glammis Rly 1835		Perth, Almond Valley & Methven Railway 1856	63
Aberdeen Railway 1845			Crieff & Methven Junction Railway 1864
Glasgow, Barrhead & Neilston Direct Railway 1845	47		
	Glasgow South Terminal Railway 1846		
			Busby Railway 1863
			Greenock & Wemyss Bay Railway 1862
			Solway Junction Railway 186
		Portpatrick Railway 1857	
			Greenock & Ayrshire Railway 1865
		Castle Douglas & Dumfries Railway 1856	
		Maybole & Girvan Railway 1856	
Ardrossan & Johnstone Rly 1827	Ayrshire & Galloway Rly 1847	Ayr & Dalmellington Rly 1853	Bridge of Weir Railway 186
Ardrossan Railway 1840			Kirkcudbright Railway 1861
Glasgow, Paisley, Kilmarnock & Ayr Railway 1837	**GLASGOW & SOUTH WESTERN RAILWAY** 1850 52	54 58	
	Glasgow, Dumfries & Carlisle Railway 1846		
Paisley & Renfrew Railway 1835		Ayr & Maybole Junction Railway 1854	
			Girvan & Portpatrick Junction Railway 1865
			City of Glasgow Union Railway 1864
Kilmarnock & Troon Rly 1808			

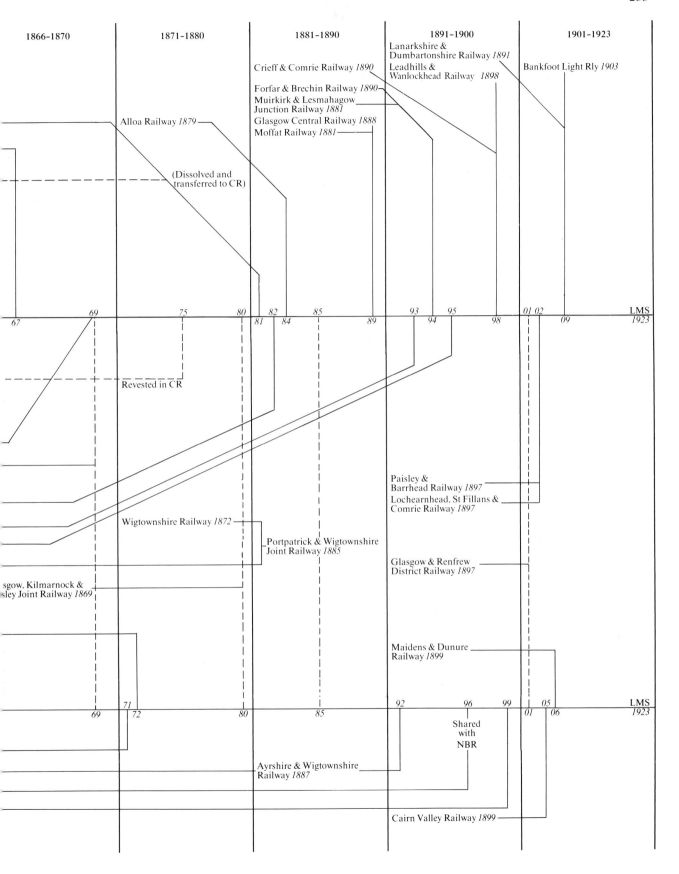

1866-1870 | 1871-1880 | 1881-1890 | 1891-1900 | 1901-1923

Lanarkshire &
Dumbartonshire Railway *1891*

Crieff & Comrie Railway *1890*

Leadhills &
Wanlockhead Railway *1898*

Bankfoot Light Rly *1903*

Forfar & Brechin Railway *1890*

Muirkirk & Lesmahagow
Junction Railway *1881*

Alloa Railway *1879*

Glasgow Central Railway *1888*

Moffat Railway *1881*

(Dissolved and
transferred to CR)

69   75   80   82   84   85   89   93   95   98   01 02   09   LMS
67   81   94   1923

Revested in CR

Paisley &
Barrhead Railway *1897*

Lochearnhead. St Fillans &
Comrie Railway *1897*

Wigtownshire Railway *1872*

Portpatrick & Wigtownshire
Joint Railway *1885*

Glasgow & Renfrew
District Railway *1897*

sgow. Kilmarnock &
sley Joint Railway *1869*

Maidens & Dunure
Railway *1899*

71   05   LMS
69   72   80   85   92   96   99   01   06   1923

Shared
with
NBR

Ayrshire & Wigtownshire
Railway *1887*

Cairn Valley Railway *1899*

6 LMS: Highland Railway and Lancashire & Yorkshire Railway

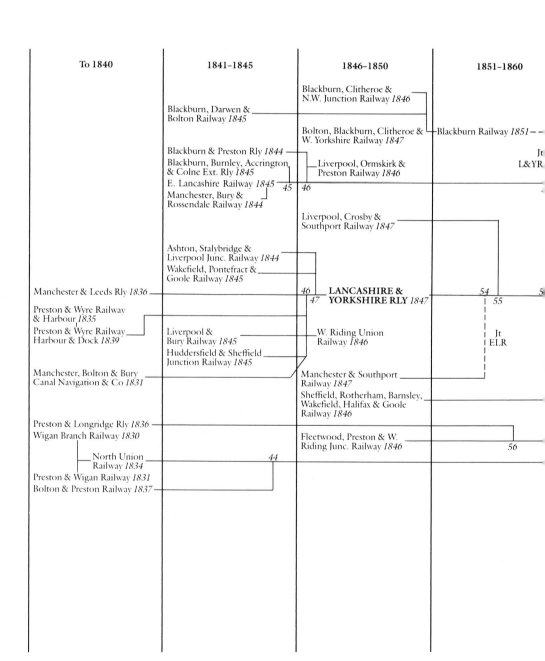

To 1855	1856–1865	1866–1870	1871–1875
	Dingwall & Skye Railway *1865*		
	Inverness & Ross-shire Railway *1860*		
	Findhorn Railway *1859*		
Inverness & Nairn Railway *1854*			
	Inverness & Aberdeen Junction Railway *1856* 61 62		
	HIGHLAND RAILWAY *1865*		
Perth & Dunkeld Railway *1854*			Sutherland & Caithness Railway *1871*
	Inverness & Perth Junction Railway *1861* 64	Duke of Sutherland's Rly *1870*	
	Sutherland Railway *1865*		

To 1840	1841–1845	1846–1850	1851–1860
		Blackburn, Clitheroe & N.W. Junction Railway *1846*	
	Blackburn, Darwen & Bolton Railway *1845*		
		Bolton, Blackburn, Clitheroe & W. Yorkshire Railway *1847*	Blackburn Railway *1851* – –
	Blackburn & Preston Rly *1844*		Jt L&YR
	Blackburn, Burnley, Accrington & Colne Ext. Rly *1845*	Liverpool, Ormskirk & Preston Railway *1846*	
	E. Lancashire Railway *1845* 45	46	
	Manchester, Bury & Rossendale Railway *1844*		
		Liverpool, Crosby & Southport Railway *1847*	
	Ashton, Stalybridge & Liverpool Junc. Railway *1844*		
	Wakefield, Pontefract & Goole Railway *1845*		
Manchester & Leeds Rly *1836*		46 **LANCASHIRE &**	54 5
		47 **YORKSHIRE RLY** *1847*	55
Preston & Wyre Railway & Harbour *1835*			
Preston & Wyre Railway Harbour & Dock *1839*	Liverpool & Bury Railway *1845*	W. Riding Union Railway *1846*	Jt ELR
	Huddersfield & Sheffield Junction Railway *1845*		
Manchester, Bolton & Bury Canal Navigation & Co *1831*		Manchester & Southport Railway *1847*	
		Sheffield, Rotherham, Barnsley, Wakefield, Halifax & Goole Railway *1846*	
Preston & Longridge Rly *1836*			
Wigan Branch Railway *1830*		Fleetwood, Preston & W. Riding Junc. Railway *1846*	56
North Union Railway *1834* 44			
Preston & Wigan Railway *1831*			
Bolton & Preston Railway *1837*			

1876–1880	1881–1890	1891–1900	1901–1910	1911–1923

80   *84* ——LMS *1923*

1861–1870	1871–1880	1881–1890	1891–1900	1901–1923

Bury & Tottington Railway *1877*

~ashire Union Railway *1864*
~kpool & Lytham
~way *1861*

Jt
L&NWR

Jt
L&NWR

66   *71*   *83*   *88*   *89*   *97*   L&NWR
                                                                                                       1922
                                                                                              (see Chart no 9)

Jt
L&NWR

Jt
L&NWR

West Lancashire Railway *1871*

Liverpool, Southport &
Preston Junc. Railway *1884*

7 LMS: Cheshire Lines Committee, Furness Railway, North Staffordshire Railway, Stratford-upon-Avon & Midland Junction Railway and Shropshire Union Railways & Canal Co

	To 1840	1841–1845	1846–1850	1851–1860
				Cheshire Midland Railway
				Stockport & Woodley Junction Railway *1860*
		Whitehaven & Furness Railway *1845*		
				Coniston Railway *1857*
				Ulverstone & Lancaster Railway *1851*
		FURNESS RAILWAY *1844*		
				Whitehaven, Cleator & Egremont Railway *1854*
			Harecastle & Sandbach Railway *1846*	
			Churnet Valley Railway *1846*	
			Potteries Railway *1846*	
			NORTH STAFFORDSHIRE RAILWAY *1846*	
	Calder Low Tramway *1776*			Potteries, Biddulph & Congleton Railway *1854*
			47	
				Silverdale & Newcastle Rly (leased to NSR from *1860*)
			Newtown & Crewe Rly *1846*	
			Shrewsbury & Stafford Railway *1846*	
			SHROPSHIRE UNION RAILWAYS & CANAL CO *1846*	
			Chester & Wolverhampton Rly *1846*	
	Pontcysyllte Tramway			

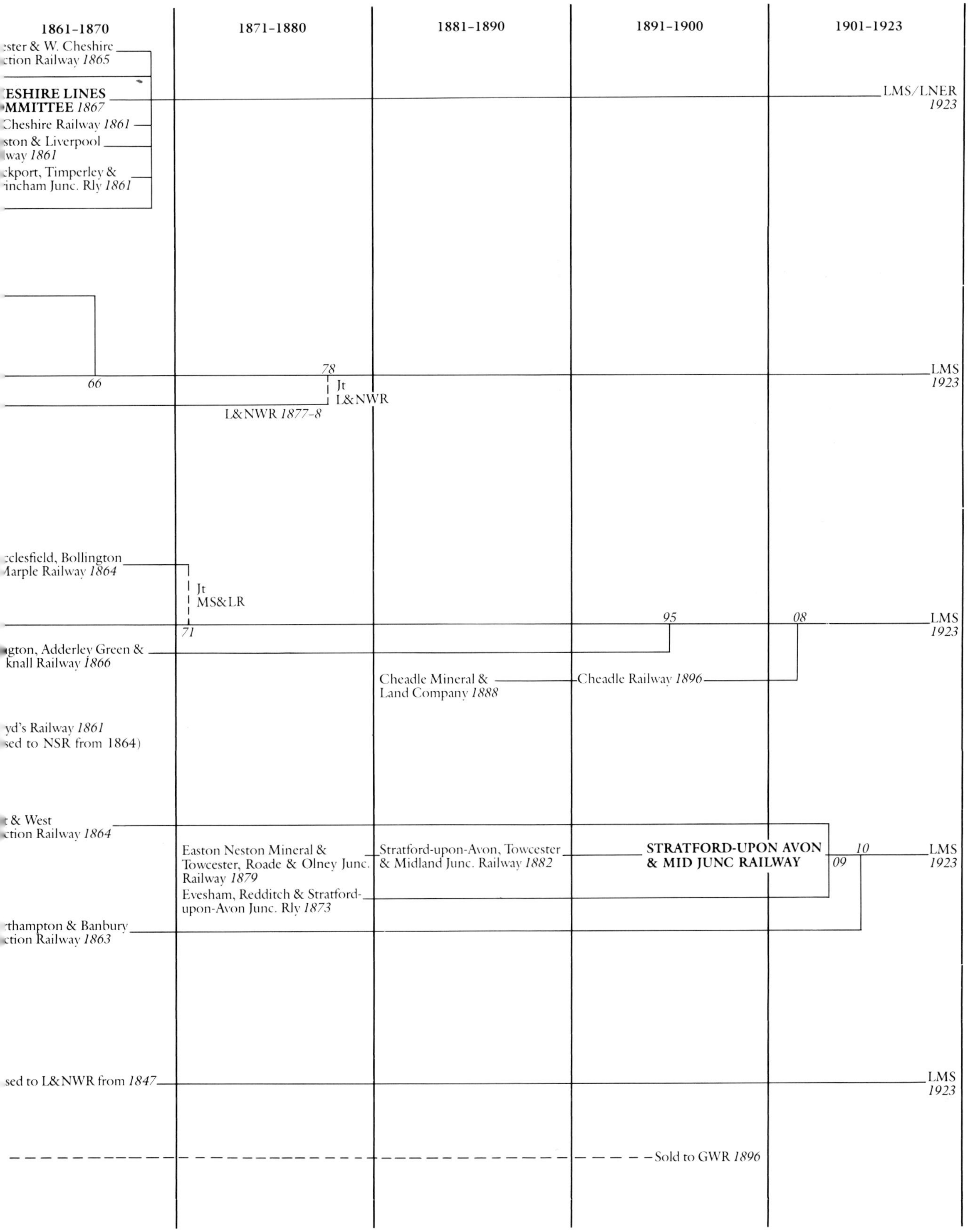

1861–1870	1871–1880	1881–1890	1891–1900	1901–1923

...ester & W. Cheshire
...ction Railway *1865*

...ESHIRE LINES
...MMITTEE *1867*

...Cheshire Railway *1861*

...ston & Liverpool
...way *1861*

...ckport, Timperley &
...rincham Junc. Rly *1861*

LMS/LNER
1923

66

78

Jt
L&NWR

L&NWR *1877–8*

LMS
1923

...cclesfield, Bollington
...Marple Railway *1864*

Jt
MS&LR

71

95

08

LMS
1923

...gton, Adderley Green &
...knall Railway *1866*

Cheadle Mineral &
Land Company *1888*

Cheadle Railway *1896*

...yd's Railway *1861*
...sed to NSR from 1864)

...& West
...ction Railway *1864*

Easton Neston Mineral &
Towcester, Roade & Olney Junc.
Railway *1879*

Evesham, Redditch & Stratford-
upon-Avon Junc. Rly *1873*

Stratford-upon-Avon, Towcester
& Midland Junc. Railway *1882*

**STRATFORD-UPON AVON
& MID JUNC RAILWAY**

10

09

LMS
1923

...rthampton & Banbury
...ction Railway *1863*

...sed to L&NWR from *1847*

LMS
1923

Sold to GWR *1896*

8 LMS: Midland Railway

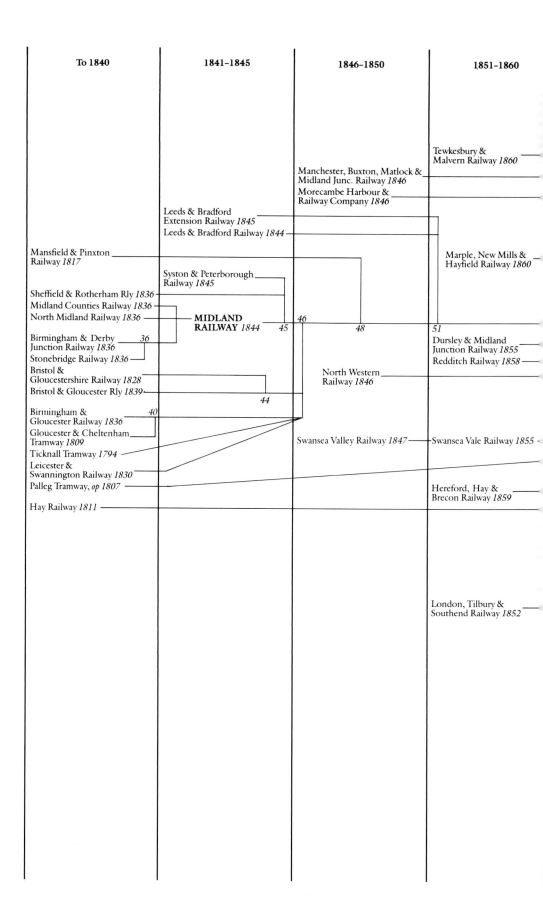

	To 1840	1841–1845	1846–1850	1851–1860
				Tewkesbury & Malvern Railway *1860*
			Manchester, Buxton, Matlock & Midland Junc. Railway *1846*	
			Morecambe Harbour & Railway Company *1846*	
		Leeds & Bradford Extension Railway *1845*		
		Leeds & Bradford Railway *1844*		
	Mansfield & Pinxton Railway *1817*			Marple, New Mills & Hayfield Railway *1860*
		Syston & Peterborough Railway *1845*		
	Sheffield & Rotherham Rly *1836*			
	Midland Counties Railway *1836*			
	North Midland Railway *1836*	**MIDLAND RAILWAY** *1844* 45	46 48	51
	Birmingham & Derby Junction Railway *1836* 36			Dursley & Midland Junction Railway *1855*
	Stonebridge Railway *1836*			Redditch Railway *1858*
	Bristol & Gloucestershire Railway *1828*		North Western Railway *1846*	
	Bristol & Gloucester Rly *1839*	44		
	Birmingham & Gloucester Railway *1836* 40			
	Gloucester & Cheltenham Tramway *1809*			
	Ticknall Tramway *1794*		Swansea Valley Railway *1847* — Swansea Vale Railway *1855*	
	Leicester & Swannington Railway *1830*			
	Palleg Tramway, *op 1807*			Hereford, Hay & Brecon Railway *1859*
	Hay Railway *1811*			
				London, Tilbury & Southend Railway *1852*

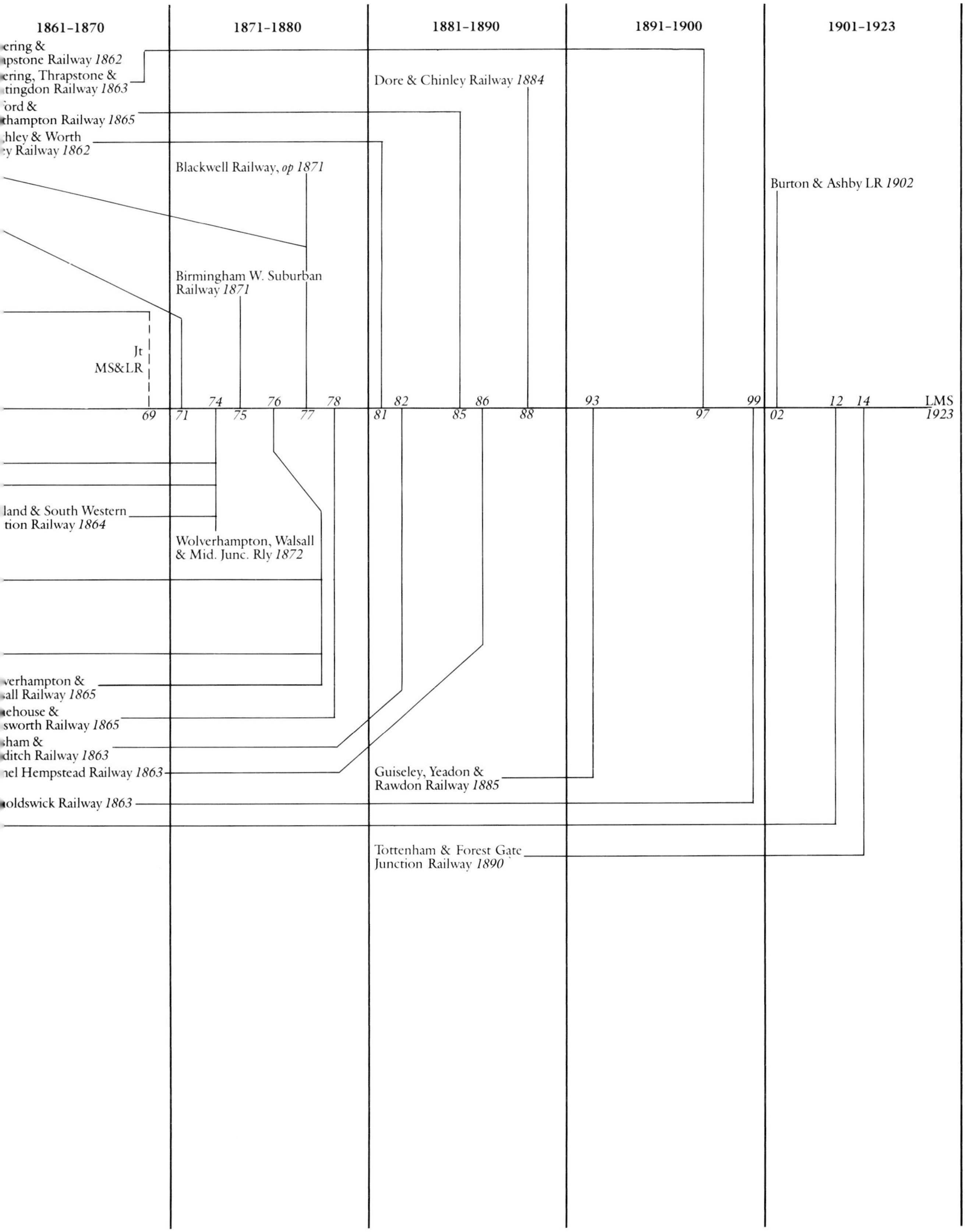

1861–1870	1871–1880	1881–1890	1891–1900	1901–1923

ering &
psstone Railway *1862*
ering, Thrapstone &
tingdon Railway *1863*

Dore & Chinley Railway *1884*

ord &
thampton Railway *1865*

hley & Worth
ey Railway *1862*

Blackwell Railway, *op 1871*

Burton & Ashby LR *1902*

Birmingham W. Suburban
Railway *1871*

Jt
MS&LR

69   71   74   75   76   77   78   81   82   85   86   88   93   97   99   02   12   14   LMS
1923

land & South Western
tion Railway *1864*

Wolverhampton, Walsall
& Mid. Junc. Rly *1872*

verhampton &
all Railway *1865*

chouse &
sworth Railway *1865*

ham &
ditch Railway *1863*

nel Hempstead Railway *1863*

Guiseley, Yeadon &
Rawdon Railway *1885*

oldswick Railway *1863*

Tottenham & Forest Gate
Junction Railway *1890*

9 LMS: London & North Western Railway, England

	To 1840	1841–1845	1846–1850	1851–1860

Watford & Rickmansworth Railway 1860

Derbyshire, Staffordshire & Worcestershire Junc. Rly 1847

Cannock Mineral Railway 18[...]

South Staffordshire Junction Railway 1846

S. Staffordshire Railway 1846

Trent Valley, Midlands & Grand Junction Railway 1846

Birmingham, Wolverhampton & Stour Valley Railway 1846

Hampstead Junc. Railway 185[...]

Warrington & Altrincham Junction Railway 1851

Warrington & Stockport Railway 1853

Nuneaton & Hinckley Railway 1859

S. Leicestershire Railway 186[...]

St. Helens & Runcorn Gap Railway 1830

St. Helens Canal & Railway 1845

Sankey Brook Navigation

Bedford & Cambridge Railway 1860

Sandy & Potton Railway, op 1[...]

Leeds, Dewsbury & Manchester Railway 1845

Huddersfield & Manchester Railway & Canal 1845

Kenyon & Leigh Junc. Rly 1829

Bolton & Leigh Railway 1825

Liverpool & Manchester Railway 1826

Chester & Crewe Railway 1837

Grand Junc. Railway 1833 — *34*

40

45

Warrington & Newton Railway 1829

Trent Valley Railway 1845

Manchester & Birmingham 1837

LONDON & NORTH WESTERN RLY 1846   *46*   *47*

London & Birmingham Rly 1833

43

Cannock Chase Railway 186[...]

Warwick & Leamington Union Railway 1842

Rugby & Leamington Railway 1846

Bedford Railway 1845

Stockport, Disley & Whaley Bridge Railway 1854

Aylesbury Railway 1836

Cockermouth & Workington Railway 1845

Whitehaven Junc. Railway 1844

Preston & Longridge Rly 1836

Fleetwood, Preston & West Riding Junction Railway 1846

56

Whitehaven, Cleator & Egremont Railway 1854

Buckinghamshire Railway 1847

Kendal & Windermere Railway 1845

Lancaster & Carlisle Railway 1844

Lancaster & Preston Junction Railway 1837

Cromford & High Peak Rly 1825

Wigan Branch Railway 1830

North Union Railway 1834   *44*

Preston & Wigan Railway 1831

Bolton & Preston Railway 1837

LANCASHIRE & YORKSHIRE RAILWAY (see Chart no 6)

East & West India Docks & Birmingham Junc. Railway 1846

North London Railway 1853-

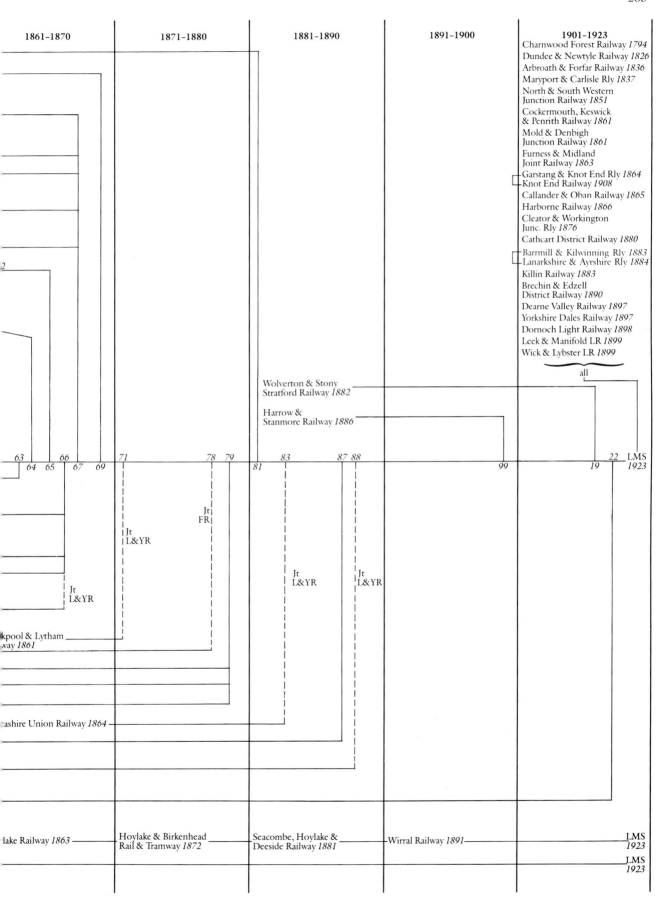

1861–1870	1871–1880	1881–1890	1891–1900	1901–1923

Charnwood Forest Railway *1794*
Dundee & Newtyle Railway *1826*
Arbroath & Forfar Railway *1836*
Maryport & Carlisle Rly *1837*
North & South Western
Junction Railway *1851*
Cockermouth, Keswick
& Penrith Railway *1861*
Mold & Denbigh
Junction Railway *1861*
Furness & Midland
Joint Railway *1863*
Garstang & Knot End Rly *1864*
Knot End Railway *1908*
Callander & Oban Railway *1865*
Harborne Railway *1866*
Cleator & Workington
Junc. Rly *1876*
Cathcart District Railway *1880*
Barrmill & Kilwinning Rly *1883*
Lanarkshire & Ayrshire Rly *1884*
Killin Railway *1883*
Brechin & Edzell
District Railway *1890*
Dearne Valley Railway *1897*
Yorkshire Dales Railway *1897*
Dornoch Light Railway *1898*
Leek & Manifold LR *1899*
Wick & Lybster LR *1899*

all

Wolverton & Stony
Stratford Railway *1882*

Harrow &
Stanmore Railway *1886*

63   66   71   78 79   81   83   87 88   99   22 LMS
  64 65   67 69   19   1923

Jt
FR

Jt
L&YR

Jt
L&YR

Jt
L&YR

Jt
L&YR

kpool & Lytham
way 1861

ashire Union Railway *1864*

lake Railway *1863*   Hoylake & Birkenhead   Seacombe, Hoylake &   Wirral Railway *1891*   LMS
                        Rail & Tramway *1872*   Deeside Railway *1881*   1923

LMS
1923

10 LMS: London & North Western Railway, North and Mid-Wales

	To 1845	1846–1850	1851–1860	1861–1865
				Holywell Railway *1864* ——
			Denbigh, Ruthin & Corwen Railway *1860*	
				Carnarvonshire Railway *186.*
	Nantlle Railway *1825* ——			
				Carnarvon & Llanberis Railway *1864* ——
			Vale of Clwyd Railway *1856* ——	
		Mold Railway *1847* ——	Conway & Llanrwst Railway *1860*	
			Bangor & Carnarvon Railway *1851*	
	Chester & Holyhead Rly *1844* —	*49*	*54*	
		LONDON & NORTH WESTERN RAILWAY *1846*		*59*
	Bailey's Tramroad, *op 1822* ——		Merthyr, Tredegar & Abergavenny Railway *1859*	
			Knighton Railway *1858* ——	
			Central Wales Railway *1859* ——	
			Central Wales Ext. Railway *1860* ——	*63*
	Nerquis Railway ——			
	Penllwyn Railway, *op c 1824* ——			
	Sirhowy Railway *1802* ——			
				Anglesey Central Railway *1863*

11 LNER: Great North of Scotland Railway

	To 1855	1856–1865	1866–1870	1871–1875
	Morayshire Railway *1846* ——			
		Aboyne & Braemar Railway *1865* ——		
		Deeside Exten. Railway *1857* ——		
	Deeside Railway *1846* ——			
		Denburn Valley Railway *1864*		
	GREAT NORTH OF SCOTLAND RAILWAY *1846*	*64*	*66*	
		Banff, Portsoy & Strathisla Railway *1857* ——		
		Banffshire Railway *1863* *63*		
		Alford Valley Railway *1856* ——		
	Banff, Macduff & Turriff Railway *1855*	Aberdeen & Turriff Railway *1859*		
		Banff, Macduff & Turriff Extension Railway *1857* ——		
		Strathspey Railway *1861* ——		
		Formartine & Buchan Rly *1858* ——		
		Keith & Dufftown Railway *1857* ——		
	Inverurie & Old Meldrum Railway *1855*			

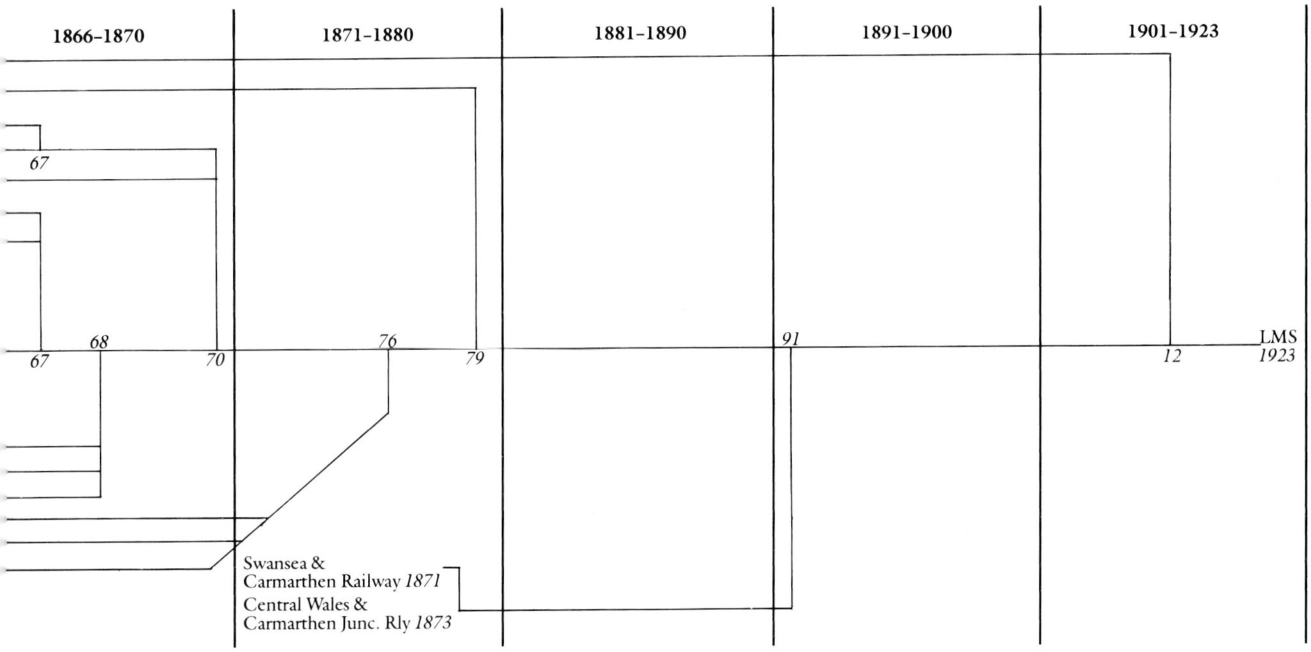

1866–1870	1871–1880	1881–1890	1891–1900	1901–1923

67

67   *68*   *70*   *76*   *79*   *91*   *12*   LMS
                                                                     1923

Swansea &
Carmarthen Railway *1871*
Central Wales &
Carmarthen Junc. Rly *1873*

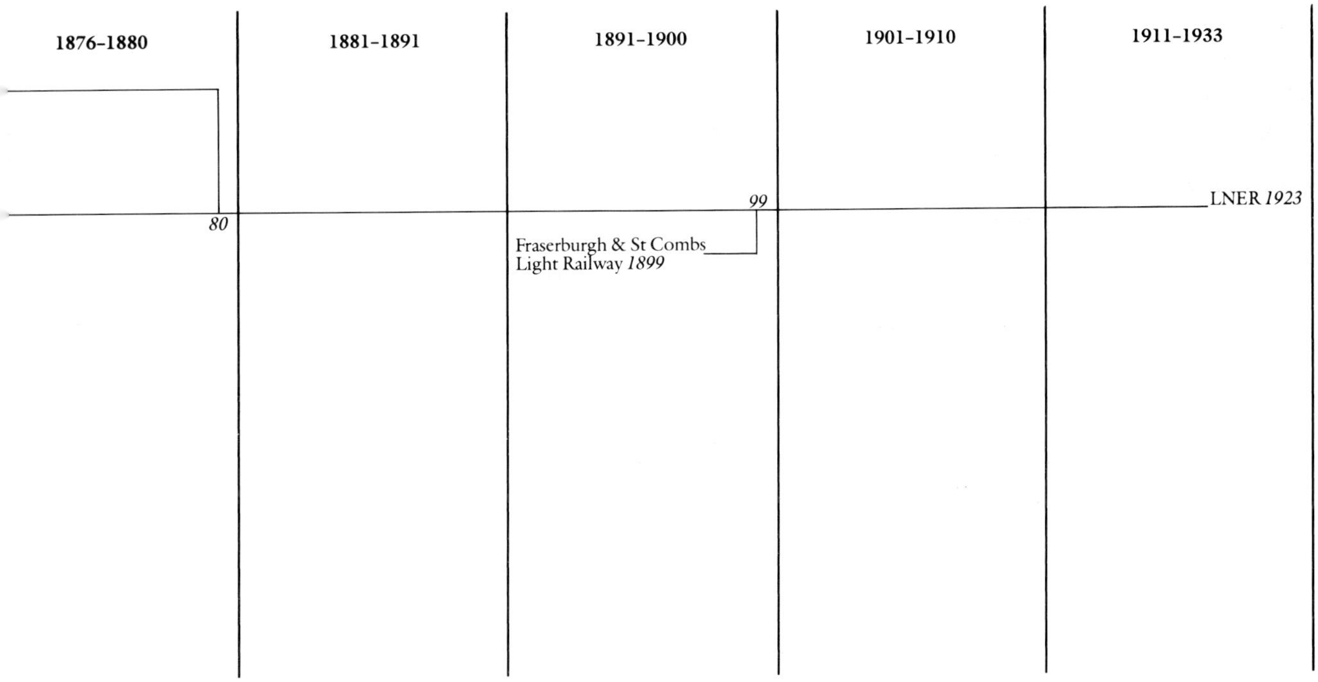

1876–1880	1881–1891	1891–1900	1901–1910	1911–1933

                                                             99   LNER *1923*

80

Fraserburgh & St Combs
Light Railway *1899*

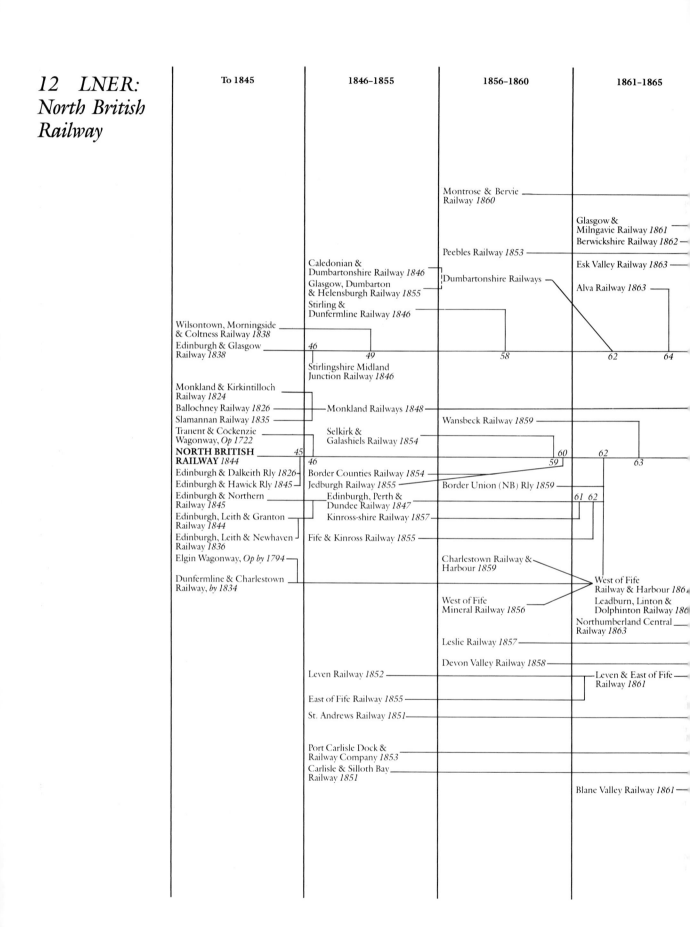

12 LNER: North British Railway

To 1845	1846–1855	1856–1860	1861–1865

Montrose & Bervie Railway 1860

Glasgow & Milngavie Railway 1861
Berwickshire Railway 1862

Peebles Railway 1853

Esk Valley Railway 1863

Caledonian & Dumbartonshire Railway 1846
Dumbartonshire Railways
Alva Railway 1863

Glasgow, Dumbarton & Helensburgh Railway 1855

Stirling & Dunfermline Railway 1846

Wilsontown, Morningside & Coltness Railway 1838

Edinburgh & Glasgow Railway 1838   46   49   58   62   64

Stirlingshire Midland Junction Railway 1846

Monkland & Kirkintilloch Railway 1824

Ballochney Railway 1826 — Monkland Railways 1848

Slamannan Railway 1835

Wansbeck Railway 1859

Tranent & Cockenzie Wagonway, Op 1722

Selkirk & Galashiels Railway 1854

NORTH BRITISH   45   60   62
RAILWAY 1844   46   59   63

Edinburgh & Dalkeith Rly 1826   Border Counties Railway 1854

Edinburgh & Hawick Rly 1845   Jedburgh Railway 1855   Border Union (NB) Rly 1859

Edinburgh & Northern Railway 1845   Edinburgh, Perth & Dundee Railway 1847   61 62

Edinburgh, Leith & Granton Railway 1844   Kinross-shire Railway 1857

Edinburgh, Leith & Newhaven Railway 1836   Fife & Kinross Railway 1855

Elgin Wagonway, Op by 1794

Charlestown Railway & Harbour 1859

Dunfermline & Charlestown Railway, by 1834

West of Fife Railway & Harbour 186_

West of Fife Mineral Railway 1856

Leadburn, Linton & Dolphinton Railway 186_

Northumberland Central Railway 1863

Leslie Railway 1857

Devon Valley Railway 1858

Leven Railway 1852

Leven & East of Fife Railway 1861

East of Fife Railway 1855

St. Andrews Railway 1851

Port Carlisle Dock & Railway Company 1853

Carlisle & Silloth Bay Railway 1851

Blane Valley Railway 1861

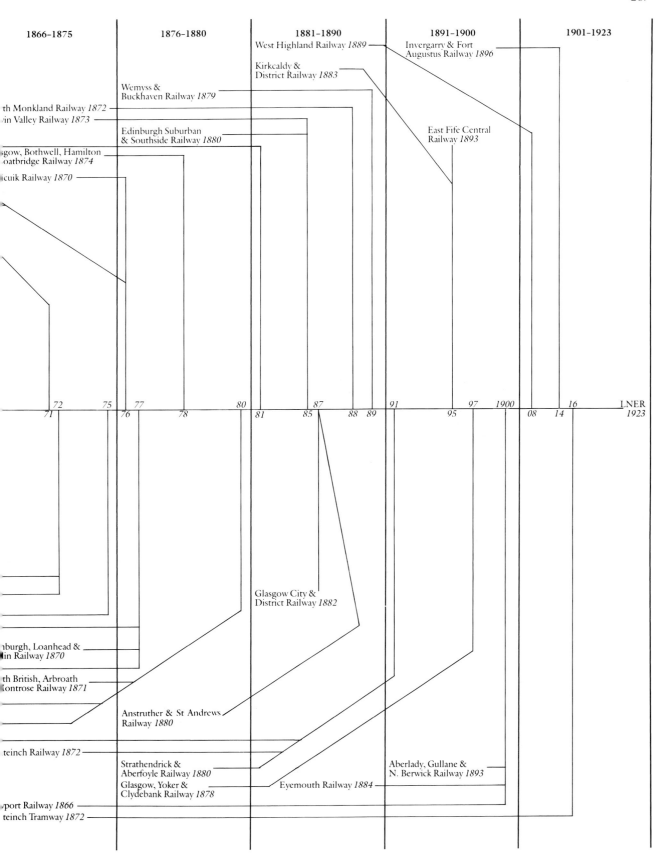

13 LNER: Great Northern Railway and Great Central Railway

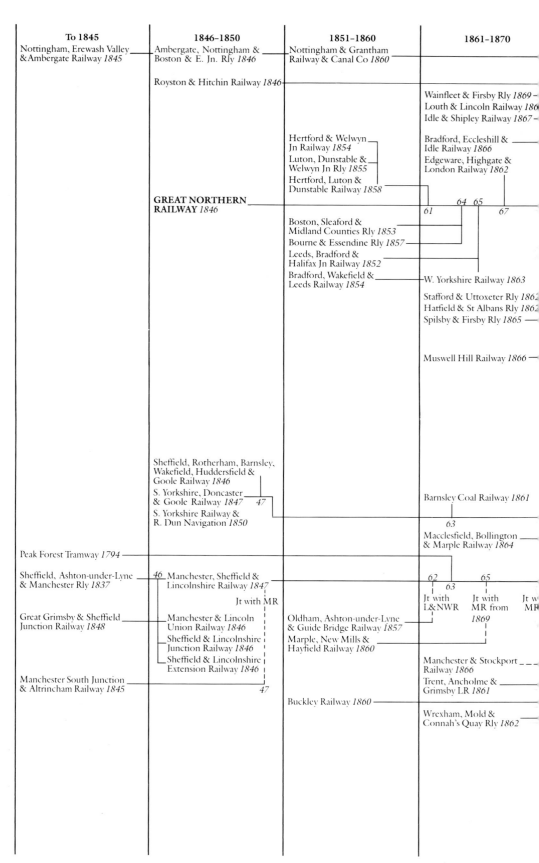

	To 1845	1846–1850	1851–1860	1861–1870

Nottingham, Erewash Valley & Ambergate Railway *1845*

Ambergate, Nottingham & Boston & E. Jn. Rly *1846*

Nottingham & Grantham Railway & Canal Co *1860*

Royston & Hitchin Railway *1846*

Wainfleet & Firsby Rly *1869*
Louth & Lincoln Railway *186*
Idle & Shipley Railway *1867*

Hertford & Welwyn Jn Railway *1854*
Luton, Dunstable & Welwyn Jn Rly *1855*
Hertford, Luton & Dunstable Railway *1858*

Bradford, Eccleshill & Idle Railway *1866*
Edgeware, Highgate & London Railway *1862*

GREAT NORTHERN RAILWAY *1846*

61   *64*   *65*   *67*

Boston, Sleaford & Midland Counties Rly *1853*
Bourne & Essendine Rly *1857*
Leeds, Bradford & Halifax Jn Railway *1852*
Bradford, Wakefield & Leeds Railway *1854*

W. Yorkshire Railway *1863*

Stafford & Uttoxeter Rly *186*
Hatfield & St Albans Rly *186*
Spilsby & Firsby Rly *1865*

Muswell Hill Railway *1866*

Sheffield, Rotherham, Barnsley, Wakefield, Huddersfield & Goole Railway *1846*
S. Yorkshire, Doncaster & Goole Railway *1847*   *47*
S. Yorkshire Railway & R. Dun Navigation *1850*

Barnsley Coal Railway *1861*

63

Macclesfield, Bollington & Marple Railway *1864*

Peak Forest Tramway *1794*

Sheffield, Ashton-under-Lyne & Manchester Rly *1837*

46 Manchester, Sheffield & Lincolnshire Railway *1847*

62   *65*
63

Jt with MR

Jt with L&NWR   Jt with MR from   Jt w MR

Great Grimsby & Sheffield Junction Railway *1848*

Manchester & Lincoln Union Railway *1846*
Sheffield & Lincolnshire Junction Railway *1846*
Sheffield & Lincolnshire Extension Railway *1846*

Oldham, Ashton-under-Lyne & Guide Bridge Railway *1857*
Marple, New Mills & Hayfield Railway *1860*

1869

Manchester & Stockport Railway *1866*
Trent, Ancholme & Grimsby LR *1861*

Manchester South Junction & Altrincham Railway *1845*

47

Buckley Railway *1860*

Wrexham, Mold & Connah's Quay Rly *1862*

1871–1880	1881–1885	1886–1890	1891–1900	1901–1923

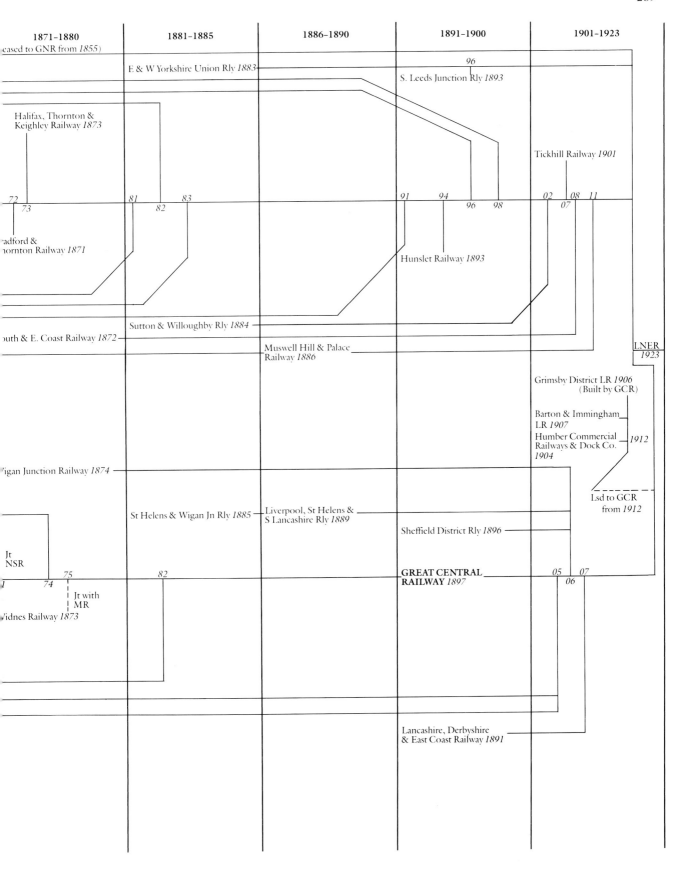

(eased to GNR from *1855*)

E & W Yorkshire Union Rly *1883*

96

S. Leeds Junction Rly *1893*

Halifax, Thornton &
Keighley Railway *1873*

Tickhill Railway *1901*

72   73   81   82   83   91   94   96   98   02   07   08   11

radford &
hornton Railway *1871*

Hunslet Railway *1893*

Sutton & Willoughby Rly *1884*

outh & E. Coast Railway *1872*

Muswell Hill & Palace
Railway *1886*

LNER
1923

Grimsby District LR *1906*
(Built by GCR)

Barton & Immingham
LR *1907*
Humber Commercial
Railways & Dock Co.
1904

1912

Vigan Junction Railway *1874*

Lsd to GCR
from *1912*

St Helens & Wigan Jn Rly *1885*

Liverpool, St Helens &
S Lancashire Rly *1889*

Sheffield District Rly *1896*

Jt
NSR

74   75   82

GREAT CENTRAL
RAILWAY *1897*

05   07
06

Jt with
MR

Widnes Railway *1873*

Lancashire, Derbyshire
& East Coast Railway *1891*

14 LNER: North Eastern Railway

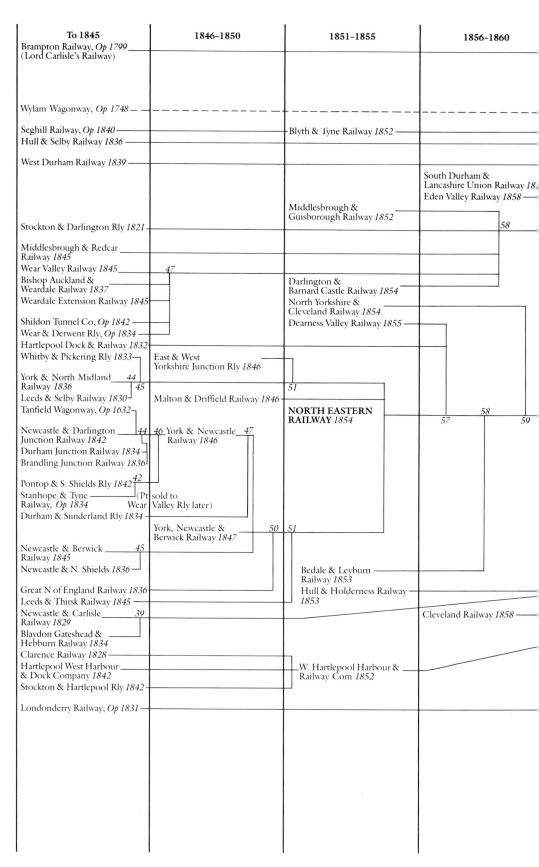

To 1845	1846–1850	1851–1855	1856–1860
Brampton Railway, *Op 1799* (Lord Carlisle's Railway)			
Wylam Wagonway, *Op 1748*			
Seghill Railway, *Op 1840*		Blyth & Tyne Railway *1852*	
Hull & Selby Railway *1836*			
West Durham Railway *1839*			South Durham & Lancashire Union Railway *18..* Eden Valley Railway *1858*
		Middlesbrough & Guisborough Railway *1852*	
Stockton & Darlington Rly *1821*			*58*
Middlesbrough & Redcar Railway *1845*			
Wear Valley Railway *1845*	*47*		
Bishop Auckland & Weardale Railway *1837*		Darlington & Barnard Castle Railway *1854*	
Weardale Extension Railway *1845*		North Yorkshire & Cleveland Railway *1854*	
Shildon Tunnel Co, *Op 1842*		Dearness Valley Railway *1855*	
Wear & Derwent Rly, *Op 1834*			
Hartlepool Dock & Railway *1832*			
Whitby & Pickering Rly *1833*	East & West Yorkshire Junction Rly *1846*		
York & North Midland Railway *1836* *44* *45*		*51*	
Leeds & Selby Railway *1830*	Malton & Driffield Railway *1846*		
Tanfield Wagonway, *Op 1632*		**NORTH EASTERN RAILWAY** *1854*	*57* *58* *59*
Newcastle & Darlington Junction Railway *1842* *44*	*46* York & Newcastle Railway *1846* *47*		
Durham Junction Railway *1834*			
Brandling Junction Railway *1836*			
Pontop & S. Shields Rly *1842* *42*			
Stanhope & Tyne Railway, *Op 1834*	(Pt sold to Wear Valley Rly later)		
Durham & Sunderland Rly *1834*			
	York, Newcastle & Berwick Railway *1847* *50* *51*		
Newcastle & Berwick Railway *1845* *45*			
Newcastle & N. Shields *1836*		Bedale & Leyburn Railway *1853*	
Great N of England Railway *1836*		Hull & Holderness Railway *1853*	
Leeds & Thirsk Railway *1845*			
Newcastle & Carlisle Railway *1829* *39*			Cleveland Railway *1858*
Blaydon Gateshead & Hebburn Railway *1834*			
Clarence Railway *1828*			
Hartlepool West Harbour & Dock Company *1842*		W. Hartlepool Harbour & Railway Com *1852*	
Stockton & Hartlepool Rly *1842*			
Londonderry Railway, *Op 1831*			

271

1861–1865 | 1866–1875 | 1876–1890 | 1891–1900 | 1901–1923

Scarborough &
Whitby Railway 1871

Hylton Southwick &
Monkwearmouth Railway 1871

Scotswood, Newburn & Wylam
Railway & Dock Company 1871

Kiltonthorpe
Railway, Op 1873

Hull & Hornsea Railway 1862

Frosterley &
Stanhope Railway 1861

3

62

62   63   65   66   70 72 74   76   82   89   94   98 1900   14   22 LNER
                                              83   12   1923

Wear Valley
Extension Railway 1892

Cawood, Wistow &
Selby Railway 1896

Leeds, Castleford &
Pontefract Jn Rly, 1873

Hexham & Allendale Rly 1865

Tees Valley Railway 1865

Whitby, Redcar &
Middlesbrough Railway 1866

Merrybent &
Darlington Railway 1866

Scarborough, Bridlington &
W. Riding Junction Rly 1885

Hull, Barnsley & W. Riding
Jn Rly & Dock Co. 1880

Hull & South Yorkshire
Extension Railway 1897

98

Hull & Barnsley
Railway 1905

15 LNER: Great Eastern Railway and Midland & Great Northern Joint Railway

To 1849	1850–1854	1855–1859	1860–1864
Colchester, Stour Valley, Sudbury & Halstead Railway *1846*			
			Ely, Haddenham & Sutton Railway *1864*
			W. Norfolk Junction Rly *1864*
			Lynn & Hunstanton Railway *1861*
E. Union & Hadleigh Junction Railway *1846*		Tendring Hundred Railway *1859*	
Ipswich & Bury St Edmunds Railway *1845*		Ware, Hadham & Buntingford Railway *1858*	
Eastern Union Railway *1844* 47			
Norwich & Brandon Rly *1844*			
Norfolk Railway *1845* 45			
Yarmouth & Norwich Rly *1842*	Wells & Fakenham Railway *1854*		
Newmarket & New Great Chesterford Railway *1846*			
Newmarket Railway *1847*			
Wisbech, St. Ives & Cambridge Junction Railway *1846*			
North Woolwich Railway *1845*			
Eastern Counties & Thames Junction Railway *1844*			
Eastern Counties Railway *1836* 46 48 47	54	59	**GREAT EASTERN** 63 **RAILWAY** *1862*
Maldon, Witham & Braintree Railway *1846*			
Lowestoft Railway & Harbour *1845*	Halesworth, Beccles & Haddiscoe Railway *1854*		
	East Suffolk Railway *1854*	58	
		Lowestoft & Beccles Rly *1856*	
Lynn & Ely Railway *1845*		Yarmouth & Haddiscoe Railway *1856*	
Lynn & Dereham Railway *1845*			
East Anglian Railways *1847*			
Ely & Huntingdon Railway *1845*	Waveney Valley Railway *1851*		
			Ramsey Railway *1861*
			Bishop's Stortford, Dunmow & Braintree Railway *1861*
			Saffron Walden Railway *1861*
			East Norfolk Railway *1864*
			Wivenhoe & Brightlingsea Railway *1861*
Northern & Eastern Rly *1836*			
Ely & Huntingdon Railway (Part)			
Lynn & Ely Railway (Part)			
Wisbech, St. Ives & Cambridge Jn Railway			
			Mid Eastern & GN Junction Railway *1860*
			Lynn & Sutton Bridge Railway *1861*
			Spalding & Bourn Railway *186.*
	Norwich & Spalding Rly *1853*		
			Peterborough, Wisbech & Sutton Bridge Railway *1862*

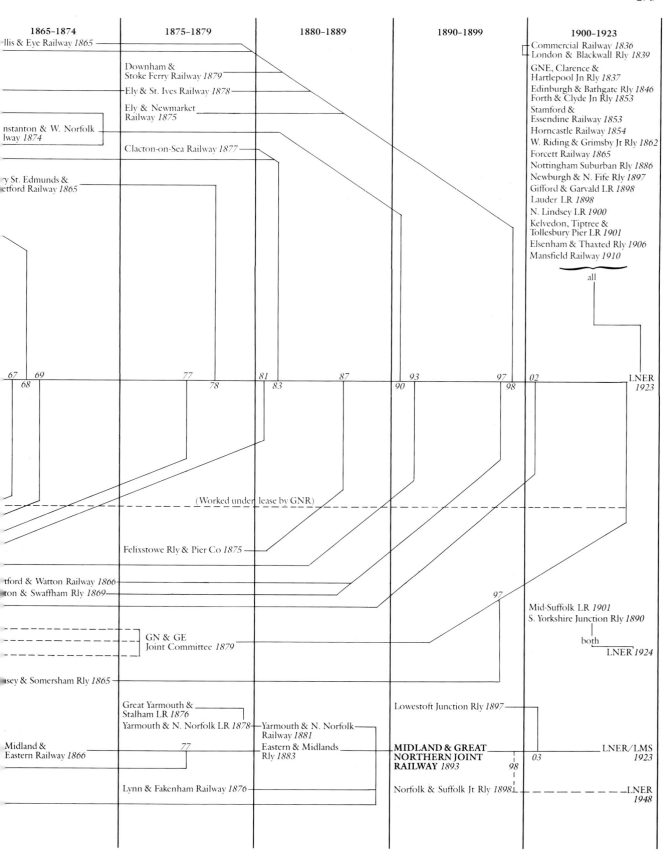

1865–1874	1875–1879	1880–1889	1890–1899	1900–1923

llis & Eye Railway *1865*

Commercial Railway *1836*
London & Blackwall Rly *1839*

Downham &
Stoke Ferry Railway *1879*

Ely & St. Ives Railway *1878*

Ely & Newmarket
Railway *1875*

GNE, Clarence &
Hartlepool Jn Rly *1837*
Edinburgh & Bathgate Rly *1846*
Forth & Clyde Jn Rly *1853*
Stamford &
Essendine Railway *1853*
Horncastle Railway *1854*
W. Riding & Grimsby Jt Rly *1862*
Forcett Railway *1865*
Nottingham Suburban Rly *1886*
Newburgh & N. Fife Rly *1897*
Gifford & Garvald LR *1898*
Lauder LR *1898*
N. Lindsey LR *1900*
Kelvedon, Tiptree &
Tollesbury Pier LR *1901*
Elsenham & Thaxted Rly *1906*
Mansfield Railway *1910*

nstanton & W. Norfolk
lway *1874*

Clacton-on-Sea Railway *1877*

y St. Edmunds &
etford Railway *1865*

all

LNER
1923

67   69

68

77

78

81

83

87

93

90

97

98

02

(Worked under lease by GNR)

Felixstowe Rly & Pier Co *1875*

tford & Watton Railway *1866*

ton & Swaffham Rly *1869*

97

Mid-Suffolk LR *1901*
S. Yorkshire Junction Rly *1890*

GN & GE
Joint Committee *1879*

both

LNER *1924*

sey & Somersham Rly *1865*

Great Yarmouth &
Stalham LR *1876*

Yarmouth & N. Norfolk LR *1878*

Lowestoft Junction Rly *1897*

Yarmouth & N. Norfolk
Railway *1881*

Midland &
Eastern Railway *1866*

77

Eastern & Midlands
Rly *1883*

**MIDLAND & GREAT
NORTHERN JOINT
RAILWAY** *1893*

98

03

LNER/LMS
1923

Lynn & Fakenham Railway *1876*

Norfolk & Suffolk Jt Rly *1898*

LNER
1948

16 SR:
London, Brighton & South Coast Railway, South Eastern Railway and London, Chatham & Dover Railway (SE&CR)

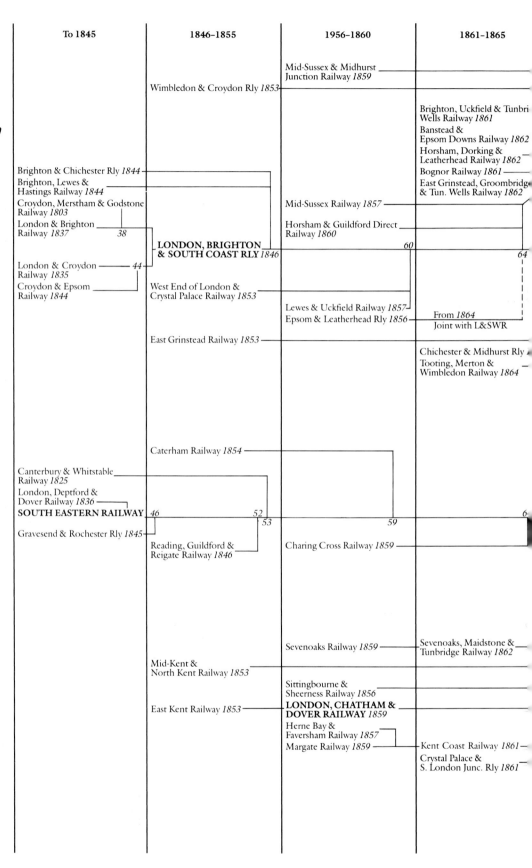

	To 1845	1846–1855	1956–1860	1861–1865

Mid-Sussex & Midhurst Junction Railway *1859*

Wimbledon & Croydon Rly *1853*

Brighton, Uckfield & Tunbri Wells Railway *1861*

Banstead & Epsom Downs Railway *1862*

Horsham, Dorking & Leatherhead Railway *1862*

Bognor Railway *1861*

East Grinstead, Groombridge & Tun. Wells Railway *1862*

Brighton & Chichester Rly *1844*

Brighton, Lewes & Hastings Railway *1844*

Croydon, Merstham & Godstone Railway *1803*

Mid-Sussex Railway *1857*

London & Brighton Railway *1837* 38

Horsham & Guildford Direct Railway *1860*

LONDON, BRIGHTON & SOUTH COAST RLY *1846* 60 64

London & Croydon Railway *1835* 44

Croydon & Epsom Railway *1844*

West End of London & Crystal Palace Railway *1853*

Lewes & Uckfield Railway *1857*

Epsom & Leatherhead Rly *1856* From *1864* Joint with L&SWR

East Grinstead Railway *1853*

Chichester & Midhurst Rly

Tooting, Merton & Wimbledon Railway *1864*

Caterham Railway *1854*

Canterbury & Whitstable Railway *1825*

London, Deptford & Dover Railway *1836*

SOUTH EASTERN RAILWAY 46 52 59 6

53

Gravesend & Rochester Rly *1845*

Reading, Guildford & Reigate Railway *1846*

Charing Cross Railway *1859*

Sevenoaks Railway *1859* Sevenoaks, Maidstone & Tunbridge Railway *1862*

Mid-Kent & North Kent Railway *1853*

Sittingbourne & Sheerness Railway *1856*

East Kent Railway *1853* **LONDON, CHATHAM & DOVER RAILWAY** *1859*

Herne Bay & Faversham Railway *1857*

Margate Railway *1859* Kent Coast Railway *1861*

Crystal Palace & S. London Junc. Rly *1861*

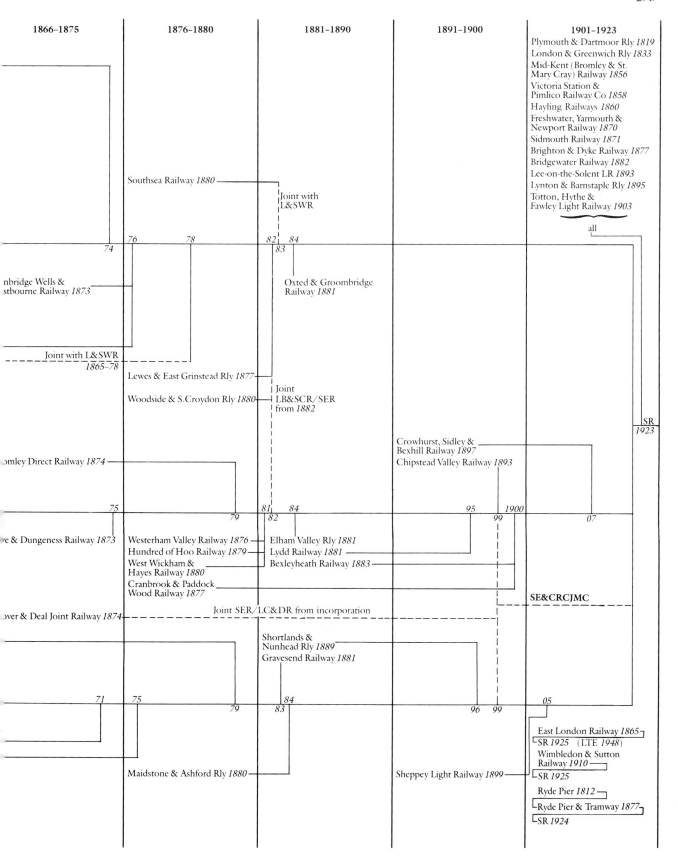

Plymouth & Dartmoor Rly *1819*
London & Greenwich Rly *1833*
Mid-Kent (Bromley & St. Mary Cray) Railway *1856*
Victoria Station & Pimlico Railway Co *1858*
Hayling Railways *1860*
Freshwater, Yarmouth & Newport Railway *1870*
Sidmouth Railway *1871*
Brighton & Dyke Railway *1877*
Bridgewater Railway *1882*
Lee-on-the-Solent LR *1893*
Lynton & Barnstaple Rly *1895*
Totton, Hythe & Fawley Light Railway *1903*

all

Southsea Railway *1880*

Joint with L&SWR

74　76　78　82　84
83

nbridge Wells & stbourne Railway *1873*

Oxted & Groombridge Railway *1881*

Joint with L&SWR
1865–78

Lewes & East Grinstead Rly *1877*

Woodside & S.Croydon Rly *1880*

Joint LB&SCR/SER from *1882*

SR *1923*

Crowhurst, Sidley & Bexhill Railway *1897*
Chipstead Valley Railway *1893*

omley Direct Railway *1874*

75　79　81　84　95　1900　99　07
82

re & Dungeness Railway *1873*
Westerham Valley Railway *1876*
Hundred of Hoo Railway *1879*
West Wickham & Hayes Railway *1880*
Cranbrook & Paddock Wood Railway *1877*

Elham Valley Rly *1881*
Lydd Railway *1881*
Bexleyheath Railway *1883*

SE&CRCJMC

over & Deal Joint Railway *1874*　Joint SER/LC&DR from incorporation

Shortlands & Nunhead Rly *1889*
Gravesend Railway *1881*

71　75　79　83　96　99　05

East London Railway *1865*
SR *1925* (LTE *1948*)

Wimbledon & Sutton Railway *1910*

Maidstone & Ashford Rly *1880*
Sheppey Light Railway *1899*
SR *1925*

Ryde Pier *1812*

Ryde Pier & Tramway *1877*
SR *1924*

17 SR: *London & South Western Railway*

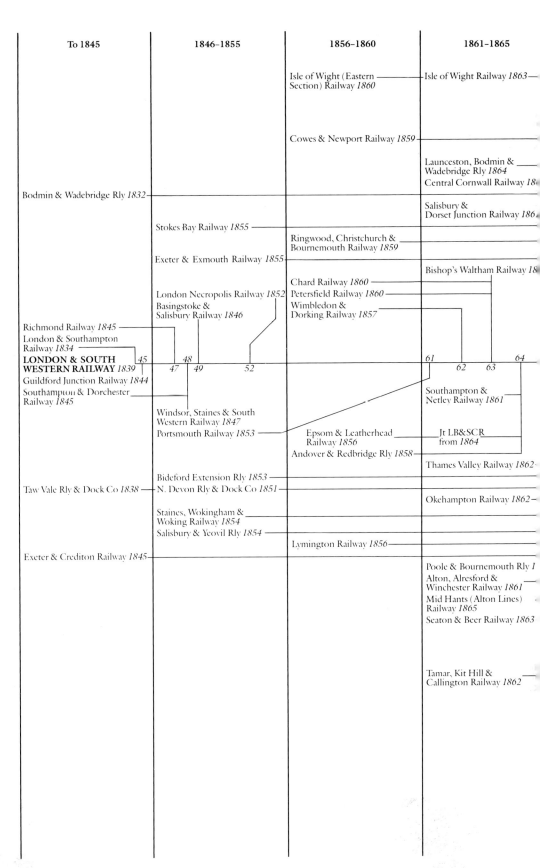

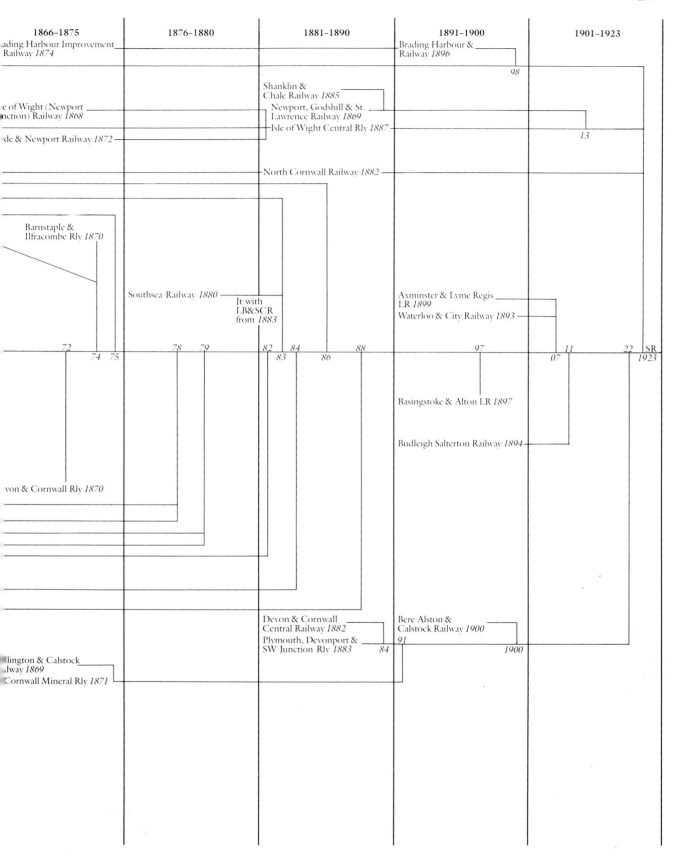

1866–1875	1876–1880	1881–1890	1891–1900	1901–1923

ading Harbour Improvement
Railway *1874*

Brading Harbour &
Railway *1896*

98

Shanklin &
Chale Railway *1885*

e of Wight (Newport
nction) Railway *1868*

Newport, Godshill & St.
Lawrence Railway *1869*

13

Isle of Wight Central Rly *1887*

de & Newport Railway *1872*

North Cornwall Railway *1882*

Barnstaple &
Ilfracombe Rly *1870*

Southsea Railway *1880*

Jt with
LB&SCR
from *1883*

Axminster & Lyme Regis
LR *1899*

Waterloo & City Railway *1893*

72 *74* *75* *78* *79* *82* *84* *88* *97* *11* *22* SR
83 *86* *07* *1923*

Basingstoke & Alton LR *1897*

Budleigh Salterton Railway *1894*

von & Cornwall Rly *1870*

Devon & Cornwall
Central Railway *1882*

Bere Alston &
Calstock Railway *1900*

91

Plymouth, Devonport &
SW Junction Rly *1883* *84*

1900

llington & Calstock
lway *1869*

Cornwall Mineral Rly *1871*

18 LPTB: London Electric Railway and Metropolitan Railway

	To 1855	1856–1865	1866–1870	1871–1875
				Wotton Tramway, *Op 1871* ——
		Aylesbury & Buckingham Railway *1860*		
		Metropolitan & St. John's Wood Railway *1864*		Harrow & Rickmansworth Railway *1874*
	N. Metropolitan Railway *1853*			
	METROPOLITAN RAILWAY *1854*		*67*	
			Jt with GWR	Metropolitan Inner Circle Completion Railway *1874*
		Hammersmith & City Railway *1861*		Hammersmith Extension Railway *1873*
		Metropolitan District Railway *1864*		*74*

1876–1880	1881–1890	1891–1900	1901–1910	1911–1933

Central London Railway *1891*

City & South London
Railway *1890*

City of London &
Southwark Subway *1884*

Baker Street & Waterloo
Railway *1893*

Brompton & Piccadilly
Circus Railway *1897*

Great Northern, Piccadilly
& Brompton Railway *1902*

**LONDON ELECTRIC
RAILWAY** *1910*

12

Charing Cross, Euston &
Hampstead Railway *1893*

Edgware &
Hampstead Railway *1902*

Oxford & Aylesbury
Tramroad *1888*

LPTB
1933

Harrow & Uxbridge
Railway *1897*

79   *81*   *82*   *91*   *05*   *13*

80

Great Northern &
City Railway *1892*

Aylesbury &
Rickmansworth Railway *1881*

Ealing &
South Harrow Railway *1894*

03

79   *1900*

ounslow &
etropolitan Railway *1880*

Bibliography

The reading required to prepare a book of this sort is vast; the list below is just some of the literature I have consulted.

Books

Allen, Cecil J, *The Great Eastern Railway* (Ian Allan, 1968)
The North Eastern Railway (Ian Allan, 1964)
Athill, Robin, *The Somerset & Dorset Railway* (Pan, edn 1970)
Awdry, Rev W./Cook, Chris (rev'd Crombleholme, Roger), *Guide to the Steam Railways of Great Britain* (Pelham, edn 1984)
Barclay-Harvey, Sir M., *The Great North of Scotland Railway* (Loco Publ Co, edn 1949)
Barnett, A.L., *Railways of the South Yorkshire Coalfield* (RCTS, 1984)
Barton, D.B., *The Redruth & Chasewater Railway* (Bradford Barton, 1966)
Baughan, Peter, *The Chester & Holyhead Railway*, Vol 1 (David & Charles, 1972)
Baxter, Bertram, *Stone Blocks and Iron Rails* (David & Charles, 1966)
Body, Geoffrey, *PSL Field Guide, Railways of the Eastern Region*, Vol 1 (Patrick Stephens Ltd, 1986)
Bonavia, Michael R., *Historic Railway Sites in Britain* (Robert Hale, 1987)
Boyd, J.I.C., *Narrow Gauge Railways in South Caernarvonshire* (Oakwood Press, 1972)
Bradley, D.L., *A Locomotive History of Railways on the Isle of Wight* (RCTS, 1982)
Borley, H.V., *Chronology of London's Railways* and supp't (RCHS, 1982)
Brown, G.A./Prideaux, J.D.C./Radcliffe, H.G., *The Lynton & Barnstaple Railway* (David & Charles, 1964)
Casserley, H.C., *Britain's Joint Lines* (Ian Allan, 1968)
Carter, Ernest F., *The Railway Encyclopaedia* (Harold Starke Ltd, 1963)
An Historical Geography of the Railways of the British Isles (Cassell, 1959)
Christiansen/Miller, *The North Staffordshire Railway* (David & Charles, 1971)
The Cambrian Railways, 2 vols (David & Charles, 1968–71)

Clew, Kenneth, *The Somerset Coal Canal and Railways* (David & Charles, 1970)
Clinker, C.R., *The Birmingham & Derby Junction Railway* (Avon Anglia, 1982)
Course, E.A., *The Bexleyheath Railway* (Woolwich & Dist Ant Soc, 1954)
Railways of Southern England, Vol 1 (Batsford, 1973)
Crombleholme/Stuckey/Whetmath/Gibson, *Callington Railways* (Forge Books, 1985)
Daniels/Dench, *Passengers No More* (Ian Allan, edn 1973)
Dendy Marshall, C.F., *History of the Southern Railway* (Ian Allan, rev Kidner, 1963)
Donaghy, Thomas, *Liverpool & Manchester Railway*, Vol 1 (David & Charles, 1972)
Dow, George, *Great Central*, 3 vols (Ian Allan, 1959–65)
Railway Heraldry (David & Charles, 1973)
The First Railway in Norfolk (LNER, 1944)
Gordon, W.J., *Our Home Railways*, 2 vols (Fredk. Warne, 1910)
Gough, J.V., *The Midland Railway – A Chronology* (J.V. Gough, 1986, and supp't)
Grinling, C.H., *History of the Great Northern Railway* (Methuen, 1898)
Greville, M.D., *Chronology of the Railways of Lancashire and Cheshire* (RCHS, 1981)
Greville/Spence, *Closed Passengers Lines of Great Britain, 1827–1947* (RCHS, rev edn 1974)
James, Leslie, *A Chronology of the Construction of Britain's Railways* (Ian Allan, 1983)
Joy, David, *Cumbrian Coast Railways* (Dalesman, 1968)
Klapper, Charles, *London's Lost Railways* (Routledge & Kegan Paul, 1976)
Lewis, M.J.T., *The Pentewan Railway* (Bradford Barton, edn 1980)
Long, P.J./Rev W. Awdry, *The Birmingham & Gloucester Railway* (Alan Sutton, 1987)
MacDermot, E.T., *History of the Great Western Railway*, 2 vols (GWR, 1927–31)
MacMillan, Nigel S.C., *The Campbeltown & Machrihanish Railway* (David & Charles, 1970)
Maggs, Colin G., *The Midland & South Western Junction Railway* (David & Charles, 1967)

'Manifold', *The North Staffordshire Railway* (Henstock, 1952)

Markham, Sir John, *History of Milton Keynes*, Vol 2 (White Crescent Press, 1975)

Martin, Don, *The Garnkirk & Glasgow Railway* (Strathkelvin District Libraries, 1981)

Moffat, Hugh, *East Anglia's First Railways* (Terence Dalton Ltd, 1987)

Norris, John, *The Stratford & Moreton Tramway* (RCHS, 1987)

Ottley, George, *Bibliography of British Railway History* (HMSO, 1983 edn)

Paar, H.W., *Severn & Wye Railway* (David & Charles, 1963)

Paye, Peter, *The Tollesbury Branch* (OPC, 1985)

Pearson, R.E./Ruddock, J.G., *Lord Willoughby's Railway, The Edenham Branch* (Willoughby Memorial Trust, 1986)

Petchey, Tim, *A List of Railway Undertakings in England, Scotland and Wales* (privately published)

Pope/How/Karau, *The Severn & Wye Railway*, Vol 1 (Wild Swan, 1983)

Robertson, C.J.A., *The Origins of the Scottish Railway System* (John Donald, 1983)

Rolt, L.T.C., *Talyllyn Adventure* (edn David & Charles, 1971)

Snell, J.B., *Railways: Mechanical Engineering* (Arrow, 1973)

Stuckey, Douglas, *The Bideford, Westward Ho! & Appledore Railway* (Forge Books, 1983)

Taylor, R.S./Tonks, E.S., *The Southwold Railway* (Ian Allan, 1979)

Thomas, John, *The North British Railway*, 2 vols (David & Charles, 1969, 1975)
The West Highland Railway (Pan, 1970)

Tolson/Roose/Whetmath, *Railways of Looe and Caradon* (Forge Books, 1974)

Tomlinson, W.W., *The North Eastern Railway* (David & Charles, edn 1987)

Tonks, E.S., *The Ironstone Railways and Tramways of the Midlands* (Loco Publ Co, edn 1961)

Vallance, H.A., *The Great North of Scotland Railway* (David & Charles, 1965)
The Highland Railway (David & Charles, 1938)

Webb, B./Gordon, D.A., *Lord Carlisle's Railways* (RCTS, 1978)

Whetmath/Stuckey, *The North Devon & Cornwall Junction Light Railway* (Forge Books, 1980)

Whishaw, *Railways of Great Britain and Ireland, 1842* (David & Charles, 1969)

Williams, F.S., *The Midland Railway: Its Rise and Progress* (David & Charles, edn 1976)

Woodfin, R.J., *The Cornwall Railway* (Bradford Barton, edn 1972)

Wrottesley, A.J., *The Midland & Great Northern Railway* (David & Charles, 1970)

Wrottesley, John, *The Great Northern Railway*, 3 vols (Batsford, 1981)

The Glasgow & South Western Railway (Stephenson Loco Soc, 1950)

Little and Good — GNSR (Stephenson Loco Soc, 1972)

Official Handbook of Stations (BTC, 1956)

All volumes in the David & Charles 'Regional History' and 'Forgotten Railways' series

Many volumes in the Oakwood Press 'Locomotion Papers' series

Local and Personal Acts of Parliament.

Magazines

Railway Magazine, British Railway Journal, Locomotive Magazine, Railway World, Backtrack, Steam World, Steam Railway.

Society Journals

Railway Observer (RCTS), the Journal of the Railway & Canal Historical Society, Great Eastern Journal, Talyllyn News, Festiniog Railway News, Bluebell News, Bulliver, numerous Society handbooks and guides.

Index

This index contains placenames mentioned in company titles, and also the names of companies which do not contain a specific placename, eg Great Central.